COMRADE PAVLIK

The statue of Pavlik Morozov in Gerasimovka, 2003.

COMRADE PAVLIK

The Rise and Fall of a Soviet Boy Hero

CATRIONA KELLY

Granta Books
London

Granta Publications, 2/3 Hanover Yard, Noel Road, London N1 8BE

First published in Great Britain by Granta Books 2005

A CIP catalogue record for this book
is available from the British Library.

1 3 5 7 9 10 8 6 4 2

ISBN 1 86207 747 9

Frontispiece photograph by Catriona Kelly, September 2003

Typeset by M Rules

Printed and bound in Great Britain by
William Clowes Limited, Beccles and London

CONTENTS

Illustrations vii
Abbreviations ix
The Morozov Family Tree xi
Dramatis Personae xii
Maps xviii
Preface xxii

Introduction: Death in the Taiga 1

1 Pavlik's World 18
2 Local Hero 43
3 Investigating the Murder 69
4 Class Warrior, Boy Martyr 110
5 All-Soviet Hero 140
6 Pavlik Eclipsed 176
7 Pavlik after Stalin 197
8 The 'Real Life' of Pavlik Morozov? 223

Afterword 261

Notes 266
List of Sources 321
Acknowledgements 340
Index 343

ILLUSTRATIONS

Frontispiece: The statue of Pavlik Morozov in Gerasimovka, 2003. ii

Map 1: The Soviet Union in 1932. xviii
Map 2: Urals province in 1932. xx
Map 3: Tavda district. xxi

Group of Pioneers hearing about Pavlik Morozov's life. xxiii
Pavlik Morozov's schoolmate, Dmitry Prokopenko. xxvi
The statue of Pavlik Morozov in Gerasimovka, 1972. 3
Propaganda photograph of a field of standing rye. 24
Anti-kulak poster. 27
'The Pioneer March'. 35
Propaganda photograph of a blast furnace, 1934. 46
Political procession in Sverdlovsk, *c.* 1930. 52
Cover of file H-7825. 70
A page from witness testimony recorded by policeman Yakov Titov. 83
A page from witness testimony recorded by district plenipotentiary Bykov. 89
First page of Pavlik Morozov's death certificate. 99
15 October 1932 report on the Morozov murders from *Pioneer Pravda*. 115
Report on the Morozov trial, *Pioneer Pravda*, November 1932. 120
The accused lined up in the courtroom. 129
Pavlik confronts his father. 135
Portrait of Maxim Gorky, 1932. 141
Gorky broadcasting to the Soviet nation from his dacha, 1932. 143
Stalin posed with Gelya Markizova, the daughter of a high-ranking Communist Party official from Buryat-Mongolia, 1936. 146

Pavlik tells the local teacher what his father has done. 154
Still from Sergei Eisenstein's film *Bezhin Meadow* (1936). 156
Timur and his friends lay their plans. 178
Maquette for the monument by Izaak Rabinovich to Pavlik Morozov, 1938. 188
Nikita Chebakov, *Pavlik Morozov* (1952). 194
Assorted gifts from Pioneers to the Pavlik Morozov Museum. 204
Mock-up of the classroom where Pavlik was educated. 205
Artist's impression of Pavlik Morozov, 1972. 206
Monument in Gerasimovka carrying Gorky's command, 'The memory of him must not be allowed to vanish'. 216
Picture of a child's funeral, early 1930s, erroneously identified as showing Fyodor Morozov. 225
Gerasimovka school photograph, 1931. 227
'Pavlik Morozov and his Mother'. 228
Painted wooden box, 1970s. 263
The site of Fyodor Morozov's murder in the woods at Gerasimovka, 2003. 264

ABBREVIATIONS

BSE (edn 1): *Bolshaya sovetskaya entsiklopediya* (65 vols.; Moscow, 1926–46)

BSE (edn 2): *Bolshaya sovetskaya entsiklopediya* (51 vols.; Moscow, 1949–65)

BSE (edn 3): *Bolshaya sovetskaya entsiklopediya* (30 vols.; Moscow, 1969–81)

ES: *Entsiklopedicheskii slovar* (41 plus 4 supp. vols.; St Petersburg: izd. Brokgauza i Efrona, 1890–1907)

GASO: State Archive of Sverdlovsk Province (Gosudarstvennyi arkhiv Sverdlovskoi oblasti)

KP: *Komsomol Pravda* (*Komsomolskaya pravda*: the official newspaper of the Komsomol, Communist Youth Movement)

LI: *Leninist Sparks* (*Leninskie iskry*: the Leningrad Pioneer paper)

OGPU (*Obyedinyonnoe gosudarstvennoe politicheskoe upravlenie*, United State Political Administration): The title of the Soviet secret police (known between 1918 and 1922 as the Cheka, and between 1922 and 1923 as the GPU). Renamed GUGB (*Glavnoe upravlenie gosudarstvennoi bezopastnosti*, Chief Administration of State Security), and integrated into the People's Commissariat of Internal Affairs (NKVD), in 1934. The organization, later retitled the KGB, and in post-Soviet times the FSB, has remained a department of the Ministry of Internal Affairs up to the present

PP: Pioneer Pravda (*Pionerskaya pravda*, the national Pioneer paper)

RAO NA: Russian Academy of Education. Scholarly Archive (Rossiiskaya Akademiya Obrazovaniya Nauchnyi arkhiv)

RGASPI: Russian State Archive of Social and Political History (Rossiiskii gosudarstvennyi arkhiv sotsialnoi i politicheskoi istorii)

RGASPI-TsKhDMO: Centre for Youth Organization Documents (Tsentr khraneniya dokumentov molodezhnykh organizatsii), a department of RGASPI since 2000

RGIA: Russian State Historical Archive (Rossiiskii gosudarstvennyi arkhiv)

TR: *Tavda Worker* (*Tavdinskii rabochii*, the Tavda local paper); for the sake of simplicity, this title has been consistently used, although the paper in fact ran under a variety of different titles in the late 1920s and early 1930s

TsA FSB: Central Archive of the Federal Security Service (Tsentralnyi arkhiv Federalnoi sluzhby bezopasnosti)

TsAODM: Central Archive of Public Associations of the City of Moscow (Tsentralnyi arkhiv obshchestvennykh dvizhenii Moskvy)

TsDOO SO: Centre of Documents relating to Public Associations, Sverdlovsk Province (Tsentr dokumentov obshchestvennykh organizatsii Sverdlovskoi oblasti); – formerly the Party archive

TsGALI-SPb: Central State Archive of Literature and Art, St Petersburg (Tsentralnyi gosudarstvennyi arkhiv literatury i iskusstva Sankt-Peterburga)

VK: *Dawns of the Commune* (*Vskhody kommuny*, the Sverdlovsk Pioneer paper)

Materials from archives are generally given in the following form: abbreviated name of the archive (GASO, RAO NA, etc.), followed by f. for 'fond' or collection number, 'op.' for opis or inventory number, 'd.' for delo or file number, and 'l.' for list or folio number. However, references to materials from the Morozov case file, held in the Central Archive of the FSB (TsA FSB H-7825 t.2), are given by folio number in the main text, thus: (44), etc.

Russian words and names are transliterated in a simplified version of British Standard. The soft sign ' is used only in the Notes and List of Sources, and names are given in their most familiar form (Sergei not Sergey, Dostoevsky not Dostoevskii).

The Morozov Family Tree

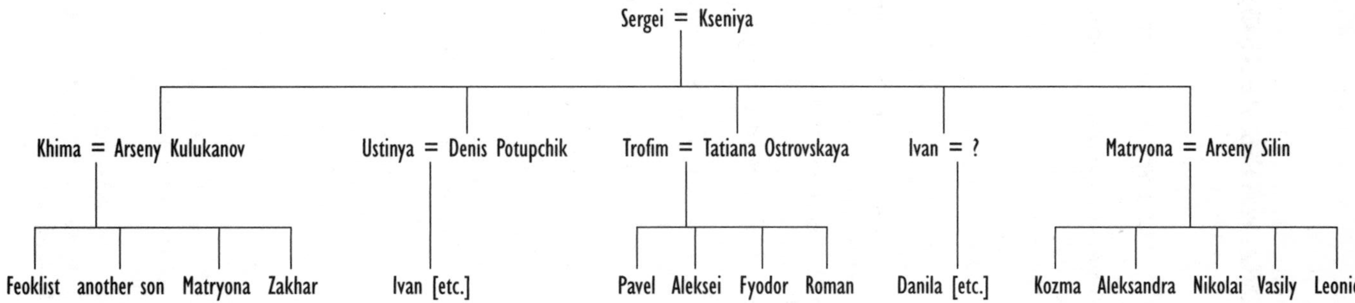

DRAMATIS PERSONAE

A NOTE ON NAMES

Russian names, as given on passports and other official documents, consist of a first name, patronymic, and surname. Polite address among city-dwelling adults consists of name and patronymic. In villages, the use of first name alone was common, sometimes in diminutive form ('Danilka'); older adults would be addressed by patronymic alone ('Sergeich' for Sergei Sergeevich Morozov). Little of this usage, though, is reflected in the written documentation of Pavlik Morozov and his milieu. Pavlik (or Pasha/Pashka, as he was known to his family) almost always appears even in witness testimony by his full name, 'Pavel'.

Official figures, such as policemen and Party secretaries, generally signed themselves by surname alone – 'Bykov' (this practice also means that the first names of most of the local officials in Tavda are now impossible to trace: the only investigator in the Morozov case who occasionally included his first name when signing was Andriyan Iskrin).

Often, the documents refer to a person by his or her surname first, followed by forename ('Morozov Pavel'). I have retained such reverse-style appellations in my translations of documents into English, given their highly specific associations (with Soviet official contexts) in Russian. I have, however, standardized spelling of the names by which people are referred to, for the sake of avoiding confusion, though in the original documents – particularly those from the first phase of the investigation – variation is rife. Pavlik's grandmother sometimes appears as 'Aksinya', sometimes as 'Kseniya', Pavlik's grandfather's name is often spelled 'Sirgei', Danila is sometimes referred to as 'Danil', 'Daniil', or 'Danilka', Mezyukhin as 'Mizukhin', Varygin as 'Vorigin', the Shatrakovs as 'Shitrakovs' or even 'Shirokovs', 'Efrem' as 'Efem' or 'Efim', and so on.

Pronunciation: In Russian, as in English, but unlike in say Italian or Polish, stress can fall on any syllable of the word, and unstressed vowels are 'reduced'. So, the surname Morozov is actually pronounced Ma-ROZ-off (with the sound of the final o as in the English word 'lemon'). In the list below, the surnames of the central figures in the Morozov case are followed by a guide to pronunciation. The main place names in the story are pronounced Sveerd-LOVSK, Tav-DAH, and Gi-RAH-see-moff-ka.

OGPU investigators

Tavda

Bykov (BWEE-koff) (first name not known). District plenipotentiary 1932–. The senior police official in Tavda: managed the third stage of the investigation.

Iskrin, Andriyan. Deputy plenipotentiary. An 'Ikrin, Andreyan Danilovich', born 1902, and with primary education, is included in a list of 'responsible officials' for Tavda region from June 1930 (TsDOO SO f. 1201 op. 1 d. 7, l. 50). This is no doubt the same person. Originated the copy of Pavlik Morozov's denunciation; silently present at some interviews conducted by Fedchenko.

Kartashov, Spiridon (Kar-ta-SHOFF, Spee-ree-DON). Rank not clear. Aged twenty-nine in 1932 (Druzhnikov, p. 10). In Gerasimovka 11–12 September carrying out the second stage of the investigation.

Likhobabin (first name not known). OGPU official, silently present at some interviews conducted by Fedchenko.

Rechkalov (first name not known). Deputy plenipotentiary. Conducted some interviews at the third stage of the investigation.

Trusov (first name not known). 'OGPU official', silently present at some interviews conducted by Fedchenko.

Ushenin (first name not known). Bykov's predecessor as district plenipotentiary in 1930–2.

Nizhny Tagil

Fedchenko (first name not known). Inspector, Operations Section, Plenipotentiary Division.

Sverdlovsk

Shepelev (first name not known). Plenipotentiary, Second Section, Plenipotentiary Division.

Police and police aides

Potupchik, Ivan (Pa-TOOP-chik, Ee-VAHN). Born 1911. Poor peasant background. Formal education to primary level. Plenipotentiary of the land society from 1930–31, shop assistant, police aide 1931–2, senior police aide 1931–2 [*sic.*] (74, 29). Son of Denis Potupchik, cousin of Pavlik Morozov.

Suvorov (first name not known). Local inspector, helped with the investigation in Gerasimovka at the initial stages (1, 21).

Titov, Yakov (Tee-TOFF, YA-koff). Born 1896. Local inspector. Party member from 1931, four dependants. Originally from Vitebsk; lived in Beloyarka village soviet (77).

Varygin, Prokhor. Aged eighteen in November 1932. Poor peasant background. Partly literate (231, 71). Assiduous provider of information to the investigation, acted as witness at the trial.

Yudov, Karp. Named in an OGPU report of December 1932 as a police aide; beaten up as an activist and grain collector by members of the Kniga family, Gerasimovka, November 1932 (TsDOO SO f. 1201 op. 1 d. 26, l. 48).

The Morozov clan

Kulukanov, Arseny – see under Accused below.

Kulukanov, Zakhar (born 1913–14?). Son of Arseny and Khima Kulukanov.

Kulukanova, Khima – see under Accused below.

Morozov, Aleksei (Ma-RO-zoff, Al-ek-SAY) (born 1921?) (67, 229). Second son of Trofim and Tatiana Morozov.

Morozov, Danila – see under Accused below.

Morozov, Fyodor (Ma-RO-zoff, Fee-OD-or) (born 1923?). Murdered with his brother Pavel, 3 September 1932. Son of Trofim and Tatiana Morozov.

Morozov, Ivan (Ma-RO-zoff, Ee-VAHN) (born *c.* 1888). Elder (?) brother of Trofim Morozov, father of Danila Morozov. Living in Kiselyovo village when the murders took place.

Morozov, Pavel (Ma-RO-zoff, PA-vel) (born 14 November 1918).[1] Murdered with his brother Fyodor, 3 September 1932. Son of Trofim and Tatiana Morozov.

Morozov, Roman (Ma-RO-zoff, Ro-MAHN) (born 1927?) (67). Younger brother of Pavel and Fyodor Morozov.

Morozov, Sergei – see under Accused below.

Morozov, Trofim (Ma-RO-zoff, Tro-FEEM) (born about 1890? Kseniya Morozova gave his age as '32' in her arrest form (132), but this cannot be right: '42' seems more likely). Father of Pavel and Fyodor Morozov.

Morozova, Tatiana (Ma-RO-za-va, Tat-YAH-na) (born 1893) (228). Mother of Pavel and Fyodor Morozov, wife of Trofim, daughter-in-law of Sergei and Kseniya.

Potupchik, Denis (Po-TOOP-chik, De-NEES) (born 1874?). Deputy chairman of the village soviet, Gerasimovka, autumn 1932. Father of Ivan Potupchik, uncle by marriage of Pavel and Fyodor Morozov.

Potupchik, Ustinya (born 1879) (132). Second daughter of Sergei and Kseniya Morozov, wife of Denis Potupchik, mother of Ivan Potupchik, aunt of Pavel and Fyodor Morozov.

Silin, Arseny – see under Accused below.

The Accused

This list includes only villagers who were formally arrested and interviewed in connection with the murder, and not those named in newspaper reports as guilty, e.g. Dmitry Shatrakov.

Kulukanov, Arseny (Koo-loo-KAHN-off, Ar-SAY-ny) (born 1862, Vitebsk province) (138). So-called 'kulak' sentenced to exile for resistance to grain surrender (96 rev.). Son-in-law of Sergei and Kseniya Morozov. Illiterate: signed with thumb print (97 rev. etc.).

Kulukanova, Khima (Koo-loo-KAHN-ava, HEE-ma) (born 1872) (92, 138).[2] Eldest daughter of Sergei and Kseniya Morozov; aunt of Pavel and Fyodor Morozov, and of Danila Morozov.

Mezyukhin, Vladimir (Mi-ZOO-hin, Vla-DEE-mir) (born 1902, Vladimirovka). Married with two children. Barely literate (95). A business connection of Kulukanov and Sergei Morozov, with a sideline in horse-dealing.

Morozova, Kseniya (Ma-RO-za-va, KSAY-nya) (born 1853, Vitebsk province) (132). Wife of Sergei Morozov, grandmother of Pavel and Fyodor.

Morozov, Danila (Ma-RO-zoff, Da-NEE-la) (born 1914, Tavda district). Son of Ivan Morozov, first cousin of Pavel and Fyodor Morozov.

Morozov, Sergei (Ma-RO-zoff, Sir-GEY) (born 1851, Vitebsk province) (135). Husband of Kseniya Morozova, grandfather of Pavel and Fyodor.

Shatrakov, Efrem (Sha-tra-KOFF, Ef-REM) (born 1912, Gerasimovka) (188). Friend – though he denied this – of Dmitry Morozov.

Silin, Arseny (SEE-lin, Ar-SAY-ny) (born 1892, Gerasimovka; family originally from Minsk province). Married with five children: Kozma (eleven), Aleksandra (nine), Nikolai (seven), Vasily (five), and Leonid (one) (129 rev.). Partially literate (could sign his own name) (99 etc.). Had fought in the First World War, where he lost two fingers (130).

Other villagers

Galyzov, Efim. Frequently used as an official witness at interviews; perhaps a police aide or an unofficial informer. 'Golyzo' (first name not given) was listed as a candidate member of the Malo-Gorodishche party cell in May 1929 (see TsDOO SO f. 1201 op. 1 d. 7, l. 64). 'Efim Gazykov' is listed as a witness at the trial (214), where he is given as a plenipotentiary of the Gerasimovka village soviet.

Kabina, Zoya. Senior teacher at the village school from 1931. Aged 17 (230).

Prozerova, Klavdiya. Junior teacher at the village school from February 1931 (230 rev.).

Sakova, Anastasiya. Schoolgirl. Aged eight (?) (169).

Shatrakov, Anton. Father of Dmitry and Efrem Shatrakov.

Shatrakov, Dmitry (Sha-tra-KOFF, Dee-MEE-try). Aged twenty-two. Elder brother of Efrem Shatrakov. Barely literate. Discovered the bodies of Pavel and Fyodor; under suspicion until he produced an alibi (16, 26, 65, 141, 159).

Shatrakova, Olga. Mother of Dmitry and Efrem Shatrakov.

Stepanchenko, Anna. Interviewed as witness to Kseniya Morozova's movements (32, 38, 170).

Timoshenko, Fyodor. Fellow-prisoner of the Morozovs who gave hostile evidence about what was said in the cell (114); here he is described as a 'special settler'. Listed as a trial witness, with place of residence as 'Gerasimovka' (214), but does not appear in the trial transcript.

Volkov, Konstantin. Aged twenty-six in 1932. (233 rev.).

Yudova, Stepanida (born 1905) (73). Gave evidence against Kseniya Morozova (the 'meat' story) (73). In the list of witnesses she was to be called at the trial (214), but she was not recorded as speaking in the transcript.

Propagandists

Alymov, Sergei (1892–1948). Author of lyrics for many popular songs, including 'Red Navy March', 'Sebastopol – Town of Glory', etc.

Chebakov, Nikita (1916–68). Prominent Socialist Realist painter, known for *Lenin is Everywhere!* and other canonical canvases.

Gaidar, Arkady (Gy-DAR, Ar-KAH-dy) (real name Golikov: his pseudonym is a Turkic word meaning 'horseman'). Born 1914. Brought up in Arzamas, the son of a first-generation-educated teacher. Volunteered for the Red Army aged fourteen. Began publishing 1925; his first hit was *The School* (1930). A prolific and popular writer for children, many of whose books (*The Blue Cup*, 1936; *Chuk and Gek*, 1939) were filmed. Killed shortly after the outbreak of war in 1941.

Gorky, Maxim (GOR-ky, Mak-SEEM) (real name Aleksei Peshkov). Born 1868 in Nizhny Novgorod, brought up by his grandparents, had little formal schooling. Began work as an errand-boy at twelve; his first published work appeared in 1892. Associated with the Left before 1917, but his criticism of Lenin led to tension, and he was forced into exile ('on health grounds') in 1921. Made lengthy visits to Soviet Russia in 1928 and 1929, returned permanently in 1931. Died 18 June 1936.

Gubarev, Vitaly (GOO-ba-reff, Vee-TAH-ly) (1912–81). Journalist, mainly for the Pioneer press, from 1931; children's writer; Party member from 1943. The article on him in the *Concise Literary*

Encyclopedia (*Kratkaya literaturnaya entsiklopediya*, 1962–78), vol. 2, misleadingly credits him with publishing the 'first materials' on Pavlik Morozov.[3]

Krupskaya, Nadezhda (KROOP-sky-ya, Na-DYEZH-da) (1869–1939). Lenin's wife and close Party ally, she was probably the single most important force in Soviet education for children between 1917 and 1932. Resolutely hostile to imaginative literature for children, she believed that reading should be based on factual material from early days.

Mikhalkov, Sergei (Me-hal-KOFF, Sir-GAY) (1913–). Began publishing in 1928 in the provincial press. Studied at the Gorky Literary Institute 1935–7. Published children's poetry from 1935; by the late 1940s, had become one of the major children's writers in the country. Author of the words for the 1943 Soviet national anthem and of the recent post-Soviet reworking of the text.

Rabinovich, Isaak (Ra-been-OV-ich, EE-sak) (1894–1961). Sculptor of the Pavlik Morozov monument in Moscow (designed 1938, erected 1948). Best-known for his work as a theatre designer, and a set designer for film, including *Aelita* (1924); his early style was explicitly modernist (unlike the Pavlik Morozov monument). A hint of this modernism remains in the handling of the banner held by Pavlik.

Shchipachov, Stepan (Shee-pa-CHOFF, Sti-PAHN) (1898–1980). From a peasant background in the Urals; the author of many different collections of poetry, mostly on patriotic themes, including 'The Pioneer Tie' (1942) telling Soviet children to cherish this item of attire, dipped as it is in the blood of their elder comrades.

Smirnov, Elizar (Smir-NOFF, El-ee-ZAR). Pioneer press journalist. On the *Pioneer Pravda* editorial board, member of the Central Children's Bureau of the Komsomol (245). Appeared as 'social prosecutor' at the trial of the Morozov murders. Druzhnikov, 1995: 11 estimates his age as twenty-four in 1932. Was to continue writing for the Pioneer press into the 1960s.

Solomein, Pavel (So-lo-MAY-in, PA-vel). Born about 1907 (Druzhnikov 1995: 11). From a poor background in the Urals. Worked for the Sverdlovsk Pioneer paper *Dawns of the Commune*, and as a 'stringer' for *Pioneer Pravda*.

Yakovlev, Aleksandr (YA-koff-leff, Al-ex-AHN-der) (1886–1953). Ran away from home aged twelve to become a hermit; then returned and finished school. In 1905, lost his faith and joined the Social Democrats. Author of many myth-making works of the Stalin era, including *The Great Stalinist Constructions* (1953). Died just over a month after Stalin himself (11 April 1953).

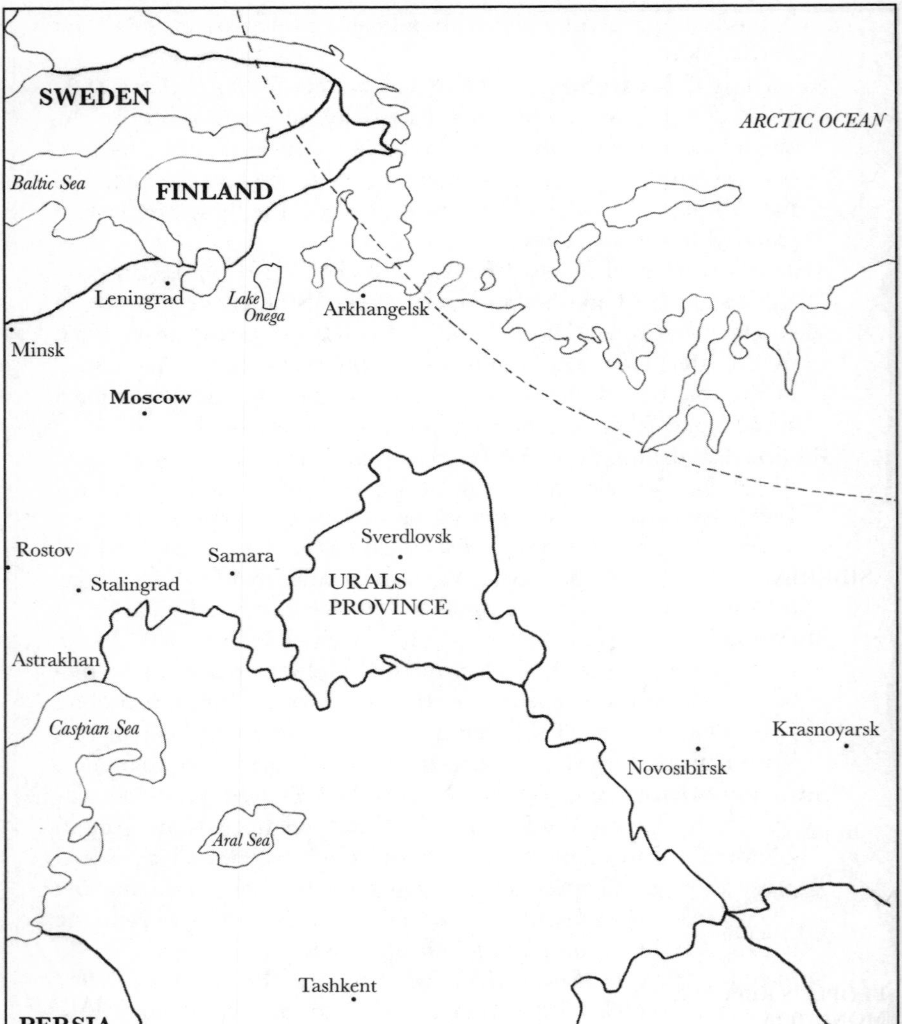
SWEDEN
ARCTIC OCEAN
Baltic Sea
FINLAND
Leningrad
Lake Onega
Arkhangelsk
Minsk
Moscow
Sverdlovsk
Rostov
Samara
URALS PROVINCE
Stalingrad
Astrakhan
Caspian Sea
Krasnoyarsk
Novosibirsk
Aral Sea
Tashkent
PERSIA
AFGHANISTAN
Kabul
INDIA

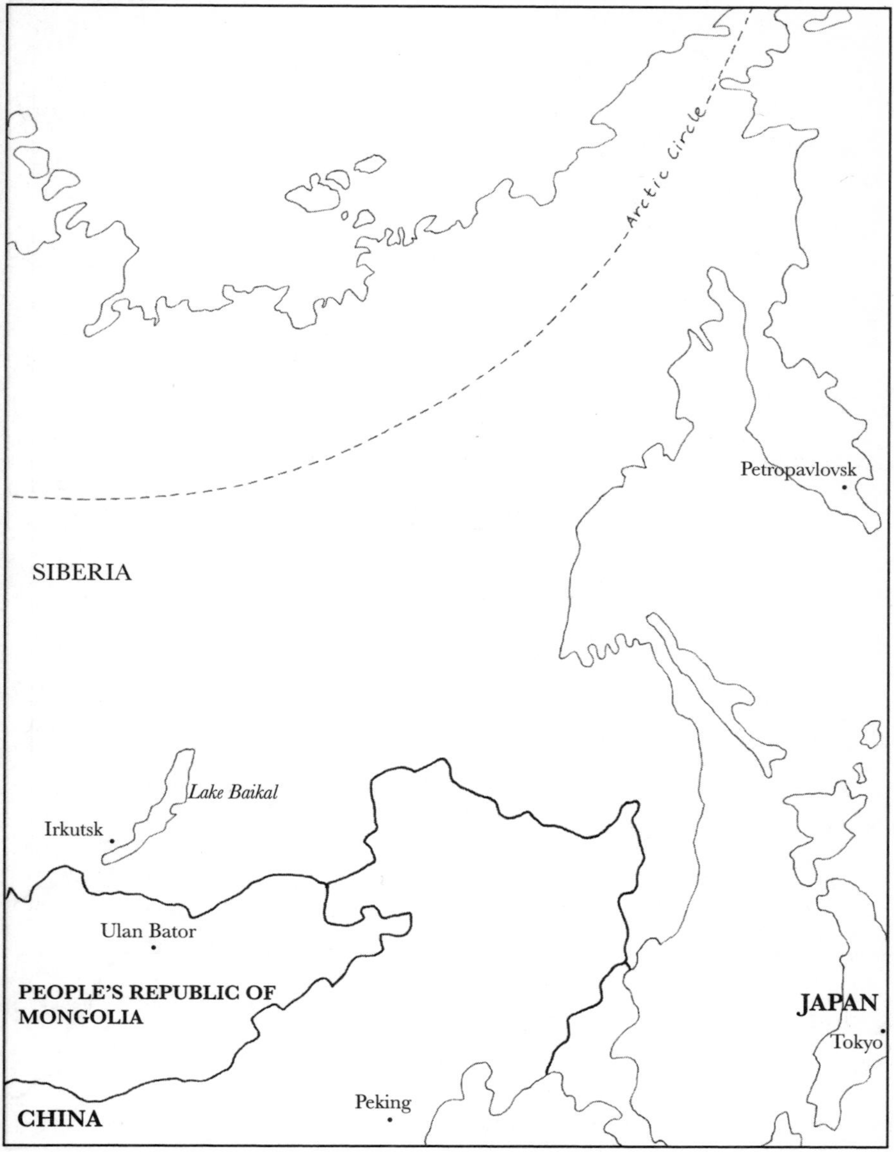

Map 1: The Soviet Union in 1932.
(After *A Pocket Atlas of the USSR* [*Karmannyi atlas SSSR*] 1934)

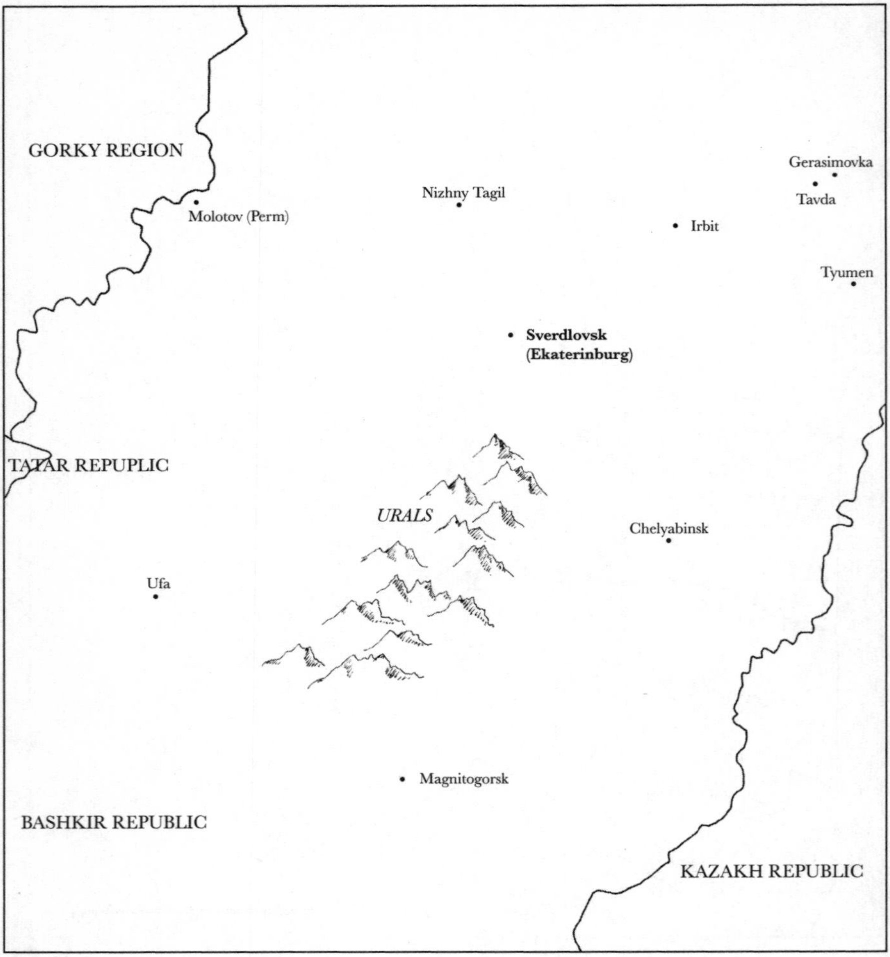

Map 2: Urals province in 1932.
(After *A Pocket Atlas of the USSR* [*Karmannyi atlas SSSR*] 1934)

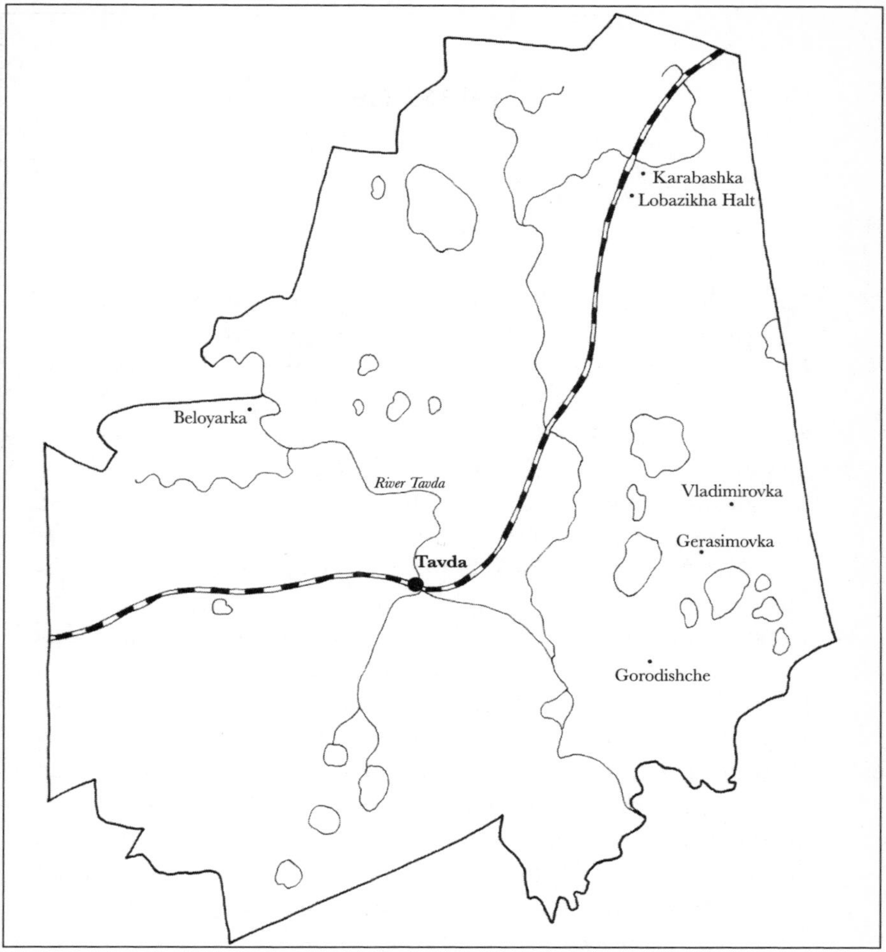

Map 3: Tavda district.
(After V. Ermolaev, *A Description of Tavda* [*Tavdinskoe mestopisanie*] 1999)

PREFACE

You are a Soviet Russian child aged ten, halfway through your first visit to a Young Pioneer camp. So far, your stay has gone quite well. It seemed strange at first, without your family, crowded into a big dormitory with forty other children, but you have made friends and enjoyed most of the activities – gymnastic drills, swimming, organized games – and even more the games you and the other children play when you have free time, the rounds of creepy stories after lights-out. Tonight you have been promised a bonfire. Sure enough, the day turns out fine, and after supper, you gather in the appointed place. Your Pioneer leader lights the cone of branches and logs, and soon the heat creeps out – welcome as the sun disappears – and the fuel is popping in the flames. You put potatoes in to bake, sing songs, and talk with your friends. Suddenly, though, your Pioneer leader starts to speak in that slowed down, deeper than usual voice she uses to say special things. She asks whether anyone has noticed the statue of a boy on the edge of the parade ground used for morning roll-call and for flying the detachment flag. Lots of hands go up, but when she asks his name, only know-it-all Sasha responds. 'Pavlik Morozov,' he says. Even he can't answer the next question, though: why should there be a statue to Pavlik Morozov? So your Pioneer leader starts to tell you.

Long ago, before you were born, perhaps even before your mother and father were born, back in the early 1930s, there was a little boy, not much older than you – thirteen – living far away, in a little village in the taiga, beyond the Urals, almost in Siberia. At that time the authorities were trying to change life in the villages, to take land, farm animals and grain away from the fat-cat peasants, the kulaks, and share them out so that everyone could be equal, and no one would be poor any more. Of course,

Group of Pioneers hearing about Pavlik Morozov's life by the original burial site of the boys in the village graveyard, Gerasimovka, 1940. (State Archive of Sverdlovsk Province, Ekaterinburg)

the kulaks didn't like this, and they did everything they could to stop it, hiding sacks and barrels of grain in their attics, under their floorboards, even inside their beds. And Pavlik Morozov found out that his own father, the chairman of the local village soviet, was in league with the kulaks, and was helping them evade justice. Of course, he was horrified: he was a good Pioneer, like you: but what should he do? He decided there was only one solution: he must report his father to the police. So he walked sixty kilometres to the nearest town, and there he went to the headquarters of the OGPU, the secret police, and told them what was going on. His father was sent to prison, of course. When his relatives found out what Pavlik had done, they got together and took revenge: on 3 September 1932, they stabbed him and his younger brother to death. They were hoping not just to punish Pavlik, but to frighten other Young Pioneers so that they wouldn't stand up for what was right. But it didn't work: the course of history rolled triumphantly on, and now Pavlik is a hero, honoured all over the Soviet Union.

Your teacher's voice gets deeper and deeper as she tells you this: she sounds as if she might be going to cry.[1] 'How could they do things like that to two little children?' she asks. You don't know: this is something much more horrible than the night-time stories in the dormitory. Imagine having to do that to your father! Could you ever do it? Suppose there ever came a time when you had to?

Soviet children did not always hear about Pavlik Morozov at a Pioneer camp. It might be at a political meeting after school, or in a lesson; or they might read a book about him as part of the extra-curricular school programme. Equally, responses to the story did not always work in the same way. Listeners might be inspired and uplifted by Pavlik's action, considering it a supreme act of self-sacrifice, or they might be indignant at anyone who could tell tales on someone else, let alone a member of their own family. Or they might have a squeamish sense that there was something not quite right about all of this – could you really walk sixty kilometres by yourself, all in a day? As the Soviet Union grew further away from its revolutionary roots, indignation and scepticism became more common. But there were always people who found the image of the boy, for one reason or another, admirable. Indeed, there still are people – a small minority, to be sure – who defend his memory in Russia today. In many ways, people's first responses to Pavlik – enthusiasm, embarrassment, indifference, hostility – would colour their responses to political education more generally: whether they found meetings and discussions enthralling, or diabolically boring; whether they later joined the Party, considered themselves unworthy of the honour, or did everything they could to avoid tangling with official politics.

Pavlik was not just a role model for children: he had meaning for adults as well. It was adults who created the story of Pavlik in the first place. The boy called Pavel Morozov really did exist, in the sense that he grew up in the place the legends describe and was murdered at the age of thirteen. Almost everything else about him, though, was undocumented, and had to be invented when it came to writing up the story of his life; almost everything, in other words, was subject to change in the face of ideological fluctuation.

Often, Pavlik's story is perceived as extremely straightforward – as a manifesto for blind fidelity to the Soviet state, in the face of which nothing, including family love, was sacred. The legend of the boy who betrayed his father is seen as part of the destruction of the family that the Bolsheviks are thought to have advocated. However, the top-level administration in the Soviet Union – as opposed to radical political groupings outside the circles of ultimate power – always took a rather lukewarm view of the idea of destroying the family. Providing state child-care for all was not only costly in economic terms, but also impossible practically speaking – where could one find the trained staff for thousands of nurseries, in a country where just a few dozen permanent institutions had been working before 1917? In any case, priority had to be given to caring for the hundreds of thousands of abandoned children, left bereft by war and revolution. And in the mid-1930s the Soviet leadership started doing all it could to build up family values – making it rather awkward to promote the cult of Pavlik, a boy locked in conflict with his father.

The Pavlik Morozov legend touched on all areas of Soviet society. This tale of a boy from a remote rural area was to a large extent created in the centre of the country, in Moscow: Pavlik was imported from the periphery, repackaged, and then exported for the edification of Soviet provincials, sold an uplifting image of themselves. The legend came at once from the ideological heart of the country, and from the muscle and bone of its provincial everyday.

I felt and lived this strongly myself, as I was researching this book. On the one hand, there are the official legends, which I absorbed – as many of their original readers would have done – far away from where Pavlik was brought up, in the relative privilege and comfort of Moscow and St Petersburg. On the other, there are the first news reports and the hesitantly typed or scrawled documents that were produced in Pavlik's home provinces, which show officials who could often barely spell gleefully absorbing new messages of righteous hatred. As I gathered materials, I also moved about in a physical sense, from quiet back streets in Moscow not far from where the writer Maxim Gorky, one of the main promoters of the Pavlik Morozov legend, lived in *style moderne* splendour, all curlicued railings, wood veneer and green tiles, to the tree-lined and straggling streets of Sverdlovsk (now Ekaterinburg), and then – after a night on an almost empty train, whose jolting, moaning, painfully slow progress suggested exhaustion and despair – to the wooden houses of Tavda and Gerasimovka.

This taiga region had a melancholy beauty in September, the time when Pavlik was killed. The river below the sand bluff on which Tavda stands was the Prussian blue of a fine day in the west of Ireland or Scotland; the handsome wooden houses built for managers in the lumber mills that used to sustain this one-industry town were locked in amber sunlight. Both here and in Gerasimovka itself, there were one or two buildings in angular concrete embellished with lavatory tiling

Pavlik Morozov's schoolmate, Dmitry Prokopenko, a war veteran, standing in front of his house in Gerasimovka, September 2003. (Catriona Kelly)

and vast picture windows, these days cracked and filthy with age – tokens of esteem from a relentlessly modernizing government back in the 1960s and 1970s – but for the most part, houses were in the timber-framed, plank-fronted style that now, seventy years after it started to replace log cabins proper, has started to look picturesque and venerable. In Gerasimovka, flowers were still determinedly out; sheep wandered the streets; the mixed, mainly deciduous, forest that makes up the taiga in these parts was a sensual combination of acid yellow and bronze. It was all a lesson in the visual appeal of the 'depths', as Russians put it. But after having spent a year in the provinces myself as a student, I was not deceived: things are very different in the desperate weeks between winter and spring, when there is mud everywhere, and stubbornly grey skies, the last sleet alternates with a particularly horrible form of precipitation known as 'mixed rain and snow', and when anything fresh disappears (the cause of famine in the past, though only of monotony now).

The Urals changed a great deal after Pavlik died. The centre of Sverdlovsk was transformed in the Stalin era by building work of the distinction befitting the capital of the vast Urals region, stretching for over 1,500 kilometres on each side of the mountain range. It was given its Lenin Street, and an enormous square fronting the city soviet, with the obligatory Lenin monument planted in front.[2] Gerasimovka now has electricity, though plumbing remains of the hole-in-the-ground and outside tap variety. In the past, the Urals had large numbers of forced-labour camps, absorbing half a million 'kulak' prisoners in 1930–31,[3] and generations of political prisoners for sixty years afterwards; now, most have been closed, and the remaining camps deal with a much smaller population, made up of people convicted for criminal offences of the everyday kind. The main problem for law enforcement now is drug-related crime – intravenous heroin use is particularly high in these parts.

But some of the past has endured, and is visible even today. Tavda retains the muddled, rustic look of a town that was rushed up under forced industrialization: there is no central square, just an open area near the railway station, with a pacing statue of (inevitably) Lenin off towards the track, and the white cuboid mass of the culture club (not the one where Pavlik's trial took place, but a newer building) dumped to one side. Older women in Gerasimovka still wear white headscarves, and life about the smallholding follows much the same round as it always did – indeed, as the collective farm struggles, traditional subsistence agriculture has become more important in recent years. And as I walked along the path that leads from the fields outside Gerasimovka village to the monuments marking the places where Pavlik and his brother were found murdered,[4] my Russian companions let out yelps of delight and rushed off the path to help themselves to wood mushrooms – a tall, handsome, rust-coloured parasol type with a greenish tinge was especially abundant.[5] Sadly, murders are common these days as well. Often alcohol is to blame, but sometimes sheer tedium and frustration, a desperation for *something* to do, plays a part.

The physical and emotional landscape of Pavlik's tale, then, is at once altered and as it was; the same could be said of the ideological landscape. In modern Russia, this tale of a boy who denounced his father out of loyalty to Party values has lost much of its force. A good many Russian citizens have forgotten who Pavlik was, or get him confused with one of the many other heroes they were told about at school. Yet there are ways in which the material is still sensitive. Many members of the generations who reached consciousness before Stalin died and were brought up with the notion that Soviet citizens were different from, morally superior to, the citizens of every other country in the world – those now sixty and above – have been deeply hurt by the constant and insistent revelations about the iniquities of the Soviet system that have poured from journalists, amateur and professional historians, writers, memoirists and commentators at large, since 1987. A phrase that one hears a great deal is, 'But not everything was bad.'

While members of younger generations were usually amused or incredulous that a foreigner wanted to write a book about Pavlik – assuming they knew what I was talking about in the first place – people in their sixties and older often became defensive. Typically, they would describe him – quite accurately – as a 'contradictory' figure. Having discovered that my purpose was not to heap mockery on the ideals of their youth from the point of view of smug historical hindsight, they heaved sighs of relief and began to pour out what the legend had meant to them. I never found anyone who told me that they thought denouncing your father (in whatever circumstances) was a good thing, but I found plenty who were eager to tell me about how much they valued the idea of selfless social commitment that they associated with Pavlik, and how much they regretted the self-seeking that they believed (not unjustifiably) to have started pervading Russia since 'savage capitalism' hit the country.

From the point of view of official attitudes to freedom of information, too, this story presents a chequered picture. On the one hand, the reluctance to give the case of the Morozov murders a thorough juridical reassessment shows the extent to which post-Soviet Russia has yet to come to terms with the Stalinist legacy. There is still a very widespread indifference to the importance of legal procedure – embodied in the idea that what happens to suspects who are certainly guilty anyway really doesn't much matter. I was once sitting in a flat with ex-dissident friends who are abrasively critical of many things about post-Soviet Russia too, and happened to see, in the street several floors down, a policeman drag a driver from his car and start to beat him with his truncheon. My distress was met with shoulder-shrugging incomprehension: 'What does it matter? He's probably drunk anyway.' Trials in which the prosecution plays fast and loose with the evidence and with the interpretation of statute to political ends are common – though not as common as those where justice is perverted in a more humdrum way, by recourse to bribery. But on the other hand, greater rigour and transparency of process are starting to make themselves felt.

Or at least, this much seemed to be clear in what was perhaps the least predictable episode of work on this book – the circumstances in which I came to see the secret police file on the Morozov murders. Even discovering where this was held was far from straightforward, and depended less on my assiduous sleuthing than on good luck. As of the autumn of 2003, my latest information was that the file was in the central office of the State Prosecution Service in Moscow, where it had been forwarded in connection with an unsuccessful application to rehabilitate one of the alleged murderers. My attempts to find someone with contacts at the Service had not worked; lengthy emails and faxes to a well-known Russian liberal politician who chairs a committee disseminating material from the archives had fallen into an abyss. Then someone in Moscow whom I'd been casually telling about the Pavlik book offered to ring round his historian friends and find out whether anyone knew anything. I was grateful, but not optimistic: often this kind of offer in the past had turned up someone who had given me a beginner's lecture on Soviet history. In this case, though, the friend of a friend in question was about to publish a selection of materials from the Morozov file in the historical journal he edits. The file, it emerged, was now in the Central Archive of the FSB (formerly the KGB).

I have a fair amount of experience of working in Russian archives, but don't collect them in the way people used to collect cigarette cards, and had never set foot in the secret police one. Indeed, I had no idea even where it was exactly or how to start applying to go there. As it turned out, there is a set procedure, but one that places daunting obstacles before anyone who wants to gain entry. The fact that it is essential to have a letter of introduction in Russian, signed, stamped and sealed, comes as no surprise – this is a routine entry requirement for all archives. However, a number of additional tasks, rather like the supposed-to-be-impossible missions set before the heroes of magic tales, is also imposed on anyone wanting to use the FSB facilities. You have to specify the details of the case file that you want to see (problematic, as no public catalogue is available), and you must either be a blood relation of the person to whom the case file relates, or have the written permission of this person's blood relations. I therefore approached the exercise of applying for permission in the only rational frame of mind – one of self-ironizing fatalism – and with the firm expectation of receiving, sooner or later, a courteous refusal.

Eventually, after some hiccups – my first letter of introduction was deemed to be 'no kind of a letter!' by an irate colonel in the FSB's Public Reception Centre, which is situated behind an ox-blood-coloured marble façade on a street of designer boutiques – I managed to get my application to the archive accepted. A few days later, I came to the end of that particular visit in Moscow, and returned home to work on something else and forget about Pavlik for a while. A month went past, and I was absolutely certain that any answer now would be a firm no. Then I suddenly got news that the FSB proposed to let me see the file. From then on, everything went smoothly. The archive reading room – not in the Lubyanka itself, but in a pleasant nineteenth-century building a hundred metres or so away – is open daily, and delivery works to appointment (in Russian archives generally, erratic openings and long delays are more characteristic). The reading-room staff are polite and helpful to their relatively few visitors, many of whom are elderly, and appear to be researching the case files of their own relations. Everyone works in a discreet hush – the occasional squealing mobile is quickly silenced. There is plenty of space, and an exuberantly prim display of busy-lizzies and rubber plants on the window-ledge. When I asked whether it would be all right to publish material from the file, I was told, 'That's exactly what we want you to do.'

What had provoked this astonishing desire to accommodate me? The staff archivist with whom I worked said to me that they could have continued to refuse permission, according to the standard rule that the case had not been reviewed and that those executed for the murder had not been rehabilitated. No doubt the 'blood relative' rule could also have been invoked (which would have been a serious problem, since Pavlik's last living relative, his nephew, also called Pavlik, was last heard of several years ago living in the Crimea, now part of a separate nation, Ukraine). But they had decided to make an exception in this instance, for several reasons: the length of time that the case had been on file; the notoriety and historical interest of the material in it; and the fact that all sorts of harmful rumours were circulating about the content of the case file.

To be frank, I think that I gained permission simply by dint of being the first serious scholar to ask to see the file, though it is possible that it also helped to be a foreigner (because that meant being safely outside the cut-and-thrust of post-Soviet domestic politics). Whichever way, the material was handed over without reservation. No attempt was made to control how much of it I saw, or to direct the way that I was to use it. There is a theory that the OGPU, the Soviet secret police, themselves killed Pavlik; the paranoid might suspect that I was shown a sanitized or forged set of documents, deliberately put together to exonerate them from blame. I can only respond that the material in the Morozov file resembles that in other case files of the day (if this is a forgery, it is at least a sophisticated one).[6] And the file does not show the OGPU in an at all flattering light. As it reveals, the process of preparing for the trial had more in common with an investigation by witch-hunters or members of the Inquisition than with a criminal investigation. But while there are certainly signs of some cover-up operations by the police, these were of a low-level kind. There is nothing to suggest that the killing itself was staged.

In terms of the broader facts of the case, though, the Morozov case file solves no problems. The 'real Pavlik' has disappeared behind hundreds of different stories: those told by his fellow-villagers, fearful of the authorities; those told by the investigators; what was said by the later journalists and biographers, and the teachers and Pioneer leaders who regurgitated their work for children; and of course, what the children said to each other about the boy. Reality lay outside these images of Pavlik: in the suffering of the peasants enduring collectivization; in the desperation to believe of self-made intellectuals, themselves from peasant or working-class roots; and in the injustices that were committed in the name of Soviet power in order to ensure that its enemies were punished, and the spirit of resistance in the villages broken. The Morozov legend was created to represent Soviet society as it wanted to show itself and to see itself; by looking at the process of its creation, on the other hand, one learns all sorts of things the propaganda makers most definitely did not want known.

INTRODUCTION

Death in the Taiga

On 15 October 1932, *Pioneer Pravda* reported that a sensational trial was about to take place in Tavda, located in the forest about 350 kilometres east of Sverdlovsk (now Ekaterinburg). Two children had been murdered just outside the remote village of Gerasimovka: a fifteen-year-old boy, a staunch and active Pioneer, and his nine-year-old brother. 'Till this very hour, the taiga [primal forest] conceals the traces of this bestial crime,' the paper declared. The 'thick undergrowth' where the boys had been slaughtered was 'spattered with cranberries', and trampled aspen and birch leaves carried traces of blood. One boy had four deep knife-wounds, the other three. The murderers, the paper asserted confidently, were the boys' cousin, aged eighteen, and one of his friends. The motive for the murder was the elder victim's selfless commitment to the Communist cause: he had 'placed the interests of the Party and the working class above his own'. Specifically, he had denounced his father to the authorities for corruption, and had been killed as an act of vengeance by the two accused.

The boy's mother was quoted, commending her son's courage. Even when beaten by his father, he had refused to back down, and, at his father's trial, he had declared fearlessly: 'Uncle judge, I am acting not as a son, but as a Pioneer![1]

Six weeks later, on 3 December 1932, *Pioneer Pravda* brought its readers the result of the now notorious murder case. Five people had stood trial. They included, besides the victims' cousin, their grandparents, and their two uncles by marriage.

The uncles were arraigned as the main moving spirits behind the murder; the boys' cousin and grandfather were said to have carried it out. The grandmother had lured the boys into the woods and covered up for her relations by washing the bloodied clothes of the perpetrators.

After a four-day hearing (25 to 28 November), four of the five accused were sentenced to 'the highest measure of punishment' – death by shooting. The case had been heard as a full 'show trial', with maximum publicity, submissions to the tribunal from the indignant public in the form of letters, petitions, etc., and two 'social prosecutors', or ideologists, sitting alongside the legal specialists to offer input into the hearing of evidence and the judgement. *Pioneer Pravda* printed in full the closing oration of one of these two 'social prosecutors', Elizar Smirnov (a young journalist on the paper). He represented Gerasimovka in the most melodramatic fashion, 'cast away in the forest amid bogs and lakes; a dim dark village with accursed olden-time traditions'. Equally colourful was the portrait of the older murder victim: 'He was not only a good pupil at school and a good Pioneer, not only public-spirited to the highest degree, but a good support to his fatherless family: the best helping hand to his mother, the best friend to his little brothers.'[2]

The subject of this eulogy was Pavel or 'Pavlik' Morozov, the first child hero in Soviet history. Canonized in 1955 in the Book of Honour of the Moscow Pioneer Palace, as 'Pioneer No. 001',[3] Pavlik had become legendary well before that, both in the Soviet Union and the West, as an example of unswerving commitment to political rectitude. He was the subject of songs, plays, a symphonic poem and even a (dreadful) full-length opera, as well as six full-length biographies, several poems and countless commemorative articles in the children's press. Streets, parks and culture clubs were named after him, as were aeroplanes and boats, not to speak of Pioneer groups and 'Pioneer corners' in schools. Monuments were raised all over the Soviet Union, and indeed beyond (there is one in Colombo, Sri Lanka).[4] He even inspired a genuine work of art – Sergei Eisenstein's film *Bezhin Meadow* (1936), in which a fanatical blond-haired boy heads his village's march into the future, leading a violent assault on the local church (at the culmination, its gold iconostasis is torn down). In the 1960s, knowledge of Pavlik's life became essential

The statue of Pavlik Morozov in Gerasimovka, photographed in September 1972: Pavlik's younger brother Aleksei is standing in the foreground. (Pavlik Morozov Museum, Gerasimovka)

for admission to the Pioneer movement, and in schools of the day, official lives were set as compulsory extra-curricular reading.

The article in *Pioneer Pravda* was not the first item about Pavlik to appear in the press.[5] However, it represented the first notable coverage of the murder and of the trial in the national (or, to use the preferred Soviet term, 'central') press. It therefore marked a vital initial stage in the process of Pavel's transformation into a Soviet hero. A dark-haired peasant boy from a particularly remote – in Soviet parlance 'backward' – village was resculpted as an exemplary Pioneer activist with chiselled blond looks and a resolute gaze.[6]

From the mid-1930s to the late 1980s, the vast majority of Soviet children between the age of ten and fourteen were members of the Pioneer movement. A Soviet equivalent of the Scout and Guide organization, the Pioneers had a similar motto – 'Always Prepared', rather than 'Be Prepared' – and a similar oath of fidelity, but children swore allegiance to the 'cause of the working class' (from 1937, to 'the cause of Lenin and Stalin'), rather than to king and country. Like the Scouts, the Pioneers had a tie, only in their case it was red – they were known as 'red-tie-wearers', or 'young Leninists'. And the movement had its own ceremonies and rituals: parades with bugles and drums; the raising of the flag at Pioneer summer camps; and the 'conversations round the bonfire', at which children were taught about Pioneer history.

In terms of Soviet propaganda, Pavlik was unquestionably a hero; but this is not the only version of his life. In the 1970s, Yury Druzhnikov, a writer and journalist then living in Moscow, began carrying out a single-handed, necessarily clandestine investigation of the real circumstances of Pavlik and Fyodor's murder. Having spoken to survivors, scrutinized the published record, and pieced together such archival materials as he could find (the secret police file on the case was not accessible to him), he came to the conclusion that the life and death of the real Pavlik Morozov had been very different from the life and death shown in the various official biographies. Druzhnikov's book had, in its first Russian edition, published in 1995, the sensational title *Denouncer No. 001*,[7] and its purpose was to debunk every aspect of the official myth. Pavlik emerges from it as a dirty, miserable, probably mentally abnormal, child, who was probably not a Pioneer and certainly not a hero. His murder was carried out not by 'enemies of the people', and certainly not by members of his own family, but by members of the security services aiming to provoke a scandal and to stigmatize the enemies of the Soviet state.

Druzhnikov's book contains valuable testimony from those who lived in Gerasimovka when Pavlik was alive, and is a rattling good yarn (it reads like a detective novel). But the case that it advances will simply not stand up. Much weight is attached to a small selection of documents from the OGPU case file – four sheets from a record that in fact stretches to around 250 pages – which are taken out of context in order to present arguments that seem very questionable when archive materials are scrutinized in depth. I was sceptical about the Druzhnikov hypothesis at the start of my research, and only had my scepticism reinforced by work in the local archives (which produce a totally different picture of the state of political control in the early 1930s). Eventually I rejected it completely after I had worked with the full case file. But I was left equally dissatisfied by the official version – which has the actual murderers being egged on to do their work by a shadowy network of kulaks. My research suggests a very different kind of murder – brutal, to be sure, but lying beyond conspiracy theories, the product of a community that had been horribly damaged by three years of forced collectivization.

I would emphasize, though, that getting at the truth about Pavlik Morozov and his murder is probably now impossible. As I discuss in detail in Chapter Three, the interrogation records are a tissue of accusation and counter-accusation, malicious gossip, self-contradiction and confessions produced under (sometimes physical) duress. Every participant in the process of collecting information about the murders – from villagers up to senior secret policemen – had his or her own prejudices about the case, and many also had something to hide. Testimony often smacks less of sincerity than of creative (or, at other times, stumbling) lying. Where statements seem most straightforward (direct confessions to the murder), they are most problematic: suspects were cajoled, coerced and bullied into admissions, often given in words that were patently not their own.[8]

Oral history does not provide a touchstone of truth either. To begin with, most of the generation who could directly recall the Pavlik Morozov affair is now long gone. In addition, when I visited Gerasimovka in September 2003, I discovered that the villagers were – exactly as one would expect – telling me about events according to a set of established stereotypes. The case is just too famous for anyone to recall what they *really* thought about it back in 1932. Indeed, Gerasimovka old-timers were often reluctant to recall the past in detail at all. 'Och, life was bad, bad, bad, back then: it's got better now,' said Pavlik's cousin

Yulianiya, who bears a striking resemblance to the picture of him used on the front cover of this book.[9] Mariya Sakova, an intelligent and fine-featured woman who eventually honoured me with some very vivid recollections of Pavlik's murder, and of her childhood in the late 1920s and 1930s, at first did not want to speak to me at all. 'What's there to say?' she demanded, sitting on the bench outside her house on Gerasimovka's one tarmacked street ('the road Pavlik brought', locals call it). 'I never had a childhood – I only worked and worked . . .'[10]

Pavlik's murder happened just as the nation he had lived in was about to undergo an important transformation. The Soviet Union was approaching the end of the First Five-Year Plan, and of the so-called 'Cultural Revolution', when 'revolutionary' and 'Bolshevik' values – in other words, an attachment to the radical transformation of society – had been paramount. From 1933, the culture would settle into an extended period of self-glorification and celebration of its own achievements, as manifested by the outstanding individuals of the nation, above all, of course, the dictator, Joseph Stalin. An entire industry for the manufacture of heroes started up. Writings about such heroes were not intended to reflect reality: like the legends of saints circulated by the Catholic Church in the medieval period, they were supposed to excite the admiration and awe of the faithful at large. Every story in the Soviet press edited out any details that did not suit the governing image of admirable behaviour, and superimposed traits that were considered desirable. Flamboyant drunks and womanizers were presented as exemplary family men, illiterate peasants as wise devotees of the works of Lenin.[11]

Portraying really famous individuals, those destined for admiration on the part of Soviet citizens everywhere, was a sophisticated and time-consuming process. They had to be repeatedly remodelled in order to reflect the latest changes in the Party line. Just as Trotsky and other 'enemies of the people' vanished from new editions of photographs showing Lenin at public meetings, so heroes lost some features and acquired others, as time went on. The remodelling of Pavlik Morozov was especially energetic. From the first newspaper reports of 1932 to the new lives of the 1960s and 1970s, his legend was transmuted to reflect changing attitudes to what children should learn about ethical values and about revolutionary politics.

The provision of role models for the young is an age-old activity, reaching back into the classical era and beyond. What was novel about the process in the early twentieth century was the rising interest, as the new discipline of 'paidology' took hold, in children's reactions to such models. In Russia, as in Britain, America, Germany and France, educationalists conducted surveys establishing who children's heroes were, and discovered a bewilderingly eclectic mix, ranging from historical figures and characters out of books to royalty, contemporary politicians and people the children actually knew ('my mother', 'my teacher').[12] In the one-party dictatorship, attempts were made to build on and control children's assumed capacity for hero-worship, and to provide them with an alternative range of 'politically correct' role models, all safely subordinated to the ultimate authority and glory of the primary hero-figure, the dictator himself. Pavlik's legend was invented at a point when Pioneers were supposed to be feisty little activists, members of a juvenile elite, addressing public meetings and laying down the law to their elders about the virtues of cleanliness and the evils of godliness. By the mid-1930s, the Pioneers was turned into a mass organization, with whole school years more or less automatically enrolled. And as organizing 'rational leisure' for children became as important as political indoctrination, Pavlik moved in step: he began to develop hobbies, friends, an interest in schoolwork, and his role as a rebel within the family started to be played down.

The significance of the legend is not at all straightforward, therefore. But often, the subject of Pavlik Morozov as role model is discussed as if it were. The motif of Pavlik's denunciation of his father is so sensational that it has, for many commentators, overshadowed everything else about the story. Anyone who has even a passing acquaintance with psychoanalytical theory is likely to come out with the obvious label. As the Russian-American cultural theorist Svetlana Boym has written, 'This is the Soviet version of the Oedipal myth par excellence – only secrets, blindness, and the metaphysical conversation with the sphinx are lacking.'[13] By extension, one could see the Pavlik myth as a mirror-image version of *Hamlet* (the favourite play of Russian intellectuals since the Romantic era) in which the son colluded with his 'uncle' the judge in order to effect the symbolic murder of his father, pouring verbal poison into the latter's ear. As with Hamlet and Oedipus, the price of Pavlik's filial rebellion was his own destruction: the myth therefore worked to warn against the instigation of generational conflict, and not only, or mainly, to endorse this.

Yet the Pavlik Morozov myth was distinct from both *Oedipus Rex* and *Hamlet* in significant ways. To begin with, Pavlik's relationship with his mother was usually marginal to his legend. The official lives represented her as innocent but helpless, sympathetic to Pavlik but incapable of giving him any real aid in his struggle with his father. Second, Pavlik did not feel the kind of ambivalence towards his father that was common to both Oedipus and Hamlet. The man had traduced paternity by his actions, made himself no longer a father: the act of rejecting him was straightforward and guilt-free. In other words, the Pavlik myth was only in a marginal sense a family drama.[14] The archetypicality of the tale lay less in the realm of psychosexuality than in the realm of politics and ethics. Pavlik's life brought to the fore the conflicted relationship between blood ties and justice, raising a question that has preoccupied European moralists for at least two and a half millennia: in what circumstances can it be right to denounce a member of your own family?

To assign Pavlik's tale such universal meaning might seem at first sight perverse. Usually the boy is seen as typical only of the age and place from which his cult came, the Soviet Union under Stalin. In words attributed to Shostakovich: 'The hero of the era was little Pavlik Morozov, who informed on his father. Pavlik was sung in poetry, prose, and music. Eisenstein took part in the praises, working long and hard on a great art film which glorified the little sneak, *Bezhin Meadow*.'[15] In similar terms, an anti-Soviet history of the Komsomol fastened on Pavlik as the supreme example of the Soviet system's commitment to fostering double-dealing: 'Deliberate lying and political denunciation are the methods of reprisal used by the government against *personae non gratae*. The government has cultivated these attributes with equal diligence among the Komsomol and among children. Remember the story of Pavlik Morozov.'[16] For Yury Druzhnikov, the story 'exactly sums up the nature of a political system with a one-party ideology'.[17]

It is certainly striking that a similar figure to Pavel, Hitler

Boy Quex, was celebrated as a children's hero in another one-party, totalitarian, state, the Third Reich.[18] But these two master narratives from one-party states should not be looked at in isolation. Denunciation of family members is not uniformly condemned even in societies that celebrate the autonomy of the family and propound strongly individualist moral values, such as late twentieth-century Western ones. Though Yury Druzhnikov has insisted that 'every type of denunciation within, or from within, the family is amoral',[19] the question of in what circumstances it would and would not be right to conceal a near relative's crime is usually seen as more problematic in ethical terms than this assertion would suggest.

To be sure, there exist some canonical texts from the Western democratic tradition questioning the virtue of the 'denouncer from within'. Plato's dialogue *Euthyphro*, for example, shows Socrates undermining the conceit of an Athenian man who proposes to prosecute his father for causing the death of a servant. The vigilante's self-satisfied notion of virtue is scrutinized, and duly exposed as logically faulty. Assuming himself bent on justice, he is incapable of exploring the complexities of guilt, and so gets locked into behaviour that looks, to a sophisticated (Socratic) observer, more like the enactment of primitive revenge than the imposition of rational punishment.

There is, then, a strong antipathy to the idea of denunciation within the family in mainstream Western philosophical tradition. In comparable vein, one notes that Dostoevsky neatly avoids, in his narratives about blood-guilt, the issue of whether denunciation within the family might ever be appropriate. Raskolnikov's relations are unaware of his part in the murder of the two women that opens *Crime and Punishment*; Ivan Karamazov, who acts as unwilling confessor to Smerdyakov, promptly goes mad, and so would be unable to cashier his half-brother for the murder even had this idea occurred to him.

However, there are other voices in Western culture too.[20] The foundation myths of Rome include a famous legend about the placing of duty higher than family connections: Livy's tale of Brutus the Elder, who condemned his own sons to death for treachery to the Republic.[21] Mayor Lynch of medieval Galway, who hanged his son with his own hands and so, in slaughtering his offspring, gave birth to a verb, is a later case of 'justice before family ties'. And Western practical morality has continued to esteem those who break emotional bonds in the face of serious offences against the common good. In the contemporary world, children who denounce parents or relations for certain types of economic crime (the organization of child sex-trade rackets, large-scale drug-dealing) as well as certain types of political crime (involvement in Mafia or terrorist activity), not to speak of crimes against the person (above all child abuse), tend to meet with sympathy and approval, rather than disgust. When Sorcha McKenna, the daughter of Northern Irish human rights activist Vincent McKenna, denounced her father as a child abuser, using words close to those of the fictional Pavlik Morozov ('I don't think of him as my father any more'), and asserting she had done what she did because of her father's public role,[22] the probity of her action was not questioned.

It is fair to say that the idealization of those who place civic patriotism above family affinity expresses something more than merely the suppression of individual autonomy that is held to be a defining characteristic of totalitarian states. The peculiarity of the Soviet version of civic patriotism did not lie in the proposition that even fathers should be denounced, if they were wicked. It lay, rather, in the extrapolation of a general principle proclaiming the virtues of denunciation in all circumstances from a decidedly peculiar and sensational example. And it also lay in the fate of those denounced, in a legal system that denied defendants the right to a fair trial, silently tolerated torture, regarded confessions extracted under duress as acceptable legal evidence, and condemned those summarily tried and sentenced to immediate execution, or to moulder in the appalling conditions of a Soviet prison or labour camp.

The Pavlik Morozov myth was about more than denunciation within the family. As more or less everyone who has written about it so far seems to have forgotten, the story was also about the killing of two children. In the first months after the Morozov murders, it was precisely for this reason that it attracted interest from the general public. The letters that poured in to the local press, and the national Pioneer press, often included formulas about continuing to fight the good fight, and refusing to be intimidated by the evil deeds of 'enemies of the people'. But their main thrust was the need to take vengeance on the monsters that had done this deed. The order of priorities is captured well in a letter written in October 1932 by a group of children in Moscow province:

> PROTEST
> We, Pioneers and schoolchildren of Kosterevskaya Factory School, attached to the Komintern Factory, have read the article in *Pioneer Pravda* about the murder of Pioneer Pavel Morozov by kulaks, and we demand that the murderers are subjected to the highest measure of punishment, execution by shooting. In our turn, we promise to step up the fight for knowledge and work discipline in our school.
>
> Sleep soundly, dear comrade Pavlusha!
>
> We will carry on your cause to the end.
>
> And the most splendid wreath and memorial for you will be our struggle for knowledge.[23]

Letters like this did not come out of nothing. 'We have read the article' actually meant 'Our teachers have made us read parts of the newspaper for homework and suggested we write to the paper.' But while the Soviet authorities stirred up emotions about the Morozov murders, they did not create these to start with. Such a brutal attack on two children – both boys were repeatedly stabbed in the neck, chest and stomach – would be an inflammatory event in any society. It is not just in the Soviet Union that child murderers are taken to be figures of supernatural evil, probably drawn from some socially abject part of the population (ethnic minorities, paedophiles), who prefer to work in groups.[24] The discovery of the headless and mutilated torso of an African child in the Thames in September 2001 was followed by deductions conforming to the classic pattern. 'Initially, the detectives wondered if the mutilation might be an attempt to disguise the identity of the victim of an accident, a family row or a sex crime. But then, two miles upstream in Chelsea, they found the remnants of an African ritual, with a Nigerian name written on a sheet, carved into seven half-burned candles. Might this be a ritual killing?'[25] If speculation of this kind can easily take hold in a country that prides itself on its rationalistic legal culture, it is hardly surprising that the Soviet Union, where justice was explicitly subordinated to the needs of the 'class war', could be gripped by wild imaginings. Those who opposed collectivization were wicked, therefore they must have perpetrated a vicious murder such as this; in turn, the murder itself became a crucial example of just how wicked the enemies of Soviet society were.

Child murder was not, according to the tariffs imposed by Soviet legislation at this period, a capital crime. Indeed, the 1926 Criminal Code of the Russian Federation did not recognize 'child murder' as a specific offence at all. Instead, the tariff of penalties specified under Articles 136 to 140 depended upon whether the murder concerned was premeditated or not. Penalties ranged from up to three years in prison for 'murder out of carelessness' (approximately equivalent to 'manslaughter'), to a maximum of ten years in certain cases of premeditated offence – where the murder had been inspired by 'selfishness, jealousy, and other low promptings', or was committed by a repeat offender, or in order to conceal another crime; or where the victim was someone in the care of the offender, or exploited by that person; or where the act was accompanied by torture, or had been committed against a pregnant woman. Children were specifically recognized in other areas of the Criminal Code – notably in Article 11, which stipulated that children under fourteen could not be subjected to 'measures of social defence of a judicial and penal kind [. . .] but only to measures of a medico-pedagogical kind'. What in practice this meant was that under-14s could not be tried, imprisoned or executed, but were supposed to have their cases considered by expert tribunals, and to receive, at most, supervision orders or referrals to special types of homes for 'difficult children'. Children aged fourteen to sixteen were usually supposed to be subjected to 'medico-pedagogical' measures as well. And such measures could also be applied to sixteen- to eighteen-year-olds if the courts deemed them to be essential.[26] Children, then, were recognized as a special category of perpetrators of crimes, including murder, but not as a special category of victims.

Children's affairs had become concerns of state in a radically new way after 1917 – as shown in Trotsky's declaration, 'A revolution does not deserve its name if it does not take the greatest care possible of the children – the future race for whose benefit the revolution has been made.'[27] But even so, child murder was not necessarily treated as a crime of primary importance. In 1928, a Nizhny-Novgorod woman, incensed when her small daughter's friend called her 'a madman's wife', stabbed the girl repeatedly with a knife, once in the chest and several times in the belly. The original sentence of a year's forced labour compares strikingly with the maximum penalty for submitting a child to illegal religious education, which at the time also stood at one year.[28]

However, the Morozov murders were not treated as a normal murder, under Articles 136 to 140 of the 1926 Criminal Code. Instead, the article applied to their case was one of the subdivisions of the notorious Article 58, for crimes against the state. Point 8 of this article embraced 'the execution of terrorist acts aimed against representatives of Soviet power, or activists in revolutionary worker and peasant organizations, and participation in the execution of such acts, even if this be by persons who do not belong to a counter-revolutionary organization'. Among such 'terrorist acts' were murder, attempted murder and grievous bodily harm aimed at a 'representative of Soviet power' or an 'activist in a revolutionary worker and peasant organization'. The maximum penalty for offences under Article 58.8, as for most other offences under this article, was execution by shooting.[29]

Once the suspects in the Morozov case had been arraigned under Article 58.8, the investigation took on a new urgency. Now, those researching the crime were concerned with the need to underline the guilt of those who were already seen as guilty before the investigation began. The investigators were collecting evidence for a show trial – which was not the objective examination of evidence presented by each side, but the demonstration of why the verdict set out in the case for the prosecution, literally the 'act of accusation' (*obvinitel'nyi akt*), was correct and appropriate. In other words, the trial was a ritual demonstration of the state's power to isolate and punish wrongdoers.[30] Hence, the records relating to the investigation and trial are ideological documents, just as the various lives of Pavlik Morozov and the newspaper reports are.

Throughout the book, I am primarily concerned with ideology and with myth, but I have always kept in mind their central target – Soviet children themselves. The myth itself was not straightforward. It drew on different, and in many respects contradictory, traditions: Christian martyrdom; beliefs about ritual killing; public disquiet about the killing of the children of Nicholas II as a 'Bolshevik outrage' (which required publicity to be given to an *anti*-Bolshevik outrage). In seeking to promote a cause they saw as rational by appeal to the irrational, Soviet propagandists were playing a dangerous game, and in fact reactions to the myth were not within their control. This especially applied to the child audience for the myth, an apparently malleable, but in fact unpredictable, public.

Soviet children grew up in a culture where politics got everywhere, but the result of this was not necessarily a precocious interest in politics. Like any other kind of indoctrination, the teaching offered by the Pioneer movement and by Soviet schools about Pavlik risked provoking exactly the opposite of the intended reaction. There was a danger that a hero promoted as assiduously as Pavlik would become an anti-hero – not that little sneak again! Jaded reactions became especially common after the Second World War, when a very different type of hero – silent even under torture – started to be celebrated in children's literature and in patriotic propaganda.

But at the same time, Pavlik's myth retained its hold – above all, in the abstract sense, as a model of supreme self-sacrifice for the good of the national cause. An interviewee of mine in Ekaterinburg compared him with Danko in Maxim Gorky's early story 'Old Woman Izergil', who destroys his own body in order to lead his people from the dark forest into which they have been driven by enemies:

> And suddenly he tore open his breast and ripped out of it his heart and lifted his heart high above his head.
>
> His heart shone brightly as the sun, and brighter than the sun, and the whole forest fell silent, lit by the lantern of great love for mankind, and the dark flew away from its light and there, deep in the forest, sank down into the rotten maw of the bogs. And the people stood astonished, still as stones.
>
> 'Let us go!' cried Danko and rushed forward, holding high above his head his burning heart and lighting with it the path that they were to walk.[31]

In that sense, the myth exemplified some of the values that held Soviet society together, and made a fundamentally artificial and wrong-headed political system last for seventy years.

Yet, at the same time, the fact that Pavlik's supreme act was *denunciation* proved embarrassing even to Soviet patriots. It would perhaps not be an exaggeration to say that the moral entropy of Soviet society – where elevated ideals were propounded by ethically questionable means, leading, eventually, to the discrediting of these ideals – is set out, in miniature, by the history of the legend. And for its part, the murder investigation provides a case study in the inequities and mendacities of Soviet police investigations and trials in the early 1930s, a glimpse into the jaws of the huge 'mincing machine' that was represented by the penal system.[32]

Arguing that the Pavlik legend is central to the understanding of Soviet history might at first sight seem strange. In its public form, the story was explicitly directed at children, a much celebrated but politically disempowered social group. The promotion of the legend at national level was the work of what one might term political 'middle managers' – ideologues and journalists from the Komsomol, many with provincial roots. The process by which the investigation and trial were carried out at the local level was also controlled, in a primary sense, by Soviet officials far down the system – only at a late stage of the investigation did officials even at the level of regional government in Sverdlovsk get involved. The trial of Pavlik's alleged murderers was held in the 'culture club of the name of Stalin' on Stalin Street in Tavda, but the hundreds of pages of unpublished material about, or related to, the case that were produced in the Urals contain not one reference to Stalin, or to any other member of the Soviet administration at its highest level. Indeed, Stalin played – so far as I can tell – no direct role in the dissemination of the cult. (If anything, he disliked and despised the story of a boy who rebelled against patriarchal authority. He is reported to have left the pre-release showing of Eisenstein's *Bezhin Meadow* with the comment, 'We cannot allow any small boy to behave as though he were Soviet power itself.')[33]

Archival evidence makes clear that the Pavlik Morozov legend was not originally invented at the top of Soviet society. A plethora of telegrams and instructions from higher instances to lower along the lines, 'You've got it all wrong,' and 'Get a move on,' indicates that this was a case which started off with only parochial significance, and gradually worked its way upwards, so that what would originally have been a hasty trial in a village hall organized for a local public turned into an extended, five-level investigation, culminating in a district-centre trial attended by the national press. In other words, the mechanics by which this cult grew resembled those by which the cults of local saints come in time to be recognized by the higher ecclesiastical authorities, to be followed by canonization and 'translation' of the relics to a resting-place of greater prestige and religious significance.

Cults are made, not born: they are the creations of living individuals. And so I look not just at the *content* of the Pavlik myth over the different decades, but at the people who put it together. Some of those who took part in this were famous: Maxim Gorky, the most powerful writer in the early Stalin era (indeed, probably the most powerful writer in Soviet history of any era). But some were rank-and-file officials: the district plenipotentiary of OGPU, as the political police was then known, and his subordinates; the members of the local Party; the overworked journalists on the Tavda local paper. And others were Pavlik's fellow-villagers in Gerasimovka, who may have had a shaky grasp of ideology, but who readily provided officials with snatches of malicious gossip and fantastic rumours that could be used as substantiation for, and embellishment of, the case against the real and imaginary enemies of the state.

In the end, what this book represents is a concentrated study of Soviet history at the grassroots, 'Stalinist history without Stalin' – a kind of counterweight to the naïve view, in popular Western historiography, of a country under the all-seeing eye of the malevolent dictator (a view that is strikingly close to the one in Soviet propaganda, though there Stalin was, of course, seen as munificent and wise).[34] The Morozov case shows how difficult it was for many people to understand what the Party leadership really wanted, and points to the struggle to articulate barely familiar new ideas, and to find role models to go with them. It also illustrates the horrors of experiencing collectivization on the ground: of a traditional peasant culture torn apart, of communities set at each other's throats, and of the tragedy of child activism in circumstances where self-assertion put children in physical danger.[35]

The traditional hierarchy of Russian villages had subordinated children to the absolute rule of their elders, and especially male heads of household. During the first decade or so of its existence, the Pioneer movement stood this hierarchy on its head, actively encouraging children to harangue their elders. It is no wonder that the result was often aggression directed against the young. For some children, then, as well as many adults, the promotion, from the mid-1930s, of dependence upon adults rather than all-out conflict with adults, probably seemed less a repression of hard-won rights than a welcome suspension of activities that had indeed led them 'way out of their depth': which had been frightening, difficult and, in the end, often pointless as well. But at the same time, the Pavlik myth gave voice to children's potential for real action in the early Soviet era – as expressed not just through their part in the collectivization campaign, but also in the activities of the children who fought in the Russian Civil War, addressed public meetings, and not least, held families together by working, and by queuing for bread in the terrible years of famine.[36]

CHAPTER 1

Pavlik's World

When the murder of the Morozov brothers took place in 1932, the Russian countryside was gripped by *de facto* civil war. On one side stood the Soviet government and its local representatives; on the other, the millions of peasant farmers, most of whom had no wish to join collective farms and to lose their hard-won independence. Collectivization – whereby peasants were coerced or forced to join co-operative units, *kolkhozy* or collective farms, to become a rural proletariat on shared holdings rather than farmers working their own land – was far more than a campaign for economic change. It was a full-scale assault on peasant tradition and on the autonomy of the village. Millions died from starvation, in imprisonment, in exile or in transit; rural life was never the same again.[1] To grasp the scale of the catastrophe, one might imagine the Highland clearances and the Irish potato famine rolled into one. The spirit of the exercise was comparable too: in the same way that British governments and so-called enlightened landlords of the eighteenth and nineteenth centuries presented their evictions (or tolerance of these) and refusal to provide food relief as the only possible response in the face of the ignorance and fecklessness of the populations they were aiming to manage, and encouraged emigration as a way of reducing the numbers of the inhabitants, the Soviet authorities evicted and deported the opponents of collectivization. And just as right-thinking, sober-minded and philanthropically inclined individuals in the late eighteenth or early nineteenth centuries in London or Edinburgh held crofters in Sutherland or Mayo as themselves to blame for the devastation that they endured, so Soviet patriots in Moscow, Leningrad, Kiev and other major cities discounted the half-starved peasants they saw begging on the streets as the necessary detritus of history.[2]

Each attack on a kulak family exacted terrible human costs. Ivan Tvardovsky and his family (including three young children) were evicted from their home in Smolensk province in March 1931, taking with them only essentials (an axe, cooking equipment, soap and bedding).

> The youngest – Pavlik, Masha and Vasilyok – were crying and pressing themselves to our mother. 'Mam! Where are they taking us? Mam!' They threw back their heads and stretched towards her face, grabbed hold of her clothes, clung to her, begging for an answer, begging for help. My mother was beside herself. She was rushing round, things falling from her hands, and crying tears of desperation, embracing the children. And in a voice not her own, she tried to comfort them: 'Now children! Now, then! What's all this! Eh, don't cry, my loves, my little ones!'[3]

Tvardovsky's family were at least lucky in that they were able to take some domestic items, and in that the official and witnesses who supervised the eviction were ashamed of what they were doing, and did not add to the misery with threats or taunts – as commonly happened in other cases.

The official doctrine of 'class war' stirred up such scenes, but exterminating 'enemies' was not the only motive behind collectivization. Those forcing through reform were also convinced that this was necessary in order to root out the 'backwardness' flourishing in the Russian village. A 1926 story by Evgeny Zamiatin, the author of the dystopian fantasy *We*, brings out the customary stereotype. In the last days of the First World War, simple-minded Styopka, whose father has prevented him from joining a monastery, and packed him off to a factory job in town, starts sending letters back to his remote home village with reports of strange events. It has been decided that God is only a superstition, and that instead of the Bible you should read someone called Marx. In Styopka's village, though, social unrest centres round the figure of the local landowner, and especially his collection of foreign statues representing strange pagan gods.

Eventually, news filters through that some kind of revolution, with processions and flags, has broken out in the city. The villagers decide to join in by storming the local manor house. Urged on by the suddenly returned Styopka, they threaten the landowner with death, and announce their intention of destroying his statues. But they spare one statue and its owner when they hear from him that the statue is of 'Marx'. Loading it on to a farm cart, they set off on a triumphal march round the village. The mistake is laid bare only much later, when a 'proper orator' from the city arrives and points out to them the difference between the Roman god of war and the author of *Das Kapital*.

Zamiatin's story, the wandering reminiscences of a man from the invented village of Kuiman, where 'nature is all spread out in thick forest', captures some of the spirit of revolution in the deep countryside: settling scores with landowners was indeed one of the main local responses to the collapse of central power. But it also travesties the motivation behind peasant political action. Revolution in the provinces did not consist of comical misunderstandings on the part of naïve boobies, but of calculated, self-interested efforts by the peasants to acquire what was of most interest to them – land. Hence the mass support for the political party which promised that land would be redistributed directly to peasants themselves, the Socialist Revolutionaries. While the nationalization of economic resources advocated by the Bolsheviks had appeal to workers because it promised to empower those in factory jobs, state ownership flew in the face of the peasant yearning for land of their own.

Like Zamiatin in 'Comrade Churygin', the Bolsheviks had a view of the Russian countryside as remote, unchanging, economically and intellectually deprived, and without local variation. As they got to grips with the colossal task of imposing central authority on the Russian hinterland from 1921, after their victory in a civil war where large sections of the rural population had supported their opponents, their actions were driven not only by an accurate belief that the Russian peasantry constituted a formidable political adversary, but also by the legacy of pre-revolutionary paternalism. The peasantry had to be tamed, by force if necessary, but it had also to be civilized, raised to the cultural levels of the urban population.

THE HARD LINE

Already during the era of 'War Communism' (1918–21), a preliminary and short-lived collectivization drive had taken place; despite fierce opposition from the peasantry, the number of collective units climbed from under 1,000 to over 15,000.[4] But momentum was soon lost with the onset of the 'New Economic Policy' in 1921, when the Party leadership allowed some freedom to private enterprise in order to attract investment to repair the economy ravaged by revolution, world war and civil war. From this point, the collectivization movement was to a large extent forced to rely on propaganda and local activism, and worked in parallel with a voluntary commune movement, according to which groups of enthusiasts set up agricultural enterprises on their own initiative (this in due course became the inspiration for the kibbutz movement in Israel).

Once the move to economic centralization and forced industrialization began with the institution of the First Five-Year Plan in 1928, however, the pressure to collectivize acquired a new urgency. With the drafting of millions of new workers into factory jobs that was essential to the expansion of industry, it was vital to ensure reliable supplies of food to the enlarging cities. Unfortunately, the 1927–8 season had seen crop failures in the main grain-producing areas of the south, promising a serious food crisis at the worst possible time. Attempts to solve the crisis through the marketplace failed, as the low threshold of government grain requisition prices made peasant producers inclined to store produce and wait for a better season (especially since the shortages of quality consumer goods meant that there was little incentive to spend). All of this lent support to hard-liners, particularly Stalin, who argued that the time for tolerance of peasant acquisitiveness (or what peasants themselves saw as trying to secure the best possible prices for produce) had come to an end. Now, the peasantry had to be forced to make their contribution to the national cause. In the short term, this meant requisitioning the grain that they refused to release. In the medium to long term, it meant creating large efficient units working to the collective good of the whole nation, rather than tolerating smallholdings allowing subsistence or the personal enrichment of the producers. At this period, the utopian dream of many top-level administrators was less the small-scale *kolkhoz* than the *sovkhoz*, or state farm, an industrial-style enterprise in which those who worked the land were rurally based industrial workers rather than co-operative farmers.[5]

The authoritarian character of these measures was played down by the perpetration of the myth that collectivization was desired by all ordinary peasants, or 'poor' and 'middling' folk, but was fiercely resisted by *kulaki*, the rural elite. The term *kulak*, derived from the word for fist, had a range of pejorative meanings in traditional peasant culture, among them a miser (as in the English phrase 'tight-fisted'), and a trader or middleman, especially one dealing in grain.[6] Both before and after the Revolution, however, the term was used by Russian populists and socialists to stigmatize members of what they held to be the evolving rural petite bourgeoisie. After the Revolution, the Bolsheviks immediately declared war on this group. In the words of Lenin, 'Kulaks and criminals are torturing the population with famine, and tens of millions are dying. We will bring them to heel by force.' Among the tasks that he placed before Party activists being sent to work in the countryside in February 1918 was 'to explain to the countryside that kulaks and parasites must be forced out of existence'.[7]

The presupposition behind this was that inequality in the countryside was the result of 'capitalism': after the Emancipation of the Serfs in 1861 created a free peasantry that was able to buy and sell immovable property, rural society had stratified, with certain 'fat cats' rapidly acquiring land, while other peasants scraped out a living on miserable holdings, or were reduced to the status of landless labourers. This view of things ignored the disparities in peasant life that long preceded Emancipation. The well-being of early nineteenth-century peasant farmers depended on physical geography (those living on the boglands of Western Russia eked out a miserable existence compared with the peasants of central Russia, let alone fertile Ukraine), on the competence and goodwill of the local landlord and his agents, and on the available opportunities for non-agricultural work (fishing, craft industries, seasonal work in the cities). All the same, the creation of a market in land, and the development of trade in produce and in manufacture, had certainly brought new opportunities for peasant entrepreneurs. Late nineteenth-century handbooks of merchant guilds in Moscow and St Petersburg recorded increasing numbers of traders able to pay the fairly high taxes that went with membership in the second and third tiers of the guild system. And in villages themselves, there emerged a Russian equivalent of the Irish 'strong farmer', a prosperous peasant who was able to employ others to work the land. In Tolstoy's *Anna Karenina*, the hero, Lyovin, visits such a family, which emerges as a kind of utopia of peaceful co-operation and wise patriarchal order. On the other hand, Tolstoy's *Master and Man*, written two decades later, expresses the disquiet felt by traditionalist landowners when peasant entrepreneurs fell into money-grubbing ways. Its anti-hero, Brekhunov, is a ruthless, asset-stripping businessman so eager to close a deal that he insists on travelling during a blizzard, bringing tragedy upon his horse, himself and very nearly upon his foreman as well. The sense that there was something not 'Russian' in such business acumen was very widespread in the Russian gentry and in the intelligentsia.[8]

Under Pyotr Stolypin, Minister of the Interior from April 1906 and simultaneously Prime Minister from July of the same year, however, support of this type of prosperous, independent farmer became official policy. Fierce unrest in many rural areas of the Russian Empire in 1905–6 had convinced government officials and landowners that the traditional form of social organization in the village, the commune or *mir*, was now the source of disorder rather than of political stability. The result was a package of legislation, issued from November 1906, which allowed communes to be dissolved and separate farms set up. According to the vision of the Tsarist administrators, peasant proprietors would now form part of a land-owning backbone of the nation, patriotic and committed to the endurance of state power.

In practice, things did not work out like this. To begin with, response to the reforms was patchy. Peasants in some regions – notably the steppe lands of the Volga – responded far more enthusiastically to the opportunity to repartition land than did peasants in other regions, for instance the far North. When peasants did respond positively to the reform, the results were also diverse: the commune might, for instance, opt for repartition defensively, as a way of containing the break-away manoeuvres of individuals who wanted to farm independently, or allocate land according to traditional views about equitable practice, rather than the projections of administrators about rational planning.[9] And, though the Stolypin reforms had brought about some attrition of the communes by 1917 (fewer than 50 per cent of peasants in the forty-seven European provinces of the Russian Empire were still members of communes at that point), they ground to a halt after the revolution.[10]

Yet the reforms had symbolic importance. Peasant landed proprietors acquired an ideological weight out of proportion to their numbers, since their existence affronted the communitarianism that was a passionate belief among many Russian intellectuals. In villages, though, attitudes to them were ambivalent. Feelings among less prosperous neighbours towards the more prosperous had always included more or less grudging admiration as well as resentment.[11] It was a good deal more prestigious to be a kulak than to be short of money: those who defaulted on taxes were deprived of their land holdings, which could lead to total destitution.[12]

For the Bolshevik regime, though, peasant proprietors were both an ideological and a pragmatic nightmare. First, they were clearly 'class enemies', part of the most despised stratum, the

Propaganda photograph of a field of standing rye, *Our Achievements* magazine, 1934.

petite bourgeoisie. Second, their opposition to collectivization was inevitable, since this would bring them few gains and many losses. Among peasants generally, the anxiety that co-operation would mean 'working for others' was indeed widespread; the more hard-working and successful a peasant was, the more likely such anxieties were.[13] Rural proprietors, therefore, were the targets not just of ideological attacks, but also of hostile policy. The methods employed included 'social pressure' (denunciation of kulaks at public meetings and in the press, the circulation of negative agitation and propaganda) and fiscal measures, such as the imposition of extra taxes upon kulaks. These methods did have effects on some of those targeted: a proportion of peasant proprietors decided to sell up and depart. None the less, in 1927, 3.5 per cent of rural holdings were still in the form of 'Stolypin farms', and 95.5 per cent were in traditional communes.[14] From the point of view of the Soviet leadership, then, collectivization of agriculture was essential; at the same time, by 1928 it was obvious that there was little support in the villages for it. A clash between the government and the peasantry was inevitable.

It came in the form of the forced collectivization campaign of 1929–33. This had two thrusts: the imposition of grain delivery quotas on the entire countryside, province by province, and an all-out assault on the kulaks as the key opponents of collectivization. Detailed work on Siberia by James Hughes has shown how these two policies worked on the ground during the early stages of the campaign. In March 1929, the peasantry's self-taxation system started to be used in the region to enforce grain requisitions on the ground. Villages would be assigned a 'norm' for grain delivery, which would then be passed down to individual houses on a 'class' basis. Defaulters were punished by swingeing ('fivefold') fines, imposed by the local village meeting, whose sessions were now directed by 'plenipotentiaries', or mobile activists, appointed by the Party.[15]

Grain requisitions were thus supposed to work on their own as a weapon against kulaks; but other weapons were used as well. Propaganda had adopted an uglier tone. In Novosibirsk, for example, the local paper *Young Worker* mounted a campaign, in January and February 1929, accusing the regional public prosecutor's office of undue leniency in dealing with kulaks who murdered activists. At this point too, another economic weapon, the boycotts of kulak produce and employment, came into play. This was followed by a more direct attack on kulak property, in the form of mass confiscations and appropriations – in Siberia, 8,000 farms had been subjected to these measures by May 1929. And in November 1929, immediate prison sentences were brought in for those who refused grain procurements.

Those mobilized to enforce grain requisitions and act against kulaks included a number of different bodies. Among them were the Party authorities, usually represented by 'plenipotentiaries' or 'political instructors', the Komsomol, or Young Communist League, and the police – the local *militsia*, or ordinary criminal police, and more particularly the secret police, euphemistically known as the General State Political Directorate, or OGPU. As well as perlustrating mail in the search for signs of dissatisfaction with government policy, and running networks of local informers to try to pre-empt local resistance, OGPU officials also participated directly in raids and evictions, sending along its own 'plenipotentiaries'. In an effort to keep up the pretence that collectivization was a democratic movement, though, so-called *bednyatskie aktivy*, or collectives of poor peasants, were, from spring 1929, charged with assigning norms for grain surrender relative to household status, and also with enforcing these.

The involvement in action against kulaks of people who had no training in 'persuasion' or in active crowd control, and who were answerable to no higher authority at the local level, made such action arbitrary, chaotic and likely to result in violence. Though there was a relatively strict official definition of kulak status, based on a sliding scale of property ownership and labour bought into the farm, in many places the majority of those who suffered expropriations were not officially kulaks at all.[16] The policy of confiscation was often just an excuse for looting: raiding parties would help themselves to anything that took their fancy, including even babies' nappies and the food for family meals. Some enforcers did not hold back from rape and assault.[17]

In late 1929, a still more vicious phase of collectivization was unleashed. In November, a month marked by the publication of Stalin's article 'The Year of the Great Breakthrough', trumpeting the contribution that would be made by collectivization to the Soviet Union's status as a world power, began the mobilization of the so-called 'twenty-five thousanders', worker activists from

Уралроста
КУЛАК НА ХЛЕБЕ СИДИТ,
А БЕДНЯК ПЕРЕД НИМ БЕЗ ШАПКИ СТОИТ...

Anti-kulak poster. (Pavlik Morozov Museum, Gerasimovka)

the cities drafted in as ancillary forces to help with the campaign. These newcomers from the cities were usually immediately assigned positions of responsibility such as kolkhoz chairman or deputy chairman, a move that of course did little to mitigate local resentment.[18] Then, on 27 December 1929, came a speech from Stalin speaking for the first time of 'the liquidation of the kulaks as a class'. A decree of the Central Executive Committee and Sovnarkom passed on 1 February 1930 put this decision in concrete form, requiring total confiscation of kulaks' property and their exile from their home region. A secret instruction of 4 February spoke more concretely of the need to target 'kulak activists', who were to be exiled to distant regions within the USSR, or to remote parts of their home regions. Once again, the mechanisms of local democracy were to be exploited: meetings of collective farmers, landless labourers and poor peasants were to draw up lists of kulaks, which would then be passed up to the Party authorities for enactment.[19]

There was a procedure for 'dekulakization'. It began with the exposure at a village meeting of a household's kulak status, which was supposed to be on officially approved grounds such as the employment of wage labour, but which (according to folk memory) in practice could fasten on some more marginal sign of status such as the possession of a horse, a cow or even a sewing machine.[20] It continued with confiscation, likely accompanied by looting and violence. A complaint from Kurgan district in the Urals recorded that, during dekulakization of a village in Belozersk, 'systematic insulting behaviour was employed during the search of properties: the women and children were stripped naked'. Rapacity among officials knew no bounds: an OGPU report from Tyumen province in early 1930 stated that brass icons had been snatched so they could be melted down for tractor parts, and that gold and garments of good quality (which were supposed to be inventoried upon confiscation) had simply been pilfered.[21]

Once the raiding party had sifted through possessions, the kulak family would be turned out of their home. Sooner or later followed – for those who were considered to belong to the most dangerous categories of kulak – exile, imprisonment or indeed execution. Execution might well have seemed a preferable fate for some, compared with incarceration in the labour camp network, now vastly expanded to accommodate the huge influx of prisoners, or with so-called 'special exile'.

Between January and May 1930, over 200,000 families were targeted for deportation of this kind: a substantial proportion (around 40 per cent) of individuals involved were children. The deportees, crammed into overcrowded wagons without sanitary facilities, were packed off the thousands of kilometres to remote, inhospitable areas, without adequate clothing, space or food supplies, and sometimes even without water. Dehydration and infectious disease were rife, and it was children who most often succumbed to them, making up, for instance, more than 80 per cent of deaths on one series of transports to the far North.[22]

Once they arrived in the area ordered to receive them, the kulak refugees fared little better. Preparations for their reception were flustered and inadequate, and in any case the sheer numbers of the arrivals (67,000 in Arkhangelsk alone, for instance) stretched resources beyond breaking point. Temporary housing, usually in places such as disused churches and prisons, was often filthy, damp, cold and without even basic plumbing and drainage. Clean water and food were in desperately short supply. Once again, it was children who suffered most: illnesses such as measles, mumps and gastro-enteritis were rife. In Arkhangelsk, 335 children died in hospital between 31 March and 10 April, and

252 outside hospital. The rate of deaths in Kotlas in early May was thirty children a day. Conditions improved a little during 1931, but worsened again in 1932–3 (a time of famine all over rural Russia): once again, 'the little ones died most', in the words of a survivor. From Arkhangelsk, a witness wrote anonymously to *Pravda* of seeing 'children's corpses [. . .] taken to the cemetery by threes and fours and even without coffins, just in boxes'.[23] Kulak children who came through epidemics and hunger could expect a life comparable to that of the very poorest children before 1917. Manual labour and begging were common from a young age, as was educational disadvantage. One daughter of an alleged kulak remembered that when the village school opened in 1935, she could not attend it as 'there would have been no one to run things'.[24] And in some places, kulak children were debarred from nursery facilities, at least during the early 1930s.[25] It was also difficult for them to enrol in the Pioneers, even after this had begun to be the norm of school-age children, rather than a privilege for children with an unimpeachable class background who had proved their ideological fervour.[26]

Though the new Soviet state had from the first been presented in its own propaganda as the world champion of children's welfare, the tendency to regard class status as innate meant that kulak children were condemned to suffer along with their parents. Even kulaks who were allowed to remain near home suffered terribly: neighbours were often too afraid or self-interested to help them, and retreat to a dugout in the forest or to a shed in someone's garden might be the only possible recourse. Well after the end of collectivization, 'unmasking' as a kulak led to expulsion from higher education or dismissal from work – unless those besmirched by the identity of their parents were prepared to purge the inherited guilt by disowning their own family.[27] If he or she survived physically, therefore, a so-called kulak was faced with another problem. The Soviet Union was, even before 'internal passports' (formal national identity cards) were reinstated in 1932, a society that was obsessed with identity documents. But a kulak needed a document that concealed his or her kulak origins – through the use of a false name and a false place of origin, for instance. Of course, being caught in the possession of false papers simply compounded the stigma. Yet at the same time the risk had to be taken, at any rate if village-dwellers proposed to move from the countryside into the cities, a step that was essential for many to escape starvation and ensure the chance of a new working life, away from suspicious neighbours.

Secret police reports indicate that forgery was widespread.[28] Memoirs and oral history confirm this, and indicate that it was a source of pride, rather than of shame. One man born in 1916, for example, thanked his lucky stars in late 1931 that he had applied himself diligently in writing classes and school, so that he found it no problem to copy the commandant's signature on papers that allowed free right of passage to 'special exiles'.[29] Ruses of this kind often paid off, allowing the abject free passage into a new life, where they felt relief they had survived, 'despite the deaths and privations, taking no revenge on those who had dealt so savagely with us'.[30] Though collective farmers were officially tied to the land (it was only in 1980 that they acquired the automatic right to be issued an internal passport at the age of sixteen), poverty and lack of opportunity in the countryside, versus the ease of finding factory jobs in cities, worked in the opposite direction.

By late February 1930, only weeks into the new phase of collectivization, the savagery unleashed by the invitation to 'liquidate the kulaks' was causing disquiet in the Party leadership. On 1 March, Stalin made the speech 'Dizzy with Success', which assigned blame for 'excesses' in dekulakization to local party officials. The call for restraint, which was extremely unpopular at the grassroots, slowed down, rather than halting altogether, the pace of collectivization. By October 1930, licence to pursue a harder line had once more been given from the top; it was only the abolition of mass deportations in May 1933 that marked the end of all-out collectivization and the effective subjugation of the peasantry to state power, even though 30 per cent of holdings remained in private hands.

In any case, whether in early 1930 or later, the procedure of denunciation, confiscation and eviction happened in much the same way, and the distress and humiliation suffered by a kulak family was identical. The crucial factor in what happened was less the year when dekulakization took place and more who was involved; according to the standard Russian saying about relations with officialdom, 'it all depends on the person'. A sympathetic kolkhoz chairman could delay dekulakization or mitigate its effects, and could also provide a family labelled as 'kulak' with the identity papers that were needed to allow migration to another place. There is evidence that quite a number of officials did help out in this way (some concrete examples will be mentioned in Chapter 2). However, as collectivization proceeded, it became harder and harder for chairmen to protect village populations, since they themselves were held responsible for enforcing dekulakization norms, and would be sacked if these were not met.

The effect of dekulakization, and of collectivization more broadly, in the shorter term was to devastate the rural economy in many parts of the Soviet Union. Sometimes villagers resisted openly, rising up against the authorities; more often, action was taken against individual political activists, who were murdered *pour encourager les autres.* In the North Caucasus in late 1932, according to notes taken by Lazar Kaganovich during a visit there from November 1932 to February 1933, 'The kulakery is conducting class war in the form of monstrous acts of terror: they inundated a plenipotentiary with petrol, and beat and mocked the woman vice-chairman of a village soviet.'[31] Still commoner were different forms of evasion and responses of a self-destructive kind – slaughter of stock before it was sequestered, drunkenness, demoralized passivity.[32] Disruption of sowing led to falling harvests and hence to famine in 1932–3, with an accompanying food crisis in major Russian cities of exactly the kind that collectivization had been meant to avert. In the countryside, cases of cannibalism were recorded during this time: in Western Siberia, for example, a woman from a family of Belorussian settlers was found to have killed her four-year-old boy and prepared him as food. Her defence was, 'I thought I might at least save the elder boy that way.' Such cases were not reported by the press, which maintained a total silence about the horrors of the famine, concentrating instead on kulak scandals, sometimes of a fantastic kind. In early 1933, an epidemic in Western Siberia, which without doubt was the result of infections ravaging the malnourished population, was reported in the press as caused by 'kulak terror': the evil enemies of Soviet power had been leaching poison into the water supply.[33]

Collectivization should not be seen simply as an injustice perpetrated on the suffering population of villages by Party leaders. The most zealous activists were often Soviet citizens of humble origins who genuinely believed that kulaks existed, and that they threatened Soviet democracy and national prosperity. The 'twenty-five thousander' campaign was a case in point. In Leningrad, it took only two weeks to sign up the quota of 4,390 worker activists that the city was supposed to provide, and across the Soviet Union as a whole, volunteers outstripped places available by almost three to one. Thirty per cent of the enrolment stayed in the countryside even after a decree of December 1931 permitted them to return to the factory floor.[34] And villagers themselves were capable of joining in the fray, whether out of fear, conviction or self-interest. Traditional methods of imposing collective disapproval, such as *samosud* (arbitrary justice, which often amounted to gang violence), or shaming rituals,[35] all too easily transmuted into assaults on so-called kulaks. Already during the Civil War, groups of peasants had used the term 'kulak' in order to pursue vendettas against others;[36] after intensive propaganda had made the word more familiar, behaviour of this kind could only become more prevalent.

Recent history played a significant part here as well. The Russian Civil War had ended only eight years before collectivization began, and animosities from that period, including the support given by many peasants to the anti-Bolshevik side, were well remembered. It was easy to believe that resistance to collectivization posed a threat to the very existence of the Soviet state, and to take on trust official claims that 'either we destroy the kulak as a class or the kulak will grow as a class of capitalists and liquidate the dictatorship of the proletariat'.[37] What was more, young activists had been inculcated in the rhetoric of the 'class war' throughout the 1920s, when traditional envy of the successful became redefined as righteous indignation directed at social parasites. Even in nursery schools, awareness of social status was heightened: in establishments run by the First Experimental Station of Narkompros, the education ministry, in Kaluga province, children were asked questions about who the 'bourgeois' were, how the rich differed from the poor and so on. Some five- to seven-year-olds had the answers off pat: the 'bourgeois' were 'the masters of the earth', 'rich people' had two-storey houses, the 'poor' had no work, 'kulaks' lived in brick houses, rather than wooden ones, and so on.[38]

Thus, the policy of 'divide and rule' was absorbed at the grassroots. Absorption was the more effective because teachers, activists, journalists and other toilers in the factory of indoctrination were usually not unprincipled opportunists and careerists; they genuinely believed the reports and commentaries they passed on to their public. Despite tight censorship of the press since 1918, there was a measure of input from ordinary citizens into newspaper coverage through the 'worker correspondent' and 'village correspondent' movement, a loose association of non-professional 'stringers' who reported on local issues and concerns to metropolitan and local newspapers and magazines. Individuals of this kind were less likely to sympathize with homeless and starving peasants than they were to feel that the punishment of exploiters was the essential price of social justice.

'DARKNESS INTO LIGHT'

To understand why these activists should have been prepared to suspend judgement and endorse, at a distance, the terrible injustices of collectivization, one needs to know a little about the second strand in Bolshevik policy for the countryside, the drive to civilize the cultural wasteland, to turn 'darkness into light'. This driving away of 'darkness' was to be achieved literally, through the electrification campaign (many Soviet villages were not in fact electrified till the 1960s or later, but the 'typical' 1920s village of propaganda was one where white-haired old women naïvely enthused over 'Ilyich's light bulb', electricity as the personal largesse of Vladimir Ilyich Lenin). But it was also to be achieved through the dissemination of enlightenment in an intellectual sense.

From the second half of the 1920s, rural children were identified as an especially important group, both as the focus of propaganda, and as potential disseminators of propaganda. This was partly because children of all kinds were considered a crucial target for Sovietization. The Tsarist education authorities had been so fearful of activities that smacked of involvement in politics that even parent–teacher organizations were allowed to develop only after 1905, and then in restricted form; social organizations for schoolchildren were hardly tolerated at all. From the first days after the February Revolution in 1917, on the other hand, political activity by children was actively encouraged. Children took part in meetings at schools and sent representatives to school councils; they also attended public meetings and political demonstrations in the towns and cities where they lived and, in some cases, set up their own political organizations. In a short-lived newspaper called *Red Dawns*, published in Petrograd in 1919, one girl from Vologda gloatingly described how she and her fellows had managed to get a meeting held by the local military cadets closed down by block voting, throwing rude messages on stage, and shouting 'Long live the working class'.[39]

Once the Bolsheviks' grip tightened over political activities, however, this free-for-all began to come under surveillance. As with social participation for adults, the end of the Civil War saw a watershed, and from the end of 1921, there were intensive discussions about how the Party might take in hand political activity by children, particularly between the ages of about nine and fourteen. Older teenagers were already catered for by the Young Communist League (Komsomol), set up in 1918. During the Civil War, younger teenagers had joined this organization in some numbers, but once peacetime arrived, rules began to be applied more strictly, and it was widely felt that the presence of children in the organization did not contribute much to the dignity of debate, or to the Komsomol's role as a force for serious political change.

By late 1921, therefore, the question of a separate political organization for children had begun to preoccupy the Komsomol authorities. A pragmatic view was that the Party would be best to take over and Sovietize the largest and most coherent existing organization for younger children, the scout movement. However, many activists objected on the grounds that the scout movement was 'imperialist' and 'bourgeois', despite the presence in it of some pro-Communist youth leaders. This view appeared confirmed in 1922, when the International Scouting Movement gave official recognition to Russian *émigré* scout groups, a development that more or less ruled out any rapprochement between scouting and the Soviet youth movement. Accordingly, in May 1922, a new Soviet movement for children, the Young Pioneers, was set up in Moscow. The scout movement was also banned in 1922, and the Pioneer movement increasingly acquired a monopoly over political activities by children and, by the early 1930s, over out-of-school activities more generally.

The Pioneer organization was not administratively autonomous, but a sub-department of the Komsomol. Unlike the Party and the Komsomol, it never held congresses and conferences, but only 'rallies', essentially celebrations of the movement's achievements rather than debates on institutional policy. It did, however, have its own, and extremely efficient, propaganda operation, issuing special books, brochures, magazines and newspapers. In early 1924, the first issue of *Pioneer* magazine (dedicated to Lenin's funeral) appeared; by 1925, the organization had its own newspaper, *Pioneer Pravda*, which in 1926 became the official paper for the whole movement.[40]

МАРШ ПИОНЕРОВ.

Радостным шагом,
с песней веселой,
мы выступаем
за комсомолом.
Близится время
светлых годов.
Клич пионеров:
— Всегда будь готов!
Грянем мы дружно
песнь удалую
за пионеров
семью мировую!
Будем примером
борьбы и трудов.
Клич пионера:
— Всегда будь готов!

'The Pioneer March', from Avgusta Dernovo-Yarmolenko, *I'm Learning to Read!* [Ya uchus], Moscow 1930.

Yet for all these diverse efforts, the most important instrument of Sovietization among the young was certainly the school system. To be sure, not all children were exposed to this right from the start of Soviet power. Universal primary education was laid down in law only in 1930, and was supposed to become a reality from 1932, but putting the command into life took much longer. Schools were also in some disarray because of lack of equipment and underfunding, and because of teachers' unfamiliarity with, or incompetence in using, or hostility to, the new teaching methodologies that were being introduced by Narkompros. The syllabus was regularized only gradually, with the first harmonizing instructions introduced in the mid-1920s. Even afterwards, teachers had a good deal of discretion in terms of the textbooks and the explanatory materials that they chose to use. All the same, by the end of the 1920s, the staff in Soviet schools included a high proportion of very young teachers, some barely older than their pupils, who had experienced all, or almost all, their education under Soviet power, and who were eager to pass on to their pupils messages about egalitarianism, internationalism, rational collectivism and social justice.[41] The nature of recruitment meant that these young enthusiasts were more likely to be posted to remote areas, as new schools were opened up in the drive to expand primary education. And the school coverage was also expanding apace: by 1939, over 80 per cent of the target age group was attending primary school, and it would be fair to assume that a higher figure than this experienced schooling at some point during their childhood, while not necessarily attending regularly and continuously.[42]

The school network was supposed not just to inculcate skills, but to provide a grounding in moral or character education, which included Soviet patriotism and social activism. In the early Soviet era, children were regarded not just as 'future citizens', to be taught about politics and current events so that they would be able to participate in public life in adulthood, but as vital participants in the process of changing society. Schoolteaching and propaganda texts represented feisty, assertive juveniles (particularly boys) as heroes; fiction published in children's magazines often selected as protagonists children who fought with the Red Partisans during the Civil War. Articles published in the press exhorted children to pass on the new values to 'backward' members of their own family, including not just younger brothers and sisters, but adults as well. This type of material was especially widely disseminated in the late 1920s and early 1930s, when the so-called 'cultural revolution' was accompanied by a widely publicized 'campaign to transform daily life' urging Soviet citizens to discard filth, mess, slack time-keeping, superstition and religious belief, in favour of streamlined living according to the rules of hygiene and science, and commitment to hard work and efficiency. The following list of new year resolutions was published by *Pioneer* magazine as the frontispiece of its first issue for 1931:

What You Must Do

Agitate with your father, brothers, relations and friends and urge them to stick with their job to the end of the Five-Year Plan.

Fight for cultured daily life, for hygiene (air rooms, take care to keep things clean, etc.)

Stamp out the drug of religion, expose priests' fairy tales for what they are.

Explain the decisive significance of the third year of the Five-Year Plan to your relations.

Make contracts of [socialist] competition with your father or with any of your brothers who are in employment.

Material of this kind was clearly most relevant to children in the urban world – not only large cities, but the factory settlements grouped round one or two large plants that were one of the main types of urbanized habitat at this point. However, by the late 1920s, the organizers of the Pioneer movement began to step up the drive to get children in villages to participate in activism, and to push recruitment of rural children to the Pioneers. The network of 'child correspondents' was expanded as well: in 1928, a new magazine, *Friendly Lads*, was set up in order to showcase work by children in villages, and in 1930 it held its first congress of 'child correspondents', essentially aimed at using these individuals as a conduit for market research on the kind of reading that would appeal to village children of the day.

Inevitably, as collectivization became the single most important issue – indeed, the single issue – in rural politics, children's magazines devoted space to it in the same way that adult ones did. They carried articles exhorting Pioneers to behave like miniature Komsomol members, or juvenile 'twenty-five thousanders', and to band into brigades to carry out propaganda for collectivization in villages (material of this kind appeared repeatedly in *Pioneer Pravda* during 1930, for instance). They reported success stories from zones under collectivization: in June 1930, *Pioneer* magazine triumphantly proclaimed that 350 kulak households had been liquidated in Berezovsky district, near Odessa. (Needless to say, the human cost of this achievement was not mentioned.) They exhorted children to take a leading role within the family in this area of politics too: 'LET'S GET OUR PARENTS INTO THE KOLKHOZ', ran the headline of an item in the Leningrad Pioneer newspaper, *Leninist Sparks*, for 23 March 1930. But above all, they exposed the evil activities of kulaks themselves.

Occasional articles conceded that kulak children might be a separate category, at least so long as they were of pre-adolescent age.[43] On the other hand, stories about kulak 'fifth columns' in schools ran in the other direction, suggesting that kulak children could be a danger as well. And there was no doubt that kulak adults were utterly monstrous and deserving of no sympathy whatever. They were prepared to go to any lengths to protect their own selfish ends, infiltrating village soviets and even communes in order to corrupt the collectivization movement. They exploited small children as a cheap workforce. Above all, they were armed and dangerous, repeatedly attacking not only adult activists and school teachers, but Pioneers and 'child correspondents' as well. A whole juvenile martyrology began to build up in the children's press. Brutal assaults on Pioneers were reported on 22 January 1930 by *Pioneer Pravda*, for instance. In December 1930 came a far more serious case. On the 13th of the month, *Pioneer Pravda* reported that a Pioneer from Gandzhi in Azerbaijan, Grisha Akopov, had actually been murdered, but the local authorities had failed to take appropriate action. In time, Pavlik Morozov would become another of these saintly victims.

Pieces of self-declared fiction supported the idea that kulaks were dangers to society at large, and particularly to its most vulnerable members, small children. A story published in *Leninist Sparks* on 20 January 1930 took as its anti-hero Terenty, a shopkeeper and kulak, who exploited little Pashka to do odd jobs. When exposed by boy correspondent Ignashka for ill-treating his small employee, Terenty brazenly went forth with his gun to shoot Pashka dead, but fortunately missed his aim. Doggerel published in the children's press took the same theme, proclaiming for instance:

The kulak sneaks up
on fox-like paws,
to kill the activist
with his sawn-off.[44]

The anti-kulak theme got bound into every other sort of campaign, for example hygienic ones. Items appearing under titles such as 'DEATH TO THE PEST!' and exhorting Pioneers to help exterminate marmots or corn-cockles invariably mentioned that infestations were a delight to the kulak, and thereby suggested that one kind of 'pest' was to be identified with another.[45] As well as every kind of accident being attributed to kulak sabotage, every sort of negative social phenomenon was assumed to be stirred up by them. 'Anti-semitism always has links with the counter-revolution', a 1931 article in *Friendly Lads* proclaimed in bold type.[46] Despite the despicable nature of kulak activity, though, in propaganda for children they were always shown as being dealt with fairly and in accordance with the strict letter of the regulations.[47]

The struggle between the authorities and the enemies of collectivization was presented as a Manichean myth, then, just as the Civil War was in Soviet fiction, or as the struggle between brave border guards and despicable Western spies (and their treacherous Soviet lackeys) was to be in the late 1930s. Children – and not just city children – responded to it at this level, siding with the underdogs, the victims of the kulaks. Propaganda had its concrete effects in agitational campaigns as villages underwent collectivization: schoolchildren might festoon the fences of neighbours with notices branding them kulaks, buttonhole and harangue neighbours reluctant to join the collective farm, or engage in more elaborate forms of activism. In Irbit district, in the Urals, for example, children tied red flags to their toboggans and went from house to house urging neighbours to surrender grain, using a special chant: 'Give me your grain, don't be a fool, or I'll get no pencils at the school!'[48]

In close rural communities, it was of course extremely likely that children campaigning in favour of collectivization would come into conflict with members of their own extended familes, or indeed with their parents. Official propaganda was absolutely rigid about what was supposed to happen on such occasions. Loyalty to the Party and to the Pioneer movement was to come before one's family. While destruction of the family in itself was never the aim of mainstream Bolshevism – as opposed to some marginal left groups in the early 1920s – the consensual view of the early Soviet government was that the traditional patriarchal family, based upon domination of women by men and of children by parents, was an unjust institution and one that socialized children into backward attitudes and might also actively exploit them. Education and political indoctrination were supposed to work as counterweights to the pernicious influence of traditional families, allowing children to proclaim their adherence to the new values and thereby to transform family relations from within.

If parents proved recalcitrant, the only option (according to propaganda dogma) was for children to call for help from outside the family. Miscreant parents should be reported to sympathetic persons in authority, who would see that the abuses they perpetrated were brought to an end. In 1930, *Pioneer* magazine ran a story, 'What Should I Do with My Father?', about a young boy, part of the 'child correspondent' movement, who had discovered that his own father carried a large load of the blame for the fact that the factory where he worked was not fulfilling its plan properly. His strategy so far had been to expose the man's misdeeds to the press.[49] The question in the title was rhetorical: it was clear that denunciation was, and would continue to be, the right way of dealing with the paternal delinquent.

This procedure was the same whatever the nature of the abuse in question – whether the child was being forced into under-age work, beaten and ill-treated, or had become aware that its parent was guilty of some criminal act, for example, belonging to the wrong class. On 19 April 1930, a schoolboy wrote to the newspaper *Red Kurgan*,

> I consider it disgraceful to rely any longer on the financial support of my idle drone of a father, who is shoring up religion, and impeding the development of socialist construction, and I therefore rupture any connections with my father, an obscurantist and a village priest, the disseminator of lies and deceit to the population.[50]

During collectivization, the number of criminal acts that parents might be guilty of expanded rapidly: grain hoarding, sabotage, theft of public property, and (if they held some official position) fraud of identity papers or insufficiently zealous prosecution of kulaks. The number of newspaper stories about brave children who were prepared to see that their parents were punished for such crimes expanded in parallel.

The 'happy ending' envisaged by propaganda for a child like this would have involved some minutes of fame in the local paper, congratulation at a Pioneer rally or other such public meeting, and in due course transfer to the paradise of a Soviet orphanage, which, in propaganda texts, was seen as the best possible place for upright, politically aware children (or any children) to be; there they would joyfully march forward to the future in the company of others like themselves. In reality, Soviet orphanages were of course often far from paradisical: children were as likely to suffer abuse, regimentation, neglect and intellectual under-stimulation as they were anywhere else in the world, and considerably more likely to suffer material hardship, given the exceptionally severe conditions endured by Soviet society generally. But in propaganda, the glorious character of the Soviet orphanage became living proof that this was the single country in the world where children's welfare was at the heart of social and political policy. Not for nothing were foreign visitors to Russia invariably taken to visit model children's institutions, so that they could return home and report (as they often obediently did) that the new society treated its children in a way not matched anywhere else.

Children who denounced were not just a figment of propagandists' imagination, however. Oral history also turns up cases where the message of 'duty before family' cut home. A woman brought up in Pskov province, north-western Russia, remembered such a story from 1932 or 1933. A man had a horse – his pride and joy – confiscated as part of dekulakization, only to see, not long afterwards, the village soviet chairman riding around on the animal. Furious, he and his brother resolved to take revenge. They murdered the chairman, threw him in the local lake and cut the horse's throat. But the chairman came up in the nets when people were fishing in the spring, even though the killers had tied a stone to his belt to keep the body down. At that point, the eight-year-old son of one of the men piped up: 'My uncle killed him [. . .] my Uncle Matvei done it, and there was blood on our gates, me mam wiped off the blood with soot from the stove.'[51]

Childhood experience during collectivization, then, is not easily classified in any one way. Children were prominent among the victims of collectivization, suffering along with their families when parents were branded 'kulaks'. When the costs of collectivization were remembered, it was naturally this side of children's lives that came to the fore. In Andrei Platonov's great allegorical novel *The Foundation Pit* (1929), the death of a young girl comes to symbolize the human tragedy and moral futility of the whole socialist building project. Robert Conquest's history of dekulakization and famine, *Harvest of Sorrow*, likewise dwells on the child victims of collectivization – the exhausted and emaciated children of the special exiles, the starving children of Ukraine. But children were not just on the receiving end of politics; they also engaged in political action themselves, whether denouncing adults or participating in brigades to force the pace of collectivization. In the particular, if not necessarily unique, circumstances of early Soviet history, a schoolchild who was part of a group acting with sanction from the Party or the Komsomol enjoyed a much greater degree of empowerment than an adult belonging to a category officially considered abject – an elderly religious woman from a 'backward' village, for example. And it is precisely this contrast – between powerful children and disempowered adults – that was acted out in the earliest account of Pavlik Morozov's life, constructed by the police investigators.

But before getting to the case file, it is important to consider the immediate milieu in which the Pavlik Morozov story took place – the far east of the Urals zone, on the borders of Siberia – since the real circumstances of collectivization, like the early growth of the Morozov legend itself, depended to a large extent on local conditions.

CHAPTER 2

Local Hero

From the mid-1930s until the end of its existence, the Soviet Union was a country where gradations of status were all-important, where towns, hotels, foodstuffs and state prizes (to name only a few things) were assigned to 'first', 'second' and 'third' (or worse) categories. It was inevitable, therefore, that heroes also should be ranked. Entry level to the Soviet pantheon was represented by promotion within one's 'collective' – an educational institution, say, or a place of work, or indeed a prison camp. A high-achieving worker might be lauded in a home-produced newsletter displayed on the works notice-board, and a prize pupil commended at a Pioneer meeting, or their names might be displayed on the 'board of honour' suspended, for the edification of all, alongside its negative counterpart, the 'board of shame'. More gratifyingly, individuals of this kind might be awarded coverage in the local press, with a laudatory biography published alongside a photograph of the remarkable individual at his or her lathe, milking-machine or desk. For a select few, promotion to the highest level then followed, represented by publicity in a 'central' newspaper (one published in Moscow and circulated throughout the Soviet Union), and – if circumstances proved propitious – by admission to a range of different honours: the award of medals, the publication of an official biography, the conferral of names on streets, buildings, institutions and even cities, the erection of busts, plaques and full-size monuments.

Once heroes had reached this final, 'all-Soviet', status, connection with their birthplace and individual roots became tenuous. The title of a 1940s hagiography of the Leningrad Party leader murdered in 1934, Sergei Kirov, *The Boy from Urzrum*, offered a coy wink to the reader, much in the way that a life of Christ under the title *The Boy from Nazareth* might. In both cases, the town was famous because of the person born there, but the equation did not work in reverse. At the same time, there were Soviet heroes whose regional origins were of some moment in terms of their myth, Stalin's connections with Georgia being a case in point.

In the course of his posthumous career, Pavlik Morozov unquestionably achieved 'all-Soviet' status. Canonical accounts, such as articles in encyclopaedias, tended to state his birthplace as 'Gerasimovka', a title derived from a saint's name that could have been attached to any Russian village, rather than dwelling on the precise location of the settlement. Few of those who had come across the legend at school or in the Pioneer movement would have been able to remember exactly where it was the boy came from, given that there was likely to be a statue of him somewhere locally. At the same time, Pavlik's origins were of central importance to the development of the cult, which started off as a Urals phenomenon. Equally, the local history and local politics of the region were fundamental to the emergence and early development of the legend.

STEEL AND MOUNTAINS

On the face of it, Pavlik's association with the Urals might seem surprising. This tale about a village boy bravely defying kulaks ran counter to the standard image of the Urals and Western Siberia in the late 1920s and early 1930s. In propaganda, this vast area was most familiar as a developing industrial power-house, the home not only of individual projects such as Uralmashstroi (the Urals Machinery Works), but of new cities, in particular Magnitogorsk, and of entire industrial regions, notably the Urals and Kuznetsk Basin (Ural–Kuzbass), celebrated as 'a World Centre of Coal and Metal'.[1] Children were regularly informed about such projects in the Pioneer press, and it was considered disgraceful if they turned out, on the ground, not to know enough about them.[2] As collectivization surged into repression, chaos and eventually famine in 1932 and 1933, the Soviet press, including the children's press, concentrated more and more on industrial success, with the Urals at the centre. So too did 'proletarian poetry' of the day. Typical is an unintentionally absurd poem by Konstantin Mitreikin, published in 1932, which is almost as abundant in mixed metaphors as the Urals were in mineral wealth:

At the cusp of Europe and Asia,
a spine of folds and gathers,
like huge mushrooms, the Urals
mountains have popped up!
Dipping its shaggy head in the Arctic,
lashing Kazakhstan with its knobbly tail,
this dragon stretches out, wreathed in clouds,
at the cusp of two countries.
The treasure-houses of ore brim over,
nothing to delight the eye is lacking:
there's only a blue moon missing
from the Soviet Eldorado:
Gold,
Copper,
Potassium,
Nickel,
Platinum,
Barium,
Iron, Manganese, Chromium,
Aluminium,
Lead,
Magnesium,
Tin,
Zinc,
Natrium,
Antimony, Wolfram . . .
And the woods! Just try to count
the timber bodies . . .[3]

Propaganda about the Urals represented a particularly acute form of Soviet gigantomania – a model state farm there was even called 'Gigant'. It did not condescend to particulars about how industrial and agricultural progress was being achieved – with hundreds of thousands of political prisoners drafted in as forced

Propaganda photograph of a blast furnace, *Our Achievements* magazine, 1934.

labour, with peasants press-ganged to act as seasonal muscle for forestry projects, and with local officials frantically trying to cope with centrally imposed targets unsuited to local conditions.[4] And in tune with 'revolutionary romanticism', the mountain range itself was at the centre of images for the masses. The vast and diverse Urals region was represented as a sort of Soviet Switzerland, where eagles soared above wooded slopes and crags, throbbing industrial centres and prosperous collective farms.

This set of clichés was faithfully reproduced in texts about Pavlik Morozov – for example, Sergei Alymov's *The Song of a Pioneer Hero*, which was sung by thousands of Soviet schoolchildren in the 1930s and 1940s:

The woods on the heights
Of the Urals are bright,
They are green through the year, without cease:
There the eagles take flight,
Over cliffs grey and white,
And still higher the aeroplanes cruise.

At the foot of the hills
A collective farm swells:
It's where our young comrade grew up.
Morozov's his name,
As a hero he's famed,
When his father thieved grain he said 'Stop!'

What a dark bitter fate!
He inspired kulaks' hate,
And they took their revenge with a knife.
They were lying in wait,
And he couldn't prevent
Savage wolves from ending his life.

Our Pioneer troop
Is of eagles that swoop,
Fierce and brave every one of us is.
And we all want to be
Like Morozov, for he
Is remembered by Young Pioneers.

On the peaks and the woods
Of the Urals the dew
Is blown dry by a light morning breeze.
Hero Pavlik is still:
He died under that hill,
Raise your voice to remember his deeds.[5]

My translation captures Alymov's doggerel, but makes his version of the Pavlik drama seem closer to the first newspaper reports than it actually was. The weapon in the original is, for metrical reasons, 'an axe', and not a knife. And just as Alymov blurred the details of the murder, so he also transformed the landscape of Pavlik's homeland. Even in the most favourable weather, no mountains are visible in Gerasimovka: it is, in fact, more than 500 kilometres from the Ural range. In the words of a local historian, the Tavda region, now at the far east end of Sverdlovsk province, but in Pavlik's day part of the enormous Urals province, stretching westwards over the far side of the mountains and beyond Perm, 'is administratively in the Urals but geographically in Siberia'. Not mountainous, not even hilly, it is made up of forested plain interrupted by stretches of peat bog, here covered by long tangled grass that turns tawny-blond by late summer.

Like much of Siberia, Tavda region was always a place of migration, a refuge for the socially abject, the poor and the desperate. Its original settlers were nomadic herdsmen, as with much of the Eurasian landmass; a recently published list of modern villages indicates that nearly fifty settlements founded between 1900 and 1940 ceased to exist only decades after the forest was first cleared.[6] A particularly large influx came into the district during the 1900s and 1910s, as a result of government policy. Migration among the landless had begun to be encouraged in 1868, when an interior ministry circular had granted resettlement rights to entire peasant communities on government lands. It had continued – despite wobbles in government approval, brought about by the sheer popularity of migration among peasants in some poor areas, such as Central Russia, Ukraine and Belorussia – throughout the late nineteenth and early twentieth centuries. Earlier waves of migrants had tended to go for fertile country, such as the Altai, in Siberia; later waves had to settle for poorer lands, such as those available in Tavda province. Nevertheless, thousands continued to be drawn to make the long journey east by the promise of land grants, subsidies for travel and building, and tax advantages. Between 1895 and 1908, nearly four million migrants crossed the Urals, just under 4 per cent of whom settled in the Urals provinces; migrants from the western areas of the European parts of the Russian Empire made up 29 per cent of the overall numbers of migrants in 1900–1904, and 25 per cent in 1905–9.[7] Gerasimovka was one of many settlements built to house the new settlers, who came, in this case, mainly from Minsk and Vitebsk provinces.[8]

Outwardly, though, Gerasimovka did not betray the ethnic origins of its settlers: it looked much like any recently constructed village anywhere in the Russian parts of the Soviet Union. It was (and is) a linear village of wood houses, built along two parallel roads. To this day, the houses are mostly one-storied. In the 1920s and 1930s, they were usually one-roomed, with the family sleeping, in traditional style, over the stove. The few living inhabitants old enough to recall the decades before the

Second World War remember the village as large – the line of houses stretched 'from that wood there to this wood here'. But the population was poor, and conditions were hard. In 1932, there was still no telephone connection – indeed, electricity was installed only in 1947, to mark the fifteenth anniversary of Pavlik's death – and though by Russian standards the distance to Tavda town, the administrative centre, was not great, journeys there were prolonged, especially in springtime, when people had to wade knee-deep in clinging mud. A trip on foot took an entire day in the best of conditions, so those journeying had to camp out somewhere on the way. It was an expedition to be undertaken only when essential.

Accordingly, the village lived shut up on itself, scarcely adapting to modern or Soviet life. Every house had its icons, though there was no church, and the distance to the nearest place of worship, Vladimirovka, was too long (at ten kilometres or so) to make regular attendance at mass a possibility. But saints' days were observed punctiliously: in the words of a woman born in 1922, 'If there was ever a holiday in summer, whether the day was dry or whether it was wet, we'd not get to work. We'd enjoy ourselves, and the men would sit down to a game of cards.' The major festivals included, besides Easter and Christmas, St Michael's Day, and also village weddings, when carts would be decorated and horses dressed in garlands, and bands of vehicles raced through the settlement, harness bells ringing.[9] Celebrations lightened the monotony of a life that was otherwise relentlessly hard, especially for women, who were taught to spin at the age of six or seven and were kept working during the winter evenings – though with gossip or singing to make the time pass quickly – while the men and boys relaxed with story-telling or, once more, a game of cards.[10]

WHITE BANDIT KULAKS

Poor, traditionally minded villages were difficult territory for collectivization at the best of times; villages of settlers who had wrenched themselves from their homeland in search of land were especially recalcitrant. In the 1900s, a Siberian settler had told a visitor from Britain, 'The land will be all our own.'[11] Survivor memoirs reveal that those who went east were tough, independent types, who brooked no contradiction.[12] Gerasimovka was entirely comparable. Holdings there were small – a few hectares of cultivable land at most – but none the less precious for that. Most locals did not want to surrender personal proprietorship to the kolkhoz. The figure of 80 per cent kolkhoz membership allegedly achieved in Tavda district by February 1930[13] was certainly a pious fiction. Even while recording it, the authorities were admitting that desertions from the collective farms had reached the level of a mass phenomenon.[14] And in January 1931, just 9.5 per cent of households in the region belonged to collective farms, and only 4.2 per cent of livestock had been collectivized. (At the same date, the average figures across the huge Urals province were 38.8 per cent and 25.9 per cent respectively.)[15] By April, the figures had improved only to 13.1 per cent and 6 per cent in the Tavda region (as compared with 32.9 per cent and 27.3 per cent for the Urals generally).[16] A report of October 1934 recorded that 31.4 per cent of Tavda district's individual peasant households were collectivized by 1 January 1932, which looked like a significant improvement. But by 1 February 1933, this figure had risen to no more than 33 per cent, and by July 1934 to only 36 per cent.[17]

As average rates of collectivization rose, pressure on local officials to bring their recalcitrant fiefdoms into line began to mount. To this day, Gerasimovka old-timers remember ever more strident demands ('they'd come for wool, they'd come for meat, and then they'd come for milk'). But resistance to surrendering land, in an area where people recalled that their families had moved thousands of kilometres to get it, remained fierce.[18] And the fact that settlements were widely scattered across inhospitable terrain also made policy imposition difficult. Reports of insubordination would take a day to reach the district centre, and then it would take another day to send in plenipotentiaries to deal with the problem. In addition, the local Party officials were notably short on experience, sophistication and even basic literacy.[19]

At the same time, political fervour was as prevalent as political subtlety was scarce. The term 'kulak' was ubiquitous in the local press and in discussions at district and local level. It was used almost exclusively in an ideological, rather than economic, sense: in this part of the world, a 'kulak' meant a class enemy, and the term was applied freely to saboteurs, hooligans and anyone at all with a socially dubious profile. Verbal assaults often invoked the still unhealed wounds of the Civil War, which had raged fiercely in the district. Tavda was under White control between July 1918 and August 1919, and thirteen Communists at the lumber factory were shot in July 1919. Before retreating, the Whites did considerable damage to the freight yards in the Tavda station. A good many workers from Tavda fled into the taiga, where some organized partisan detachments, but among village-dwellers themselves, support for the Reds was not so clear. In January 1921, peasant risings began all over Western Siberia; in March, villagers in Tonkaya Grivka, only twelve kilometres from Gerasimovka, attacked six Red Army soldiers who had been sent in to confiscate grain, killing five of the group.[20] During the collectivization campaign, the phrase 'White bandit kulak' was ubiquitous, and alleged saboteurs, arsonists or simply members of the local Party whose turn had come for purging usually had service with the White forces dredged up.[21]

'Class war', then, was taken very seriously in this locality, and dekulakization, when carried out, was as gratuitously brutal as anywhere, with wholesale confiscation of property and arbitrary selection of victims. In February 1930, for example, a forest ranger came back from a professional conference to find his homestead ransacked on the grounds that he was a 'kulak'; in the same month, a dekulakized peasant was stripped of his new shirt and overcoat, and humiliatingly dressed in a skinny, sleeveless, disreputable old jerkin.[22] Incidents like this – involving draconian fines on poor peasants as well as kulaks, harsh confiscations, and sale of confiscated properties for private gain – continued throughout the next two years.[23]

None of the material about problems with collectivization got into press reports even at local level, however. Indeed, agriculture, in whatever respect, was a marginal concern of the Tavda journalists. As with the central press, the focus was on industry and the achievements of the First Five-Year Plan. Even the title of the Tavda paper, published by the District Committee of the Communist Party, reflected this set of priorities. Originally known as *The Saw*, it became in 1930 *The Tavda Sawmill*, before adopting, in 1931, the less vivid, but longer-lasting name of *The Tavda Worker*. The paper was above all preoccupied with events in the enterprise that kept this settlement on the Tavda river alive – the lumber mill plus wood-finishing enterprises, which made plywood and, by the late 1930s, skis, canoes and other finished products – and with decisions at the top that were likely to affect the life of industry. More marginal items dealt with day-to-day conditions in the town, generally affecting an optimistic tone: a new culture club was to be opened; Tavda nursery schools were expanding; the pupils at the model primary school were making tremendous progress.

The urban, proletarian bias was combined with a strong degree of intolerance towards the hinterland. Sketch portraits of prize kolkhozes went alongside an understanding of the traditional village as a world peopled by intransigent or actually anti-Soviet individuals, who needed to be taken in hand from outside. 'SMASH THE OPPORTUNIST CLIQUES', screamed an article published on 30 November 1930, attacking peasants in the district who had failed to surrender their corn. Kulaks were held to blame for all untoward events in Tavda itself – a fire at

Political procession in Sverdlovsk, *c.* 1930, with Komsomol and Pioneers participating. (State Archive of Sverdlovsk Province, Ekaterinburg)

a local club in late December 1930, for instance. And of course, here as everywhere, attacks on activists were recorded and the alarm sent out: the usual pattern was for a report of the murder to be accompanied by invitations to local factory workers to send in petitions demanding tough justice, which were then printed in later issues of the paper.

'IGNOMINIOUSLY DRAGGING IN THE REAR'

Often, particular villages, or indeed individuals, were singled out for attack. Here the paper relied on a network of 'village correspondents'. Individuals of this kind had a preference for florid bylines – 'The Scourge' – and displayed a bitchy command of character traits and of personalities that bespoke local knowledge. So-and-so 'white bandit kulak' had been slaughtering pigs on the sly; so-and-so chairman was forever boozing with the kulaks.[24]

Over the next two and a half years, the local paper carried many similar reproachful reports about foot-dragging in the villages with regard to every index of social participation – grain surrender, tax payment and supply of workforce when the local industries were under pressure ('storming weeks'). Bottom marker on many occasions was Gerasimovka, which almost always figured on the 'board of shame', or was castigated for 'ignominiously dragging in the rear'. Alleged bad management by the chairmen of Gerasimovka village soviet was the subject of two major scandals, in 1930 and in 1931. On 24 October 1930, *Tavda Sawmill* reported that only 44 per cent of the annual grain norm had been fulfilled in Gerasimovka, and that kulaks had surrendered hardly anything. 'Here the class enemy has grown impudent to a revolting degree, and the 900 poods [17 tons] of potatoes and 11,130 poods [200 tons] of hay scheduled for collecting have still not been gathered,' it claimed. The district plenipotentiary was in league with the village soviet, whose chair, Filippov, was in turn in league with the kulaks: he had, for instance, spared a kulak from being exiled, among other derelictions of duty. In large letters, the paper called for retribution: 'PUT THE KULAK AGENTS ON TRIAL.' On 31 August 1931, another chairman, Novopashin, was attacked for inertia and dereliction of duty – instead of attending to his proper duties, he had been helping his wife complete an inventory in the co-operative shop that she managed.

These reports, and the many others from the village, point to two significant features about Gerasimovka. On the one hand, there clearly were problems with the local administration, at a level exceptional even for this difficult region. Plenipotentiary after plenipotentiary was sent to Gerasimovka, but with little effect – one, as reported by *The Saw* on 25 September 1930, confined his efforts to nationalizing a single goat. An internal Party survey of collectivization results for August 1931 recorded that there was 32 per cent collectivization across Tavda district, but that this average concealed huge variations from village soviet to village soviet: 'fluctuating from zero (Gerasimovka village soviet) to 93 per cent'.[25]

As branded in local propaganda, Gerasimovka was a 'nest of kulaks'. In reality, collectivization was indeed proceeding extremely slowly. But the problem was not in a superabundance of kulaks: the community members ranged between poor and even poorer. According to official figures of 1927, there were no kulaks at all in the whole of Tavda district, and only 27 per cent of the population fell even into the 'middling peasant' class.[26] In the circumstances, deciding who should be 'dekulakized' was an almost impossible task. Survivors recall that the selection of victims was entirely arbitrary; 'anyone who worked hard' or 'anyone with a cow' might be under threat.[27] In other parts of the Urals, a 'kulak' might be somebody with two houses surrounded by stable-yards, orchards, workshops and storehouses, who ran a small business alongside.[28] Here, such wealth was simply unknown, and dividing up villages meant making unreal decisions.

The bitter poverty of Gerasimovka life is brought out vividly in the personal and property records relating to the Morozov family itself, and to the network of blood relations and relations by marriage which surrounded it. Sergei Morozov, who had, according to his own account during interrogation (105), been born in Vitebsk province, in 1851, came from a landless family; his father had been a prison warder. As a youth, Sergei had lived with relations (probably as a hired labourer – this kind of arrangement was common in rural areas of European Russia); at twenty, he had moved to the land-holdings of his wife's family.

(Usually, the tradition was that women moved in with their husbands, so the reversal of it pointed to Sergei's low status in property terms.) He and his wife, Kseniya (born in 1853), had moved to the Urals in 1910, where they were allocated forty-five desyatinas (roughly forty hectares) of ploughed land, most of which was bog. Sergei had managed to put ten desyatinas of this under the plough, and to set himself up with two horses, two cows and five 'small animals' (probably pigs, sheep and hens).

In the Soviet period, things got worse. To begin with, Sergei made over some of the land to his grown sons, Trofim (probably born in 1890: he and his wife Tatiana, born in about 1893, were the parents of Pavel and Fyodor Morozov) and Ivan (born in about 1888). He was left with only half a desyatina for his own use. His stock was also reduced: in 1927, he was in possession of only one horse and one cow, along with a pig, a sheep and five hens, and in 1932, an inventory compiled for the purposes of the murder investigation indicated that most of his movable property consisted of farm equipment – a cart, some cartwheels, two sickles, a saw, a harrow, four axes and various items of horse harness (including a *sedyolka,* or harness saddle, which goes over the animal's spine and to which the traces – the straps attaching the harness to the shafts of a plough or cart – are fixed; it was to figure dramatically in the murder investigation). There was also a milking bucket and four other wooden buckets, eighteen and a half poods of rye grain and a wagonload of hay.[29] Possessions for domestic and personal use were scanty. Certainly, the family had a samovar, which indicated that they were not actually destitute, and a lamp. But there were only two plates, a skillet, and some cast-iron utensils and vessels listed in terms of household equipment. Like all Gerasimovka at the time, the Morozovs evidently made clothes from homespun: eight pieces of linen cloth were in the house in September 1932.[30] The range of dishes and so on indicates that they ate together from a communal dish – the universal custom in Russian villages during the early twentieth century. The wooden spoons that would have been necessary for cooking and serving food are not listed in the inventory, presumably because they were deemed to have no value (56–7).

Two of the Morozovs' three daughters, on the other hand, had done rather better for themselves. Khima, the eldest, was born in 1872, the same year the Morozovs got married. If

Kseniya had a 'bun in the oven' at the time, it might explain why she became involved in what otherwise might have looked like a poor match with the landless Sergei. Certainly, Khima's own marriage – contracted in 1899, according to her own recollections (92) – was a good deal more successful, in socio-economic terms. Unlike most of the other settlers in Tavda, Arseny Kulukanov (born in 1862) came from a landed family, though, with only five desyatinas between nine children, there was not much to go round. Accordingly, Arseny had worked from the age of fifteen as a farm labourer, and from twenty-five in 'various jobs'. After he and his wife came to Gerasimovka in 1909, however, their situation changed. From then on, Arseny had about eight and a half desyatinas of pasture and sown land; in the late 1920s, this had shrunk by half because of gifts to his two sons, but he still had two horses and some small animals. When he was arrested for grain-hoarding in 1931, and sentenced to five years of exile, with confiscation of property, his movable property included not only two sets of horse harness, and a cart and some cart-wheels, which were to figure prominently in the case, but also 'two trunks of clothes' (96). The Kulukanovs still had their last two children – Matryona, aged seventeen, and Zakhar, aged fifteen – living at home when the murders of Pavel and Fyodor occurred.

Arseny Kulukanov had had no formal education – like Sergei and Kseniya Morozov, he signed his name with a thumbprint to the end of his days. But he comes across in testimony and in the trial transcript as a man of intelligence and determination (in the newspaper court reports this was translated as 'kulak cunning'). He had, for instance, taken the step – which in Tavda district was unusual – of going to appeal against his sentence of exile, and had managed to win his case and get the sentence reversed (97). And his testimony in the murder trial – unlike that of the other accused – was consistent. He refused right through the Morozov case to admit his guilt, and was no doubt the prime mover in the appeal that was mounted after the convictions were handed out.

The Morozovs' youngest daughter, Matryona, born in about 1897, had chosen a similarly solid type for her husband. Arseny Silin, unlike many of the Gerasimovka villagers aged thirty and above, had actually been born in the settlement; in 1932, he gave his age as forty, five years older than his wife. Beginning with only a third of a desyatina of land in 1918, he had managed to increase his holdings to one and a half desyatinas by 1929, and to acquire two horses and two cows. However, in 1931, he too was tried for grain-hoarding, and fined 200 roubles – almost an entire year's income (98 rev., 184). Silin had five children aged eleven and under in 1932, four boys and a girl (129–30).

The second Morozov daughter, Ustinya, born in 1879 or so, had not managed to set herself up quite so well – at least, according to the lights of the traditional Russian village. Her husband, Denis Potupchik, was less prosperous than Kulukanov and Silin, and himself claimed – in a statement on the kulaks of Gerasimovka – to have worked for the former as a labourer in 1922 (44). But Denis was, in terms of the new Soviet order, on the side of the angels. In the autumn of 1932, he was acting as deputy chairman of the village soviet, and energetically contributed to the case incriminating materials about the property status of the accused (for example, the inventory of Sergei Morozov's property). He was also to accuse both Arseny Silin and Arseny Kulukanov directly of being kulaks, in a paper that he submitted to the investigation on 12 September (44–6). Some of Denis's fervour in serving the authorities may have come about through a desire to escape from a questionable past: he was described in the trial transcript as 'having undergone criminal trial', but no details were given as to the alleged crime or the date of the case (231 rev.). Denis's son, Ivan, born in 1911, was an even more striking example of the new age than his father: he was literate – whether his father was or not is unclear – and had a responsible role in the Soviet administration as a member of the 'special police' or 'corps of police aides'.

Neither of the Morozovs' two sons, Trofim and Ivan, was around at the time of the murder, for different reasons. Ivan seems to have been the elder of the two: his mother, who, like most illiterate, many-times mothers, was not a totally reliable source about such things, estimated him to have been forty-four in 1932. He had moved out of Gerasimovka by 1932, and taken up residence in Kiselyovo, some twenty kilometres away – this settlement is of interest as the site of one of the very few successful collective farms in Tavda district at the time, 'Red October', set up in 1929.[31] According to his son, Danila, he had separated from his first wife at some point – perhaps in 1927, when Danila himself had gone to live with his grandparents (78–78 rev.) As for Danila, he appears to have been born in 1913 or 1914, and – as was becoming commoner in the Soviet countryside at this point – had enjoyed at least some education. He claimed at one interrogation to have spent three years at primary school (78 rev.) (even if this was probably not continuous), and could certainly write his name in a neat and legible hand.

Trofim, the Morozovs' second son (who was a couple of years younger than Ivan) was missing from the village for a different reason. In his father's words, he had been 'exiled somewhere up North' for an offence to do with forging documents in 1931 (106). Whatever the truth of this statement – as we shall see, there is no evidence beyond the Morozov case file to corroborate Trofim's conviction – there is no doubt that Trofim was not in Gerasimovka when his two sons were killed, or else he would certainly have been a prime suspect for the investigation. Because of his absence, all information about him is second-hand. Through the eyes of his wife Tatiana (some three years his junior), he appears as something of a rustic villain: a drunken consorter with kulaks, and a philanderer who had dumped his first family to set up with another woman, a relation of the Kulukanovs (228 rev. etc.). Tatiana also stated consistently from the beginning of the investigation that she had been at loggerheads with her husband's family for some time – 'I wasn't friendly with them' (1). One giveaway detail that emerges from the case file is that she may not originally have been from Gerasimovka. When Tatiana first reported her sons missing, the police sent off to Kulukhovka, a village fifteen kilometres away, to find out whether they might be with their grandmother (234).[32] Certainly, Tatiana does not appear to have had blood relatives or near allies in Gerasimovka, and, according to traditional attitudes, a widowed or separated woman had a low status in her husband's family. Whatever the truth about Trofim's disappearance, her position was, at best, beleaguered. Materially, too, life must have been hard – at nearly fourteen, Pavlik was certainly old enough to help out with the farm duties, but working such rough land would still have pushed a single woman and a teenage boy to the limits. But as no records of Tatiana's property have survived, one can only say that she and her sons are unlikely to have lived better than Sergei Morozov and his household.

Some Morozov family connections did not get caught up in the group of the accused. The Potupchiks' place in the Soviet apparatus removed them from suspicion; also ruled out were most of the adolescent and pre-adolescent children from the extended family, with the exception of Danila Morozov.[33] No interest was taken in Matryona Silina, who may have been unwell in early September.[34] The hard core of suspects were all drawn from the Morozov clan, but a few other locals also became involved, one way or another. Mostly, they simply figured as witnesses, reporting sightings of the suspects, or snatches of conversation they had overheard. But three themselves became the subjects of suspicion.

The first of these was Vladimir Mezyukhin, who first floated into the investigation on 12 September, when Sergei Morozov told a long and involved story about how he had pretended to 'buy' a colt from Kulukanov that the latter was in fact trying to conceal from confiscation. Pavlik Morozov had denounced the incident to the police, and Mezyukhin had gone round saying, 'That child needs killing' (41). The combination of property misdemeanours and threatened violence struck the investigators at this stage as conclusive, and Mezyukhin was duly arrested. He did not, however, long remain a suspect, and his relations with the Gerasimovka community were in fact fairly distant – he was even resident in a different village, Vladimirovka, some kilometres away. More consistent interest, though, was devoted by the investigators to another group of suspects, from the Shatrakov family.

The Shatrakovs had no ties of blood or marriage to the Morozovs, but some of the fields belonging to the two families lay alongside each other, and one of the elder sons in the family – Efrem – was much the same age as Danila Morozov. The other members of the family included the parents, Anton, who was fifty-five, and Olga, aged forty, and Efrem's seven brothers and sisters. Most of these played no part in the Morozov story at all.[35] The exception was Dmitry, who discovered the bodies of Pavel and Fyodor, and was briefly under suspicion. Efrem and Dmitry both described themselves as 'barely literate', and their handwriting would suggest that they were less competent writers than Danila. The Shatrakovs' tie to the Morozov murders lay in the fact that Pavlik was supposed to have denounced them for possessing an unlicensed gun,[36] an offence that they did not deny. They also acknowledged that someone must have denounced them to the police in order that the latter could come to know about the gun. However, once the case had started to hot up, Efrem began to deny that they had any suspicions Pavlik might be that person; eventually, the investigators were, for one reason or another, to accept this story, and to drop the case against him.

According to official records, the actual differences in property ownership between the Morozovs, the Kulukanovs and the Silins were not large. Kulukanov's land holdings amounted to 2.8 desyatinas, according to an official village soviet 'Form on the Property Holdings of Tavda District Resident . . .' probably compiled in late autumn 1932; records for the Morozovs and the Silins were around one and a half desyatins (181–6). But Kulukanov, and to a lesser extent Silin, evidently counted as slightly more prosperous than average. Rightly or wrongly, Kulukanov was reported in the local newspapers as the owner of a two-storey house; both he and Silin were said by their brother-in-law Denis Potupchik to have employed wage labour (44–6). Most important of all was the fact that the two had been convicted of resistance to grain surrender. To be sure, Kulukanov had had his sentence overturned; but in the suspicious atmosphere of the early 1930s Soviet Union, the fact of the original negative sentence weighed far more heavily than the reprieve.

If 'wealth' did not mean much in Gerasimovka, 'poverty' was relative as well; as is clear from Sergei Morozov's list of possessions, it did not mean destitution. Equally, the post-mortem examination of Pavlik Morozov's body describes his nutritional threshold as 'average' – rather than 'emaciated' or 'showing signs of hypertrophy', as would have been the case had the boy been severely malnourished (10). Indeed, children in rural areas – unless these were famine-struck – could expect a superior level of subsistence to those in towns at the time.

But life must have been a struggle for Pavlik and his brothers, with a single mother and an absent father. At going on fourteen, Pavlik was old enough to be considered the 'man' of the family, and the case file does suggest that he took on this role, getting into conflict with his grandfather and cousin over farm property that the latter had removed 'for safe-keeping' when Trofim disappeared from sight. Pavlik would also – according to normal practices in peasant families up to the 1960s – have been expected to look after his younger brothers. On the day of the murder, child-care duties had been devolved, with eleven-year-old Aleksei left to mind five-year-old Roman (67), while Pavlik himself took Fyodor out for berries. Like other village children, the Morozov boys would have been dressed in home-made, homespun clothes (Pavlik had a shirt and a padded jacket on the day of the murder (10) – and presumably trousers as well though these are not mentioned in the post-mortem report). Hygiene would have been taken care of on occasional trips to the bath-house,[37] plus dips in local water-courses during the summer. Though the nickname 'Pavlik' has an affectionate, slightly patronizing flavour – of the sort expended by kind adults on little boys – it is misleading. The boy known in full as 'Pavel' Morozov was abbreviated by his family to 'Pashka', a much more rough-hewn style of diminutive, just as his older cousin was known locally as 'Danilka'. But Soviet official taste held names ending in 'ka' to be vulgar: what Pavlik was called at home smacked of teenage hooliganism. And so the name 'Pavlik' or indeed 'Pavlusha' – 'dear little Paul' – was attached to the boy, taking him out of the Gerasimovka fields and putting him back in the nursery.

The Morozov family network was not only divided by property ownership; it was also divided by levels of allegiance to Soviet power, which ran along generational lines. Or to put it a different way, maybe the younger members of the family had a better idea of how to answer questions about 'political convictions', when these were put by Soviet officials. 'I have no political convictions,' declared Arseny Kulukanov at an interrogation in September 1932 (96). Kseniya Morozova gave her answer in the same terms (100); Sergei Morozov added, still more provocatively, 'I couldn't care who's in power' (105). According to the prevailing official attitudes of the day – 'those who are not with us are against us' – such an answer was tantamount to a declaration of hostility for the system.

All the younger people under suspicion of the Morozov murders, on the other hand, gave a more acceptable answer: 'I am sympathetic to Soviet power' (e.g. 78). And in addition, some of the younger Morozov connections demonstrated their allegiance to Soviet power in a more positive way: besides Denis Potupchik, these included his son Ivan, who may have worked as a paid informer for OGPU as well as a police aide.[38] They perhaps also included Pavlik and Fyodor, though – as we shall see in Chapter 8 – the question of whether these two were 'Pioneers' (or some other kind of juvenile activists) or not is hard to resolve.

In the aftermath of the Morozov murders, these divisions of generation and ideology would make themselves strongly felt, with some of the extended family (Tatiana, Denis, Ivan) testifying voluntarily for the prosecution, and others (Khima, Arseny Silin) contributing discreditable information about their relations, probably in the effort to clear themselves.[39]

MURDERS, MUGGINGS AND DRINKING BOUTS

Quite a lot of information can be pieced together about those sitting on the wrong side of the table at the investigations into the Morozov murders. What of those conducting the interrogations? So far as the very limited material in terms of Party records and interrogation protocols indicates, they were entirely typical provincial officials of the time. Yakov Titov, the 'local inspector of the Worker and Peasant Militia', or beat policeman, lived in Beloyarka village soviet, in the far west of Tavda district (77). He came originally, like most of the Gerasimovka villagers, from Belorussia. He was thirty-five or thirty-six when the Morozov murders took place, and had joined the Party in 1931, but was clearly a man of little sophistication, outclassed, in terms of education, by Ivan Potupchik, his supposed junior. At later stages of the investigation, once OGPU had taken over, things were conducted with a degree more professionalism, but an arbitrary and accidental flavour persisted.

Apart from their working practices, nothing remains of the 'responsible' officials from OGPU: Bykov (his initial appears to be a Russian N or I), the 'district plenipotentiary', or local director, of the OGPU, and his various deputies; Fedchenko, called in from Nizhny Tagil at the third stage of the investigation; or Shepelev, who wrapped the case up. Ushenin, Bykov's predecessor as district plenipotentiary in Tavda, turns up on a document of 15 May 1941 as the holder of quite a high position in

Sverdlovsk, Head of the Second Section, People's Commissariat of State Security (the successor to OGPU).[40] But he is the only person in the Morozov case to have left further traces.

If the archives give little information about individual biographies, they are eloquent about the conditions in which officials had to work. The divisions within the Morozov clan reflected those in the Gerasimovka community more broadly. Local newspaper reports illustrate not only official intolerance of a poor and 'backward' local community, but also the fissured nature of that community. The very fact that Gerasimovka's problems got reported so assiduously laid bare the presence of a politically aware contingent in the village – in the shape of 'village correspondents'. And while it was often claimed, after Pavlik Morozov's death, that Gerasimovka had no Party organization, and that there were not even any Komsomol members there,[41] the situation was in fact less straightforward. A Party cell – admittedly with only three members – was set up there in early March 1931.[42] Even before that, the occasional villager was recorded as belonging to the Party cell in another village, Gorodishche, or as applying to join the cell.[43] And there was a Komsomol group active already in 1925.[44]

The hard core of Party members remained very small, however: even in November 1933, the Party had only four full members and three candidate members; earlier that year, with three full members and two candidates, Gerasimovka had one of the two lowest memberships in the entire Tavda district.[45] Another index of political awareness, subscriptions to newspapers, also pointed to low impact: even in 1933, Gerasimovka received a mere three issues of *Tavda Worker*, and single issues of a few other papers – *Pravda*, *Izvestiya* and *The Peasant Gazette*, among central publications, and *The Urals Worker*, *The Way to the Kolkhoz* and the Sverdlovsk Pioneer newspaper *Dawns of the Commune* among local efforts – which were clearly destined for the school and the local reading room.[46]

Not much support was available to the Gerasimovka 'front guard', as they would have described themselves, at district level. In Tavda generally, Party membership figures were low – never more than a few hundred.[47] In 1932, there were only seventeen Komsomol cells across the district, with a total membership of 143.[48] As well as being sparsely educated in terms of the jobs they had to fill, therefore, the Tavda officials were also chronically overworked, with at best weak backup from the rank and file.

The risk of over-stretch applied as much to representatives of OGPU as to Party and Komsomol members. In 1929, even before collectivization had started, Stepan Iosifovich Mokrousov (Wet Whiskers), OGPU plenipotentiary in Tavda since 1927, and later district investigator, became so overburdened with counter-revolutionary cases that he succumbed to acute TB and had to be hospitalized.[49] And in 1931, rank-and-file workers of the Tavda OGPU and police passed a resolution lamenting their heavy load of work in a town 'stuffed with class enemies and alien elements'.[50] The problems of coping with the workload were recognized higher up in late 1930, when the Urals Regional Committee sent round a circular warning district committees that they should exercise consideration when dispatching OGPU operatives for tours of duty in the countryside. 'Bearing in mind the disadvantages of OGPU operatives, their extreme overload of basic duties [. . .] sending OGPU operatives on campaigns to the village at the expense of their basic duties is to cease forthwith.'[51]

Disinclined as one might be to sympathize with a group that caused so much misery to others, the workload of such local officials was indeed formidable. In this area, unlike in some others in the Urals, armed uprisings do not seem to have been a problem, but attacks on activists were. In the four months from October 1930 to January 1931 alone, there were five murders or attempted murders across Irbit region, the intermediate administrative area into which Tavda district then fell, and at the same period, four activists were badly beaten.[52] Attacks of this kind continued into 1932, including not only the famous Morozov murders, but also the murder of an adult activist, Kozlov, killed by a gunshot wound to the stomach in Gorodishche in December 1932.[53] And in November 1932, two members of the special police force and Komsomol members, Karp Yudov and Prokhor Varygin, were severely beaten in Gerasimovka by five members of the Kniga family, who allegedly shouted at their victims as they worked, 'Take that for your activism over the grain collection and for your links with the police.'[54]

Lower-level political protests were also common. For example, in March 1931, a libellous leaflet, which the authorities attributed to a disaffected former worker, was discovered at the Tavda lumber mills. 'We inform you that we will set light to the hay what you have snitched. You're behaving like yids. What you want to do next[,] build a factory or pull a house down? Well we'll build a grave for you that'll fit so tight you can't turn round but first we'll burn the office down or blow it up[,] we'll give no quarter to the yids, we're not scared of you we'll cut your throats every one of you!'[55] And in November 1931, an informer discovered anti-Soviet graffiti in a lavatory at the Tavda lumberworks: 'Get out of your grave Vladimir Ilyich [Lenin], my love, the people running the five-year plan don't know stuff', the doggerel poet had written, and had contributed more literary masterworks too, this time prophesying an end to Communism in 1932.[56]

Less aggressive, but far more prevalent, and therefore just as worrying to police and party officials, were the hostile rumours and mutterings of dissatisfaction overheard by informers in crowds and queues. A few days before the 1 May holiday in 1931, a man was overheard complaining (to general grunts of assent), 'They've been deceiving us thirteen years [. . .] We just work our butts off, with not even a kilo of meat in return, we sit hungry, and now what do we get? Some f[ucki]ng salt herring!' Even among Party members, dissent was recorded, such as a rank-and-file Tavda Communist who complained at a drinking session with friends (including one false friend, who duly told all to the secret police) over the May holiday in 1931 that collectivization should have adopted a gradualist approach, beginning with well-funded voluntary communes to make the system popular in the first place.[57]

Dissatisfaction like this tended to be dispersed in grumbles alone, even among those who fantasized about the Soviet system's imminent collapse, but there was also a minority who went in for truly lawless behaviour. For example, in late 1931, it came to the attention of OPGU operatives that a gang of five bandits was living out in the taiga, sixty-five kilometres from Tavda, using hunters' shacks as shelters. The five – who were armed – had managed to escape over the border into the lower Tavda district before they could be apprehended.[58] The men concerned were described as 'dekulakized peasants', which was possibly correct – those who evaded exile automatically put themselves on the wrong side of the law, and recourse to violence in order to evade capture was a natural next step. However, they may equally well have been actual criminals, since the crime rate in the district was high, and many incidents occurred that even the hypersensitive authorities were reluctant to class as 'political terrorism'. In March 1931, a man was attacked on the streets of Tavda at about seven in the evening by muggers, who removed his outer clothing. He had the temerity to report the incident to the police, and on his way back was again attacked by the same muggers, this time seeking vengeance, and armed with a knife. He received stab wounds to his back, chest and neck, and would have had his throat cut had he not been able to grab hold of the knife and fend off the blow.[59] And in 1931, the district suffered from the depredations of horse-thieves and cattle-rustlers, whose ringleader was (allegedly) a Tatar.[60] Indeed, theft of all kinds was extraordinarily common, with up to two incidents a day being reported in some months.[61] And there were also some more offbeat crimes: in the autumn of 1932, the OGPU spent a good deal of time dealing with a case involving the sale of mushrooms at Tavda market: an unscrupulous trader had been passing off fly agarics, a particularly noxious type of toadstool, as edible.[62]

By far the largest problem for the local forces of law, however, was the presence in Tavda district of a very large number of special settlers. By the summer of 1931, over 11,000 had moved in (increasing the local population by more than 50 per cent), and were housed in conditions that were almost indescribably bad. In one logging camp (most of the exiles were deputed to help with tree-felling, or, if they were too young or enfeebled for this, packed off to collect brushwood), the main source of water was a fetid, fly-infested puddle. Families camped in earth dugouts till they were able to build their own barracks, a process that was slow and painful, since most of the exiles came from treeless areas of the Kuban and Ukraine, thousands of kilometres to the south, and had no idea how to work with the materials they were given. The food situation was dire: a mere 800 grams of bread a day was issued to full-capacity workers, while family members got six kilos of bread a month. Unsurprisingly, relative luxuries, such as clothes, footwear and textbooks for the children, were in chronically short supply. Epidemics were frequent, and the mood of those incarcerated in what were essentially labour camps by another name was demoralized and resentful.[63]

The special settlers were a particular source of anxiety to local officials, since it was suspected that serious political resistance was likely in the displaced. Such fears had some foundation: the network of informers using penny-dreadful names such as 'The Swallow' and 'The Signalman', some recruited from among special settlers themselves, brought back disturbing information about individuals concealing arms, threatening to kill the local commandants and work supervisors, exulting in the murders of local activists, and thrilling to the thought that soon war would come and precipitate a political coup.[64]

Escapes from the logging camps were frequent. Between October 1931 and April 1932, 426 special settlers made off, of whom only eighty-eight were recaptured.[65] Escapees were helped by the fact that there was a lively trade locally in false papers, which were known to be available for sale in Tavda.[66] Special settlers did not necessarily even have to go so far to get supplies. In one of the logging camps, Vaskin Bor, a woman was overheard by an informer in April 1931 boasting, 'My husband's a worker in Leningrad, but he knows a village soviet chairman and so he's got papers saying he's a poor peasant and now he's seeing to me, and if he doesn't manage to get me out, then I'll get hold of some documents and I don't care whether they're false [. . .] I'll go off by myself, I've got an identity card saying I'm not an exile, and not an individual farmer, and I've another set of papers too, and I got them from the chairman of a village soviet.'[67]

OGPU representatives and Party officials, then, were subject to a variety of contradictory imperatives. They had to respond to commands issued from the centre, coping with influxes of settlers, and with the political threat these were thought to pose; they had to ensure that dekulakization quotas and grain and stock surrender targets were fulfilled, in a district without kulaks, and with a population so poor that the surrenders brought destitution. And at the same time they had to manage the devastation that these policies caused on the ground. Party and secret police reports make it clear that local officials had a penchant for bureaucratic tidiness and paper-pushing that seems particularly incongruous in this remote and chaotic district.[68] But the same files also make it clear that officials recognized the connection between economic deprivation and political unrest: for example, the high level of escapes from special settlements was explicitly linked to poor living conditions in a report of early 1932.[69] Hence the attempts to improve living conditions and supplies that took place over the course of late 1931 and early 1932.[70]

Yet the size of the task made large-scale improvements impossible. Even outside the special settler camps, conditions were dreadful. In early 1931, there was no salt available anywhere in Tavda district. Bread could be baked only once a month 'so that it goes stale and is unfit for eating'; the total non-availability of soap had led to an epidemic of scabies, for which medical treatment could also not be offered (again, because of shortage of supplies).[71] While Party and OGPU officials lived better than the general run of the population, their own conditions were not exactly enviable, and energy had to be expended also on the backslidings and misdemeanours of colleagues and subordinates: Party disciplinary files make it clear that the main leisure pursuit of many rank-and-file members was going on drinking bouts, sometimes followed by acts of vandalism or social nuisance such as brick-throwing and loud accordion-playing in the street, and that corruption was not uncommon.[72]

Material from the archives and from oral history, and even from the local paper, presents a very different picture of the Urals from that favoured in propaganda produced in Moscow and Leningrad. Tavda, set in marshy and flat – though hauntingly beautiful – landscape, is a remote, deprived area of unstable living and broken dreams. In such a place of poor communications – aside from the railway line to Sverdlovsk, and the Tavda river itself – intractable countryside, and poverty, pressing forward crash industrialization and mass collectivization was an almost insuperable task. Yet the practical difficulties did not reduce the ideological fervour of the thin layer of fervent activists, who drew on the heritage of the Civil War as well as on the 'divide and rule' policies of dekulakization in order to stoke their own, and others', commitment. It was into this fissured world, where traditionalism and defensiveness, and the need to survive in the most basic sense, were met head on by class-war fanaticism and abstract belief in the 'bright future', that the Morozov case erupted.

CHAPTER 3

Investigating the Murder

The first news reports on the Morozov murders did not appear even in the local press for two weeks; it took almost a month for the case to reach *Pioneer Pravda*. The length of the delay may seem incredible in a news-driven culture, but the communication of news as such was never an official function of the Soviet press; information about recent events was released only after careful vetting from the authorities. The general public got to hear about the murders only at a point when Party and police officials thought they had matters under control, and that the organization of a popular response would be helpful. The publication of the first story, on 17 September, came a day after the Morozov murders had been discussed at a meeting of the Tavda District Committee of the Communist Party, whose resolutions had included 'responding to kulak terror with a new surge of working-class enthusiasm'.[1] The outlet for the story was the Party's local newspaper, *Tavda Worker*, with consequences that will be described in Chapter 4. However, far from the public eye, and even from the scrutiny of the local Party bosses, the investigation into the murders started almost immediately the bodies were found, on 6 September 1932, three days after the killings were supposedly committed.

The transcripts of these early investigations were in time placed in the official case file on the Morozov murders, two fat volumes of documents stamped on their front covers, like other materials once considered top secret, with the ambiguous formulation *khranit' vechno* (keep in safety, and/or away from the public eye, for ever). The case file was stored in the closed archives of the NKVD (later KGB and FSB) in Sverdlovsk/Ekaterinburg until 1997, when it was forwarded to the State Prosecutor's Office in Ekaterinburg, and from there to the Central Procuracy in Moscow. Since then it has remained in the capital, and it was recently transferred to the Central Archive of the FSB.[2]

The first volume of the file mostly comprises a selection of around 500 letters from Pioneers and schoolchildren demanding the death sentence for the murderers.[3] The second contains the documents in the case as such – around 250 pages of mostly handwritten testimony.[4] Making sense of these is not easy. This is not a tidily docketed, well-organized case record. Rather, it is

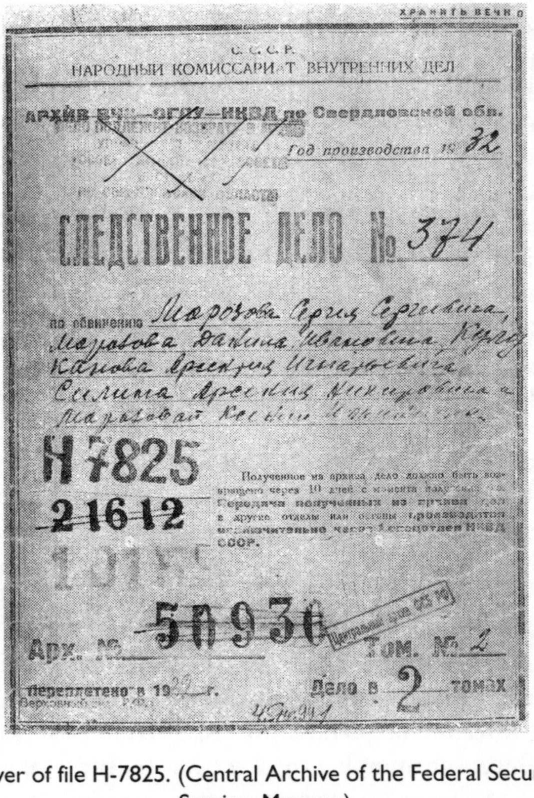
ХРАНИТЬ ВЕЧНО
С. С. С. Р.
НАРОДНЫЙ КОМИССАРИАТ ВНУТРЕННИХ ДЕЛ
АРХИВ ВЧК—ОГПУ—НКВД по Свердловской обл.
Год производства 1932
СЛЕДСТВЕННОЕ ДЕЛО № 374
по обвинению
Н 7825
21612
Арх. №
Том. № 2
Переплетено в 19 г.
Дело в 2 томах

Cover of file H-7825. (Central Archive of the Federal Security Service, Moscow)

a bulging compendium of materials dating from different stages of the investigation, which have been arranged by the archivists in more or less chronological order, though this is not necessarily the sequence in which the materials were originally used. The documents are not glossed or annotated in any way; many are on badly yellowed, high-acid paper that is now crumbling, and written with oxidized ink (or worse, rubbed pencil) in a variety of often rough hands. The grammar and spelling of some of the characters involved, particularly Yakov Titov, the district inspector in Gerasimovka, are appalling: words are run together, case endings are garbled, and formulations such as 'give evidence according to the substance of the matter' come out as 'give evdens akording to the sustis ofthemater'. Fortunately, words can often be guessed from context, and most of the contributors to the file are represented by enough documents to allow one to get a sense of how to puzzle out scribbled words by analogy – making the greater part of most of the texts accessible.

Once meaning of a superficial kind is grasped, though, it emerges that meaning at a deeper level is equally recalcitrant. File H-7825 certainly does not offer an instant solution to an unsolved crime. Instead, it shows how a brutal child murder became the centre of a variety of different narratives, with each separate set of investigators trying to impose on the contradictory and wayward testimony of the Gerasimovka villagers their own more streamlined version of *what really happened* – with not one of these versions including, or even addressing, all the details that the villagers supplied. To borrow a phrase from Natalie Zemon Davis, the Pavlik Morozov file is 'fiction from the archives': a collection of stories each representing the Pavlik Morozov case in a different way. But alongside the stories that the file *is* telling, equally important are the ones that it is not.

HEARSAY AS PROOF

The Morozov investigation did not adopt the stereotyped patterns of the police procedural, with its meticulous sifting of small pieces of material evidence on the one hand, and psychological profiling on the other. Striking for an observer brought up in a different criminological tradition is the almost total lack of scientific evidence. No scene of crime procedures of any kind were undertaken. There was no attempt to establish whether the boys had been killed where they were found, or to reconstruct the likely nature of the attack upon them from the injuries that they had suffered. No fingerprint tests were done, and there was no search of the area to look for discarded weapons, evidence of the killers' movements, and so on. Further, there was no recourse to scientific techniques later on. No autopsy was performed on the bodies, which were examined superficially by Titov and the medical orderly from the first-aid point in Maloe Gorodishche, a large settlement roughly halfway between Gerasimovka and Tavda. The examination was entirely external, though Pavel's details were entered on an official form that included space for material on the condition of the internal organs. The reason for this was no doubt that rigor mortis was still in place. Even so far as the externals were concerned, the orderly filled in only a few sections:

> Clothes: weskit has cuts in two places.
> Sex: male
> Age (going by appearance): 14
> Height: (left blank)
> Build: (left blank)
> Nutritional threshold: Average
> General skin colour: White
> Post-mortem skin changes: Red and crimson patches on the back
> State of rigor mortis: Rigor mortis still there
> Hair colour: Reddish-brown
> Length: (left blank)
> Face: White
> Eyes: Open
> Corneas: (left blank)
> Pupils: (left blank)
> Inner eyelids: (left blank)
> Mouth: Closed
> Interior of mouth: (left blank)
> Gums: (left blank)
> Tongue: Behind teeth (10).

Where the observers did give a little more detailed information, though once more presented without regard for the specifics of medical knowledge, was on the wounds. The official form completed for Pavlik stated that these were six in number: two in the thorax, two in the stomach, and two on the 'upper limbs' (11). A more detailed note at the end added,

> Death resulted from four knife wounds 1) a 4 cm. wound on the rib cage on the right-hand side near the fifth and sixth ribs 2) a wound to the solar plexus region; 3) a wound on the left-hand side of the stomach below the ribs 3 cm. in length with some of the guts sticking out of it. The fourth wound is on the right-hand side close to the partal ligament,[5] 3 cm. in length with some of the guts sticking out of it, this was the cause of death. Also on the left hand by the thumb a wound about 6 cm. long (11 rev.).

The material on Fyodor's corpse was even less informative. The report on his body, set out on a scrap of ordinary paper, simply makes a list of his wounds.

> The *fatal* wound was made with a knife in the right side of the *neck* under the ear and is 2 cm. long. The second wound is *in the Right-hand Side in the stomach* below the last rib and is about 3 cm. long and through this part of the guts are sticking out, which was the cause of death. In addition on the top side of the right arm 4 cm. above the wrist bone is a wound 4 cm. long (7: emphasis original).

The lack of professionalism with which these examinations were carried out and recorded is not surprising. In the early Soviet period, a medical orderly was likely to be someone whose education amounted to a few years of primary school and an accelerated course in medical practice that did not go much beyond first aid.[6] The Soviet Union had had state pathology facilities since the 1920s, and the performance of some tests, for example on under-fingernail samples, was established practice.[7] But laboratories were very far away from Gerasimovka, and village policemen would scarcely have heard of their services, let alone known how to make use of them.[8]

More surprising, in terms of practicalities, is the absence of forensic material from later on in the case. The district plenipotentiary, Bykov, who handled the investigation in Tavda, was evidently a man of some education (he wrote reasonably accurate Russian in a neat hand), and a bureaucratic stickler (his handwritten protocols, unlike those from other investigators, invariably include the date and almost always his own name). He took action in order to produce evidence useful to the case in some areas – for instance, having a subordinate make a copy of part of the trial record of Pavlik Morozov's father, or what purported to be this (113). But he commissioned no forensic investigations at all. In fact, just one such investigation was carried out, in early November (i.e. a full two months after the murders took place), at the time when Fedchenko, the Operations Section representative from Nizhny Tagil, had taken over the investigation. Clothes and knives found at Sergei and Kseniya Morozov's house were sent to a forensic chemist, who attempted to produce a fluorescence reaction using ultraviolet light, which would have indicated the presence of blood, and to generate haemoglobin globules by applying potassium chlorate (205).

Not only was forensic investigation sparse to the vanishing point, but it was also more or less ignored where it did exist. For example, the fluorescence and haemoglobin tests on the clothes in fact proved negative – much to the disappointment of the OGPU representatives, who (absurdly) suggested testing the water they had been washed in as an alternative (204). But despite the forensic chemist's categorical statement, 'On the basis of this investigation, one must conclude that no blood has been found on the exhibits in the case' (205), the clothes and knives were forwarded as material evidence with the prosecution dossier for the trial (213). Equally, a rough-and-ready measurement test carried out by Bykov on 16 September, which was held to demonstrate that a pair of possibly blood-spotted trousers found soaking at the Morozovs fitted Danila Morozov, but not his grandfather (83), was ignored at later stages of the investigation. When Danila, in a bizarre fantasy of cross-dressing, suggested that the trousers were his own, but his grandfather had still been wearing them on the day of the murder, this was apparently taken seriously (177).[9] No inferences were drawn from the record that Pavlik's corpse was still in rigor mortis on 7 September, a point that might have suggested to the investigators a later date for the murder than 3 September (though perhaps rigor was prolonged by cold weather at night).[10] And none of the – once again extremely sparse – personal medical information about the suspects was called on. The arrest form made out for Sergei Morozov on 16 September 1932 stated that he – just over a week after having been confined for the first time – was 'elderly and frail' (136 rev.). The same statement was made about Kseniya Morozova (133). This suggests that neither of them is likely to have been, in early September, the sturdy, resourceful old people evoked in the later investigator narratives, which assigned major parts in the murders to each of them. But questions of physiological practicality were never allowed to arise.

The evidence in which the investigators *were* interested was not 'scientific', then. Indeed, they were remarkably uninterested in mundane practicalities, such as establishing exactly when the crime had happened. According to her own story, as given to the investigators at different stages, Pavlik and Fyodor's mother Tatiana Morozova had left Gerasimovka on 2 September and returned only on 5 September, at which point it had become clear the boys were missing (1, 69). In theory, therefore, the boys could have been murdered at any time on 4 September or early the following day. None of the investigators was remotely interested in considering this possibility. Common sense and local knowledge probably played some part in this: a berrying expedition would not have needed to last more than a day at most, and, if the boys had got held up by being lost, they would not have returned with full baskets, but would have eaten the contents to keep going. The discovery of the bodies with the berries strewn across them therefore suggested a return to the village at some point on the Saturday afternoon. But the readiness to accept 3 September as the murder date right from the beginning was also connected with the determination, common to all the investigators in the case, to regard the murder as part of a plan. The murderers – whoever they were – had seen the boys leave the village, and knowing Tatiana was away in Tavda, had seized their chance.

The certainty that the murder had to have been committed on 3 September in turn generated a rather primitive kind of filtering process. Anyone who could demonstrate an alibi for that day was ruled out of the investigation, at any rate as a primary suspect. This applied in particular to Dmitry Shatrakov, who had found the bodies while helping with the search in the forest. At an early stage in the investigation, Danila Morozov claimed that the murder had been carried out by Dmitry and his brother Efrem Shatrakov, and that he himself had seen them with their hands covered in blood (22). This version lost conviction, so far as the investigators were concerned, when it turned out that Dmitry was able to produce a written statement indicating that he had spent the whole of 3 September in a call-up post for the army (65).[11] Another beneficiary of the 'alibi rule' was Arseny Silin, who – though tried as an accessory to the murder – was never seriously considered as a suspect because he was able to claim that he had been away in Tavda between 3 and 5 September (a story for which he produced no backup, but that was credited without question) (98 rev.).

A good deal of the investigation was in any case driven by Tatiana Morozova's voluntary statement, delivered to Titov's colleague, local inspector Suvorov, on the morning of 6 September, in which she claimed that she was at loggerheads with her husband's family because she had split up with her husband after he began issuing false papers to kulaks, and because they were angry about Pavel's denunciation of his father. 'And my husband's dad and mam got cross with my son because he told on his dad and they made threats to kill him and that bad feeling is still lasting and my nephew as is also my father-in-law's grandson he did give my son a vicious beating' (1).

From the beginning, the police were convinced of the Morozovs' involvement; all their interrogation was aimed at establishing this, and links with other individuals who might have helped with the murder, or encouraged the Morozovs to carry it out. As we know, Gerasimovka was a large village, of perhaps a hundred families. But only thirty or so witnesses were interviewed, most of them from the immediate area where the Morozov households – both Tatiana's and Sergei Morozov's – were located. Only two house searches were carried out: at Sergei Morozov's, where the bloodied clothing (a shirt and trousers) later sent for testing was removed (8), and at Arseny Kulukanov's (47). Although, at the first stage of the investigation, Efrem Shatrakov was under suspicion, the Shatrakovs' house was not searched. And the police were not consistent about holding follow-up interviews with individuals who had been mentioned by suspects as able to confirm their stories. For instance, on 8 September Efrem Shatrakov claimed that Vasily Anushenko could confirm his story about having gone straight from the fields to the Prokopenkos' house on 3 September (24), but this individual was apparently never contacted and interviewed.

The investigation was not, then, primarily concerned with the identification of possible suspects, or indeed with establishing whether suspects were guilty. Rather, its purpose was, at every stage, the collection of incriminating evidence about individuals who had been identified as guilty from the outset, preferably from informants who could be regarded as trustworthy. Prokhor Varygin, for instance, was interviewed several times not just because he was an assiduous purveyor of sensationalist tattle, but also because he was a police aide and a Komsomol member, and hence ideologically above board.[12] Dominance of the witness pool by 'trusties' in turn meant that the number of statements where the person expressed lack of knowledge or uncertainty was very low.[13]

Even had the investigation not had a pronounced ideological bias from the outset, there would not have been time for really thorough work. Later complaints in newspapers about its 'protraction' have to be seen in the context of an era when an entire investigation was sometimes fitted into less than three days.[14] Though the process of preparing the dossier of evidence was drawn out over more than two months (the investigation began on 6 September (1) and continued until 16 November (216)), the number of actual days involved was not large – just four working weeks of interrogation.

If the investigation did not cast its net wide, however, it did gather fairly large amounts of evidence from the witnesses who were interviewed. Much of this evidence was, from the point of view of a modern criminal justice system, highly eccentric. Rather than discounting hearsay, investigators did their best to encourage informants to provide this. They eagerly took down gossip, rumours and comments allegedly overheard from one or other of the defendants when they were sitting in the barn that was being used as a temporary lockup. For example, Prokhor Varygin reported to Bykov on 23 September that he had overheard Danila telling Efrem Shatrakov not to admit anything, even if he was beaten, and that he himself proposed to blame the blood on his trousers on a case of bloody flux from which his grandfather had been suffering (71).

The most resonant case of gossip was a story occurring repeatedly in different witness testimony about an exchange between Tatiana and Kseniya Morozova on the day when the children's bodies were brought back home. According to the version preferred by Tatiana, and first cited on 11 September, Kseniya had said to her, 'Tatiana, see the meat we've brought you, and now you can eat it' (5, 70). This version was also reported by Varygin on 23 September (the same day that Tatiana cited it for the second time) (72). Four days later, Stepanida Yudova, another villager, reported it again (73). Kseniya's story, on the other hand, was, at first, that she had never said anything to Tatiana about meat (100), and later, that she had arrived with bread for Sergei and Danila when they were sitting in the barn that was being used as a lockup, and that Tatiana lammed into her, 'Why are you taking bread to those murderers when you could take that meat?' Kseniya herself had replied, 'Let those who made the meat eat what they have made' (102 rev., 103).

The purpose of collecting gossip had several purposes. The investigators, of course, wanted to collect incriminating material about the alleged murderers. This included vengeful comments – Kseniya's taunt about meat, or, as Sergei Morozov claimed he had heard Mezyukhin say, 'That child should be killed' (41 rev.). But it also included information about the class status and political opinions of the participants. On 12 September, for example, Iosif Prokopovich recalled the following exchange between himself and Stepanida Kniga:

> When they brought the bodies to the reading room I felt pity for em and i sed if anyone ud give me a gun i sed i'd get half the village together and let rip and my words was heard by Kniga Stepanida and she sed to me if thats not enough for you she sed we can add a whole lot more weer not bothered about them and some women heard every word only they pretended not to and Varygin Prokhor he heard it all too. And Kniga Stepanida, her husband ustin fyodorovich is carying out [kulak] agitation, he says all the people what have been dekulakized will get their stuff back and they'll let the special settlers go home

> from the camp and they'll put our poor peasants in those houses, and special settlers do visit him and even some live with him as he feeds with his bread and instead of a farm worker he kept this young chit this kulak woman aged about 35 from Troitskaya [special settler] camp (37–37 rev.).

The tale offers a complete vignette of the Knigas' anti-Soviet lives: not only snide comments about collectivization, but insinuations about active fraternization (indeed, it is implied, more intimate relations than that) with special settlers.

In this particular case, the accusation went nowhere – the authorities did not arrest and interview any members of the Kniga family, or attempt to implicate them in the murder,[15] but in other cases, accusations had more mileage. For instance, the investigators' concentration on Kulukanov and Silin seems to have been dictated less by the two men's economic standing (while Kulukanov was officially designated a kulak on the 'property ownership' form supplied by the Gerasimovka village soviet during the course of the investigation, Silin was not),[16] than by what was supposed in the locality. The crucial document here was a character reference written by Denis Potupchik on 12 September, which stated that Kulukanov had run a 'kulak farm' from 1921, and had employed wage labour until 1931; the ultimate source of this information was Denis Potupchik himself, who had 'earned his bread' from Kulukanov during 1922 (44). For his part, Silin was also said to have employed wage labour and to have speculated in cattle (44 rev.). Additional damning testimony (in this case from Efim Galyzov) about him included the fact that he had sold a wagonload of potatoes to the special settlers (34 rev.).

If Sergei Morozov's house was searched for bloodied clothing, Arseny Kulukanov's was the subject of a rather different type of search – aimed at turning up property hidden from confiscation when he was dekulakized. On 12 September 1932, Titov, in the company of police aide Karp Yudov and of Iosif Prokopovich, visited Kulukanov's and tracked down the cab and shafts of a cart that had been hidden here; the wheels were later dug up in Silin's vegetable patch (47). Here was 'documentary' proof of collusion between Silin and Kulukanov to nefarious ends, and the cart was to be cited repeatedly in later testimony by the defendants.

The investigators were interested in collecting from witnesses concrete 'tokens' that could be evoked in order to prove the kulak links of the accused, whether at first or at second hand. They were operating like members of the Inquisition in early modern Spain, who transcribed testimony from neighbours about pork being eschewed in this household, and fires not lit on Saturdays in that, and used this to identify and persecute 'backsliding' Jews and Muslims. In a similar way, the testimony of peeking neighbours watching their neighbours burying cartwheels in the vegetable patch was used to identify 'backsliders' from the virtuous paths of collective ownership.

The OGPU also had other ends in view. One was carrying out a sort of public relations exercise according to which consultation (who do *you* think the kulaks are?) became an end in itself. Justice was not so much supposed to be done as it was supposed to be seen to be done. The question of who the general public thought was to blame was therefore fundamental. Collection of gossip went right up the line: if it leaked into the early testimonies accidentally as a result of the closeness of the investigators to the attitudes of their informants, it was gathered more systematically by the senior officials who took over the investigation later on. Operations Inspector Fedchenko, for example, solemnly transcribed a statement from one Grigory Matsuk[17] recording that his wife had told him some neighbours had seen Sergei and Kseniya Morozova together in the woods on 3 September (164).[18] And he also took down from another villager a statement to the effect that 'public opinion' in Gerasimovka held that Efrem Shatrakov was not guilty of the murder, and had been implicated wrongly because of hostility to Pavlik Morozov (162 rev.). From the point of view of the investigators, there was only a small distinction between a resolution passed at the Poor Peasants' Assembly, a report by a village soviet official on which of his neighbours was a kulak, and an off-the-cuff opinion from a trusted person. All of these were counted as evidence, and examples of all these genres were included in the case file (58–60, 44–6, 162 rev.).

Last but not least, the purpose of collecting gossip was to pick up motifs which could be stitched into an impressive narrative of guilt and wickedness at a later stage. No material was too fantastic to be absorbed. When Danila Morozov told the investigators that Kulukanov had stolen gold from a special settler living in his house, this was taken perfectly seriously (86). Not surprisingly, the less bizarre assertion that Kulukanov had given Danila thirty roubles (a fairly considerable sum in the Russian countryside in the early 1930s) for carrying out the murder (84) was immediately believed, and later, 'proof' was found for the allegation in the form of a payment Arseny Silin said that Danila had made him for some cloth after the murder took place.[19] Equally, Danila's alleged declaration on 3 September – reported at second hand – that 'Pavel had two wounds, and Fyodor three' (12, 103, 106) was given as much weight in the evidence-gathering as the information on the post-mortem report that in fact Pavel had six wounds, and Fyodor four (11 rev.).

FROM VILLAGE FEUD TO 'KULAK PLOT'

Despite basic similarities in procedure and in the types of evidence that they were looking for, the interrogators varied as to how they then chose to use the material. District Inspector Titov believed from the first that the murder had been committed by Danila Morozov and one or more of the Shatrakov brothers. Aside from filing the 'Dead Body Removal' document (6) and the documents relating to the examination of Pavel and Fyodor's bodies (10–11, 7), Titov and his helpers, Suvorov and Potupchik, concentrated their efforts on pursuing proof along those lines. On 6 September, Titov conducted the house search at the Morozovs' (8), and questioned Anna Stepanchenko, who had seen Efrem Shatrakov and his father working in the fields on the morning of 3 September, and had encountered Kseniya Morozova, she said, in the company of two other villagers going out for berries (28). On 7 September, he interviewed Sergei Morozov (12) and Kseniya Morozova (19). And on the same day, he took down a deposition from Prokhor Varygin, a neighbour of the Morozovs' as well as a police aide, to the effect that the Shatrakovs had been feuding with Pavel because of a suspected denunciation for having illegal firearms (13). Titov's helper Ivan Potupchik pursued the same direction, taking down statements from Dmitry Shatrakov (who denied involvement) (16), and Danila Morozov (who admitted his guilt) (22) on 7 September.[20]

On 8 September, Titov interviewed Efrem Shatrakov (24), his mother Olga (18), and two witnesses with knowledge of Efrem's movements, Ivan Pulyashkin (25) and Vasily Prokopenko (27). Pulyashkin was the first to mention a story that was later to become a crucial element in the case for the prosecution. At some point (a date was not given), Pavlik and Danila had had a violent and very public row over the harness saddle. Meanwhile, Ivan Potupchik occupied himself with Anton Shatrakov, Efrem's father (17), his only recorded interview on that day.

At this stage, the investigators were not much interested in the possible ideological background to the conflict between the Shatrakovs and Pavel and Fyodor. Instead they saw it as a straight tit-for-tat attack, with the murder a response for Pavel's informing on the Shatrakovs' unlicensed gun. As Dmitry Shatrakov supposedly stated at his interrogation by Titov on 6 September:

> Morozov Pavel he went and told on us that we had a second gun hid[,] the [first] gun was taken off of us in 1931 when they took guns off of the kulaks and that was when they took that one And the other one we hid it in 1932 [.] On 22 July they took that second gun off of us and the person who told on us that we had that gun[,] who told on us over it was Morozov Pavel and maybe my brother Efrem was cross over that I dunno (26 rev.).

Possibly Titov made up this testimony himself, in order to pin something on a suspect. But even so, what he credits – or rather, does *not* credit – to his informant is significant. Pavlik is not described anywhere as a Pioneer, or as a resolute participant in public meetings: instead, he is just someone who 'told on' a neighbour for doing something forbidden.[21] Equally, Titov's protocols are extremely sparing in their references to 'kulaks' (and when there are such references, they are quotations from 'authority-speak', as in Dmitry Shatrakov's statement above: 'when they were taking guns off the kulaks'). The same is true of the protocols taken down by Ivan Potupchik (see e.g. 17, 22). Of all the witness or suspect statements transcribed in the first days of the investigation, only one, the voluntary statement by Tatiana Morozova, given to Inspector Suvorov and dated 6 September,

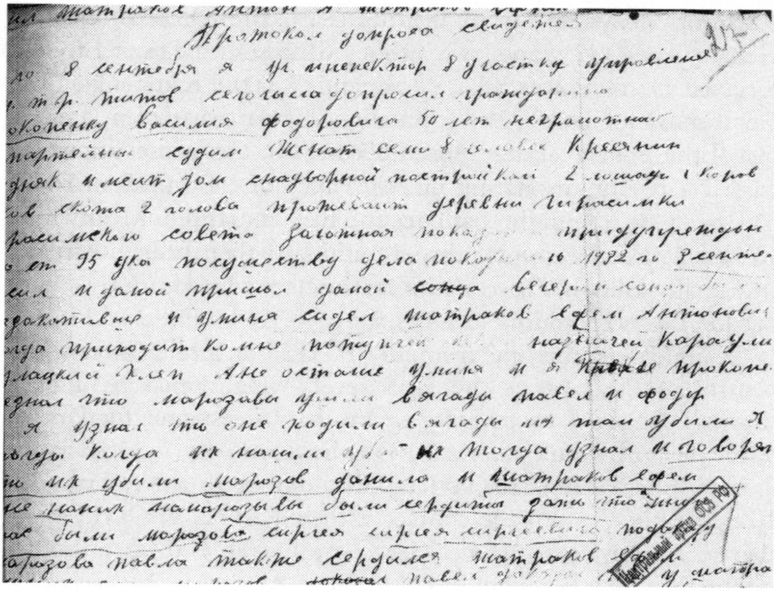
Протокол допроса свидетеля

A page from witness testimony recorded by policeman Yakov Titov. (Central Archive of the Federal Security Service, Moscow)

refers to Pavlik as 'a Pioneer' ('my son was an active Pioneer' (1)); in the others, the boy is merely someone who did a lot of 'telling on' other people.

This picture changed once Spiridon Kartashov, from the district office of OGPU,[22] became involved in the investigation on 11 September. Kartashov had come prepared with a small stock of official interrogation forms – in the pressure of the first few days, Titov resorted to writing on the backs of post-mortem certificates. Kartashov interviewed Ivan Potupchik on 11 September (29), and the schoolgirl Anastasiya Sakova on the same day (31), along with two other schoolchildren, Pavel Fokin and Pelageya Kovalenko (33).[23] He also received a written statement from the local 'village correspondent' about the reasons for the crimes: 'The Morozovs ended up killed not long after the search for a gun and for hidden kulak grain and a cart [. . .] the people who killed the Morozovs were the people who had the search done for the gun and the grain' (40).[24]

On 12 September, Kartashov interviewed the horse trader

Vladimir Mezyukhin from Vladimirovka, a few kilometres from Gerasimovka (42), and two other witnesses.[25] The team also received Denis Potupchik's document, 'On the Kulak Group in Gerasimovka Village' (44–6). Finally, they participated in a meeting of the Poor Peasants' Assembly held in Gerasimovka, which passed a resolution setting out the story of the murder (Pavlik had been on the right path to socialist construction, exposing kulaks vigorously despite threats, and had then been beaten up and finally killed). The resolution also demanded death by shooting for the perpetrators (58–60).[26]

One element missing from file H-7825 is information about control of the case at the local level, which must have been through face-to-face meetings. One has to assume that either Titov or Potupchik, or both, left Gerasimovka for Tavda on 9 September, arrived there later that day or in the morning of 10 September, and made contact with the offices of OGPU, and that Kartashov was sent back to Gerasimovka with them, arriving on 10 or 11 September. Or perhaps Kartashov happened by accidentally: on 8 September, the District Party Committee in Tavda passed a top-secret order directing that district inspectors reporting to OGPU should supervise work on the harvest and prevent sabotage. Kartashov could conceivably have arrived to see this order enacted.[27]

Whichever way, there are signs of a much more ideology-heavy approach to the suspects in the work that Kartashov did. In Tatiana Morozova's first statement, she had referred to the Kulukanovs and Silin in one precise context, alleging she had seen them all creeping around the village and visiting each other's houses in the early morning of 3 September (2). In her second statement, to Kartashov, she spoke in much more abstract terms:

> . . . suspicion falls on the following citizens: Morozov Sergei and his wife Aksen'ya Il'inichna and his grandson Morozov Danila Ivanovich and also Kulakanova Khima, Kulukanov Arseny, and Silin Arseny, because all that kulak band always used to gather to gether in a group and they had discussions about how much they hated Soviet power, and the people supervising all the measures being taken, and the Party, and my son Pavel Trofimovich Morozov aged 13 a Pioneer who with all his

> strength fought for the measures being taken by Soviet power and was devoted heart and soul to the cause despite being only a Pioneer, who mercilessly [exposed?] his father Morozov Trofim Sergeevich for making documents, that is, [Trofim] was the chairman of the village soviet and sold those documents to class hostile elements in the kulakery, to special settlers, and that Pioneer Pavel denounced [*donosil*] him for that, forwhich Trofim got 10 years as a measure of social defence [i.e. was sentenced to 10 years' imprisonment] and the victim's father Trofim is own son to that Sergei Morozov (3).

As my English translation suggests, Kartashov was not in total command of grammar and punctuation, and was not a good organizer of syntax, but he had absorbed some key phrases from contemporary propaganda: 'kulak band'; 'for/against the measures being taken' (meaning, essentially, 'collectivization'); 'devoted heart and soul to the cause'; and not least, 'denounced' rather than 'told on'.

The second stage of the investigation, then, was concerned with laying bare a 'kulak band', and material pointing to its existence was collected assiduously. This included not only the search of Kulukanov's house, and Denis Potupchik's report on the local kulaks, but several witness statements. Ivan Potupchik, in his witness statement to Kartashov, talked about Pavlik speaking at citizens' meetings and exposing kulaks, and reporting grain hoarders to the village soviet. He also stated that Pavlik had exposed his own father to the authorities (29). The investigators were concerned to expand the number of those suspected of participation: as well as interesting themselves in Mezyukhin, they looked for a witness who could say Kseniya Morozova had been seen with the boys (31, 32). On the other hand, it was at this point that Dmitry Shatrakov was removed from the investigation because he was able to provide an alibi (65).

Another significant part of the investigation was the attempt to accord the victims, in particular Pavel, the status of juvenile activists. Witness statements were collected to this end. Varygin, in his second witness statement as given to Kartashov, now described Pavel (who in the first statement had been simply one of 'the brothers Morozov') not only as 'a Pioneer', but as someone who had 'spoken at the general citizens' meetings and spoken for the suksess of the measures being taken, and also at the meetings had spoken about Kuluks, that they was hiding things and grain' (14). And a character reference on the two boys was commissioned from Denis Potupchik. This piece, dated 12 September, talked up Trofim Morozov into the ringleader of a whole gang of document-forgers, 'and heealso had Agents working from him, at the trial Pavel gave all the details about his father' (61). For the first time, it was suggested that Pavel had been under constant threat from his grandparents and others for his denunciatory activities, but had refused to give way (61 rev.).[28]

Phase Two of the investigation culminated on 16 September, with seven suspects being formally charged under Article 58.8: Arseny Silin, Kseniya Morozova, Sergei Morozov, Arseny Kulukanov, Khima Kulukanova, Efrem Shatrakov and Danila Morozov (48–54) (an eighth suspect, Vladimir Mezyukhin, was charged under the same article on 3 October (55)).

On 16 September, the third phase of the investigation began, this time in the rather more professional hands of district plenipotentiary Bykov, with occasional help from one of his deputies, Rechkalov. On the first day, Bykov conducted long, thorough interviews with Sergei Morozov (105) and with Danila Morozov (78), and instituted a face-to-face confrontation between the two (82). Danila had now retracted his confession to the murder; Sergei continued to implicate his grandson, but admitted to a sense of guilt about Pavel's and Fyodor's deaths, and particularly about not reporting Danila's suspicious statements earlier. He also insisted that Danila had not acted alone in carrying out the killing: the latter was (here the words were certainly Bykov's, not Sergei's) 'the instrument of a kulak plot'.

At this point, Sergei seems to have been in a state of some mental confusion. In the arrest form compiled on 16 September he gave the name of his dependants as Aksinya (Kseniya) and 'Pavel Ivanovich' Morozov (by the latter, he meant *Danila* Ivanovich Morozov) (135 rev.). And in his interview on 16 September and at the face-to-face confrontation, he gave different accounts of who had worn the shirt and trousers found in the house search on 6 September. Bykov seems to have interpreted this behaviour as evidence of Sergei's guilt. In a report to his superiors written on 17 September, he identified Sergei

Morozov as the main suspect, but described the murder as carried out by the 'local kulakery'. Members of this had 'taken offence' at Pavlik's repeated denunciations, not only of his 'own father', but also of some locals (unnamed) who had 'unregistered guns'. Bykov's report named as suspects Khima and Arsenty [*sic*] Kulukanov, Arsenty [*sic*] Silin, and the three Morozovs, who, he said 'have regularly appeared in police reports as persons of an anti-Soviet mood' (149–51).

The remainder of Bykov's investigation, though, devoted much more attention to Danila than to his grandfather. The younger man was called in on 22 September (84), when he admitted that a squabble over a piece of horse harness had indeed taken place, dating this to 26 August. Bykov saw Danila again on 1 October (86) and on 4 October (87); on 23 September, a confrontation was organized between him and Arseny Kulukanov (81), and on 5 October, one took place between him and Efrem Shatrakov (89). At these various sessions, Danila contributed incriminating material about Kulukanov (for instance, the story about the gold stolen from a special settler, and about the payment of thirty roubles).

Alongside working on Danila, Bykov attempted to flesh out the 'local kulakery' argument. For instance, he commissioned an inventory of Sergei Morozov's property, carried out on 17 September, perhaps in the hope that this would show Sergei also to be a kulak, or that hidden kulak property might be discovered there (56–7). He recorded an allegation by Sergei Morozov on 3 October that Kulukanov had stolen corn from the village soviet in August 1932, and that Danila had gone to Tavda to sell the corn on 11 August (111). And Khima Kulukanova was encouraged to produce negative testimony about her husband – she admitted the family had relations with special settlers, and that they had hidden property to avoid confiscation. She also provided incriminating detail about her father, stating that she said to him, 'You were always sinning against those Morozov boys, and now they've found your shirt covered in blood' – and had been greeted by a meaningful silence (93, 93 rev.).

Bykov also worked on Arseny Kulukanov himself. He brought the latter to an admission that he had 'cheated' Soviet power by hiding items from confiscation, including a cart, horse harness and cartwheels. However, Kulukanov still refused to accept any connection with the murder (96–7). But Bykov was working from another angle to implicate him. On 28 September, Arseny Silin not only confirmed that the cart owned by Kulukanov and hidden in his vegetable patch had originally been hidden at the Morozovs' (therefore establishing an anti-Soviet plot involving all three families), but also made the allegation about selling cloth bought in Tavda to Danila for thirty roubles (99). In Bykov's eyes, this evidently amounted to proof that Danila's story about being given the thirty roubles by Kulukanov was true, and that he had indeed been lured into the role of killer by the evil kulaks.

Bykov displayed relatively little interest in Efrem Shatrakov. To be sure, Potupchik and Titov were interviewed about the earlier interrogations, reiterated their suspicions of Efrem and Danila, and insisted that the two had confessed freely (74–6, 77). But at a re-interview on 22 September (90), and at his face-to-face confrontation with Danila on 5 October (89), Efrem himself denied all responsibility for the murder, insisting he had no resentment against Pavel, and denied he had ever been friends with Danila. For his part, Danila, while maintaining that he and Efrem had been friends – he painted a touching picture of the two going round Gerasimovka together with an accordion (89) – was no longer telling the story about having committed the murder with his friend. And Bykov made no attempt to get them to repeat the admissions they had made earlier.

Equally, he seems quickly to have decided that Silin and Khima Kulukanova were more useful as witnesses for the prosecution than as potential suspects. Both had alibis for 2–5 September; both seem to have been very willing to implicate others. Perhaps physical abuse, or the threat of it, was behind this; perhaps the promise of clemency in return for co-operation was the key. It is not beyond the bounds of possibility that Bykov suspected that they were innocent, or that the case against them would not stand up. During the Great Terror of 1937–8, investigators were keen to push as many suspects through the interrogation process to confession and sentence as quickly as possible, because they were working to quotas (there were targets for the proportions of 'guilty as charged', as for everything else in the planned economy), but in the early 1930s, the situation was different. This was, after all, a legal system where Arseny

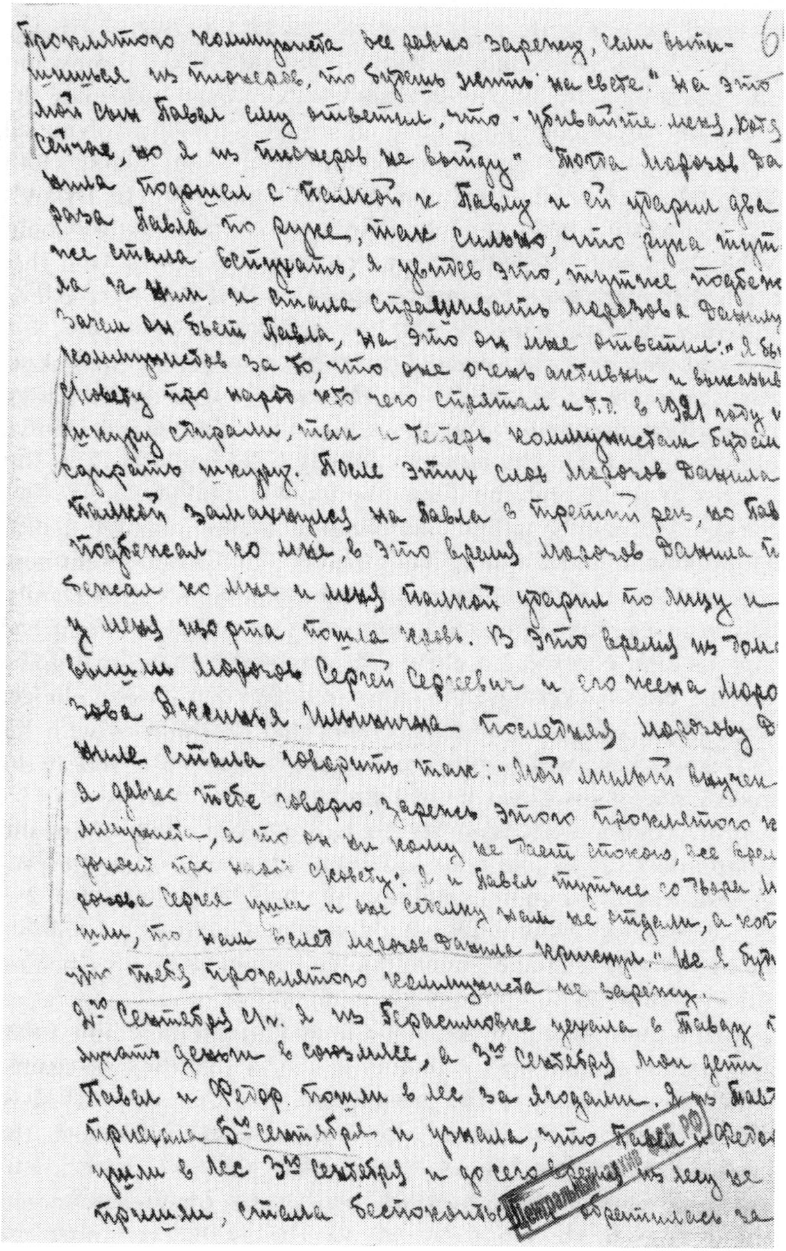

проклятого коммуниста все равно зарежу, если выпишешься из пионеров, то будешь жить на свете." На это мой сын Павел ему ответил, что "убивайте меня, хоть сейчас, но я из пионеров не выйду". Тогда Морозов Данила подошел с палкой к Павлу и ей ударил два раза Павла по руке, так сильно, что рука тут же стала вспухать, я увидев это, тут же подбежала к ним и стала спрашивать Морозова Данилу зачем он бьет Павла, на это он мне ответил: "Я бью коммунистов за то, что они очень активны и высказывают [illegible] про народ кто чего спрятал и т.д. в 1921 году [illegible] стреляли, так и теперь коммунистам будем [illegible]". После этих слов Морозов Данила палкой замахнулся на Павла в третий раз, но Павел подбежал ко мне, в это время Морозов Данила подбежал ко мне и меня палкой ударил по лицу и у меня изо рта пошла кровь. В это время из дома вышли Морозов Сергей Сергеевич и его жена Морозова Аксинья Ильинична последняя Морозову Даниле стала говорить так: "Мой милый внучек я двух тебе говорю, зарежь этого проклятого коммуниста, а что он ни кому не дает покою, все время доносит про нашу [illegible]". Я и Павел тут же со двора Морозова Сергея ушли и все [illegible] нам не [illegible], а [illegible], то нам вслед Морозов Данила крикнул: "Не я буду что тебя проклятого коммуниста не зарежу."
2го Сентября с/г. я из Герасимовке уехала в Тавду [illegible] деньги в [illegible], а 3го Сентября мои дети Павел и Федор пошли в лес за ягодами. Я из Тавды приехала 5го сентября и узнала, что Павел и Федор ушли в лес 3го Сентября и до сего времени из лесу не пришли, стала беспокоиться, обратилась за

A page from witness testimony recorded by district plenipotentiary Bykov. (Central Archive of the Federal Security Service, Moscow)

Kulukanov had managed to get his sentence of forcible exile reversed by going through the Urals cassation court (97). So, suspects had some chance of legal redress, and there was a genuine possibility that an over-zealous OGPU official might end up doing his career damage.

Another suspect in whom Bykov rapidly lost interest was Mezyukhin. Here the cause was perhaps a sentence reported by Kseniya Morozova in testimony that was intended to implicate Mezyukhin, and allegedly uttered by Mezyukhin to Pavel: 'I'll teach that snot-nosed Pioneer to squeal on Red Partisans' (101). Whether this was true or not, the authorities could not, for political reasons, have tolerated the suggestion that a former Red Partisan might be responsible for the murder of an activist. Any information suggesting sympathies with the old order was meticulously recorded – the fact that Arseny Silin had served in the Tsarist army during the First World War (129 rev.), or that Sergei Morozov's father had been a prison warder (105). Mezyukhin's custody form has vanished from the case file – it was perhaps against the rules to keep records of arrestees who had been cleared – but circumstantially, it might be supposed that his early disappearance from the case was because he had the 'wrong' class background (or rather, exactly the right one, in the sense of his being virtuous and committed to the cause).

Bykov, then, was beginning to narrow down the case to an inner circle of suspects who had strong ties with each other, who had in common an inability to demonstrate fidelity to the Communist cause, and who had been implicated by more than one witness, or by another suspect. Much of his collection of evidence revolved around Danila. It was now starting to look as though Danila had acted alone, though incited to do the deed by Arseny Kulukanov.

Cross-questioning of the suspects and witnesses at this stage also aimed to build up the picture of Pavlik's political activities, which was essential to the prosecution of a case under Article 58.8, 'murder of an activist'. By now, Tatiana Morozova was down as saying that her son 'belonged to a Pioneer troop', and detailing accounts of an attack on her by Danila, who had shouted, 'I'll slit your throat all the same, you damned Communist' (68 rev., 69). Even Kseniya was recorded speaking of 'Pioneer Morozov Pavel' (101).

A final touch was added to the investigation when Rechkalov interviewed, on 18 October, a special settler, Fyodor Timoshenko, who had shared a prison cell for a week with the alleged murderers of the Morozov boys, and who may have been a stool pigeon placed with the group to gather information (this was standard practice in Soviet prisons). Timoshenko reported conversations that he had overheard going on between his cell-mates. Allegedly, the group had been trying to persuade Efrem to take the blame for the murders, since he was a legal minor and would hence get a milder sentence. Sergei Morozov was planning to claim that he had been beaten during testimony. And Silin and Kulukanov had received a note which they had pored over together before tearing it up and throwing it in the prison latrine (114).

A number of the details in Timoshenko's account were shaky. For instance, Kulukanov was definitely illiterate, Silin almost completely so (to judge by his handwriting and by the claims on his interrogation records), so the note looks like an invention. This did not, however, deter Rechkalov from taking the essence of the evidence seriously. On 20 October, he reported to Bykov that Timoshenko had overheard Kulukanov saying to Sergei, 'It's all because of you, you old snake, we'll have to pay because you sneaked on us,' and Sergei replying, 'If it hadn't been for you, Kulukanov Arsenty, me and my grandson Daniil wouldn't be stuck here now' (124). The authorities' response to this information was to have Sergei placed in a separate cell, less to impede collusion, one suspects, than to try and break him down by isolation.

Bykov's work for the dossier was almost finished, and he himself considered the case pretty well closed. He had anyway received by wire on 8 October an order to forward the results of his investigation to the Secret Political Section of the OGPU in Sverdlovsk, and to send the materials for examination by a *troika* (three-man tribunal) (148). On 13 October, an 'Urgent' telegram repeated this order in more peremptory terms: 'SEND FILE MURDERS PINEERS [*sic*] MOROZOV IMMEDIATELY' (147). On 14 October, Bykov applied to the Tavda District Committee of the Communist Party for a month's leave, and was duly granted this.[29] On 16 October, he signed the order releasing Mezyukhin and Khima Kulukanova. Just over a week after having been told to forward the file, on 21 October, Bykov did transfer this and the list of suspects to the director of the Secret Political Section (146).

Bykov's report to his superiors at this stage has not survived, but the course of the investigation from mid-September suggests that he had changed his mind about Sergei being the chief murderer, and now suspected that Danila had done the deed, urged on by Kulukanov. Whichever way, the investigation was not yet – as he supposed – closed. Bykov had, after all, elicited no confessions, and his interrogation records showed suspects refusing to stick to a coherent story, and all implicating each other. More clarity and focus needed to be introduced.

In early November began yet a fourth phase of questioning, under Operations Inspector Fedchenko, who was apparently drafted in from Nizhny Tagil, 150 kilometres north-west of Sverdlovsk.[30] Questioning was now extremely intensive and aimed at obtaining full confessions. It is not impossible that the suspects were subjected to the form of psychological torture known as 'riding the conveyor' (i.e. being interviewed continuously, without sleep, for several days). Certainly, numerous interviews were carried out over a short time (Danila took part in three extended sessions over 5 and 6 November alone). Whichever way, efforts were concentrated more or less entirely on the central Morozov trio, though Fedchenko did see Efrem Shatrakov once (175), and originated a copy of his birth certificate (188) on 4 November. He also collected one witness statement reporting on Shatrakov's movements on 3 November (160) and spoke about the results of the earlier interrogations to Ivan Potupchik (163). Much more material, though, was collected about the Morozovs, and all of an incriminating kind. There was a search for witnesses who could say they had seen Kseniya with the children on 3 September (164, 169, 170) – in the event, a single second-hand account of a viewing was all that could be found (164). More overheard snatches of horrible talk were transcribed ('we should have shoved those bodies in Petrushensky Bog' (165)).

The most important part of Fedchenko's work, however, was to extract confessions from Danila, Sergei and Kseniya Morozov. Kseniya was the first to make detailed admissions, on 2 November, when she presented a long and involved story about a family feud. Sergei Morozov had hated Pavel because of squabbles about what happened to various bits of movable property after Trofim was exiled. Pavel had protested not only over the horse harness, but also about the removal of axles for a cart and an axe. He had even brought a court action against his grandfather, making relations still more acrimonious. Eventually, a major row had taken place, roughly two days before the murder,[31] with the piece of horse harness at the centre. When Pavel asked for it back, Sergei 'hit him hard and threw him out of the *izba* [peasant hut], he gave him a punch on the back'. Pavel then threw a stick through the windows and Sergei said, 'Just you wait you son of a bitch, you're not long for this world, I'll soon finish you off.' Her husband had been acting strangely the day of the murder: when asked why he was not going fishing, he had said, 'I've got some farm work to *finish off*' (here the interrogator added meaningful italics). After the murders, Sergei had said he regretted not burning the bodies (154). On 5 November, Kseniya confessed that she had indeed known about the murders on the day they happened: Sergei had told her, 'Danila and I have dealt with [i.e. killed][32] the Morozov boys' (173). However, she had been too frightened of possible reprisals to tell the police.

As for Danila and Sergei, they both confessed in detail to participation in the murder. On 6 November, Danila presented his interrogators with a full and sequential narrative. His grandfather and 'Pioneer' Pavlik Morozov had been enemies because Pavlik had tried to expose Kulukanov. Sergei had repeatedly tried to persuade Danila to do it, but there had never been an 'opportune moment'. Then had come a day when Arseny Kulukanov told him the children were off berrying, and gave him thirty roubles to deal with them. His grandfather had urged him on in similar vein. He and Sergei had gone into the woods together at 2 p.m.; Sergei had stabbed Pavel, Fyodor had run off, his grandfather had called out, 'Hold him,' and Danila had obeyed, at which point Sergei had come up and 'struck him several blows with the same knife'. Scared by the boys' yells, Danila had headed off home, while his grandfather remained in the woods for around an hour. They had changed their clothes after the murder, and told Kseniya nothing about it (176).

Sergei's evidence the same day was similar as to the main

points. He had stabbed the boys; Danila had held them. He had changed his clothes after the killing. However, he said nothing about contact with Kulukanov, though he did state that he had been under the latter's influence, and that he had thoroughly resented Pavlik. He also insisted that the crime had not been premeditated:

> I didn't know what I was doing, it's only now I realize. I only told Danila about the need to get ready for the killing the day of the murder. And when I got home and took off my bloodied clothes, we didn't intend to wash them and conceal our crime. And I repeat that the cause for the whole murder was my hatred for Morozov Pavel because I heard him saying, he said to me he'd burn my house down and give me no mercy (179 rev.–180).

A decision must have been made at this stage that confessions were necessary from only some of the suspects. Fedchenko had Arseny Kulukanov in only twice: on 1 November – for a face-to-face confrontation with Danila, who repeated his story about the thirty roubles' blood money – and for a solitary interview on 2 November (153, 157). At both, Kulukanov resolutely stuck to his previous story of knowing nothing about the murder. Perhaps Fedchenko realized that Kulukanov was not going to crack, or perhaps he decided that the blood-money story, plus the evidence of Kulukanov's kulak connections (his sentence of exile, his admission to hiding property to avoid confiscation) would be enough to impress the court. Or perhaps the schedule was jolted on before he could come back to Kulukanov again. In any case, he now had Danila and Sergei in the bag, and at this point Fedchenko signed off.

The final interviews, by Shepelev, an official at the regional level, essentially pulled the threads of the investigation together. The one major change was that *Danila* now admitted to having done the murders. On 11 November (192–4), he set out a coherent and, from the point of view of kulak-haters, convincing story, ornamented with many of the details that he had hitherto provided one at a time. Property had been hidden at his grandfather's, and Pavlik had reported this to the village soviet. Iosif Prokopovich, a member of the commission for grain surrender who was a connection of Kulukanov's by marriage, had told

Kulukanov about Pavlik's denunciation, leading to a burst of rage: 'You scum, if you go telling on me like that you've not got long left!' It was Kulukanov who had told Danila the boys were going berrying, and who had given him the thirty roubles as a sweetener. He had agreed with his grandfather they would do the harrowing and go (Sergei had been approached by Kulukanov separately). Sergei still resented the fact that Pavlik had betrayed his father, which explained his part in the killing. After dinner, Danila and his grandfather had gone out, Sergei urging his junior not to lose his nerve. 'I ran up with my knife in my right hand and cut him in the belly.' Pavlik had cried out, 'Fedya, little brother, run away.' 'But my grandfather (Sergei Sergeevich) already had him[.] I cut Pavel with my knife a second time and ran to Fyodor and stabbed him with my knife in the belly.' Danila had then shaken the berries out of the sack and his grandfather had suggested he put the sack on Fyodor's head so he could not get home. Danila acknowledged that his earlier evidence had been very different, but said this had been because he hoped to provoke Kulukanov into admitting giving him the money, and because Kulukanov had told him to say nothing. Efrem Shatrakov, he now declared, was entirely innocent.

The same day (195–6), Sergei Morozov confirmed Kulukanov's part in the murders, saying that Kulukanov had blamed Pavel for all the searches going on and had insisted he must be 'exterminated' (the unlikeliness of the verb did not seem to bother Shepelev). He no longer claimed responsibility for the murders: instead, he backed up Danila's story of having done the stabbing while Sergei held the boys. This agreed narrative was then presented to Kulukanov, who continued to deny everything at two successive 'confrontations', one with Sergei (198) and one with Danila (200). At his final interview, Silin said he had known nothing about Pavlik's denunciation of his father, and had not remarked on the boys' denunciatory activities: 'They were just little boys: I paid them no mind' (197).

Shepelev could perhaps have gone further to rehearse the last details of the story, but the investigators were by then under high-level pressure to wrap up their work. Once the news of the murder reached the central press in early October, preparation for the show trial was given a degree of attention much larger than these provincial officials can ever have experienced. By the second week of November, the *Pioneer Pravda* journalists were bellyaching about 'delays' in bringing the case to trial. On 15 November, the paper printed a report of further hitches, with a fuming editorial note alongside. 'Despite the protests and demands for a speedy trial of the murderers arriving from all over the Soviet Union, the investigation is being carried out without care, and without due concern to bring it to a speedy conclusion. Yesterday, the editorial board of *Pioneer Pravda* contacted the State Prosecutor of the Republic, Comrade Vyshinsky, to ask him to step in.' Vyshinsky had immediately sent a telegram giving the Sverdlovsk officials three days to wrap the trial up.[33] The telegram is not included in the H-7825 materials, but the dates of other documents make it likely the *Pioneer Pravda* story is in substance true.[34] The prosecution case was ready by 15 November (206–13), and on 16 November the Urals District Procuracy sent the files, with a letter marked 'urgent', to the Urals Regional Court, requesting immediate progress to a 'show trial in the district[;] the prosecution case will be supported by the Procuracy' (216).

STITCHING UP THE CASE

The prosecution case set out what would, at the trial and in the early biographies of Pavlik published afterwards, become the first orthodox version of the boy's life and death. On 25 November 1931, he had

> given notification to the organs of investigation of the fact that his father, Morozov Trofim Sergeevich, being the chairman of the village Soviet, and having links with the local kulaks, was occupying himself with the forgery of documents and the sale of these to kulak special settlers, for which Morozov Trofim was duly sentenced to 10 years' exile.[35]

Pavlik had then denounced his grandfather for hiding kulak property. In the winter of 1932, he had also denounced Arseny Silin for not complying with grain surrender norms, and for selling a wagonload of potatoes to the special settlers. After stealing fifteen poods of rye grain from the village soviet, Kulukanov had said to Sergei Morozov that he was afraid Pavlik would denounce *him* to the village soviet. Danila had threatened him with death if he did not leave the Pioneers. A fight over the horse harness (here referred to, because of a comical typing error, as 'salt herring') had ensued on 25 August. And on 3 September had come the culmination of the plot against Pavlik, when Danila had murdered him and his brother out on the berrying expedition. As for Kseniya, she had gloated to Tatiana in front of various neighbours, jeering, 'Tatiana, see the meat we've brought you,' when the boys' bodies were brought in (206–13).

In terms of a presentation of the evidence as collected so far, this narrative was deeply suspect. It cited material – Danila's threat to Pavlik to leave the Pioneers, for instance – that had not appeared in witness testimony. It was also extremely selective in terms of the confused and contradictory evidence accumulated over the weeks of the investigation. But it told a coherent, compelling and (from the point of view of Soviet justice at the time) persuasive story. A Pioneer who was brave beyond his years in supporting the Soviet cause and in bringing to account those who had betrayed it – including his own father – had been murdered by vengeful kulaks, whose instrument had been his own aggressive and anti-Soviet cousin, supported by his grandfather and grandmother. And as the prosecution document also stated, all three Morozovs had made a full confession. All that remained was for this story to be set before the 'Soviet people' at the trial itself.

The words 'show trial' seem first to have been used publicly by *Pioneer Pravda* on 15 October, when the imminence of such a trial 'in the next few days' was predicted (as it turned out, over-optimistically). From the point when the investigators were aware that a show trial would be the culmination of their efforts, they were grooming the witnesses and the defendants for their role in a public drama, a celebration of 'proletarian justice' that was to crown the investigative process, and present its results to the public at large. The panel presiding at a real-life show trial such as this (the term was also used for agitational 'trials' of fictional characters, or for events at which the political achievements of Soviet leaders, such as Lenin, were debated)[36] exercised full judicial authority. The chairman was a 'people's judge' or other member of the Soviet judiciary, and the other members were also drawn from the legal profession. Defendants and witnesses were sworn in, called forward and cross-examined in the usual way. But the case for the prosecution was put not only by the procuracy, but also by 'social prosecutors' drawn from the agitprop sections of the Soviet establishment. In the case of the Pavlik Morozov trial, these were, alongside Elizar Smirnov from *Pioneer Pravda*, a senior representative of the Communist youth movement at provincial level (Urin of the Urals Province Central Committee of the Komsomol).

The setting for the trial was chosen and decorated so as to suggest a spectacle or a memorial meeting, rather than a mere 'session of the Urals Region circuit court', as this officially was. Demonstrations and political gatherings were held all over Tavda district to honour the start of the proceedings, and enormous piles of letters and telegrams demanding punishment for the 'kulak beasts' were assembled as tokens of public opinion.[37] The meeting was convened in Tavda's culture club ('of the name of Stalin'), and the judges, witnesses and defendants were seated on the stage. An enormous picture of Pavlik Morozov was used as a backdrop; and the defendants sat crammed together, in a straggling, uncomfortable row, guarded by two young men with fixed bayonets. They embodied perfectly the role of contemptible villains brought low by the authority of the state.[38]

Since a show trial was as much a theatrical as a legal occasion, conceptual gaps between the prosecution's case, the prepared speeches of the 'social prosecutors', summing up the case in retrospect, and the defendants' testimony would have turned the event into a débâcle. It was vital that the defendants enact their assigned roles, and taking them through their statements again and again was a way of ensuring that their performance was word-perfect. During the Great Purges, when defendants were tried by secret tribunals, the principles of the investigation were different: now, the rituals of investigation were turned inwards, with the humiliation and 'reworking' of those accused enacted *in camera*. The interrogation records from later years are therefore less copious, and the central act of acquiescence became the moment of signing the statement, rather than of articulating it in the courtroom.

Its public nature made a show trial potentially a nerve-ridden business for the authorities. When the entire process of investigation and trial was secret – as it generally was during the Great

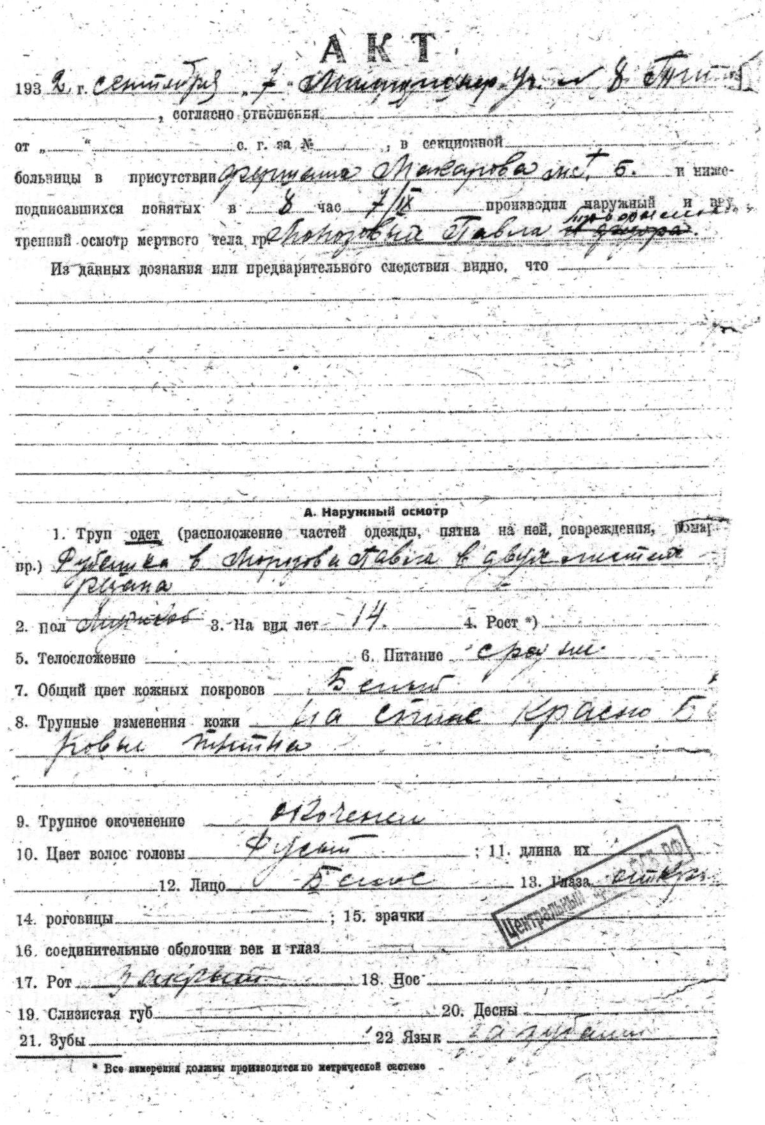

АКТ

193 2 г. сентября 7

, согласно отношения

от „ “ с. г. за № , в секционной

больницы в присутствии фельдшера Макарова и ниже-

подписавшихся понятых в 8 час 7/IX производил наружный и внутренний осмотр мертвого тела гр. Морозова Павла

Из данных дознания или предварительного следствия видно, что

А. Наружный осмотр

1. Труп одет (расположение частей одежды, пятна на ней, повреждения, и пр.)

2. Пол мужской 3. На вид лет 14. 4. Рост *)

5. Телосложение 6. Питание средне

7. Общий цвет кожных покровов белый

8. Трупные изменения кожи на спине красно-багровые пятна

9. Трупное окоченение окоченел

10. Цвет волос головы русые ; 11. длина их

12. Лицо белое 13. Глаза открыты

14. роговицы ; 15. зрачки

16. соединительные оболочки век и глаз

17. Рот закрыт 18. Нос

19. Слизистая губ 20. Десны

21. Зубы 22 Язык за зубами

* Все измерения должны производится по метрической системе

First page of Pavlik Morozov's death certificate, H-7825. (Central Archive of the Federal Security Service)

Purges – the fact of an accused person's taking back his or her testimony at a late stage did not matter. (Occasionally defendants did this: a case in point was the writer Isaac Babel, who defied his interrogators once he knew he would be shot whatever he said.) On the other hand, a defendant who retracted testimony at a show trial could discredit the entire process, since the accusatory narrative presented in the case for the prosecution was constructed precisely on the basis of close reference to the testimony collected earlier. As the Collegium of the Central Executive Committee of the Communist Party had stated in 1924, the trial was intended to show that a decision already made was correct, and not to examine the whys and wherefores of that decision.[39] Hence the need to make absolutely certain that witnesses and defendants knew what to say. According to the official protocol of the Morozov trial (no full transcript exists), things generally went smoothly.

The witnesses in any case presented the authorities with fewer problems than the defendants, because they could easily be selected and primed in advance. To judge by the trial protocol, too, little cross-questioning of witnesses – as opposed to bullying of defendants – went on, so that the danger of a witness becoming confused or self-contradictory was reduced. But even so, a significant amount of work was done on choreographing witness testimony in the most useful way for the prosecution case. Most of the witnesses who had given evidence in the ordinary course of the investigation simply disappeared from the record (though in some cases, their testimony was picked up by other witnesses). Several who did appear – Tatiana Morozova, Prokhor Varygin, a young villager called Konstantin Volkov and Efim Galyzov – told stories that were rather different from those they had told before. Tatiana now revealed that her husband had left her and gone to live with the Kulukanovs, 'where they married him off'. None of the accused had bothered to come and enquire for the children after they disappeared. After the Morozovs were arrested, Kseniya had uttered a string of obscenities, and then said, 'We drank the blood, now you eat the meat' (229 rev.).

Tatiana's new material consisted of points of detail – the central part of her story, concerning her in-laws' hatred for her and the children, and the Morozovs' especial detestation of Pavel because he had denounced his father, remained the same. But some of the other witnesses said things that were fundamentally different from those they had said before. In a witness interview of 23 September with Bykov, Varygin had told the story about hearing Kseniya say to Pavlik's mother, 'Tatiana, see the meat we've brought you' (72). At the trial, on the other hand, he repeated *Kseniya's* version of the story, where Tatiana had protested about bringing food to her children's murderers, and Kseniya had said, 'Let them who made this meat eat it' (231). Konstantin Volkov, whose function earlier had been to provide information about Efrem Shatrakov's movements and the to-ings and fro-ings of Kulukanov's cart, produced an entirely new story about a fight between Danila and Pavel while they were both out fishing (233 rev.). And Efrem Galyzov, previously one source of the rumour that the accused had been overheard lamenting not having pushed the bodies in the Petrushensky bog, became the mouthpiece of information about one of Pavlik's civic denunciations – of Arseny Silin for hoarding potatoes so that he could sell them (233 rev.).

A great deal of the parade of witness testimony at the trial was directly aimed at building up the character of Pavlik Morozov. The local schoolteacher, Zoya Kabina, was brought on to describe him as 'a determined, active lad who always went ahead of everyone else in the measures being taken', despite the local population's intolerance of Pioneers. His friends had been Yakov Yudov and Yakov Kovalenko (the former was the son of one of the local police aides, so this indicated an impeccable choice of companions) (230 rev.). Klavdiya Prozerova, another schoolteacher, described Pavlik as someone 'who was always first in the measures being taken' (230 rev.). Denis Potupchik, the deputy chairman of the village soviet, spoke in a similar way about Pavlik's political commitment (231 rev.). And Aleksei Morozov, one of Pavlik's younger brothers, claimed that he had energetically recruited other children for the Pioneers (230). The murderers had, it was clear, put an end to an exceptional individual.

The only discordant note in the witness testimony was struck by Efrem Shatrakov, who used his time before the court not just to implicate Danila (who, he said, had already been out in the fields when Efrem arrived there), but also to defend himself. He had been friends with Pavel, and had been forced to sign an interrogation protocol confessing to his murder that had not been read aloud to him (231). For their part, Titov and Ivan Potupchik denied this tale of police malpractice, and Titov's testimony referred to a further sighting of Efrem and Danila close together in the fields (231 rev.). The only impact that this unsightly squabble made on the court decision was that the procurator moved Titov should be called to answer under Article 111 of the Criminal Code, on account of not taking steps to safeguard the murder victim (234 rev.). In the authorities' eyes, the Shatrakov story was definitely dead.

The five accused turned in generally creditable performances, in the sense that these were consonant with the scripts written for them in advance. The star role was acted by Danila, who contributed the bulk of the testimony, and followed the final version of his story that had been set out in his interviews with Fedchenko and Shepelev – Kulukanov as the moving spirit behind the murder and informant about the boys' movements on the day of the crime, Sergei as Danila's helper with the murder itself, the removal of the bloodied clothes when the deed was done. Danila now added, though, that Kulukanov had given him a cup of vodka to buy his silence on the day after the crime. And he explained that the motivation for the crime had been the lure of the thirty roubles, though the fight on 26 August over the horse harness had also been a factor (223 rev., 224, 226 rev.; cf. 176, 193 rev.).

Kseniya Morozova was equally obliging about embellishing her former accounts with new detail. The horrors of the Morozov home life were made clear. 'My old man was very severe and hard to live with and he didn't like it when people contradicted him.' He had hated Pavel as well. 'The grandchildren like me,' she stated, but when the boys visited, Sergei would complain, 'Why have the little ratbags come over now?' Sergei's threat to Pavlik after his father's trial was repeated, but in a more genteel form, with the expression 'son of a bitch' modified: 'You mangy young dog, you've not got long left.' Kseniya presented her nephew as a radiant alternative to this grim picture: standing up to his grandfather over the piece of harness, and generally asserting what was right: 'If anyone had done anything wrong, Pavlik would tell on them' (219–20).

Everything also went according to plan so far as the two

'accessories' to the murder, Arseny Silin and Arseny Kulukanov, were concerned. Silin once again stated that he had been in Tavda when the murder happened and knew nothing; that he had got on perfectly well with Pavel, and had not known he was an activist; and that he had no idea how Pavel and his grandfather got on. He repeated the story about the sale of the material to Danila, and described Sergei Morozov as 'very severe' (228). For his part, Kulukanov continued to deny the murder, and repudiated Danila's testimony with contempt: to the story about the cup of vodka, he objected, 'I never touch spirits' (226). He asserted once again that he had never possessed any gold, and that he knew nothing about who had denounced him for the hiding of the cart (226–226 rev.). All of this was – from the point of view of Kulukanov's place in the murder narrative – perfectly acceptable. Had he broken down and confessed to involvement in the killing while in the courtroom, this would have made for high drama, but as it was, the part he was playing suited the script well. He was, after all, being presented as a ruthless, manipulative, mendacious kulak, so it was fine for him to deny his guilt; everyone in the courtroom would know just how much value to attach to such denials. So far as the majority of the audience went, his insistence that he never touched spirits would likely come across as preposterous, an indication that the man was lying through his teeth all along.

The one defendant whose testimony introduced dissonance was Sergei Morozov. To be sure, at first things went according to plan. He confirmed his earlier statements about his place in the killing: 'I held my grandson Fyodor and Danila stabbed him.' He also stated that relations between him and Tatiana, and him and the children, had been very bad. Tatiana had always been on at him to hand over pieces of property and animals that had belonged to her husband; he detested the boys because they were always laughing at him. Pavel's denunciations, not just of his father, but of Kulukanov, had rankled. Sergei also had unpleasant things to say about his wife: yes, she had known about the murder, and she was also an untrustworthy type herself, with a conviction for theft dating back to pre-revolutionary days. He had helped Kulukanov remove grain from the communal fields and stash it away, even though members of the village soviet had told him not to touch it (221 rev.–223).

All of this represented, as with Kseniya's or Danila's testimony, a redecorated and improved version of what Sergei had said before. The problem was that after saying all this, Sergei suddenly changed heart. The protocol does not record his exact words, but states that 'Morozov rejects his statements. In answer to a question from the procurator, "Does he want to tell us the truth?" defendant Morozov answered, "It's wise to hold your tongue"' (223 rev.). One of the central suspects was now refusing to admit that he was guilty.

In terms of the court's decision, this hiccup made no difference. Sergei, Danila and Kseniya, along with Arseny Kulukanov, were found guilty of the crime for which they had stood trial. In passing sentence of death by shooting, the tribunal repeated the version of the murder that had been set out by Danila and Sergei: the two had collaborated in the killing of the boys, but had been urged into the act by Kulukanov. For her part, Kseniya had tried to obstruct the course of the investigation. In the case of Silin, on the other hand, there was no evidence of involvement in the crime (235–9). This last decision, the single surprise in the whole trial process, from the audience's point of view, had, however, been foreshadowed by the infrequency, brevity and lack of intensity of Silin's interrogations. One may suspect that the investigators did not really expect him to be convicted. But his story about the cloth was an important part of the evidence against Dmitry. He could, of course, have been called as a witness to repeat the narrative, but this would have been less dramatic – the fact that Dmitry had been involved in financial dealings with someone who was also suspected of guilt in this terrible crime made his purchase of the cloth seem particularly sleazy. It seems very likely that Silin stood trial simply in order to fill the purpose of a dramatic catalyst.

WORKING OVER THE SUSPECTS

At every stage of the investigation, the OGPU officials and their colleagues in the ordinary police and in the public prosecutor's office were working towards confecting a gripping 'true crime' story.[40] At later stages of the investigation, they were concerned with creating a narrative that would justify before the audience in the courtroom, and before public opinion in the outer world, the decision to punish the group on trial. The rules applied were those of 'campaign justice' – where legality was subordinated to the demand that enemies of the state should be exposed and made to pay for their crimes.[41]

At the same time as recognizing the ideological, and the artistic or fictional, nature of the interrogation and trial records, though, one should not forget that they involved real people, who were being subjected to both physical and psychological bullying. The protocols consist almost exclusively of signed statements, transcribed as sequential narratives. The process by which the information was actually obtained from the witnesses is not recorded, but some material in Fedchenko's interrogations suggests the extensive use of leading questions.[42] A similar aim of forcible suggestion lay behind a much-loved technique of all the interrogators, the setting up of 'face-to-face confrontations'. These generally followed a pattern according to which a suspect who was already 'telling the right story' was brought together with a suspect who was still recalcitrant. For instance, early in the investigation, Danila Morozov, who was protesting his innocence of the murder, was lined up with his grandfather, who stated that Danila had known at a suspiciously early stage that the boys had been stabbed, and also the number of their wounds (21).

The interrogators also had other methods of getting their meaning across. Undoubtedly, an unofficial variant of what in the modern American justice system is formalized as 'plea bargaining' was practised. Suspects were told that if they confessed, their sentence would be lighter; the same would apply if they implicated others. Offers of this kind do not appear directly in the protocols, but there are hints of them in the files – in the release of Khima Kulukanova and acquittal of Arseny Silin for example, or in the details of testimony by the other accused. On 6 November, for instance, Sergei Morozov told Fedchenko, 'after my return home and taking off the bloodied clothes, we didn't intend to wash them and destroy the traces of the crime' (179 rev.–180). Probably, the investigator had told Sergei (quite inaccurately) that a confession to non-premeditated murder would ensure a less severe punishment than he would receive if others' testimony pointed to his involvement in a crime that had been planned in advance.[43]

Beatings were not recorded in the protocols either, but it is possible to guess where they occurred. For example, at an early stage in the investigation, Danila Morozov and Efrem Shatrakov, both of whom had been denying the murder, suddenly changed their testimony in mid-interview (22 rev., 24 rev.). The former was being interviewed by Ivan Potupchik, the latter by Yakov Titov. Efrem was later to make allegations that he had been beaten, allegations that were eventually endorsed by the tribunal at the show trial (234 rev.).

Another point of the interrogation when violence seems to have been used was after Operations Inspector Fedchenko was drafted in from Nizhny Tagil. At the trial of the Morozovs, a criminal investigation of the use of beatings against Kseniya Morozova was instituted (264 rev.). This tallies with a doctor's note dated 6 November which states, 'Comrade Morozova has had to undergo an operation for removal of an ovary. At the moment the lesion is healing and has to be dressed every second day' (190). On 5 November, Kseniya Morozova had been subjected to an interrogation at which not just Fedchenko was present, but also a second OGPU operative by the name of Trusov, and had testified to hearing Sergei state that he and Danila had 'offed' the boys (173). Other interrogation records confirm the correlation of admissions and confessions on the part of suspects with the presence of more than one officer at a session.[44] To be sure, the regulations apparently required that confessions be witnessed: the 'confession protocol' relating to Danila's interview on 6 November (178) was signed by Arseny Silin, as well as Andriyan Iskrin and Likhobabin, OGPU deputy plenipotentaries. But it is hard to believe that the OGPU reinforcements were brought in simply to sit and watch. And the fact that the medical certificate for Kseniya was issued the day after a multi-interrogator interview supports the hypothesis of systematic brutality at such interviews in order to force confessions.

Sadism was not just a means to an end, though – a way of making the prisoner tell the right story – it was also an end in itself. The interrogations were occasions of ritual humiliation, where suspects were forced into contradictory testimony and patently false confessions as a way of making them lose touch with their former selves and prepare for re-education. The 'guilty' (and from the point of view of the interrogation procedure, no suspect was assumed innocent) were meant to be brought to a condition of self-abnegation and recognition of the all-consuming power of the state. According to the trial protocol, Danila Morozov is recorded as being in this condition by the end of the case: 'I ask the proletarian court to judge me as the law dictates' (232). Making a request for mercy rather than punishment – as Arseny Kulukanov did – was a sign that a person had only imperfectly absorbed the lessons of interrogation. Just so, Kulukanov refused to make any confessions under interrogation, even as the other suspects all meekly articulated the words that had been put into their mouths, and he was eventually to make the ultimate gesture of defiance – moving an appeal against his sentence.

Yet the paradox was that admission of guilt did not invite a pardon: Kulukanov was sentenced to execution, but so too was Danila. The process of purgation required not simply that suspects be broken and remade at the interrogations, and forced to speak to command during the trial, but that they were physically driven out of existence – 'exterminated'. No one in the courtroom seems to have felt uneasy about this decision, despite the curiosities and even minor contradictions in the testimony that was given. The 'social prosecutors' read their concluding orations, which called, in the name of the Soviet population at large, for the severest possible punishments to be imposed upon those who had stood trial. The defence lawyer – who had hitherto taken no part at all in the proceedings – formally renounced all responsibility for the accused. And when the verdict was read out, according to the *Dawns of the Commune*, the assembled masses voiced their 'unanimous approval', and rose to sing the *Internationale*.

The outcome of the trial was everything the investigators could have wished. The death sentence was pronounced, and – after the failure of an appeal – implemented on 7 April 1933 (240).[45] A great deal of hard work lay behind this: evidence had to be collected – or, more accurately, forced out of suspects, reworked and, in some cases, invented. Presenting the murder as a casually brutal act deriving from a small-scale fight over property (a confiscated gun, a disputed piece of horse harness) would not do. The investigators needed to turn the Morozov murders into a political act, the killing of an activist. And once it had become such an act, it needed perpetrators who were appropriate in ideological terms – kulaks. Suspicion, therefore, automatically focused on Arseny Kulukanov and Arseny Silin, both of whom had convictions under anti-kulak legislation. The Shatrakovs, who seem to have been kulaks by local reputation alone, did not fit the picture so well.

What was more – a gift for the investigators – their chief 'kulak suspects' were relations of the Morozov boys by marriage, members of the extended patriarchal family against which Pavlik himself had fought. The fact that Kulukanov and Silin were the sons-in-law of Sergei Morozov was constantly stressed during the investigation: the understanding was that Morozov was what was traditionally known in villages as 'the big man', the senior male in the extended family. No one investigating the case chose to contemplate the inconvenient fact that another of Morozov's sons-in-law, Denis Potupchik, was a useful instrument of the investigation, or that his daughter, Khima Kulukanova, chose to give evidence against him. This would have laid bare the uncomfortable truth that the extended family was, during this era of covert civil war in the countryside, not as solid a unit as the investigators suggested.

The 'kulak conspiracy' did not figure in the earliest interrogation records, but by the time that Spiridon Kartashov had finished his round of testimony-gathering, it had been roughed out. It was then elaborated in the work done by Bykov in his interviewing from mid-September until early October, during which most of the (very meagre) supporting documentation for the case was collected – in particular, property records for the suspects. Yet two further stages of investigation were required before the case could be wrapped up. The reason for this was not the need to collect qualitatively different evidence: only one forensic report, as we have seen, was obtained. And it was only partly to do with rehearsing suspects for the show trial, cowing them into giving formal confessions. The fact was that the Morozov murders – an event of Tavda district interest in mid-September – had, by late October, begun to be notorious at the national level, attracting the attention of journalists who were also members of the Komsomol Central Committee. These journalists duly unleashed ready-made tirades about the 'inertia' and 'incompetence' of the provincial hicks who were dealing with this explosive case, just as they had with Grisha Akopov, and, as in that case, bounced the Morozov trial into a major public event. But they did more than that: they also – as we shall see in the next chapter – did their best to stir up public opinion in the broadest sense, to arouse a national clamour for the culprits' blood, and to initiate a celebration of the life of Pavlik Morozov as a Soviet saint.

CHAPTER 4

Class Warrior, Boy Martyr

The show trial of Pavlik and Fyodor Morozov's murderers was without doubt the most significant occasion of the year in Tavda, and indeed probably in the entire Urals. The estimates published in the contemporary press – 2,000 crammed into the Stalin club in order to catch a glimpse of the proceedings, 1,000 children demonstrating with flags and banners outside – were no doubt inflated. But if the club, which officially held 600, was full to overflowing, as a story in *Dawns of the Commune* suggested, then 700 or 800 people may certainly have been present.[1] There was also a large 'long-distance' audience for the trial, which was given wide coverage both in the local Komsomol press, and in the national Komsomol and Pioneer press.

Publicity about the Morozov murders began modestly, however. When the very first press story about the case came out on 17 September 1932, it did not get front-page space, or indeed any space at all in the main paper. Instead, it was consigned to the 'Komsomol page', *The Shift*, an occasionally published newsletter that was usually a round-up of local administrative news, and of rewritten snippets from the national and international press. And the story made no attempt to squeeze pity or horror out of the killing of the two children. Instead, it reported a characteristic act of kulak aggression in bold and extremely clumsy prose:

A KULAK BAND HAS KILLED PIONEER MOROZOV

THESE DESPERADO[2] KULAKS AND SUB-KULAKS SHOULD BE SHOT

Pioneer Morozov Pavel of Gerasimovka village, aged 14, and his brother Fyodor, aged 9, realized that kulaks and sub-kulaks were enemies of Soviet power and that nothing could be expected from them but harm, and therefore the Pioneers tried with all their strength to unmask their wrecking activities.

Pioneer Pavel, who had actively co-operated with the work of the police, managed to expose a kulak band right on the spot where they had hidden their kulak property, grain, and other things of that kind.

The kulaks tried to force Pioneer Pavel to leave the Pioneers, and if he wouldn't, they were threatening to kill him, only Pioneer Pavel didn't only not leave the Pioneers, he all the more stubbornly began carrying on his work, and for this on 3rd September he and his brother Fyodor were killed.

A desperado kulak band, nine in number, has been detained. The investigation is complete, the murderer-executioners, comprising a group of kulaks and sub-kulaks, have admitted responsibility: Morozov Daniil Ivanovich, Shirokov [*sic*: i.e. Shatrakov] Efrem Antonovich, Morozov Sergei Sergeevich, Morozova Aksinya Ilinichna, Kodukanov [*sic*: i.e. Kulukanov] Arsenty, Kodukanova Khima Sergeevna, Shitrakov Anton Nikolaevich, Shitrakov Dimitry, Silin Arsenty Nikolaevich, [these people] waited for a chance when it would be convenient to mete out reprisals on Pavel and Fyodor. They seized their opportunity when the boys' mother went to Tavda, and Pavel and Fyodor had gone berry-picking, and the kulaks began waiting for the boys to return, who had gone there in the morning.[3]

The unsuspecting brothers Pavel and Fyodor, on their way back encountered on the way home Danila Morozov and Efrem Shitrakov [*sic*], who, not allowing the brothers to return home, killed them half a kilometre away from Gerasimovka, inflicting 4 knife wounds on Pavel in the chest and 3 knife wounds on Fyodor Morozov in the same place, which caused their immediate death.

The fact that the kulaks and their agents still exist and are carrying on kulak agitation right up to the level of terrorist acts is blatant. Sensing their immediate kulak doom, kulaks and their agents are still hoping to return to the past and to keep hired workers and poor peasants in bondage, but they are not

> succeeding in this. The slogan 'the liquidation of kulaks as a class' will be carried out without protest, decisively and finally.
>
> The kulakery should be shot for the murder of the Pioneer and his brother! That is the sentence expected by the labouring people of Tavda and its district.[4]

Laboured as it was, the piece conveyed two things clearly: the boys who had been murdered were activists who had made tireless efforts to 'expose' the evil-doings of the kulaks in their village; and the kulaks themselves, along with their lumpen accomplices, the 'sub-kulaks', would stop at nothing.

The story belongs with the second stage of the investigation – when the 'unfocused' kulak group theory held sway. But as a piece from this layer of the Pavlik cult's development, it is remarkable, in the first instance, for what it does *not* include. Pavlik's denunciation of his father is absent; so too is any material about his commitment to the Pioneer cause and his exemplary life. Instead, the story shows two boys, 'Pioneer Pavel' and his younger brother, pitted against 'a group of kulaks and sub-kulaks'. The Morozov murders are seen purely and simply as an act of class war.

Tavda Worker continued to push this line through the next months,[5] up to and including the trial (of which more later). Soon after this piece appeared, however, the paper lost exclusive control of the story about the Morozov murders. On 20 September, the Regional Bureau of the Children's Communist Organization in Sverdlovsk (the local head office of the Pioneer organization) discussed the Morozov affair at its meeting, and the Tavda District Committee of the Komsomol came under strong censure. It had failed, the Regional Bureau fulminated, to pass on the information about the Morozov murders in a properly detailed and timely fashion. The Tavda officials had had the temerity to wait until the investigation of the murders was concluded before consulting up the line, and had then coolly posted to the Regional Bureau a cutting of the 17 September article reporting the murders, as though the Bureau's opinion were of no value. The Regional Bureau resolved to report the incident to the next link up in the chain of command, the Regional Committee of the Komsomol; to send an investigator of its own to Tavda to find out what was going on; to urge the organization of meetings about the murders in Sverdlovsk schools; and to publicize the murders, as well as the need to step up class vigilance against kulaks, throughout the Sverdlovsk Pioneer organization.[6] This set of decisions, alongside the stinging rebuke to the Tavda District Committee, was duly published in *Dawns of the Commune* on 23 September. Here, too, was published the first report of the Morozov murders to appear outside the Tavda district; a day later, the Sverdlovsk Komsomol newspaper, *Let the Shift Begin!*, also carried coverage about the murders.[7]

The way the story was presented in *Dawns of the Commune* and in *Let the Shift Begin!* was not in the event much different from the way it had broken in *Tavda Worker*. *Dawns of the Commune* simply reported that Pavlik ('aged 14') and his nine-year-old brother had 'exposed and unmasked' a '9-man strong kulak band', and that Danila Morozov and Efrem Shatrakov had taken revenge by murdering them. Much the same was communicated in *Let the Shift Begin!*, which printed a piece by a 'youth correspondent' stating that Pavel had 'helped the work of the police' and 'managed to unmask a kulak band, catching it red-handed in the act of hiding grain, property, and other objects'. The paper named the same garbled list of suspects as *Tavda Worker*. Once the story had reached the central press, on the other hand, the presentation of it began to change in quite fundamental ways.

PAVLIK IN THE CENTRAL PRESS

The mechanics by which the story spread beyond the Urals cannot be described with certainty.[8] But Elizar Smirnov, the *Pioneer Pravda* journalist delegated to work on the Pavlik Morozov case, later reminisced about what had happened:

> In the autumn of 1932, somebody working for *Pioneer Pravda* was looking through local newspapers in the hunt for interesting material about the lives of Soviet Pioneers and schoolchildren. In a paper from Tavda district, Sverdlovsk Region, he noticed a little item somewhere on the fourth page. It was about a bestial murder in the village of Gerasimovka. The victims of this bloody act of reprisal were two brothers – Pioneer Pavlik Morozov and his nine-year-old brother Fedya.[9]

Smirnov's memory that the story came from a cuttings file seems plausible, given that the first report in *Pioneer Pravda*, on 2 October 1932, did little to modify the manner in which the provincial press had handled the Pavlik tale. A short piece appearing on page 4 of the paper set out, in dry documentary style, the murder of what was then described as 'two' Pioneers, aged fourteen and nine. The boys were represented as tireless activists – they had relentlessly exposed a 'kulak band' in their village, and had been dispatched with three and four blows of the knife on their way back from the forest on 3 September. Already, it was asserted, Pioneers had held demonstrations 'all over the Urals' demanding justice. Even the mistake about the number of kulaks involved (nine) was repeated passively from *Tavda Worker*.[10]

Yet there were important differences between the *Pioneer Pravda* story, even in this preliminary form, and the earlier newspaper versions. To begin with, no paper had previously mentioned Pavlik's denunciation of his father – or, as *Pioneer Pravda* originally put it, the denunciation by *both* Morozov boys of their father. To quote the paper,

> The activist Pioneers Pavel and Fyodor exposed and unmasked a kulak band which was carrying out its wrecking work in the village soviet, work directed at the undermining of all the measures being taken by the Party and by Soviet power. They did not even stop at the unmasking of the counter-revolutionary activity of their father, the chairman of the village soviet.[11]

And on 15 October, *Pioneer Pravda* – by then having decided that only one of the boys had 'unmasked' his father – blew this part of the story up into a whole narrative. Pavlik had renounced his father publicly: 'Uncle judge, I speak not as a son, but as a Pioneer: my father has betrayed the cause of the October Revolution.[12]

Pioneer Pravda, then, built up the 'activism' line, for the first time introducing the motif of the boy so dedicated to the cause that he would stop at nothing. Another innovation was the introduction of photographic material. The 15 October story appeared below a picture of Pavlik, based on what appears to be a genuine group photograph of the Gerasimovka school, cropped and retouched to give the boy a defiant stare. The most important new element of

ВЫШЕ КЛАССОВУЮ БДИТЕЛЬНОСТЬ!

ЗВЕРСКОЕ УБИЙСТВО ПИОНЕРОВ МОРОЗОВЫХ

ОТВЕТИМ НА ВЫЛАЗКУ КУЛАЧЬЯ УДАРНОЙ БОРЬБОЙ ЗА ЗНАНИЯ

Убитый кулаками пионер Павлуша Морозов.

Ежедневно в редакцию поступают десятки протестов против зверского убийства шайкой кулаков двух пионеров-активистов. Со всех концов Советского союза приходят эти протесты. В них пионеры и школьники требуют расстрела кулаков — убийц пионеров.

Сотни протестов получены и выездной сессией суда, выехавшей на место убийства — в Тавды.

ПРОЛЕТАРСКИЙ ОТПОР КУЛАЧЬЮ

По всему Уралу прошла волна протеста против убийства шайкой кулаков пионеров-активистов Морозовых.

Рабочие ЛЕСОЗАВОДА Тавдинского района в ответ на убийство об'являют себя ударниками, обязуясь перевыполнить задание по экспорту.

Рабочие УРАЛЬСКОГО КИРПИЧНО-МЕХАНИЧЕСКОГО ЗАВОДА отвечают стопроцентным выполнением производственной программы.

КОЛХОЗ «ТРЕТИЙ ИНТЕРНАЦИОНАЛ» в ответ кулакам—убийцам пионеров досрочно выполнил план хлебозаготовок; семь единоличников подали заявление о вступлении в колхоз.

НАШ ОТВЕТ — СБОР ПОДАРКОВ ДЛЯ ДЕРЕВНИ

Мы, пионеры и школьники 4-й школы ФЗД им. Ленина (Казань), присоединяемся к требованию уральских пионеров о расстреле шайки кулаков.

В ответ на контрреволюционную вылазку классового врага мы обязуемся еще сильнее вести борьбу за увеличение пионерских рядов, за поднятие качества учебы и сознательной дисциплины в школе, за боевое проведение сбора подарков для пионеров и школьников деревни.

ПИОНЕРЫ ШКОЛЫ № 4.

ЗАМЕНИМ ПОГИБШИХ ТОВАРИЩЕЙ

Мы, пионеры и школьники старорусской ФЗС № 5, узнав об убийстве пионеров Морозовых, требуем немедленного расстрела убийц.

На зверскую вылазку кулаков мы ответим умножением своих рядов, усилением борьбы за учебу.

Наших товарищей, погибших от руки классового врага, мы заменим десятками новых стойких борцов, продолжающих их дело.

140 подписей.

ВЫСШУЮ МЕРУ — УБИЙЦАМ ПИОНЕРОВ

Обсудив сообщение «Пионерской правды» о зверском убийстве двух пионеров — братьев Морозовых, мы, учащиеся Озерецкой школы (Средняя Волга), требуем применения к шайке кулаков высшей меры наказания.

Учащиеся Озерецкой школы.

ПО СОВЕТСКОМУ СОЮЗУ

ДНЕПР РАБОТАЕТ НА СОЦИАЛИЗМ

Пущенная на-днях Днепровская гидроэлектростанция дает ток огромному промышленному металлургическому комбинату Запорожстали. На снимке — комсомольская домна № 2 Днепрокомбината, которая будет задута в этом году.

В ШКОЛАХ ДНЕПРОГЭСА

10 октября пущен Днепрогэс. К пуску пионерорганизация и школы пришли с новыми достижениями в борьбе за качество учебы. Все школы включились в социалистическое соревнование. Организованы буксирные бригады помощи отстающим. К пуску 115 пионеров переданы в комсомол, двести учеников вступили в пионерорганизацию.

Пионеры и школы организуют изучение строительства. Управление строительства отпустило средства на постройку оздоровительной детской колонии на острове Хортице. Ударники школ премируются.

КУЛАЦКАЯ РАСПРАВА

(От нашего спец. корреспондента)

Как только в редакции было получено сообщение об убийстве пионеров Морозовых, на Урал, в Тавдинский район, выехала специальная бригада из представителей «Пионерской правды» и «Колхозных ребят».

Совместно со следственными органами при помощи тавдинского райкома партии удалось установить полную картину преступления.

Сегодня мы печатаем первую корреспонденцию, рисующую обстановку, в которой произошло зверское убийство пионера Морозова и его девятилетнего брата.

В ближайшие дни в селе Герасимовке Тавдинского района состоится общественно-показательный суд над кулаками-убийцами. Судит выездная сессия уральского областного суда. В качестве общественного обвинителя выступает член редколлегии «Пионерской правды» тов. Дубах.

Тайга до сих пор хранит следы этого зверского преступления. В кустах клюквы, где были убиты 13-летний пионер Павел Морозов и его 9-летний братишка Федя, [illegible] У Павла на теле 4 глубоких ножевых раны, у Феди — три. Убили и Федю: боялись свидетеля.

Убийц двое: Данила Морозов и Шатраков Ефим. Но перед пролетарским судом вместе с ними встанут и будут держать ответ Арсений Морозов, Сергей Морозов, Кулуканов Арсений, Шатраков Ефим и другие герасимовские кулаки и подкулачники — главные организаторы убийства пионера Павла.

Классовый враг сопротивляется

За что убит светловолосый, голубоглазый Павел? Вспомним слова тов. Молотова, сказанные им на 17-й партконференции:

«Ликвидация капиталистических элементов сопряжена с огромными трудностями, с проявлением отчаянных попыток сопротивляться со стороны кулачества и буржуазных элементов вообще. Классовая борьба не только не прекращается, но особенно на отдельных участках и в отдельные периоды может и будет значительно обостряться».

Чувствуя свою близкую гибель в ширящейся коллективизации, остатки кулачества упорно пытаются тормозить социалистическую перестройку деревни путем вредительства, запугивания, путем отдельных убийств лучших, активных товарищей.

Но ничем не запугать нас. Об этом говорит, в этом убеждает успешное строительство социализма на всех участках. Под руководством партии наша страна добилась величайших побед. Наша страна прочно утвердилась на социалистическом пути. Кулачество ликвидируется на основе сплошной коллективизации как класс и будет окончательно ликвидировано. Более 60 процентов бедняков и середняков Союза об'единились в колхозы.

„Я выступаю как пионер"

Пионер Павел ставил интересы партии и рабочего класса выше своих личных интересов. Когда его отец — председатель сельсовета — связался с кулаками, помогая им выполнять контрреволюционные цели, Павел уверенно разоблачил своего отца. Пролетарский суд приговорил отца Павла к 10 годам заключения. На суде в качестве свидетеля выступал светловолосый пионер Павел, и голос его не дрогнул, когда он говорил:

— Я, дяденьки судьи, выступаю здесь не как сын, а как пионер! И я говорю: «Мой отец предает дело Октября!

Не раз кулаки угрожали Павлу смертью, не раз он был избиваем. Но разве может что-нибудь остановить пионера-ленинца? Нет такой силы! Павел продолжал выявлять перед органами милиции и советской власти проделки кулаков, открывая запрятанный ими хлеб, спрятанное оружие.

„Бей — не бей, — буду пионером!"

Мать Павла рассказывает, как однажды его избивал Данила. Давясь слезами и, увертываясь от ударов палки, он выкрикивал:

— Отца не боялся и вас всех не побоюсь... Бей—не бей, — буду пионером! Будет всем кулакам конец!

Герасимовским кулакам стало ясно: Павел Морозов — их ярый враг. От него надо избавиться. Убийство Павла они обещали Даниле Морозову и Шатракову Ефиму заплатить золотом.

И вот 3 сентября Павла и его брата Феди не стало. Дорого стоила ребятам прогулка в лес за ягодами.

Быть бдительными

Беспощадна наша ненависть к классовому врагу. От пролетарского суда пионеры и школьники, рабочие и колхозники Тавдинского района, Уральской области, и всего Союза ССР требуют применения к кулакам-убийцам высшей меры социальной защиты — расстрела.

Лучшего из лучших вырвали классовые враги из наших рядов. На смену ему — в ответ на убийство — в пионерскую организацию идут и еще придут новые сотни и тысячи ребят. **Ударной учебой с помощью партии и комсомола в деле социалистической перестройки деревни отвечают пионеры на убийство своего товарища.**

Жизнь, борьба и смерть Павла Морозова займут славную страницу в истории пионерского движения СССР.

Будем же, как пионер Павел. Будем всегда и везде помнить: «классовая борьба продолжается, быть бдительными к классовому врагу!».

В. Губарев.

Дер. Герасимовка.
Урал.

15 October 1932 report on the Morozov murders from *Pioneer Pravda*

all, though, was the intense, even ghoulish, interest that *Pioneer Pravda*'s journalists took in the details of the murder that had been committed. The boys, in the paper's account, had been vilely and picturesquely slaughtered by the kulaks, with cranberries everywhere, and scattered leaves among the blood. Their wounds were 'deep'. In *Tavda Worker*, the boys were murdered activists; in *Pioneer Pravda*, they became martyrs. According to *Pioneer Pravda*'s interpretation, the murder was meant not just to enact revenge, but to inspire fear as well. 'Sensing their imminent doom as collectivization gains strength, the remains of the kulakery are trying to impede the socialist reconstruction of the village by wrecking activities and intimidation, by means of individual murders of the best and most active comrades.'[13] This was nothing less than an act against the entire Soviet system, aimed at undermining the loyalty of those who supported the 'measures being taken' by the state.

The 'martyrdom' theme was taken up once more in the next issue published by *Pioneer Pravda*, on 17 October. The Pioneers and schoolchildren of Gerasimovka, it stated, had held a meeting resolving to continue the work of their fallen comrade, whose physical remains were still fresh: 'The rains of autumn have not yet washed away the blood on the leaves where [he] was lying.'[14] Biologically speaking, of course, this statement was absurd, but it was intended in a transferred sense: the traces of the murdered boys were crying aloud to the Soviet nation to avenge its slaughtered saints.

The next items to appear in *Pioneer Pravda* made little contribution to the growth of the legend. On 17 October, the paper reported that a crazy prophetess who was actually a kulak agent in disguise had been seen in Gerasimovka; six days later, it stated that schools everywhere were collecting gifts (for example, exercise books) to send to the children of Pavlik's home village.[15] The paper then, without explanation, dropped the case for some three weeks. But in mid-November, the Morozov murders resurfaced with a splash. First came the fuss about delays in the investigation, leading to the intervention by Vyshinsky on 14 November. On 21 November, *Pioneer Pravda*'s front page was able to report that a date for the trial had been fixed:

> We have received a telegram from Tavda that the trial of the kulak murderers of Pioneer Pavlik Morozov and his brother will

> be held on 25 November in the village of Gerasimovka, Tavda District, Urals Region. E. Smirnov, a member of the editorial board of *Pioneer Pravda*, yesterday flew out by aeroplane to Sverdlovsk to help in the preparations for the trial.

The pleonasm 'flew out by aeroplane' brought home how important this trial was – in the early 1930s, aviation was used for extreme contingencies, such as rescuing Polar explorers, or record-breaking flights across Soviet territory.[16]

'THE KULAKS SNARLED LIKE DOGS'

The local papers covering the Morozov case departed little from the official protocol in writing up the trial.[17] The differences mostly related to simplification of the evidence. The testimony of witnesses was more or less ignored: attention was concentrated on the statements by the suspects. These were summarized fairly closely, but sometimes details were simplified. In the trial protocol, Danila said, 'The old man has told you everything right, but I should emphasize that my crime was committed in participation with my grandfather' (225), but in the 30 November issue of *Dawns of the Commune*, he said, 'Me and my grandfather killed them.' More importantly, the altercation between Pavlik and his grandfather over the piece of horse harness was turned into a much more one-sided incident than the protocol had suggested, becoming a confrontation in which the boy had acted with dignified restraint, rather than a village brawl.[18]

If they omitted certain things, though, the local papers – as with their reports on the murders – added little or nothing. The situation with *Pioneer Pravda* was once again different. For instance, the paper had Kseniya Morozova giving a verbatim account of Pavlik's denunciation of his father, an event that had not appeared in the trial testimony.[19] With the court reports, it also printed accompanying materials that were quite unlike anything in the dry trial dossier. On 27 November, alongside the first day of testimony, a tear-jerking item about Pavlik's funeral appeared. The occasion had been marked by the local Pioneers singing 'The Little Drummer Boy':

Our young drummer boy has been martyred,
But our memories of him will not fade.[20]

The paper was naturally keener to dwell on this edifying moment than it was upon another aspect of the funeral, the embarrassing determination of Tatiana Morozova that her sons should have a cross as grave-marker. The existence of this inappropriate memorial did, however, allow a topically anti-religious point to be made: it was described as 'a curiosity of a kind, and the result of the cultural backwardness and illiteracy of Pavel's mother', and the reader was assured that 'the bodies of Pavlik and Fedya Morozov were of course committed to the earth without the presence of a priest'.[21]

The Morozov murders went on being milked by *Pioneer Pravda* after the trial had ended. On 3 December, the paper printed an extract from the lyrical summing-up made by the 'social prosecutor', Elizar Smirnov. 'The grain collections began – Pavlik was the first to surrender his surplus grain. Loan contributions were being collected – Pavlik was the first to purchase a bond. The school year began – and Pavlik was the first to have educational success.' Gerasimovka, on the other hand, was a

> far-off village, remote from the centres of culture, cast away in the woods among the bogs and the lakes. A dark, unenlightened village with accursed old-fashioned traditions, with age-old ignorance and illiteracy, all-pervasive religion, and property-grubbing attitudes. [. . .] And suddenly into this dismal dump surges the radiant, heroic life of Pioneer Pavlik Morozov. The kulaks snarled like dogs and bared their fangs.

Finally, on 17 December, the paper summed up with Smirnov's even more sonorous tribute to this 'coeval of the October Revolution' and hero of the heroic surrender of corn to the Soviet authorities.[22]

Pioneer Pravda's coverage – though always pretending to the status of documentary journalism – represented the Morozov case with much more dramatic colour than the original investigation, or the local papers. Gerasimovka was turned into an identikit backward village, where religious beliefs were rife, the haunt of vicious resistance to the 'measures being taken'. Pavlik and his brother came across less as fallen soldiers of the class war than as the tormented victims of warped, cruel killers. Not for nothing was the murder routinely described as 'bestial'; equally, the photographs of the courtroom showed on one side the gnarled, twisted faces of the accused, and on the other, Tatiana Morozova with Pavlik's brother Aleksei, Madonna-like in her white headscarf.[23] And Pavlik himself was now not just the principled denouncer of every offender in the village, but the boy whose central act was the denunciation of his own father. The lineaments of the Pavlik Morozov myth were being set in place.

Later contributions in the Pioneer press continued to elaborate Pavlik's story along the same lines. A piece by Oleg Shvarts published by the journal *Pioneer* in June 1933 also dwelt at length on Pavlik's denunciation of his father. 'I, uncle judge, am speaking not as a son, but as a Pioneer. And I say: my father is betraying the October Revolution.' It added a list of Pavlik's other denunciations – of Kulukanov over the hidden cart, of the Shatrakovs – and detailed the attacks on him by Danila. It gave a still more bloodthirsty account of the murder than *Pioneer Pravda* had. Pavel's stomach had been 'split open', and his hands and chest 'cut to pieces'. And the boys were said to have gone off looking for berries in a direction where no berries grew, suggesting that they had been lured to their doom by the lies of wicked adults.[24]

The trial was presented just as melodramatically. Kseniya's account of how Pavlik had been ill-treated by his grandfather and by Danila was given in detail. Her claim to have loved the boys attracted jeering from Shvarts: so why had she done nothing, if so? 'No, the wolf cannot hide itself in sheep's clothing.' Danila's testimony was given in equal detail, as he described how Pavlik had told his brother to run, and Danila had stabbed him, and the two miscreants had grabbed Fyodor, and then put the sack over Pavlik's face. A new touch – not in earlier press reports – was added: Sergei had dragged Fyodor off to the left after the boy was murdered. And comments from the accused that did not appear in the trial transcript were stitched in. According to Shvarts, Sergei Morozov had made clear his determination to keep silent not with a peasant saying about the benefits of keeping mum, but with a sonorous Christian analogy: 'I shall take upon myself all this sin, as Jesus Christ did in the Judaic court.'

СУД НАД УБИЙЦАМИ ПАВЛИКА МОРОЗОВА

Выше знамя классовой боеспособности

Никакой пощады классовому врагу!

(Из речи общественного обвинителя от „Пионерской правды" тов. СМИРНОВА)

3 сентября в селе Герасимовка, Тавдинского района, Уральской области, кулаки зверски убили активного пионера Павлика Морозова и его братишку Федю. С 25 по 28 ноября в Тавде происходил суд над убийцами Павлика и Феди Морозовых. Суд вынес приговор — расстрелять: кулака Кулуканова — организатора и вдохновителя убийства, Морозова Сергея — деда Павлика, Морозова Даниила — двоюродного брата Павлика — непосредственных убийц и Морозову Ксению — бабку Павлика — соучастницу убийства.

На суде выступил общественным обвинителем от «Пионер. правды» член редколлегии ТОВ. СМИРНОВ. Ниже мы печатаем выдержки из речи тов. Смирнова.

— Товарищи, убийство в Герасимовке есть одно из проявлений классовой борьбы в стране. Озверелое кулачье, разбитое в открытом классовом бою, осмелилось, вырвало из наших рядов одного из лучших юных ленинцев—Павлушу Морозова и его братишку Федю.

Владимир Ильич Ленин говорил: **«Кулаки — самые зверские, самые грубые, самые дикие эксплоататоры, не раз восстанавливавшие в истории других стран власть помещиков, царей, попов, капиталистов»**... Зверская расправа кулаков над Павликом Морозовым и его братом подтверждает слова Ильича.

Мы приступаем ко второй пятилетке, к построению бесклассового общества. Нам предстоят новые большие победы. Но они дадутся не легко. Рост Советского союза, наше социалистическое наступление по всему фронту не могут проходить «гладко» и без трудностей, без борьбы, без преодоления бешеного сопротивления классовых врагов.

«Новые успехи социализма, —подчеркнула 17-я партконференция, **— рабочий класс обеспачит лишь в борьбе с остатками капитализма, давая беспощадный отпор сопротивлению гибнущих капиталистических элементов, преодолевая буржуазные и мелкобуржуазные предрассудки среди трудящихся и ведя настойчивую работу по социалистическому их перевоспитанию».**

17-я партконференция указала также, что **«и в дальнейшем еще неизбежно обострение классовой борьбы в отдельные моменты и особенно в отдельных районах и на отдельных участках социалистической стройки...»** Это надо помнить. Об этом надо знать.

ПОГИБ „ПАШКА-КОММУНИСТ"

В лице Павлика Морозова мы потеряли юного красно-галстучника, беззаветно боровшегося с кулачьем за дело партии, за дело социализма.

Павлик ясно сознавал свои классовые задачи и, как пионер, стойко боролся за них. Каждый свой шаг Павлик рассматривал с точки зрения успехов нашего социалистического строительства. Это проходит красной чертой через всю его короткую, но столь славную и содержательную пионерскую жизнь.

Начались хлебозаготовки — Павлик первый сдал свои хлебные излишки. Пришел на деревню заём — Павлик первый приобрел облигации. Начались занятия в школе — Павлик впереди всех успевает в учебе.

Он не только хороший школьник, примерный пионер, не только прекрасный общественник, но он и в семье — без отца — хороший хозяин, лучший помощник матери, лучший друг своим младшим братишкам.

Вся Герасимовка знала «Пашку — юного пионера». Его кличка была «Пашка-коммунист». Почетная кличка!

КЛАССОВО-ВОСПИТАННЫЙ ПИОНЕР

Вспомните речь Павлика на суде своего бывшего отца-подкулачника.

— Дяденьки судьи! Мой отец творил явную контрреволюцию. Я, как пионер, обязан это сказать. Мой отец — не защитник интересов Октября. Он всячески помогает кулаку, стоит за него горой. И я не как сын, а как пионер прошу привлечь к суровой ответственности моего отца».

В этих словах весь Павлик. Юный и, вместе с тем, необычайно твердый, классово воспитанный пионер. Для него интересы Октября, интересы социализма превыше всего.

Посмотрите в какой обстановке жил Павлик. Герасимовка — глухая деревня, далеко от культурного центра, заброшенная в лесу среди болот и озер. Темная деревня с проклятыми старыми традициями, с вековой неграмотностью, религиозным засильем и мелкособственническими устоями.

СВЕТЛАЯ, ГЕРОИЧЕСКАЯ ЖИЗНЬ

И вот, в эту глухомань врывается светлая, героическая жизнь пионера Павлика Морозова. Кулачье ощетинилось, оскалило зубы.

Но Павлика не испугаешь.

Он разоблачает отца и ведет неустанную борьбу с кулаками. Во главе небольшой группы деревенских пионеров он идет по селу и вывешивает позорные доски на домах зажимщиков хлеба. Он разоблачает кулака Кулуканова и др. скрывавших хлеб от государства. Он борется против кулаков, спекулянтов, против всех врагов советской власти.

Стал предателем отец — Павлик выдал его. Укрыл кулацкое

Мать убитых Павлика и Феди Морозовых.

имущество дед — Павлик раскрыл его. Украл кулак Кулуканов общественный хлеб — Павлик выдал его. Укрыл кулак Шатраков оружие — Павлик разоблачил его. Спекулировал кулак Силин — Павлик вывел его на чистую воду.

Не испугали Павлика кулацкие угрозы. Из него рос недюжинный большевик. Это чуяло кулачье и решило убрать его с дороги.

И вот Павлик погиб. Нож классового врага вырвал жизнь у светловолосого «Пашки-коммуниста».

ЮНЫЙ РЕВОЛЮЦИОНЕР

Павлика вырастила и воспитала пионерская организация. Убивая его, кулаки знали, что наносят глубокую рану детскому коммунистическому движению, они знали, что вырывают из рядов юных ленинцев одного из лучших, активных борцов за дело партии.

Пионерская организация в нашей стране выросла во многомиллионную коммунистическую организацию детей трудящихся.

Юные пионеры растут революционерами, растут достойными гражданами великой Страны советов. Павлик Морозов — яркое подтверждение этому. Вместе с партией, вместе с комсомолом, вместе со всем рабочим классом юные пионеры участвуют на всех фронтах социалистической стройки, борясь активно с классовыми врагами.

СУРОВО КАРАТЬ КЛАССОВЫХ ВРАГОВ

Кулацкая расправа над Павликом Морозовым вызвала волну негодования и протеста миллионов школьников и пионеров всего Советского союза. Весть о зверской расправе в Герасимовке облетела всю страну. В ответ на кулацкую месть пионеры и школьники высоко подняли знамя соцсоревнования и ударничества в школе, усилили борьбу за знания, за лучшую учебу. Пионеротряды еще крепче сплотились вокруг партии и комсомола.

Многотысячные протесты и резолюции пионеров и школьников, полученные «Пионерской правдой» — это демонстрация величайшей преданности третьего поколения революции делу партии, делу социализма. Миллионы детей рабочих и трудящихся требуют расстрела убийц Павлика и Федора Морозовых. Пролетарский суд должен сурово покарать классовых врагов.

ВЫПОЛНИТЬ ЗАВЕТ ЛЕНИНА

Перед лицом пролетарского суда, перед лицом всей пролетарской страны миллионы юных ленинцев заявляют, что они будут такими, как Павлик Морозов. Они крепко помнят завет Ильича, что **«коммунистом стать можно лишь тогда, когда обогатишь свою память знанием всех тех богатств, которые выработало человечество».**

Лучший наш ответ на классовую месть — выполнить завет Владимира Ильича Ленина, лучше учиться, овладеть знаниями и готовить из себя всесторонне развитых и активных строителей социализма.

Пусть помнит кулачье, что дни его сочтены. Победоносное социалистическое наступление под руководством партии сотрет с лица земли последний капиталистический класс — кулачье.

15-летний герой, юный, бесстрашный боец против врагов, красногалстучный Павлик убит. Но **«то поколение, которому сейчас 15 лет, оно увидит коммунистическое общество и само будет строить это общество. И оно должно знать, что вся задача его жизни есть строительство этого общества».** (Ленин).

УБИЙЦЫ ПАВЛИКА И ФЕДИ МОРОЗОВЫХ. Слева направо: кулак Кулуканов, дед—Морозов Сергей, двоюродный брат — Морозов Данила и бабка — Морозова Ксения.

Report on the Morozov trial, *Pioneer Pravda*, November 1932.

In some contexts, this could have been meant to sound noble; according to the lights of the proselytizing atheism that reigned in early Soviet propaganda, however, its resonance could only be contemptible. *Pioneer*'s junior readers were told that laughter had rung through the court at this point.[25]

To be sure, *Tavda Worker* had reported this comment too. But the effect was rather different, because the journalists gave Sergei's words an unambiguous gloss: 'Old Morozov is trying to make himself look like Jesus.'[26] Oleg Shvarts, on the other hand, did not explain what Morozov might have meant by his reference to the 'Judaic court', even though he was writing for a younger audience. It hung in the air, acquiring a sinister meaning.

In the local papers, the Pavlik Morozov case signified only one thing: the state's political enemies were at it again. The animosities of the Civil War were being rewritten in confrontations between those who stood for 'the measures being taken' and 'White kulak bandits'. *Tavda Worker* accordingly devoted space not to Elizar Smirnov's closing tirade at the trial, but to the tirade by the other 'social prosecutor', Comrade Urin of the Sverdlovsk Central Committee of the Komsomol, who referred to the 'construction of Soviet society', the 'liquidation of capitalist elements and classes generally', and to a 'sharpening of the class war' as an instrument of this.[27] *Pioneer Pravda* and *Pioneer*, on the other hand, had a more complex, culturally layered, view of the case. In the words of Oleg Shvarts, Danila had 'told everything like it was',[28] but such plain documentary realism was definitely not the effect created by these new press reports. So what was the function of the additions – Pavlik's denunciation of his father, the slavering particulars of the murder scene, Sergei's comments at his trial?

CIVIC DENOUNCER

The embellishments in *Pioneer Pravda* had a double effect: the elevation of Pavlik into a civic hero and the denigration of his killers. The 'denunciation of father' motif was more closely relevant to the first purpose. In terms of this motif in the abstract, the journalists dealing with the Morozov case had invented nothing new. Stories of this kind were – as we saw in Chapter 1 – scattered throughout the Soviet press of the late 1920s and early

1930s. There was also a prominent instance of such a denunciation in a National Socialist propaganda text published in the very year when the Pavlik story emerged, *Hitler Boy Quex*, by the South German writer Karl Aloys Schenzinger. Schenzinger's novel (adapted in 1933 as a film directed by Hans Steinhoff, which was to be even more popular than the book) is at first sight very like Pavlik Morozov seen in a looking-glass. Despite abusive treatment by his brutal, drunken, *Communist* father, Heini Völker (whose Fascist *nom de guerre* is later to be Quex), none the less bravely adheres to his decision to try to become a member of the Hitler Youth Movement. Soon he unmasks a planned Communist attack on the Hitler Youth, and (after nearly being poisoned by gas) is allowed to join the movement and to take up residence in one of its hostels. But before long the wicked Communists exact revenge by murdering the saintly child. On his deathbed, Quex astonishes his comrades by somehow managing to sing a Nazi marching song with his dying breath.[29] While Quex, unlike Pavlik, was presented to the public as fictional from start to finish, and was more hesitant and vulnerable than his Soviet counterpart[30] (or at least than Pavlik was in the early versions of the story), the correspondence between Quex and Pavlik is otherwise close.

The resemblance between these two boy heroes might seem coincidental, had the denunciation story emerged in the local, rather than the central press. It is hard to imagine the toiling drudges of *Tavda Worker* or even *Dawns of the Commune* having much awareness of Nazi propaganda. But in fact the denunciation was first reported in *Pioneer Pravda*, whose staff was fervently internationalist, and which frequently reported on youth movements overseas. In this context, direct influence cannot be ruled out. Possibly knowledge of the plot of *Quex* led Soviet propagandists to search for a Soviet equivalent to this alarmingly popular hero, and to fix on an actual murder victim whose biography included the same motifs as those in Schenzinger's novel (the defiance and then denunciation of the father), or to whose biography these motifs could be added.[31]

On the other hand – and this may be more likely – both Pavlik and Quex could be independently derived from a standard figure in late 1920s and 1930s German Communist mythology, the boy brutally slaughtered by the opposing side. Both Fascism and

Communism had death cults at the heart of their quest for legitimacy, and the early 1930s saw both sides jostling to claim child martyrdom as their own. Among the German Communists circulated a song called 'Der kleine Trompeter' (1925), in which a boy 'Red Guardist' who succumbed to an 'enemy bullet', was tenderly buried by his surviving comrades. The song was later to be adapted as the 'Horst Wessel Lied', in which a 'swastika wearer', likewise cut down by an 'enemy bullet', was just as respectfully committed to the earth.[32] The Soviet poet Mikhail Svetlov, who rewrote the lyrics in Russian, displayed slightly more originality: the 'little trumpeter' became a 'little drummer boy', who, after being struck by the inevitable bullet and falling on the 'moist earth', went on living in the minds of his comrades. It was this song that *Pioneer Pravda* had claimed was rendered at the Morozov boys' funeral by the local Pioneers: a real-life murder was being absorbed into the world of fiction. In the late 1920s, stories about abused and threatened foreign Pioneer martyrs were starting to be replaced by stories about abused and threatened Soviet Pioneer martyrs; it was natural that texts dealing with the former should slide sideways and be transformed into texts dealing with the latter.

BOY MARTYR

But there were also other sources for the portrayal of Pavlik and Fyodor's martyrdom. At times, Pavlik was presented as a kind of Communist Christ: in *Pioneer*'s version of the trial, Danila was said to have been paid not in the mundane 'five three-rouble coins and three five-rouble coins' of the interrogation records, but in 'thirty pieces of gold'. But though Danila regularly appeared as the Gerasimovka Judas, the analogy between Pavlik and Christ was fleeting and undeveloped. Christ was, of course, a mature adult at the time of his crucifixion and his death had, in any case, been a public execution, not a murder. Saintly figures closer to home provided more striking parallels for the Morozov deaths.

As innocents supposedly killed by wicked adults, Pavlik and his brother shared the fate of two of the most important saints in medieval Russia, Boris and Gleb, murdered, as tradition had it, by their evil elder brother Svyatopolk; and also of Tsarevich

Dmitry, slaughtered in 1591, allegedly at the order of Boris Godunov. These murders led to the vilification of Svyatopolk and of Boris Godunov as 'King Herods'. As with the Morozov murders, publicity about them had a strong political resonance, with the denigration of the killers assiduously promoted to secure the political legitimacy of the denigrators. A major sponsor of the Boris and Gleb cult was Prince Vladimir, the brother of Boris, Gleb and Svyatopolk, and Svyatopolk's rival for the throne in Kiev. And the denigration of Godunov worked to the advantage of Prince Mikhail Romanov and his successors, whose claim to the throne, in terms of ancestry, was no better than Godunov's, and who rose to power after a period of civil strife resembling that which had preceded the accession of the Tudors (who, of course, cultivated the legend of Richard III as child-killer with equal fervour). There was, then, a long tradition in Russia of child murders getting sucked into struggles over political power.[33]

The murder also had more immediate resonance. Pavlik's cult chimed with a more recent instance of 'child martyrdom' – the killing of Nicholas II's children in Ekaterinburg, the capital of the province in which Pavlik's own village lay. Though seldom mentioned in official Soviet sources,[34] this murder (above all the killing of the Tsarevich, Aleksei) had a huge significance for Russians opposed to, or ambivalent about, Soviet culture. There was an established 'underground' intellectual tradition of writing about the murder in the 1920s. At best, Aleksei's death was seen (for instance, in a poem by Mariya Shkapskaya using the fate of Louis XVII in order to evoke the murder of the Tsarevich) as the regrettable, but historically essential, spilling of innocent blood. At worst (as in Marina Tsvetaeva's poem 'Tsar and God – forgive them, for they know not what they do', written for the first anniversary of the October Revolution in 1918) it was perceived as an act depriving the regime of all possible legitimacy.[35] Given the politically explosive potential of the fate meted out to the Tsar's children, it would have been useful to stress that the enemies of the Soviet state were far more ruthless in their attitudes to juveniles than the Bolsheviks had been. Certainly, the publicity given to the murder in the Urals area itself probably had something to do with persisting memories of the atrocity against the Romanovs: the recollections of some local people who grew up there before the Second World War and even immediately after suggest that the fate of the former royal family was the subject of fascination and rumour. While some believed that two of the children (Aleksei and Anastasia) might have survived, most people thought that everyone had perished, and the general attitude among local children to the murder of the Tsar's family was bewilderment. The rationale behind the execution of the Tsar was clear enough, but the reasons why his wife and children had to die eluded comprehension.[36]

However, if desire to play on 'Herodism', and to contrive an alternative figure to Tsarevich Aleksei, were possibly at some level *motives* behind the creation of 'Pavlik Morozov', they had little effect upon the *motifs* of the legend at an overt level. In an atheist republic, it was less important to identify Pavlik and martyred princes than it was to emphasize the difference between them. The defiance with which Pavel *invited* his fate, according to the depictions of the Pioneer press, stood in vivid contrast with the non-combative manner in which St Boris *accepted* his killing: 'If my blood is spilled, then I will be a martyr for my Lord's sake', or St Gleb's pitiful plea to his murderers: 'Do not lay your hands on me, my dear sweet brothers! [. . .] Do not harm me, lords and brothers, do not harm me! What injury have I done you and my brother, my brothers and lords?'[37]

In saints' legends, the villains might bear some relation to Pavlik's evil relations (the wicked Svyatopolk in *The Tale of Boris and Gleb* has much in common with Pavlik's cousin Danila), but the virtue of the martyr himself was of quite a different order from the self-righteous civic pride so amply demonstrated by Pavlik. Indeed, it is quite possible that Pavlik's brother Fyodor disappeared from later versions of the legend less because he was too young to be a Pioneer – he could in principle have been turned into a model 'Octobrist' (member of the Communist organization for seven- to nine-year-olds) – than because a tale representing the murder of *two* young innocents would have made an uncomfortably obvious parallel with the life of Boris and Gleb.[38]

RITUAL MURDER: PAVLIK AND THE BEILIS CASE

In fact, the nearest parallel to Pavlik's case, as it was presented to readers at the outset, was a murder much closer to the boy's own era than that of Boris and Gleb, and with a political significance that was easier to manipulate than the killing of the last Romanov heir to the throne. In the 1910s had come the first case of an unexplained child murder in modern Russian history to exercise an obsessive fascination on the Russian public. This was the so-called 'Beilis case'.

In 1911, a thirteen-year-old schoolboy, Andrei Yushchinsky, had been discovered in a cave on the fringes of Podol district in Kiev half-naked, and with multiple stab wounds. The local police had originally treated the Yushchinsky murder as a routine affair, concluding that the likely perpetrator was a person or persons involved with the mother of a schoolfriend of Yushchinsky's, Zhenya Cheberyak, who was the hostess of a low-life drinking den much favoured by local criminals. However, after political demonstrations had been orchestrated by members of extreme nationalist groups at Yushchinsky's funeral, the affair came to the attention of chauvinist members of the central Tsarist administration, and a search was launched for a more politically expedient guilty party. A scapegoat was located in the person of Mendel Beilis, a Jew living in the vicinity; his trial, which lasted the best part of two years, gripped the whole of the Russian educated community.[39]

Beilis's trial is generally remembered – quite rightly – as a high-water mark of late Imperial Russian anti-Semitism, on the one hand, and a triumph for liberal legal values, on the other. The preposterous allegation that Beilis, as well as a group of other persons unknown, had murdered Yushchinsky in the pursuit of blood sacrifice, was believed and supported by disturbing numbers of well-educated and cultivated Russians, some of whom appeared at the trial as witnesses and as members of the prosecution team.[40] However, liberal opinion, in the person of the defence lawyers, eventually carried the day, and Beilis was allowed to go free. In the process, the allegations of ritual murder were undermined, not only because Beilis's non-involvement in the crime was demonstrated, but also because effective arguments were marshalled against the myth of blood sacrifice in the first place. Was it likely, a defence witness from the Kiev Theological College asked early in the proceedings, that Jews, forbidden from consuming even animal blood by Talmudic law, would be prepared to pollute themselves with human blood? If any cases of cannibalistic murder like this had been known, they were a manifestation of 'vicious superstition and monstrous behaviour on the part of individuals', and not of general religious practice.[41]

But the Beilis trial was more than a legal defeat for anti-Semitic fantasy. It was also the trial of an alleged child murderer. The statements both inside and outside the courtroom made it clear that Yushchinsky's age was crucial. Already at Yushchinsky's funeral, leaflets circulated by the chauvinist 'Black Hundreds' group had exhorted participants: 'Russian people! If you love your children, beat the Jews! Beat them till not a single one is left in Russia! Pity your children! Avenge the suffering innocents!'[42] At the trial itself, A. S. Shmakov, a member of the prosecuting team, referred to Yushchinsky's 'martyr's death', and called the boy a 'gentle, innocent martyr for the Christian faith'.[43] At the same time, though, Yushchinsky was represented as a person who was not admirable in the ordinary sense: 'The boy grew up in abnormal family circumstances, subject to no control.'[44] The prosecution hit back by presenting Yushchinsky as a hero of quite a different kind: a monument of civic virtue, a boy slaughtered by bandits because of his distaste for the activities carried on at the Cheberyak thieves' den. 'If he had been a member of that clutch of thieves, then he would not have died a martyr's death,' P. Karabchevsky asserted.[45] For his part, Mendel Beilis himself concluded his brief final speech in his own defence with a passionate appeal to the jury: 'I beg you to clear my name so that I will once more be able to see my unhappy children, who have been waiting for me these past two and a half years.'[46]

Every side involved in the trial, then, attempted to establish probity by appeal to a romanticized image of childhood. Beilis pleaded his status as an ideal family man and loving father. For the prosecution, Yushchinsky was a sacred martyr, albeit also a child who had been brought up badly; for the defence, he was a secular martyr and a hero of civic virtue, and the scion of a poverty-stricken, but essentially respectable, working-class family (despite evidence that the boy had in fact been ill-treated at home, and the local police's probably not unfounded suspicions that his murder was likely to be what in popular British English is called 'a domestic').[47] Had Yushchinsky been discovered with the same terrible stab wounds and in the same eerie location, but been a grown man, it is doubtful whether the charge of ritual murder would have had comparable potency. Most of the other alleged cases of ritual murder in the Russian Empire during the late nineteenth and early twentieth centuries also involved children.[48]

In all of this, there is an uncanny resemblance to the circumstances of the Morozov case. Pavlik's murder was also treated as routine by local investigators, and was raised by visitors from the capital into an affair of central political importance. Both Yushchinsky and Morozov were found in a place that was close to where they lived, but at the same time, slightly out of the way; in both cases, slack procedure at the time the body was discovered meant that forensic evidence was lost, allowing leeway to wild speculation.[49] In both cases, multiple stab wounds had been the method of dispatching the victim, and the bodies had been found curiously arranged – in the Morozov case, smeared with cranberry juice, with a sack over Pavlik's head, and with Fyodor 'dragged off to the left'.[50] If the reference, in the Beilis trial judge's summing up, to Yushchinsky's loss of blood evoked a measurement used in food preparation – 'five glasses' – the cranberry juice smeared on Pavel worked like an inversion of cannibalistic myth: Jews were said to drink their victims' blood: here, a red, sticky, but edible substance (cranberries were often consumed with meat in the Russian kitchen) stood in for human blood.[51] And, in both cases, the murderer or murderers were said to have acted in concert.

Of all these details, only the first, the assumption that the murderers must be part of a wider conspiracy, was characteristic of other child murder allegations of the 1930s. When Nastya Razinkina and Olya Skalkina were found raped and murdered in 1934, the killing was (just as with Pavlik's) quickly ascertained, by the percipient central authorities, to be the work of a 'robber band' composed of 'kulak dregs' – the 'political' nature of the case having been overlooked by the short-sighted and ideologically incompetent local authorities.[52] But if the attribution of evil-doing to a counter-revolutionary gang echoes the Morozov case, the technicalities of multiple stab wounds and pollution by food were absent here. In invoking such details, reports on the Morozov case were, in the contemporary context, unique. On the other hand, the murder, as presented in the Pioneer press reports, carried several hallmarks of a ritual murder as perceived in anti-Semitic fantasy. These included the youth of the victims, the mode of death (by stabbing) and the cannibalistic overtones.

To be sure, the representation of the Morozov case as ritual murder was not explicit. No one referred to the kulaks' 'blood guilt', or explicitly accused them of having involved the Morozov boys in foul rites before they were killed. And some of the details played on by the Pioneer press (the sacks, the arrangement of the bodies, the scattered cranberries) were taken from the case file. However, the young journalists writing for the Pioneer press were precisely not inclined simply to parrot material from the case file. They altered what they found, omitting details and adding details. Hence, their decision to home in on the 'bloodthirsty', 'cannibalistic' elements in the Morozov murders is striking. Notable, too, is the presentation of some of the courtroom photographs, in which Sergei Morozov, in particular, is shot from the side, so as to make him appear to have a hook nose.[53] Equally, the presentation of Kulukanov in the articles about the trial as crafty, money-grubbing, manipulating the murders at one remove also recalls stereotypes about the 'elders of Zion'.

The propagandists of *Pioneer Pravda* and *Pioneer* were not, of course, intending to suggest that the Morozov murderers actually were Jews, or were acting in league with Jews. The laudability of internationalism, and the despicable character of all prejudice based on ethnic affinity (or 'nationality', as the Soviet term was), were sacred tenets in the Pioneer movement in the late 1920s and 1930s. The Pioneer press spent more space on reporting 'International Children's Week', a propaganda event marked by

The accused lined up in the courtroom. (Pavlik Morozov Museum)

festivals of co-operation between Pioneers across the world, than it did on reporting collectivization.[54] It regularly brought news of the internationalist movement more broadly, and assailed signs of inter-racial infighting in school playgrounds or on streets where these were encountered.[55] One major charge against kulaks was that they were anti-Semitic.[56] Despite all this, though, there was an established history of representing the 'enemies' of Soviet power in terms derived from traditional anti-Semitic fantasy,[57] on which anti-kulak propaganda drew.

The Morozov murders happened just as the anniversary of the Beilis trial was occurring – 1933 was marked by the publication, in Soviet Russia, of Tager's *The Tsarist Regime and the Beilis Affair*, an in-depth analysis of the Yushchinsky murder, and of the circulation of 'blood libel' legends in the Western Russian Empire generally at this period. The assault on anti-Semitism had a specific rationale: there was an established tradition, among monarchists in the Russian emigration, of seeing the Romanov murders as a case of ritual murder by Jews,[58] and one cannot rule out the existence of such a tradition in Soviet Russia itself. Certainly, anti-Semitic feeling had – to judge by sources such as letters to Soviet politicians and official organizations – considerable currency among the Soviet masses.[59] And monarchist groups do seem to have led an underground existence in some places, including Ekaterinburg, during the 1920s and 1930s.[60]

The authorities, then, had two aims: they wanted to stigmatize kulaks, and they wanted to encourage positive feelings about Jews. The two aims came together in an attempt to present kulaks as anti-Semitic, yet also as inheritors of the negative stereotypes traditionally used to vilify Jews – particularly the blood libel legend. At any rate, this seems the most effective explanation for the citation of the comment from Sergei Morozov about the 'Judaic court' where he was being tried. The court where Christ was tried was of course a Roman one, but the denomination of it as 'Judaic' drew attention to the 'Jewish theme'.

It might seem perverse to attempt to discourage anti-Semitism by giving covert credence to 'blood libel' in the first place, but it was routine for Soviet propaganda to have this kind of aim, which was, indeed, in harmony with the laws of Marxist-Leninist dialectic. For instance, rather than discourage religious feeling altogether, propagandists attempted to divert this into secular celebrations – colourful examples in the 1920s and early 1930s included 'red weddings', 'red christenings' and 'red Easter'.[61] The idea was something analogous to the 'new wine in old skins' formula of Socialist Realism, 'socialist in content, national in form'. Pavlik Morozov's case may have been selected for national publicity in the first place, then, not only because he was a Sverdlovsk martyr who seemed fit to lay the ghosts of the children murdered in the city in 1918 to rest, but because he was a cleansing ideological opposite to Andrei Yushchinsky, the thirteen-year-old boy who had supposedly died a martyr's death at the hands of Mendel Beilis. Making kulaks equivalents to the Jews of legend appealed because it at one and the same time diverted popular hatred away from its traditional target, and allowed the enemies of the new state to be painted in vile colours.

That said, later versions of Pavlik's murder on the whole did not attempt to brand the kulaks as 'anti-Semitic ritual murderers', even though a hint of this strategy still remains in a life by Aleksandr Yakovlev published in 1936. Here, the phrasing used by Sergei Morozov, 'Beat Pashka!', recalls the infamous Black Hundreds slogan, 'Save Russia! Beat the Jews!'[62] The 'incriminating' photographs of Sergei and Kseniya Morozov were not reprinted or imitated in the canonical lives, and Danila and Sergei were represented there as violent in a banal way, like characters from detective literature: 'At that moment something sharp and painful thrust into his spine. "Owww!" Pavlik yelled, spreading his arms and falling on his knees. But immediately he got up. Danila struck out again [. . .] then crushed Pavlik under him, and at the fifth blow of the knife in his chest Pavel lay dead.'[63] In other words, the link between the Morozov case and the Beilis case was something of immediate importance to the status of the case in 1932–3, rather than to the promotion of the Morozov legend in the long term.[64]

ZERO TO HERO

The motif from the Beilis case that was in fact most relevant to the invention of Pavlik was the representation (by the defence lawyers in the Beilis case, the prosecution in the Morozov case) of the murder victim as a civic hero. Both boys came from a deprived background, and yet both had been ready to stand up for justice and to denounce misdoings. This combination of deprivation and principle was not prefigured in the lives of the saintly martyrs of 'Herodist' tradition. The classic martyr of early Christian, and medieval Russian, literature came from a princely, or at the very least, aristocratic household, even if he or she chose to defy its values by a descent into willed poverty; the classic Communist martyr, on the other hand, had humble roots.

This applied also to child martyrs. In the words of a handbook on the Communist children's movement published in 1932, 'Children are part of their class'.[65] According to the stereotypes set out in, say, Vladimir Mayakovsky's children's poem 'Fat Petya and Thin Sima' (1925), which shows the revolting, fat, greedy and stupid bourgeois Petya literally bursting from self-indulgence, while thin Sima leads a life of dignity and self-sufficiency in his slum, poverty was a guarantee of virtue in children as it was in adults. It was not just a question of innate merit: peasant and working-class children, it was believed, grew up faster, and hence would more quickly become the politically astute child activists that were regarded as the ideal in early Soviet propaganda for children. The governing ethos of an accelerated childhood, where the gap between birth and adulthood was kept as short as possible, was piquantly expressed in Samuil Adlivankin's 1932 painting *A Visit to the Tank Drivers*, which showed a small baby held aloft among the bevy of steely soldiers, his head crowned by an over-sized Budyonnovka cap decorated with a red star, and in David Moor's poster for the anti-God movement, 'I am a militant atheist!', which showed a small boy draped in his father's military greatcoat and, once more, Budyonnovka cap.[66]

There was also a preference, at this stage, for making child heroes out of what *Pravda* was in 1934 to describe as 'smut-nosed street urchins living in tar-boilers', and 'spunky little cripples'.[67] Self-assertion was all: indeed, one child-care book even informed parents that well-behaved children were likely to be suffering from psychological trauma:

> Parents want to have the sort of child that is quiet, obedient, silent, and so on, but they have no idea that quiet, obedient,

> silent children are, in essence, simply abnormal, sick children. And parents who have children like that should, instead of feeling joy and delight in them, consult a good doctor as soon as possible in order to find out how to cure them of their morbid condition.[68]

A favourite hero of the 1920s and early 1930s was the neglected orphan or street waif who, transmuted in the crucible of the Soviet orphanage, turned into a person of exemplary social and political commitment. In the extremely popular film *Road into Life* (1931) an orphaned street boy and former petty thief, Mustapha the Tatar (which in the language of the time signified member of an oppressed and 'backward' ethnic group), became the leader of the orphanage collective, and a living illustration of 'reform through labour'. As the film illustrates, fomenting activism among children from working-class and poor-peasant roots was seen as a way of enacting 'dictatorship of the proletariat' in miniature. Children of this kind, mythic texts underlined, would stop at nothing to uphold the Soviet system from which their enlightenment had come. *Road into Life* concluded with Mustapha defying the leader of the gang he had lived with, and paying with his life for this act of defiance. Discovered by his orphanage comrades, his body was placed with ceremony at the front of the first train to make the trip along the railway line the reformed waifs had built, his funeral at the same time celebrating their transformation into useful members of society.

Given the attachment of propagandists in the Urals to 'class war' stereotypes and to 'proletarian values', it is not surprising that the transformation narrative – zero to hero – dominated representations there too. The most important purveyor of these was Pavel Solomein, a young journalist from the Sverdlovsk area who covered the Morozov murders for *Dawns of the Commune*. On 8 October, Solomein sent his first detailed report from Gerasimovka. The village was a full sixty kilometres from the administrative centre in Tavda (a considerable exaggeration – the true distance is under forty kilometres). 'There is no party cell there, no Komsomol cell,' Solomein wrote (which also adapted real circumstances for dramatic effect). There was, however, he asserted, a Pioneer troop, and hence, Pavel and Fyodor Morozov had realized that one should fight the kulaks tooth and nail. Having found out about his father, Pavel had asked himself, 'What kind of poor peasant is he? What kind of chairman? What kind of father, if he sold himself to the kulaks?' He had then walked to Tavda 'and reported his father's misdeeds'. In the wake of this one hero's actions, Gerasimovka was now transforming itself: once the news of the murders had come through, there had been meetings, entries to the Komsomol, and action in Tavda.[69]

On 27 October, Solomein took up the story once more, this time describing Danila's violence towards Pavlik (he had beaten the boy and shouted, 'I'll bash you Communists'), and moving inexorably into the murder scene. As Danila and his grandfather struck, the boys fell, and 'the kulak knife thrust into [Pavlik's] neck. Before he called out, Pavlik heard Fyodor's dying scream.' After the murder, the kulaks had rejoiced and called out, 'Praise the Lord!' But, as Solomein threateningly concluded, 'For how long?'[70]

In comparison with the chronology of the case investigation that was proceeding in parallel with trial by newspaper, Solomein's accounts are interesting. Danila and Sergei did not make their formal admission of guilt till 6 November, but Solomein confidently 'fingered' them on 27 October, at a stage when earlier newspaper accounts had named Efrem Shatrakov and Danila Morozov, or else a whole string of 'kulaks and sub-kulaks' as the culprits. Possibly information in Gerasimovka was the source of Solomein's assertion, or perhaps OGPU operatives in Tavda tipped him off.

Solomein's reports were the first to present a more or less coherent account of Pavlik's life. Later, he was to write them up into the first full-length biography of Pavlik Morozov, published in 1933, which adopted a similar pseudo-documentary style to the newspaper reports. Both Solomein's articles and his book were based on fairly extensive interviewing in Gerasimovka,[71] and he – unlike later biographers – used quite a lot of the material that he collected. He represented Pavlik Morozov's story as the tale of a boy from a desperately poor and ignorant family in a poor and backward village who was stirringly committed to the Communist cause.

Solomein emphasized the lawlessness and volatility of the place where Pavlik had grown up. Tonkaya Grivka had been the site of a 'kulak rebellion' led by a White officer in 1921; fifteen Communists had been eliminated.[72] He relentlessly underlined Pavlik's economic deprivation. The reader was told that he worked the land from a young age, ploughing, harrowing and sowing. 'It won't work any other way. After all, he's the boss – the head of the family. And what kind of boss will he be if he doesn't sell his bread to the state? Pavlik bore all this in mind, though work was tough.' The family from which he came was not just poor and backward, but actively abusive. At best, Pavlik had had to endure taunts: 'I won't feed a Pioneer – out, you damned Communist!'[73] – at worst, actual physical danger. In a horrific scene, Pavlik was punished for his defiance by having chip fat poured over him by his father, leading to severe burns.

> It was only when the dirty towel, which was stuck to his septic wounds, had to be taken away [so the wounds could be cleaned] that he would wrinkle his face and grit his teeth. But he never cried. And he would often get angry with his mother: 'What yer staring at, mam, like dog Kitai at the moon? I'm not dead yet. And I'll get better.'[74]

After his father's arrest, too, Pavlik had been repeatedly beaten by his cousin and grandfather; Danila had attacked him when out

Pavlik confronts his father. (Illustration from Pavel Solomein, *In the Kulaks' Nest* 1933)

fishing, and then there had also been the confrontation over the horse harness. The aggression towards Pavlik had never ceased.

All the more remarkable, then, was Pavlik's determination to improve himself, to make use of all the educational opportunities on offer. According to Solomein, the boy had grown up 'a restless child': his impatient energy was so great that he had sprung out of his cradle in infancy, leaving himself with a lasting scar; as a toddler, he had pestered his mother with wails of 'Send me to school!' Later, he had become an exemplary pupil, despite having to study in a school with only one teacher to 100 pupils.[75] And then there was his devotion to the cause. He was the first to take part in the surrender of grain ('I'm little, but I'll be the first to give up the two hundred grams they want from me,') and the leader of the 'red wagon', the Soviet harvest festival procession, into the village, with his 'streaming red banner'.[76] He was untiring in performing his work of civic denunciation, exposing all wrongdoers, including, of course, his father. And he was a leader of the other children in civic actions, steering a raid on Silin's grain-pits, and co-ordinating the pasting of slogans around the whole village.[77]

Thus Pavel's biography was brought to embody both the present horror and the future promise of the Russian village. In the more poetic versions of the tale published in the central Pioneer press, the contrast was schematized: Pavlik was turned into a blond (the *Pioneer Pravda* story of 15 October 1932 described him as 'radiant haired'). Solomein's more downbeat version retained the reddish-brown hair that the boy had actually had when he was alive. Whichever way, he was a perfect instrument and symbol of the transformation being experienced by his home region – throughout the early 1930s, the taiga was one of the key settings for the 'darkness into light' cliché narrative of Stalinist propaganda[78] – and by the Soviet Union as a whole.

The 'transformation narrative' was not the only literary stereotype with which Pavlik had become associated by 1933. He was also portrayed as a revolutionary martyr, the Soviet answer to the child victims of revolution (the Tsar's family), and to the Christian boy saints of the past; and as the slaughtered prey of vicious ritual murderers who had adopted the role traditionally assigned to Jews in anti-Semitic fantasy.

The early 1930s saw a number of other stories about Pioneer murder victims appear in the Pioneer press. About three weeks after Pavlik's trial was concluded, *Pioneer Pravda* reported that in another part of the Urals, Kurgan district, Kolya Myagotin, the son of a worker killed in the Civil War in 1920, and a Pioneer activist and 'shock pupil', had been murdered as an act of revenge for exposing thieves and grain-hoarders in his home village.[79] A year later, in December 1933, *Leninist Sparks*, the Leningrad Pioneer newspaper, printed an account of the murder of Pioneer Kolya Yakovlev, of Luga, who had been attacked and stabbed three times by unknown men, and who had later died of his injuries.[80] And a secret report compiled in early 1933 in the offices of the Komsomol Central Committee listed the Morozov brothers alongside no fewer than eight other children supposedly murdered by kulaks.[81] Here, Pavlik appeared not as *the* victim of kulak aggression, but as *a* victim of kulak aggression – one among many others.

Pavlik was not even the first murdered child whose killing was represented in the press as the death of a Pioneer activist. That honour goes to Grisha Akopov in December 1930. Here, too, the *Pioneer Pravda* journalists had accused the local administration of foot-dragging, and got the case high-level attention; here, too, the paper had covered the story extensively. Later stories – the tale of Kolya Yakovlev, for example – also got a lot of press coverage. And some of the victims – for instance Myagotin – might well have seemed like more promising candidates for canonization than, on the face of it, Pavlik did. Why should this particular hero have gone on to outshine all the others?

A retrospective answer to this might suggest that his story was just that much more gripping than those of other murder victims, because of the denunciation of his father, above all. But in fact, as we shall see, the denunciation motif was in some ways an embarrassment in the long term. The photographic illustrations to the Pavlik story (visual material associated with the case was unusually abundant) may have helped. However, the portrait photograph of Pavlik, while widely reproduced as a cult image, never acquired the kind of iconic status of more recent images of child murder victims – James Bulger being led away by his killers on video, particularly. Lives of the boy regularly ignored it in favour of line drawings.

More important to the growth of the cult was where Pavlik had lived – in a frontier zone of Russian settlement, 'between Europe and Asia', in the words of the proletarian poet Konstantin Mitreikin, but also somewhere explicitly *Russian*, a province at once remote and definitely 'ours'. The death of Grisha Akopov, in a wild, 'oriental', zone, did not present the same drama of civilization under threat: the effect of such stories was likely to be, 'What else do you expect in a place like that?' The Urals–Siberian borders, on the other hand, were debatable land, with significant populations of ethnic minorities,[82] but the Russian sense of entitlement was strong. What was more, Pavlik's very name – Pavel *Morozov*, derived from 'frost' – was seductive. It did not seem quaintly Belorussian, as 'Potupchik' or 'Kovalenko', for instance, would have done. It was an emphatically Russian-sounding name. Authentically plebeian (Morozovs are two a kopeck), it was at the same time redolent of myths about Russians as a northern people, tough and stoical. It was, in effect, not too different from the name 'John Bull', a figure who is both 'everyman' and embodies particular, thoroughly masculine, traits of national identity.

In the early months after the murders, Pavlik's death and life history became more and more famous, and acquired added layers of cultural significance. Yet the story was not all-dominant, in terms of public profile, at the time when it first happened. Between the autumn of 1932 and the autumn of 1933, mentions of the Morozov murders were confined (at the level of the metropolitan press) to newspapers and magazines intended for a child audience. It was specifically the Pioneer press that was exhorted to publish the case in one of the regular TASS bulletins of news intended for dissemination in the provinces.[83] Neither *Pravda* nor *Izvestiya* carried coverage, though *Izvestiya* was, during late 1932 and early 1933, demonstrating the centrality of Pavlik's home region to high-level propaganda by repeatedly printing blacklists of supposedly criminally negligent state farm and industrial enterprise chairmen from the Urals and Western Siberia in its central pages. In the world of show trials, the *cause célèbre* of late 1932 and early 1933 was the arraignment of some English engineers accused of industrial sabotage, and not the summary execution of several members of the Morozov family somewhere in the taiga. Where adult audiences were concerned, the Morozov trial did not rate a mention even on *Pravda* or *Izvestiya*'s back page. The special 'rural interest' paper, *The Peasant Gazette*, did not make room for it, while *Pioneer Pravda*'s sister paper for older readers, *Komsomol Pravda*, carried only sparse and sporadic reports.[84] Indeed, even in the children's press, the Morozov murders were – at the first stages – not front-page news. Except when the trial was in progress, they appeared on pages 3 or 4, the place for subsidiary reportage, and often – during collectivization – for news of 'grisly kulak horrors' from the provinces.

All this was to change in late 1933, when Pavlik became far more famous than any Pioneer hero to date. In a country ruled by press censorship, where public opinion was subject to severe regulation, this process could not come about just 'like that'. Rather, it signified assent from the highest levels – and in this case, sponsorship from one of the most powerful men in the Soviet Union, Maxim Gorky.

CHAPTER 5

All-Soviet Hero

PAVLIK AND GORKY

The decisive moment in the elevation of Pavlik to all-Soviet heroic status came in September 1933: Pavel Solomein sent a copy of his Pavlik biography to the writer Maxim Gorky. Gorky, then in his early sixties, had made his reputation before the Revolution as the author of mythically coloured realist prose, socially critical dramas, and an autobiographical trilogy that celebrated his own ascent from a backward petit-bourgeois family, with an abusive stepfather, into the sweetness and light of education and political awareness. It is possible Solomein genuinely thought that Gorky would be interested in the story of a boy whose life history was not unlike his own. A humble desire for self-improvement should also not be ruled out: since the 1890s, Gorky had been receiving fan letters from worker-writers eager to emulate his path from errand-boy to literary master. Like other Russian authors, he believed that replying to such letters, and passing on advice, was one of his professional duties.

It could be, though, that Solomein's motives were not only or mainly idealistic. Gorky, who had spent most of the 1920s in foreign exile, latterly in Sorrento, had begun responding at the end of the decade with increasing warmth to the suggestions from figures in the Soviet establishment, up to Stalin himself, that he should return to the motherland. He started regularly making visits to his homeland from 1928, during the era of the 'cultural revolution', and by the time that he finally returned for good in

1931, he commanded unparalleled authority in the Soviet literary establishment. No other writer had the ear of Stalin and of the Politburo as he did – in 1932, there was even a plan for him to write an official Stalin biography – and none exercised such influence on the shaping of cultural policy, above all the emergence of the doctrine of 'Socialist Realism' in 1932.

What is more, Gorky had for several years explicitly associated himself with children's affairs. Letters written by him to Stalin between the end of 1931 and the late summer of 1934 refer to the 'childhood' theme on several occasions. For instance, in November 1931, he emphasized the propaganda value, in terms of relations with the West, of the Soviet concern for children's welfare. In the following month, he called for the publication of a book on 'mother and child care' as an example of 'books we do not yet have, but which ought to be written'. On 2 August 1934, he promised that he would shortly address the subject of the nation's young in print (the result was a *Pravda* article, 'Soviet Children', which saw the light of day on 8 August). He

Portrait of Maxim Gorky, 1932.

also referred to the need to protect children from what he described as petit-bourgeois infections.[1] Concern with such topics was public, as well as private. In 1929, Gorky was a guest at the First (and, as it turned out, only, till the end of the Stalin era) All-Soviet Pioneer Rally, and he was regularly photographed with groups of children in the late 1920s and early 1930s (before Soviet political figures generally began to cultivate this practice).

Given Gorky's authority and his established interest in the 'childhood' theme, it was customary for those directing artistic projects aimed at children to seek his advice in the first instance.[2] He was in every way an ideal patron for a provincial journalist with a particular interest in writing for the juvenile market who was seeking to break into the rarefied world of metropolitan letters.

In terms of any ambition for self-promotion, however, Solomein's action had disastrous consequences. Having received, and skimmed through, *In the Kulaks' Nest*, Gorky sent him one of the most brutal letters that a novice writer can ever have hoped not to receive. 'Pioneer Pavlik Morozov's heroic deed, if it were narrated more skilfully, and with a power like the one Pavlik discovered in himself, would acquire a huge and edifying value in the eyes of Pioneers,' Gorky conceded. But no such power was evident in Solomein's account:

> Your book is written in such a way that neither children nor adults will be able to understand the deep significance and social novelty of the facts that you describe. The reader will exclaim when he reaches the end of it: this is all an invention, and a badly thought-out invention too.
>
> The material is original and new, but it's been ruined. The effect is as though you'd made a hook for the door of a hen-house out of pure gold or built the hen-house out of the kind of cedar-wood best used for making pencils.[3]

While Gorky signed off slightly more kindly – 'the people who made you ruin this invaluable material are more guilty than you are, of course' – the general effect of the letter was annihilating. Solomein's biography was to be reprinted only in the 1960s, and then posthumously, and in reworked form.

However, if sending a copy of *In the Kulaks' Nest* did nothing to advance Solomein's interests, it did a huge amount to boost the prominence of Pavlik Morozov. Before he opened Solomein's book, Gorky does not seem to have been aware of Pavlik Morozov's existence. Indeed, in an attack on the kulaks published in *Pravda* on 23 November 1933, he observed: 'Not long ago, this very year, 1933, they killed a small boy, the Pioneer Pavlik Morozov.'[4] The serious inaccuracy in dating must indicate that Gorky had heard nothing about Pavlik's murder when it happened (and incidentally that the editorial staff of *Pravda* were unfamiliar with the salient details of the boy's biography too, since they did nothing to correct Gorky's mistake).[5] Gorky's ignorance is easy to understand. It is unlikely that he followed the Pioneer press in detail, and anyway, in the autumn of 1932 he was very busy with celebrations for the fifteenth anniversary of the Bolshevik Revolution, and with the festivities for his own jubilee as a writer (an event commemorated by, among other things, the renaming of Moscow's main thoroughfare as 'Gorky Street'). There was no reason why Pavlik Morozov should have meant something to him before he received the book from Solomein.

Once he did catch up with the Pavlik Morozov story, though, Gorky did everything he could to make it famous. His influence

Gorky broadcasting to the Soviet nation from his dacha, 1932.

was, one may be sure, behind the appearance of Aleksandr Yakovlev's new, and more 'appropriate', life of Pavlik, first published in 1936. It is even tempting to speculate that this was a project Gorky originally intended to take on himself, and then delegated because other commitments, and his own increasingly poor health, got in the way. While these things are not matters of record, Gorky's commitment to getting a memorial erected to Pavlik is. He first raised this subject in October 1933, in a speech delivered to a rally of the Komsomol:

> The campaign against petty wreckers – weeds and rodents – has taught our children how to fight against big wreckers, ones of the two-legged variety. It is appropriate to mention here the heroic deed of Pioneer Pavel Morozov, the boy who understood that a person who is a relative by blood may well be an enemy of the spirit, and that such a person is not to be spared. Relatives by blood and by class murdered Pavlik Morozov, but the memory of him must not be allowed to vanish – this little hero deserves a monument, and I am certain that the monument will be built.[6]

By 1934, the 'monument' theme had become an *idée fixe*. At the First Congress of Soviet Writers in August 1934, Gorky led a whip-round to help fund a memorial to the child, with prominent authors stung for a contribution. As if this had not been enough, his closing address named the construction of the monument as a prime objective of the Writers' Union over the next few years. 'We must request the government to allow the Union of Littérateurs [*sic*] to erect a monument to Pavlik Morozov, killed by his relations when he discovered their wrecking activities and chose to assert the interests of the toiling people over blood ties.'[7] Six months later, in February 1935, he was chundering to A. S. Shcherbakov, Secretary of the Writers' Union, about the inexplicable delays in construction of the monument to which he had so publicly committed himself.[8] As a further echo of this activity, the files of the Secretariat of the Komsomol Central Committee from March 1935 record a decree commanding the erection of a Pavlik monument (though without specifying a location).[9] From here, the monument campaign trickled upwards. 'The construction of a monument in Moscow to Pioneer Pavlik Morozov, who died at the hands of kulaks', an agenda item at the Politburo meeting on 17 July 1935, was duly passed by consensus.[10] In all of this, Gorky was certainly not working alone: his general position in the Stalinist establishment was as a kind of one-person clearing-house for ideas on their way to becoming (or not becoming) cultural policy.[11] But he was the most prominent figure in the Soviet Union ever to promote Pavlik's cult openly.

PAVLIK AND STALIN

Notable, by contrast, is the apparent passivity of Stalin himself. In 1938, one of Pavlik's biographers, Elizar Smirnov, was to claim backing for the monument from the highest places:

> A year ago Comrade Stalin suggested to the Moscow City Soviet that they should raise a monument to Pavlik Morozov by Red Square. The best sculptors and artists, and also hundreds of Pioneers, pondered on the monument. Now the project has been approved. Soon, next to the Alexander Gardens, by the entrance to Red Square, the monument will be raised.'[12]

But the claim – which is not supported by available material in archives[13] – was never repeated, and it seems to be no more than a garbled reference to the Politburo decision three years before.

Stalin's appetite for detail is known to have been formidable. As a eulogistic entry in the *Great Soviet Encyclopedia* put it:

> The circle of problems that occupy Stalin's attention is boundless: the most complex problems of Marxist-Leninist theory – and school textbooks; Soviet foreign policy – and daily concern for the good order of the proletarian capital; the creation of a Great Northern marine route – and the draining of the swamps of Colchis; the development of Soviet literature and art – and reorganizing daily life on the collective farm.'[14]

Notwithstanding the unintentionally comical phrasing here, it is a matter of record that Stalin did take a personal interest in school textbooks. For instance, he directly participated in the revision of the school history syllabus that took place in the mid-1930s. He also condescended to particulars in the area of children's literature, acting to prevent publication of a book about his childhood aimed at a juvenile audience.[15] He certainly must have known about the Morozov cult and decided that it should be tolerated. Yet at the same time he refrained from giving it explicit personal backing.

Important here is the sense of hierarchy that is evident in the eulogy from the *Great Soviet Encyclopedia*. Children's issues were placed on the circumference of the 'circle' of preoccupations in which Stalin moved – they were important, but not *that* important. It simply did not do for the premier politician in the Soviet Union to spend too much of his time on nursery matters. And in any case, Stalin's preferred relationships with children involved a very different psychological type from Pavlik. Once the genre of 'ruler icon with small child' took off in 1935–6, Stalin generally chose to be photographed with small girls, preferably pretty, beribboned ones; and his warm love for his daughter

Stalin posed with Gelya Markizova, the daughter of a high-ranking Communist Party official from Buryat-Mongolia, 1936. Reproduced here from *Soviet Children* (*Sovetskie deti*), Moscow 1940.

Svetlana – the recipient of affectionate and even flirtatious letters as his 'little housekeeper' and so on – stands in stark contrast to his vexed relationships with his two sons. Again and again, we see the Pavlik Morozov legend polarize observers according to whether they identify with the father in the story, or the son. It is clear that Stalin identified with the father. His own father was (according to the standard version of his biography) an abusive drunk, but he had responded to this by turning himself into an ideal patriarch. While undoubtedly perceiving the dissemination of the Pavlik legend as expedient, and hence to be encouraged (or, at least, not forbidden), he did not warm to its hero. Stalin never commented publicly on Pavlik Morozov, whichever way, but gossip reported that his private attitude to the boy was anything other than approbatory. He is even said to have once remarked, 'What a little swine, denouncing his own father.'[16]

FROM RED SQUARE TO THE SCHOOL DESK

The rise in status of the Pavlik Morozov legend cannot thus be directly attributed to Stalin's personal influence. In a strange way, too, it was out of kilter not only with the dictator's personal tastes, but also with the tone of the times more broadly. The mid-1930s saw huge and significant changes in the understanding of what an ideal childhood should be. Like everything else in Stalinist culture, this understanding was tied to the priorities outlined in five-year plans. The First Five-Year Plan of 1928–32 had given little specific attention to children's issues. At this point, in harmony with the preferred understanding of the ideal child as a precocious political activist, children had been drawn into campaigns around the general issues of the day, such as collectivization, industrialization, and the transformation of culture. The Second Five-Year Plan, instituted in 1932, on the other hand, specifically named education, and especially the achievement of learning targets and the maintenance of discipline in schools, as a central priority.[17]

During the 1920s, educational policy favoured collective forms of learning, such as 'the brigade method', which meant that children were not assessed individually on their classroom performance, but on the performance of their 'brigade', or 'team', in its entirety. (In practice, this meant that the hardest-working and most competent pupils were usually 'elected' by the brigade to act as their representatives when oral testing took place, a procedure that, obviously, provided shelter for the bewildered, the terrified and the idle.) In 1932, however, the 'brigade method' was officially declared dead, and pupils began to receive assessments on their performance as individuals. The 'shock workers' at that time being celebrated in factories were given a miniature equivalent in the 'shock pupil'. The pages of *Pioneer Pravda* began to feature pictures of determined schoolroom stars, who, unlike the child activists of the 1920s, were usually female, rather than male, and who – the admiring articles about them suggested – managed to combine a sense of commitment to the general good with the achievement of excellent results in formal education.[18] And also in 1932, the Pioneer movement began to have 'the quality of learning' as a central part of its brief. It became entrenched far more firmly in schools: these, rather than workplaces or apartment blocks, now became the usual location of Pioneer troops.[19] On the one hand, this meant that school discipline could be reinforced by Pioneer discipline (a slack or disruptive pupil could be disgraced by being expelled from the Pioneers). But on the other, it meant that academic achievement began to carry prestige within the Pioneer movement. High-achieving pupils would be singled out for fast-track entry to the Pioneers, while lazy, disruptive or incompetent ones would have their admission delayed. They might even (if their behaviour were exceptionally improper) be denied permission to enrol at all.

These measures set out a view of children that would have been considered reactionary and bourgeois in the 1920s. They heralded an era in which more and more distance was put between children and direct involvement in politics and in social issues. This idea was brought out also at the First Congress of Soviet Writers in 1934, where prominent children's writers insisted that the 'fairy tale', seen by many professional educationalists in the 1920s, including Lenin's wife, Nadezhda Krupskaya, as a pernicious distraction from real life, was the ideal form of literature for children. On top of this, in 1936 came a wide-ranging official endorsement of the kind of traditional family values that were anathema to Party activists in the 1920s. That year saw the banning of abortion, and the institution of a range of measures that included more support for expectant and new mothers, an expansion of the child-care network and a tightening-up of divorce legislation. Rather than being seen as rebels against the family, children were now cherished, but subordinate, family members.

'THANK YOU, DEAR STALIN, FOR A HAPPY CHILDHOOD'

Even before this, propaganda had begun dwelling insistently on the joys of childhood and the joys of having children. The second half of 1935 and first half of 1936 might justly be described as the Soviet 'Year of the Child': children's issues were more prominent than at any other period of the country's history. During 1935 and 1936, the august Party newspaper *Pravda* carried coverage not only of new legislation, such as the Decree on Mother and Child Protection of 27 June 1936, or the lowering of the age of criminal responsibility on 7 April 1935, but also of a huge range of child-related themes – kindergartens, films for children, Pioneer palaces, child prodigies, even the manufacture of toys and of special chocolates and sweets for children. The contrast with the near-absence of 'soft' items of this kind in the early 1930s, or indeed from the beginning of 1937 onwards, is very striking.

The material about consumer goods for children had a political background that went beyond the status of the family. In 1933, Stalin had declared that all Soviet citizens had the right to a 'prosperous life'; in 1935, he had come out with a famous dictum, 'Life has become better, life has become jollier'. The preferred image of the nation was now 'one big friendly family', united in celebration.[20] By extension, the miniature version of a 'prosperous', 'jolly' existence was the 'happy childhood' that propaganda now insisted all Soviet children enjoyed. The official slogan, 'Thank You Dear Stalin for a Happy Childhood' was launched in 1935.[21] And the first issue of *Pioneer Pravda* for 1936 carried an item called 'The Daydreams of Happy Children', in which children talked about their fantasies of learning to ski or skate, or ride, or play chess, as well as, of course, their fantasies about meeting Stalin.

The Pioneer movement also began to offer more and more practical help to children with 'daydreams' of this kind. From 1934 onwards, the 'hobby circle' facilities in the movement were expanded. In 1936 came the opening of the first 'Pioneer palaces', opulent leisure centres in the major cities which provided showcases for hobby activities and for Pioneer festivals – especially New Year's Day celebrations with decorated fir trees, singing and dancing, and gift ceremonies compèred by 'Father Frost' and 'The Snow Maiden'. Local 'Houses of Pioneers' had humbler facilities for children who could not be accommodated in the main 'palaces', so that most children had access to a 'hobby circle' of one kind or another, though not necessarily the one it would have been their 'daydream' to join.[22]

As notions of ideal childhood shifted, new child heroes came to the fore. From the mid-1930s, there was an upsurge of images of child prodigies. Writers, musicians and artists were showcased in the 'Young Talents' programme, taking part in concerts at the Bolshoi Theatre, touring the country, and being introduced to Party leaders.[23] Really outstanding school pupils or artistic *vunderkindy* (Soviet *Wunderkinder*) might even be introduced to Stalin himself – and then write a memoir, for the envy and amazement of other children.[24] The apolitical character of these model children's achievements, as written up by the press, is striking. Not one of them had, say, distributed 2,000 election leaflets, organized a large-scale political meeting in a school or set up an exhibition to mark the twentieth anniversary of the Revolution, let alone confronted an 'enemy of the people'. Certainly, the fact that they were Pioneers was usually mentioned, but much greater emphasis was placed on their capacity for outstanding achievement in some non-political field: music, school work or, occasionally, manual work, than on their ideological rectitude.[25] Large numbers of them came from major cities and from middle-class families, a point that further underlined how unpolitical the ideal image of the child had become by that time.

Not surprisingly, given this background, the mid-1930s, the point at which Pavlik Morozov became famous throughout the Soviet Union, also marked the high-water mark of his reputation. The extraordinary Politburo decision of 17 July 1935 to raise a statue to him was not in fact followed by the erection of a monument. And though the decision was reiterated the following year, at the Politburo's meeting on 29 June 1936 (and this time with an exact location specified, 'next to the Alexander Gardens by the entry on to Red Square along the Zabelin Approach'), this, too, had no consequences.[26] Gorky, Pavlik's number one patron, had died suddenly on 18 June 1936;[27] the reiteration of the monument measure eleven days after his demise was no doubt intended as a tribute, but there was now no one with real power who backed the idea of a central-Moscow monument.

Perhaps sensitive to the patronage vacuum, *Pioneer Pravda* journalists mounted a high-profile campaign during 1937 and 1938 in the effort to jump-start the memorial project. On 2 September 1937, the paper lambasted the procrastination of the Moscow city authorities. Three successive deadlines for the monument's erection had been missed, the designs for the statue were all unsuitable, and the original funds budgeted had all been used up. These strictures appear to have had some effect: the following year, a competition was held to choose a design for the monument, and a model by Isaak Rabinovich was selected for reproduction in bronze.[28] But in the event Pavlik was never to get his statue on Red Square: a plan that would have made him the most prominent child in Soviet monumental history (indeed, perhaps the monumental history of any nation) was silently shelved. And Eisenstein's film *Bezhin Meadow*, which was directly inspired by the story of Pavlik Morozov, ended up banned. According to rumour, Stalin's damning judgement – 'We cannot allow any small boy to behave as though he were Soviet power itself' – was the decisive factor in this.[29]

The extent to which Pavlik's reputation declined at this point should not be exaggerated. Pioneer journals continued to print material about him, and texts about the boy proliferated. Apart from Yakovlev's biography and other 'factual' accounts of the life, they included Eisenstein's *Bezhin Lug*, Alymov and Aleksandrov's *Song of a Pioneer Hero* (quoted in Chapter 2) and a poem by Sergei Mikhalkov. This last was an immensely ambitious young poet who was in time to become not only the *de facto* Soviet 'poet laureate' for children, but also the author of the words to the 1943 national anthem (Mikhalkov, a great survivor, lived long enough to rewrite the text when it was reinstated as the Russian national anthem in 2001). In Mikhalkov's poem about Pavlik, the boy, growing up in the (clearly symbolic) 'grey fog' of a taiga district lying 'to the side of the great route', fearlessly exposed his father's misdeeds:

Morozov Pavel the enemies he pillaged,
He taught others how to fight the fight.
Standing up in front of the whole village,
He brought his father's crimes into the light.
(Repeat last two lines)

Behind the village thick lush grass was growing
The corn was ripe and standing in the fields.
Pavlik's family with vengeance they were glowing,
Threatening him with murder for his deeds.

And one day, on a tranquil eve in summer,
In a tranquil hour, when even leaves don't stir,
From the taiga with his little brother
Pasha the Communist did not return.

[. . .]
Raising the flag of dawn, red freedom's banner,
In this place so far from the great road,
Pavlik Morozov by kulaks he was battered,
In the woods the Pioneer was stabbed.[30]

Mikhalkov's lyrics drew heavily on extant legends about Pavlik, including Yakovlev's book and Alymov's song, from which the motif of 'non-return' was lifted directly. However, in Mikhalkov's version Pavlik was killed in the orthodox way – by stabbing – and the father's crime was left unspecified.

A comparison of these three texts already indicates an extremely important feature of Pavlik legends – their instability. This applied to incidental motifs – the person to whom Pavlik made his denunciation might be the local teacher or an OGPU representative, who in turn might be named Bykov, Dymov or something else again (or indeed not named at all); the father's crime might be forging papers or hiding grain; the murder might be committed with a knife or with an axe; Pavlik might be blond or there again dark-haired. But it also applied to more fundamental constituents of the legend – the boy's character, his actions and the reasons why he had done what he had done. As notions of ideal childhood shifted, representations of Pavlik were manipulated to take account of the new qualities that were considered admirable in children.

SCHOOL SWOT AND PRIZE PIONEER

The process of writing in new qualities began very early. Already on 15 October 1932, the first detailed *Pioneer Pravda* report was topped not only by a headline screaming 'Let Us Increase Class Vigilance!' but by a second header, in rather smaller print: 'We Shall Respond to Kulak Wiles by a Shock Campaign for Knowledge'.[31] In fact, Solomein's biography, where Pavel's main contact with school was to agitate for a Pioneer troop to be opened there,[32] and where far more emphasis was placed on the boy's political campaigning than on his dedication to his homework, was already out of phase with the times when it appeared in 1933. Part of this can perhaps be ascribed to Solomein's own lack of grasp of what was required when constructing the life of a Stalinist hero.[33] He was, after all, only a provincial journalist, and a man of little education. But emphasizing Solomein's disadvantages ignores the fact that even a more sophisticated writer might have been caught unawares by the shifting aesthetic values of 1932–3. When repudiating Solomein's book, Gorky was not measuring his picture of Pavlik Morozov against an already congealed image of the boy: rather, he was seeing Pavlik's *potential* for transformation into a heroic legend of a new, Stalinist kind.

Whether because of Gorky's direct influence, or as a result of the tone of the times generally, or both, later biographies of Pavlik were far more hagiographical in presentation than Solomein's. For instance, the motif of 'Pavlik as outstanding pupil' was added to the brew. Yakovlev turned the boy into the 'top pupil' in the class, able to keep up even when he was forced to miss school because of work responsibilities.[34] In Valya Borovin's epic poem, also published in 1936, Pavel 'knew his lessons so well he always got "excellent"'[35] (a considerable achievement, bearing in mind that the mark of 'excellent' did not exist until the autumn of 1932). According to Smirnov, it was not just Pavel's 'independence' but his 'intellect' that irritated his grandfather.[36]

Alongside the new commitment to educational targets and to discipline in schools, accounts of Pavlik's life faithfully reflected the shift in the Pioneer movement from an emphasis on revolutionary

Pavlik tells the local teacher what his father has done.
(Aleksandr Yakovlev, *Pavlik Morozov*, 1936)

consciousness to an emphasis on ritual – or, in the jaded words of the poet Naum Korzhavin, who joined the Pioneers in 1935, 'the suppression of the revolutionary spirit that had so attracted me by some kind of magical-mystical mumbo-jumbo'.[37] A 1934 *Pravda* article described Pavlik as having 'spread pro-kolkhoz propaganda', which reduced his activities to the level of leafleting or addressing meetings.[38] And Smirnov's 1938 biography gave more attention to military-style drilling than to Pioneer activism, and focused more on the process of Pavlik's swearing the Pioneer oath than on his revolutionary convictions.[39] By the late 1930s, the Pioneer tie had acquired the status of a religious object, and Pioneers were hectored about the need to wear one at all times. Accordingly, Pavlik's photographic portrait was retouched in 1939 to show a tie proudly displayed round the boy's neck: a tie also formed a focal point of Rabinovich's design for the monument.[40] In the 1920s, ties had not been obligatory even on demonstrations, and Pioneer uniforms had been so scarce in rural districts that they were even awarded as prizes for good behaviour; ten years later, the past was reinvented to suggest that tie-wearing had always been an intrinsic part of Pioneer affiliation.[41]

The playing-down of Pavlik as an active political force, and representation of him as a kind of boy cadet, was not the only change. The new emphasis on the Pioneer movement as a force for disseminating 'cultured leisure' to children also came through. Yakovlev's 1936 biography opened with a scene of Pavel going hunting – not for the sake of obtaining food supplies (as would have been the reality of the time), but as a sport. In a tribute to the contemporary obsession with *vunderkindy*, Pavel's unusual abilities were stressed: where his father came home with nothing, the boy managed to shoot two birds all by himself.[42]

As the Pavlik myth was accommodated to the mid-1930s ideology of 'happy childhood', the 'junior vigilante' theme began to be soft-pedalled. Even in the early 1930s, denunciation of a parent had not always been treated with unqualified admiration. Certainly, the Pavlik tale was not unique in its insistence on children's duty to denounce criminal parents, but the gloating tone of the early *Pioneer Pravda* reports was not the only alternative. In Aleksandr Afinogenov's 1931 play *Fear*, Natasha, a ten-year-old Pioneer, reported her scientist father to one of his work colleagues for lying about his social origins on careerist grounds. She made the denunciation in extreme distress:

NATASHA: But why do I want to cry so much? Pioneers don't cry, Pioneers are always jolly. (*Bursts into tears and covers her face with a cushion.*)

Enter BOBROV.

BOBROV: Natasha, little girl, look at you here all alone . . . (*Takes her hand.*)

NATASHA: I can't cope any more . . . I . . . I wanted to tell Auntie Klara. I'm so sorry for Papa, and I'm not saying anything. The silence is weighing me down.

BOBROV: Did Papa do something nasty to you?

NATASHA: It's not me he did something nasty to. He's deceived everyone. Oh, Uncle Kolya, why do I want to cry so much? Can I tell you all about Papa's mother? We're friends, you and me, aren't we?

BOBROV: Of course, friends understand everything.[43]

Still from Sergei Eisenstein's film *Bezhin Meadow* (1936). (British Film Institute)

According to this view of things, denouncing parents was seen as something about which Pioneers were likely to hesitate: it was a tragic necessity, rather than a task to be relished.

Interesting in this context is the treatment of the Pavlik story by Eisenstein in his film *Bezhin Meadow* (1936). Eisenstein himself claimed that the film was directly based on the Morozov story.[44] But many changes were made. The fact that dark-haired, surly Pashka Morozov (as depicted by Solomein) turned into Styopok, an animated Aryan blond à la Quex (a transformation requiring the use of hair dye on the child actor),[45] was not remarkable. Even in *Pioneer Pravda*'s second report in 1932, Pavlik had been 'radiant haired'. More significant was the fact that the circumstances of the boy hero's murder were altered. In *Bezhin Meadow*, Styopok discovered his father's dishonesty accidentally, while taking part in surveillance of the kolkhoz barns as one of the local Pioneers. In this way, the exposure of the man's dishonesty became a collective, not just a personal, affair. And, though Styopok duly became the victim of a murderous attack, the denunciation *followed*, rather than preceded this. Styopok did not deliver a ruthless condemnation in court: instead, he conveyed with his dying breath to his Pioneer comrades that the man who had killed him was his father: 'My father . . . shot me . . . he's in the woods . . . over there . . .'[46]

Though the denunciation motif usually figured in later histories of Pavlik,[47] it was presented in more muted fashion by the versions dating from the mid-1930s than by the earlier ones. According to *Pioneer Pravda* in October 1932, 'At the trial bright-haired Pavel appeared as a witness, and his voice did not tremble when he said: "I, uncle judge, do not appear here as a son, but as a Pioneer. And I say, 'My father is a traitor to the October Revolution!'"'[48] Oleg Shvarts, also reporting on the trial not long after its occurrence, in 1933, stated that Pavel had given his evidence 'unhesitatingly and clearly'.[49] Yakovlev, on the other hand, writing three years later, described Pavel as telling his teacher 'anxiously and confusedly', and then 'anxiously' making his statement to the court.[50] Even in the versions of the text that appeared during the Great Purges, Pavel was usually a less than enthusiastic denouncer. In Smirnov's version, he needed to be reassured by his teacher that, yes, 'you even have to inform on your father if he's an enemy'. He also had to have his courage bolstered by his friends ('Look out, Pavlik, don't be scared! Tell the whole truth') before the court hearing.[51] Similarly, in the anniversary item published in *Pioneer Pravda* on 4 September 1939, Pavlik gave his evidence at the court in a spirit of humility and hesitation: 'It hurts to say this, but my father is an enemy of the Party and the people, and he should be punished!'

In tandem with the growing reluctance of the son to act as witness for the prosecution went the systematic blackening of the father in order to make him seem a more worthy object of denunciation. In later versions of Pavlik's biography, such as Smirnov's (1938), the man was represented not just as a swindler and a drunk, but also as an abusive husband and parent, routinely violent to his wife as well as his children.[52] Now Pavel's denunciation had become a matter not only of civic duty, but of self-defence. The new material recalled a well-publicized case of 1930, during which Kostya Chekletov had reported to his Pioneer troop the behaviour of his drunken and abusive father and stepmother, who meted out daily beatings with sticks, boots and bottles, leading to criminal proceedings and eventually to a show trial.[53]

TERROR AND SILENCE

Reworking of the Pavlik legend during the mid-1930s, then, included not only writing *in* of a new motif – Pavlik as exemplary schoolboy – but the writing *down* of two of the original motifs – Pavlik as vigilante within the family, and Pavlik as instrument of social vigilance at large. This motif manipulation in turn raises questions that at first sight seem puzzling. Why should Pavlik have been 'elevated' precisely at a point when the concept of the ideal relationship between parents and children was changing? And why was so much done to promote a new child hero on the 1920s activist pattern at a moment when Pioneer work was supposed to be anchored in the institutional work of the school? Finally, why should the denunciation motif have been played down during the years of the Great Terror, when denunciation as social practice was more prevalent than ever before?

The answer to these questions lies partly in the ideological tenor of the times. Present-day Northern Ireland has been described by the novelist Bernard McLaverty as a society with 'an elephant in the living-room': a problem so embarrassingly large and intrusive that nobody ever addresses it. Stalinist culture, on the other hand, resembled a living room where everyone knows that the tea-cosy in the corner conceals a severed head, rather than a silver teapot, but no one alludes to this distasteful fact, while talking constantly and obsessively about the beauty of the tea-cosy. As political terror spread on a scale unseen even under Soviet power, so too did a rhetoric of 'humaneness' prohibiting direct references to denunciation, arrest and incarceration.[54] In this society where everything was constricted by censorship, references to the existence of censorship were forbidden; equally, the underpinnings of the terror process, such as denunciations, were carefully concealed from view. So far as the Soviet press was concerned, the Great Purges existed solely at an elevated level, in the form of the bringing to book of state criminals. These men were openly vilified in the Soviet press by persons who had the authority to speak with the voice of the nation, such as the State Prosecutor, Andrei Vyshinsky, but the mechanics by which they had been brought to trial were never discussed. In the circumstances, an informer – however public-spirited his action in bringing criminals to justice – made at best an uneasy sort of hero. Such a person exposed mechanisms that were supposed to be kept hidden; he was also, in Stalin's accurate diagnosis, an insignificant individual who took the power of the Soviet state on himself. It therefore began to be emphasized that denunciation of the right kind was not only a supremely disinterested action carried out for the purest of motives, but also a *mediated* action – one carried out with the sanction of higher powers. Hence the presence, in later versions of the Pavlik story, of an adult – a local schoolteacher, an OGPU plenipotentiary – to whom the hero lays bare his soul.

The transformation of Trofim Morozov into a domestic tyrant, and Pavel into a victimized child, muted the disturbing force of the original myth – the son who would stop at nothing to see his father eliminated. This was in harmony with the elevation of Joseph Stalin, from 1935 onwards, as a supremely good, kind, yet also stern, father for children. It also fitted with a drive, evident from the mid-1930s, to enforce the authority of parents over children, rather than vice versa. For example, new rules for Pioneers promulgated in 1937 made it incumbent upon members to show not only respect to their elders, but also 'love to parents'.[55] In this context, Pavlik's denunciation of his father became an embarrassment. It is notable that Pavlik was recommended to the Politburo in 1935 merely as 'a victim of the kulaks', rather than as the implacable instrument of justice within the family.[56]

Of course, the problem could neatly have been solved had Pavlik been shown as denouncing one father (his relation by blood) in order to espouse another (Joseph Stalin). But the practical difficulty here was that Pavlik's cult came into existence before the wholesale promotion of Stalin's to children began. Accordingly the 'devoted to Stalin' motif came up only in later accounts of Pavlik's life, and was rare even there.[57] On the whole the motif of betrayal of the natural father in order to pay tribute to the symbolic father was implied rather than stated.

It was in any case not so much Pavlik's betrayal of his father *in itself* as the commitment to horizontal surveillance in the abstract, and to collective rather than personal ties, which was considered the boy's main virtue. Gorky, as we have seen, regarded the boy as a hero for whom 'ties of the spirit' were more important than 'ties of blood'.[58] Denunciation in this generally socially interested way continued to be propagandized well after the motif of Pavel as denouncer of his father had begun to be played down. Especially celebrated were children who brought to the attention of the authorities suspicious foreigners lurking in border zones; they were evoked in dozens of newspaper stories and works of fiction from 1936 onwards.[59]

This general attachment to civic denunciation remained in later versions of the Pavlik story. The boy might expose his father's guilt with reluctance, but was still an energetic denouncer of grain-concealing kulaks in the village.[60] This ties in with a general effort to propound denunciation, among both children and adults, as a clinical public ritual, rather than as shameful and furtive sneaking. A pedagogical manual published in 1940 instructed teachers that pupils should be exhorted to mount accusations publicly. If teachers could not induce pupils to do this, they should refuse to proceed on the basis of the information. In the same way, this manual emphasized the disinterested and overt character of Pavlik Morozov's actions: he, alongside 'other children who protected and are still protecting public property', was to be used as an example in pep talks about the importance of respect for such property.[61]

But the most significant reason for the apotheosis of a hero who was in many ways so out of kilter with the new expectations of child behaviour was that encouraging emulation of Pavlik's activities in a precise sense was not the only, or even the main, purpose of disseminating the legend. It is highly questionable whether the Soviet authorities wanted to encourage large-scale denunciation by children. Such records as exist of contacts between children and the security services suggest that the latter were often unprepared to treat the former as serious informants. A teenage girl who took the extraordinary step of voicing her dissenting views directly to the NKVD could barely persuade the authorities to take her into custody. And when the future poet Lev Druskin and his companions from the children's writing club in Leningrad attempted to telephone the NKVD to defend the club's director, who had been arrested in 1937, they were roughly told by the operative who answered to mind their own business.[62] The Stalinist authorities never provided anything resembling the confidential hotlines for children now operating in many Western countries (and Russia). There was no number that you could dial to squeal on Papa, or indeed on anyone else. Denunciation of children by children as a means of regulating discipline in schools and in the Pioneer movement was encouraged; denunciation as a way of vying for authority with adults, and of participating in the world of politics, was regarded with deep suspicion.

'A LIFE FOR THE MOTHERLAND'

All in all, one has to conclude that Pavlik was meant to be something both more, and less, than a model of denunciation. He was supposed to be a model of Pioneer behaviour, an epitome of the code that the local teacher expounded to her class in Yakovlev's biography: 'A real Pioneer is someone who studies very well, maintains discipline, does work in the troop, reads books and newspapers. A real Pioneer is an example to all.'[63] Yet at the same time, he was propagandized not as an everyday and imitable hero of this kind, but as an *impossible* hero, a child who took patriotism and civic duty to the point of no return. Not for nothing did a 1934 *Pravda* article begin by describing him as 'murdered by his grandfather' – underlining what placed him beyond the ken of most children.[64] In similar vein, the citation for the sixth anniversary of the boy's death in *Pioneer Pravda* presented him as an object of emulation in a very abstract sense: 'All Soviet children want to be like Pavlik Morozov, they are ready to give up all their strength, *and if necessary even their lives*, for the beloved motherland.'[65] In accounts of this kind, Pavlik was an outstandingly vivid example of children's 'revolutionary consciousness and courage' precisely because he had performed the supreme act of self-sacrifice, and laid down his own life. It was the sheer implausibility of his heroism that made it so admirable.

Generally, in twentieth-century children's literature, as Alison Lurie has pointed out, the death of a protagonist was an unusual or exceptional event.[66] During the late Soviet era, death was one of the topics that children's publishing houses deemed intrinsically inadmissible for their audience.[67] In the 1920s, Soviet literature – for all its willed non-conformity in some respects – conformed to the general rule. Stories for older children often represented a world of almost unbearable bleakness. In Vitaly Bianki's story 'Karabash' the young heroine's favourite dog died of rabies, and in Aleksandr Neverov's novel *Tashkent the Abundant*, a small boy crossed half Eurasia during the famine year of 1921, enduring the death of his younger travelling companion on the way, only to find, when he reached the city of fabled promise, 'they're hungry here too'. Yet even in texts like these, the central character survived.

Deaths of political heroes, however, were allowed to breach the taboo – indeed, they were honoured with grisly fervour from the early days of the Revolution. In 1920, a schoolgirl wrote in the newspaper put out by a provincial section of Proletkult, the 'proletarian arts' association, how deeply moved she had been by the funeral of a Bolshevik political martyr: 'I have quite often been present at funerals, even sometimes those of people close to me, but I have never before sensed the feeling that suffused me at comrade Zhabrov's obsequies. This was no petty feeling of pity, no! I even envied the fact that he had been able to fight and to perish so gloriously for a better future.'[68] Lenin's death in 1924 was the occasion for national mourning, and children were drawn into this as well, being encouraged by their schoolteachers to write commemorative poems and to sketch designs for a memorial to the dead leader.[69] Not only adults, dead children, too, were heroically commemorated. In May 1925, for example, a troop of Pioneers in Sverdlovsk were celebrating 'Soviet Sailors' Day', and hearing talks on the 'Kominter' [*sic*]. But they were also organizing 'the funeral of an Octobrist', and absorbing didactic material on 'funerals in the old style and the new style'.[70]

In the early 1930s, the death of a child hero became a regular occurrence in texts intended for consumption by young audiences. These included not only Ekk's film *Road into Life*,[71] but also Eduard Bagritsky's poem 'Death of a Pioneer Girl', where Valentina defied her parents on her deathbed by refusing to make the sign of the cross, and raising instead her feeble arm in a Pioneer salute.[72] However, the most extended treatment of child martyrdom was *The Military Secret* (1933), a story written by Arkady Gaidar, a former boy partisan in the Civil War, and one of the most popular adventure story writers of the 1930s.

The Military Secret was serialized by *Pioneer Pravda* a few months after the Morozov story was reported. This stirring tale, which was a staple of the school syllabus for the best part of five decades, consisted of two intersecting narratives, a frame and a story-within-a-story, both dealing with heroic death. The frame narrative, an entertaining and mostly light-hearted account of children enjoying their summer at a Pioneer camp on the Southern coast, took an unexpectedly bitter twist when one of the children, Alka, the son of a Communist engineer overseeing construction work nearby, was murdered by the brother of a corrupt foreman recently sacked by his father. The story-within-a-story was narrated by Alka (in collaboration with Nata, the children's Pioneer leader), and so worked as a kind of oblique prophecy of his death. Its burden was as follows: after the bellicose *Burzhuiny* (a distortion of 'bourgeois') attack the peaceful Soviet Union, the inhabitants rise to defend their motherland. Eventually, when the adults have all departed, and help is still needed, little Malchish rounds up a team of boys and goes off to the front. Only the perfidious Plokhish refuses to join the detachment, and later, he is directly responsible for Malchish's capture by the *Burzhuiny*. Interrogated by his enemies, Malchish dies under torture, but without giving anything away. He is buried with full battle honours, and his monument becomes the focus of the nation's tributes:

> The ships sail past – greetings to Malchish!
> The pilots fly past – greetings to Malchish!
> The trains run past – greetings to Malchish!
> And the Pioneers go past – greetings to Malchish![73]

The cluster of these various fictions of child martyrdom – the reports of Pavlik Morozov's death, the stirring tales of Valentina and Malchish – around the fifteenth anniversary of the October Revolution (the autumn of 1932) is highly significant, given Soviet culture's obsession with mathematically exact commemoration. Already in the summer, the Pioneer press was carrying 'hero' items, but having to make do with humdrum cases, like that of Pioneer Abrosimov, who saved a train from an accident by alerting the driver to a broken rail.[74] A more romantic child hero came as a godsend. In November 1932, the children's magazine *Friendly Lads* placed Pavlik Morozov, whom it described as having 'perished heroically at the hands of kulaks in the struggle for the victory of socialism', at the centrepiece of a spread dedicated to the October Revolution.[75] In some accounts (such as the 15 October 1932 *Pioneer Pravda* story), Pavlik's age was given as fifteen, though this would have made him too old to be a Pioneer, or indeed a primary-school pupil.[76] The point was that he needed to have been born in autumn 1917 to fit the 'revolutionary martyr' role. Evoking the 'coevals of the Revolution', young people who were the very lifeblood of the new society, was more important than sticking to bald facts.[77]

The connection with the Revolution gave the Pavlik legend a specific significance in representational terms. It, like texts such as Bagritsky's 'Death of a Pioneer Girl' and Gaidar's *Military Secret*, was intended as a Soviet foundation myth for child audiences. Heroes of this kind were the equivalents to the adult martyrs whose funerals had been one of the first legitimating acts organized by the Bolshevik regime on coming to power.[78] Pavlik and his contemporaries reminded children of the sacrifices that had been made so that they could live in what was then routinely proclaimed to be the most paradisiacal country in the world for children.

At the same time, the continuing emphasis on martyrdom brought home to children who had won all-Soviet piano or chess competitions, who had exceeded adult cotton-picking norms or (to descend into bathos) come top of their class at school, that their achievements were negligible before the achievements of a hero such as Pavlik or Malchish, who had laid down his life for his country. The emphasis on rewards for outstanding children had been accompanied by a good deal of anxiety about 'spoiling' and the likelihood that those rewarded would get above themselves and become 'whiny and capricious'.[79] The lives of heroes such as Pavlik Morozov or Malchish reminded achievers that there were higher destinies than their own, and therefore encouraged 'self-criticism' and 'work on the self', two of the central techniques by which a Stalinist identity was manufactured. As a 1935 article in *Pioneer Leader* demanded, in a series of troubling rhetorical questions: 'Does it take courage to unmask one's own father, if he turns out to be a class enemy? And can you be courageous at all, if you are not a pilot, a stratonaut or a deep-sea diver, but just an ordinary Pioneer?'[80]

NATIONAL HERO

As he was raised to 'apotheosis', Pavlik developed in several ways. First, he became the ideal Pioneer hero, exemplifying the fashionable virtues of the day – diligence in the schoolroom, concern for his fellows, modest participation in the political causes of the day.[81] Second, he became the most important star in a constellation of child martyrs, whose supreme sacrifice on behalf of their nation reminded children who had achieved notoriety in other ways that they had still much 'work to do on themselves'. Third, his vigilante role was softened, with his denunciation of his father becoming more reluctant and more hesitant. It was seen now as an unpleasant and extreme civic act, rather than as a glorious feat of revolutionary zeal.

Evolved at the centre of Soviet cultural politics, the altered Pavlik myth spread out to the provinces as well, affecting perceptions of the boy in his home district of the Urals as well as everywhere else. In the first months after Pavlik's death, as we have seen, the local papers maintained some independence, continuing to push their 'class war' line even at the trial, more than two months after the central press had got hold of the story. Equally, the first anniversary of Pavlik's death was a major local event. On 24 August 1933, the 'Komsomol page' of *Tavda Worker* published a long list of what was planned to mark the occasion. As a build-up, there would be 'early completion of the harvest targets', Pioneer rallies, and Komsomol gatherings. Then, on 3 September itself, would come a special number of the 'Komsomol page', celebratory meetings for Pioneers (including one addressed by Tatiana Morozova), radio talks and speeches and the organization of Pavlik Morozov shrines in every school in the district. Generally, the occasion was to be used to spearhead the development of Pioneer work: 'The Komsomol and Pioneer organizations are to be mobilized so that from the very first days of the school year it is possible to ensure the development of children's initiative and energy towards carrying out work of the right kind in Pioneer troops and schools [. . .] all under the slogan "Let our Pioneer troop train many more Pioneers like Pavlik Morozov!"'[82]

On 3 September, *Tavda Worker* followed this wish-list up with an interview with Tatiana Morozova, looking saintly in a kerchief, and an item reporting that Gerasimovka was now the home of a flourishing Pioneer troop, with a membership of fourteen children. And in the late autumn a campaign began to collect funding for a monument to Pavlik.[83] Indicative also of Pavlik's 'local hero' status in the first year after he died was the fact that the first biography of him was not published by a metropolitan 'youth interest' press, such as Young Guard, but by a Sverdlovsk publishing house, Uralkniga (Uralbook). To be sure, it is uncertain how much currency the cult had among locals at the grassroots – in December 1933, *Tavda Worker* was fulminating about the very small amount of money that had actually been collected to fund the Morozov memorial.[84] But local Party and Komsomol officials certainly put efforts into promoting it.

By 1934, however, things had changed. Now, *Tavda Worker* marked Pavlik's anniversary by only a single item, a pious article that could have appeared in any Soviet magazine or book, wherever published. 'Pavlik combined all the best qualities. He was a good Pioneer, the most excellent among all excellent pupils,[85] public-spirited, the best helpmate to his mother, and the best friend to his little brothers.' Local readers, who must have known very well where Gerasimovka was, were told that it was forty versts [*sic*] from the district centre, and given all sorts of (not very accurate) information about its backwardness in late 1932. The only 'personal' element in the article was a statement at the end that the number of Pioneer troops in Tavda district had risen to fifty-three from thirty-six, that there were now several hundred more Pioneers than the previous years, and that there was 'more than one collective farm' on the land where Pavlik had roamed.[86] But all of this could perfectly well have appeared in the central Pioneer press.

Hearing about the local hero at second hand continued to be the pattern right up until the 1960s. Certainly, work was still done in the Urals to commemorate the boy. In 1934, the newly formed collective farm in Gerasimovka was named after him; by October, it was reported to be leading the district at large in production terms.[87] In July 1939, the Provincial Executive Committee of the Communist Party in Sverdlovsk resolved to restore the dwelling in Gerasimovka where he had grown up, and to raise a statue to him there; this decision was confirmed by the Provincial Soviet of Deputies in August of the following year.[88]

The push to commemoration was felt in Gerasimovka as well. In 1940, the Executive Committee of the village soviet commissioned a portrait bust of Pavlik, carefully organizing a viewing by Pavlik's brother Aleksei, his cousin, and two friends in order to check that it was a true likeness (the witnesses dutifully agreed that it was).[89] In 1941, a Pavlik Morozov museum opened in Gerasimovka, using the former village soviet building.[90] Yet at the same time, there was a strong feeling now that Pavlik was no longer local property. In the words of a woman exposed to the Morozov cult in the late 1930s: 'Everyone was proud that he was from the Urals. But he was definitely an all-Soviet hero. [. . .] We thought of him as a Hero of the Soviet Union.'[91]

From the second half of the 1930s onwards, local papers contentedly printed texts generated at the centre that falsified not only Pavlik's biography, but also the geography of the Urals, subscribing to the generalized propaganda myth of the area disseminated across the Soviet Union. In local newspapers, as in Moscow ones, Gerasimovka was portrayed as a wonder village, a place with exemplary Pioneers, who kept up faithfully with their civil defence training when not attending classes in the spanking new village school, named after Pavlik Morozov, and with its very own Pavlik Morozov shrine.[92] *Tavda Worker* reported reverentially on a visit by these Pioneer paragons, accompanied by Tatiana Morozova and Pavlik's brother Aleksei, to Moscow in 1934.[93] Even the pressure to monumentalize Pavlik's life did not originate on his home patch: the first call for a memorial at Tavda level, in 1933, quoted Maxim Gorky as authority for the decision.[94] And from 1936, all the canonical texts about Pavlik would be published outside Sverdlovsk, at the heart of the Soviet publishing world, in Moscow.

'WE FELT SORRY FOR HIM'

By 1936, then, Pavlik was a universal legend, one that had broken free of its original setting and significance. But how did children themselves respond to the cult? Yury Druzhnikov has argued that the impact of Pavlik Morozov on real life was enormous. 'One has to confess, that Stalin and his mafia were able to raise an army of Morozov imitators. The myth became a reality of Soviet life.'[95] The evidence for this assertion is the torrent of stories in the juvenile press during 1933 reporting the deeds of child denouncers, and the rewards they received in the form of trips to Pioneer camps and the like.[96] But Druzhnikov's central premise, throughout his book on Pavlik Morozov, is that Soviet propaganda bore practically no relation to the truth. It seems odd in the circumstances to use Soviet propaganda as an uncorrected source for information about how children *really* responded to the legend. If one looks beyond press reports – towards sources such as memoirs and oral history – a more complicated picture emerges.

There is no doubt that the cult was in tune with the views of many young people, if not children. Much of the impetus behind its growth came, as we have seen, from the journalists at *Pioneer Pravda*, all of whom were young and identified strongly with Pavlik's supposed rebellion against patriarchal authority. They also believed fervently in the rightness of the collectivization struggle. A journalist working at *Pioneer Pravda* in the 1930s, Fruma Treivas, twenty-seven when Pavlik died, recalled in a later memoir the atmosphere of the times. When she saw starving peasants in Chelyabinsk province in 1930, she felt only limited sympathy: 'It was awful to see, but then they were kulaks, exploiters, against Soviet power. Now Pavlik Morozov, that was a real hero, so what if he betrayed his father?'[97]

Many of the early mythographers of Pavlik had additional reasons to identify with his side: they themselves came from impoverished, and in some cases unhappy, home backgrounds. Gorky's vexed relationship with his stepfather has already been mentioned. Pavel Solomein, for his part, had gone from a poor family with a brutal stepfather into a Soviet youth offender institution,[98] and, like many former inmates of such institutions, had emerged with a fierce loyalty to the system that 'saved' him. Mikhail Doroshin, who devoted a section of his narrative poem *Hate*, a fiery evocation of the collectivization campaign, to Pavlik, was another example of a provincial boy from a poor background whose imagination was moved by the legend.[99]

The message of 'duty before family' carried weight with ordinary young people from the skilled working class too. Devotion to Pavlik among women's groups and Pioneer groups at the Trekhgorka factory in Krasnaya Presnya (which played host to a delegation of Gerasimovka Pioneers and to Tatiana Morozova in 1937) endured well after the surge of top-level support for the cult had passed.[100] Audiences in cities hit by famines felt little sympathy for those they thought were the cause of their misery. In the words of a woman born in 1927, and brought up in a workers' family in Sverdlovsk, 'We all thought Pavlik had done the right thing [. . .] because his father was a kulak.'[101] Pavlik's father was, of course, not in fact (or even in the early versions of the legend) a kulak, but the later convention that he was simplified the story and made Pavlik's action readily comprehensible.

Yet Pavlik's primary meaning even among young people from the working class and peasantry was as a symbol of self-sacrifice and relentless commitment to the cause, rather than as a denouncer. A man who had served as a Komsomol activist in the 1930s, and whose memories carry particular weight because he later ended up a political exile (and so had no inclination to defend the Soviet system), insisted that the latter role had little appeal. 'I can't recall any instance of children being inspired to denounce their parents in the spirit of Pavlik Morozov, though I do know of cases where Komsomol members left their parents because they could not reconcile themselves to their views.'[102] Equally, young adults might desert their parents for self-serving reasons, as happened with Alexander Tvardovsky. Later the liberalizing editor of *Novyi Mir*, where Solzhenitsyn's *One Day in the Life of Ivan Denisovich* was published in 1962, Tvardovsky was, in the early 1930s, an ambitious provincial poet. He cut off all attempts by his family to make contact with him after his father was dekulakized: 'I can't write to you. And don't write to me.'[103]

Oral history confirms the general pattern of repudiation of relations *after* they were labelled 'enemies of the people', rather than denunciation beforehand. A woman from a Sverdlovsk working-class family very proud of its revolutionary heritage told me in September 2003 that her uncle had been so appalled by her father's arrest during the Great Purges that he had refused to allow his own mother, niece and nephew, into the house. When the three turned up to collect their New Year presents in 1938, they were not permitted to join other guests by the tree, but were received furtively in a back corridor. At the same time, she also remembered that elaborate systems of watch were maintained by the families in this proletarian area of the city in case any snooper should report the holding of parties with New Year trees to the authorities.[104] Committed to revolutionary probity they might be, but the members of this community did not hold with 'squealing' to the outside world.[105]

Much the same complex of attitudes – admiration for Pavlik in the abstract, rather than commitment to following him in every particular – seems to have obtained in children's reactions to the story. Any child who experienced institutionalized education from the mid-1930s onwards (the vast majority) was likely to have heard of Pavlik Morozov. And children readily internalized myths in the sense that they obediently wrote essays in class about whichever official heroes were on the agenda of the day. In January 1933, a group of eleven-year-olds from a school in Moscow province wrote to Nadezhda Krupskaya boasting of their progress in education and political nous, and citing Pavlik Morozov and Kolya Myagotin as role models:

> We've begun subscribing to *Pioneer Pravda* and *The Pioneer's Rallying Call*. And we've begun reading them as well. We've read about Pavlik Morozov and about Kolya Myagotin. We read about them and then our whole class told Anna Semyonovna [their teacher] that we'd be like them too. If we saw something going on at the factory [that shouldn't have been] we'd announce it to the Pioneer troop or the factory management committee. We know that women are swearing in the queues and they're swearing at the Party leaders, [and that's] because they don't know anything about the Party leaders. If someone has clawed his way into the Party because he wants to do some wrecking, then you can't blame the whole of the Party for that. We're going to help the Party, when we find out who in the Party is doing the wrecking. All of us in the class are Pioneers now, and there are 20 'shock pupils'.[106]

To be sure, exercises of this kind reflected not just children's own views, but also their awareness of what adults in authority were likely to want them to write. Anna Semyonovna, the teacher of this group of children, may not have actually dictated this letter, or directly supervised its writing; but the effects of her moral and political guidance stand out in every line. Yet children did celebrate the cult spontaneously, as can be seen in the case of Valya Borovin, sixteen at the time that he published his narrative poem about Pavlik, in 1936. Borovin had grown up in an outlying village in Vologda province, Northern Russia; he was a fervent Pioneer. And his poem represented Pavel according to the original tradition of fearless insubordination to paternal authority:

> Pashka stood up and gazed directly, boldly [. . .]
> 'As a Pioneer, I declare:
> My father is a traitor to October [. . .]
> I demand stern judgement
> On my father, a traitor to the kolkhoz.'[107]

Significantly, in Borovin's version Pavlik also appears as something less than the usual plaster saint. While he was described as an 'excellent' pupil, he was also said to have 'often got people off the hook'. What was meant by this was that he had acted as prompter when schoolmates were submitted to an oral cross-questioning by a teacher on their homework. While this practice was widespread in the schoolroom, it was clandestine, and attracted adverse commentary in the Pioneer press.[108] No life of Pavlik by an adult would ever have suggested that the boy hero could have acted as an accomplice to 'cheating'. Borovin's invention suggests he found Pavlik both a plausible and a sympathetic figure.[109]

There are other attested cases of children who absorbed the notion that fearless denunciation of ideologically suspect adults (and children) was admirable. Even if one chooses to discount reports in the children's press, the actual texts of such denunciations do turn up in archives. In 1938, for example, a provincial schoolboy wrote to *The Peasant Gazette*, ostensibly in order to enquire about the fate of A. V. Kosaryov, purged from his position as Secretary of the Central Committee of the Komsomol in that year, but actually in order to denounce two figures closer to home. He complained that the head of his school's Komsomol organization 'doznt keep dissipline', and that a fellow-pupil annoyed him by talking and joking around in class, and hogging the billiard table during recreation.[110]

Yet for all that, 'sneaking' was no more popular in Soviet schools than it was in pre-revolutionary ones, or indeed in schools the world over. In the words of Pyotr Kruzhin (born in 1921), who grew up in a Tver province village:

> I subscribed to *Pioneer Pravda* and I subscribed to *Dawn* newspaper. I swallowed at one gulp the articles that told how Pioneers of the border areas helped to arrest frontier-jumpers [. . .] I read a serial about little Pavlik Morozov's murder and dreamt about unmasking kulaks myself. Once again, however, these ideas co-existed with my dislike of tattle-tales and informers, my admiration for many kinds of illegalities, and my belief in loyalty among friends.[111]

In other words, Kruzhin found Pavlik attractive primarily as a modern alternative to the heroes of the massively popular adventure stories by Jules Verne, Mayne Reid or Fenimore Cooper, somehow spared violent death and translated to immortality.

Certainly, the fact that Pavlik had denounced his *father* was something that even patriotic Soviet children, provided they came from secure and harmonious families, tended to find more alienating than inspiring. There were, of course, exceptions, such as a Leningrad Pioneer, who, horrified when she heard her father comment sarcastically on the trial of Bukharin and Zinov'ev in 1937, 'If they're enemies of the people, then I'm a Japanese spy' (a comment she took in deadly earnest), dashed straight off to pass the information on 'to the right place'.[112] Yet behaviour of this kind was extremely rare, and should not be seen as the product solely of Soviet brainwashing. Before the Revolution, there had on occasion been children who had at least fantasized about reporting their parents to the authorities. The future writer Vasily Rozanov and his siblings, annoyed by their over-strict mother, had dreamt of denouncing her to the Tsarist police, though at this period the law offered far more muscle to parents' desire for revenge on recalcitrant children than it did to disaffected minors.[113] It is doubtful whether there was a significant growth, during the Soviet period, in the numbers of children from 'normal' homes who considered 'shopping' their parents to outsiders, though children could feel empowered by propaganda to criticize adults' behaviour in private.[114]

Early Soviet children, like many children in other cultures, had a pronounced taste for stories in which adults were represented as enemies and subjected to dreadful fates. However, in such texts retribution tended to take the form of carnival knockabout, and was not directed at parents.[115] Even if one (in psychoanalytical mode) chooses to argue that such stories reflect hidden resentment against parents as authority figures, the significant word is 'hidden'. It is clear that Russian children did not wish to recognize their hostility directly, let alone to enact it. In circumstances where the arrest and execution of parents were a real possibility, deep-seated desires for violence against parents were particularly unlikely to reach the surface. Memoirs and oral history overwhelmingly suggest that political oppression worked to encourage solidarity within the family, more than to undermine this.

Far more widespread among children than the desire to emulate Pavlik's denunciatory achievements were two other kinds of reaction. The first was fear and horror at Pavlik's fate, as recalled particularly vividly by a woman born in 1931, and of Bashkir-Tatar extraction (her father was a successful engineer in the Urals). Her first visit to the theatre was also her first encounter with the Morozov legend:

> I'd been brought up at home by my parents – I was the only daughter – with a lot of care and affection, a lot of kindness, and I'd had all these fairy stories, *The Three Little Pigs*, Huff-Huff, Huff-Puff, and Puff-Puff, all those lovely Grimm and Perrault stories,[116] that's how I'd been brought up, and then suddenly I was taken to the theatre in Chelyabinsk just after I'd started school, and there was a play – my hair still stands on end remembering it – about Pavlik Morozov, and it feels just like yesterday, and that drunken uncle of Pavlik's arrives, that Danila, and sings this song, 'Stamp the earth, my shoes, my big bast shoes, let grandpa Trofim[117] go wherever he should choose.' It was all so frightening, and my head started aching, and I went home feeling sick . . . because . . . well, they dealt with Pavlik. Of course we felt sorry for him, Pavlik, of course. That kulak, that Danila, arriving drunk, like a bandit, and singing that song [. . .] And they came in drunk and dealt with Pavlik. So were we supposed to feel sorry for those kulak bandits? Or Pavlik, who suffered because he wanted to help the starving children of St Petersburg, the peasants, the workers, the hungry doctors? That was the truth as we saw it, that's how we were brought up.[118]

To many younger children, such as this, Pavlik represented above all a tragic and hair-raising instance of martyrdom: a boy who suffered because he wanted to do good.

Among older children, admiration for Pavlik's commitment to the cause could generate a further reaction: a sense of shame at one's own level of dedication. Typical was Yakov Avidon, who remembered working hard at school and relishing the formal discipline of the 1930s classroom. But even an 'outstanding pupil' of this kind found the Morozov legend guilt-inducing rather than uplifting. 'I enjoyed the story and appreciated why Pavlik Morozov was a hero, but the story troubled me more than a little. I didn't think I could ever turn in anyone, no less a parent, but how could I be sure?'[119] Perhaps the best way to understand Pavlik's effect on children is to compare his life with the effect of the stirring but strange legend of the boy stoically refusing to cry out when his innards were gnawed by a wolf that was read in British schools with a classical curriculum during the first half of the twentieth century.[120]

In practice, therefore, even during the Stalin era, Pavlik was more important in ideology, and more appealing to children's imaginations, as a martyr and fulcrum of 'self-criticism', than he was as a model of denunciation. None of this is meant to play down the *actual* significance of denunciation. Throughout the Stalinist era, it remained a strongly encouraged social practice: indeed, 'failure to denounce' was a crime.[121] But archival research in recent years on real-life denunciations has shown that these took very varied forms, in which self-interest and petty desire for revenge played as large a part as civic virtue (in however perverted a sense). Many denouncers were not modelling themselves on Soviet heroes when they put pen to paper; they were driven by the desire to get hold of other people's living accommodation, jobs and spouses.[122] In other words, Soviet citizens would have denounced each other energetically without Pavlik Morozov, and schoolrooms would have contained tattle-tales without his example as well. The most that could be said is that Pavlik Morozov may have made the perpetrators of such activities feel ennobled. But more often, his legend gave the more politically conscientious of his readers pause for thought: would their heroism ever measure up to such high ideals? And thus they experienced exactly the sense of insecurity and dissatisfaction with one's own achievements that stories of this kind were supposed to foster, nurturing in themselves two of the quintessential Stalinist emotions, since authoritarian governance depended as much on people's readiness to blame *themselves* as it did on their readiness to blame others and report their misdeeds.

For the Soviet mythic system, it was vital that the central Pioneer hero should have been, at some level, a real character (and not just a fictional creation, like Hitler Boy Quex). Perhaps the only connection that 'Socialist Realism' had with reality (though not, of course, with literary realism) was that some of its heroes had once been alive. It was also important that Pavlik should have perished (a hero who had defied adults and lived would have conveyed too great a sense of juvenile empowerment). Yet the celebration of child martyrdom, such an effective part of the myth so far as adult audiences were concerned, also constrained the impact of the Pavlik Morozov legend on children themselves. The border-guards, Polar aviationists and Red Army soldiers also celebrated in propaganda fiction genuinely did fill children with aspirations.[123] It is interesting to note also that Schenzinger's Quex, who celebrated the most important insight given to him by the Hitler Youth Movement as 'learning to obey', had more popular appeal, at any rate judging by the numbers of editions published, than did Pavlik Morozov.[124] The most important legacy of Pavlik's death was to be an indirect one: in the mood of the Russian adolescents prepared to fight to the death in defence of their motherland once war broke out, though in at least some cases here, despair over the apparently incorrigible state of the Stalinist dictatorship was as strong a prompting as the positive desire to act as became a Soviet hero.[125] Among most children while they remained children, though, Pavlik inspired at best reluctant admiration. It was another Pioneer hero – the assertive yet submissive Timur – who was to become the object of genuine love and emulation. The next chapter will trace the process by which he came to be.

CHAPTER 6

Pavlik Eclipsed

During the late 1930s, the contents of *Pioneer Pravda*, like those of other Soviet periodicals, had a ritualized predictability. The first issue of the year was certain to contain a New Year spread, probably with pictures of a decorated fir tree and beaming children; later issues in January were likely to include articles about what fun the children were having tobogganing and ski-ing, and playing 'hunt the spy' games, during their winter holidays; and the anniversary of Lenin's death on 21 January would be marked by hagiographical tributes to the great leader, and celebration of his supposed bosom friendship with Stalin. Coverage continued this way in later months, with spreads for Red Army Day (23 February), the death anniversaries of Communist heroes, and important Soviet festivals, such as Constitution Day (5 December). Throughout the 1930s, Pavlik Morozov had been slotted into this calendar, and an issue around the anniversary of his death on 3 September had always contained a memorial item about the boy. This remained the case even after August 1935, when legislation was passed to harmonize the starting date of the school year all over the Soviet Union, and when 1 September became an important new festival, 'Study Day', celebrated by the arrival of pupils bearing flowers for their teachers, and by ceremonial drills and speeches in school halls and yards reminding pupils of their duty to study diligently in order to display patriotism and gratitude to motherland, party and their great leader Joseph Vissarionovich Stalin.

Given that Soviet festivals were marked almost as punctiliously in the press as they were in printed calendars – a boom genre of the late 1930s and 1940s (niche products for the juvenile market included a *Children's Calendar*, with colour pictures of Lenin, Stalin, fairy-tale characters and Soviet happy families), any alteration to the schedule was unlikely to be purely accidental. In the circumstances, then, it was astonishing that nothing about Pavlik was published during the first week of September 1940. Instead, on 5 September, the day when such coverage might have been most likely, *Pioneer Pravda* began serializing a story about a very different kind of Pioneer hero.[1]

TIMUR AND HIS TEAM

Unlike Pavlik, this hero was not based on a real-life prototype. He came straight out of the head of the adventure story writer Arkady Gaidar, the author of *War Secret*. *Timur and His Team*, appearing over the next few months in *Pioneer Pravda* (and later in many editions as a printed book), was a typically lively, well-crafted and entertaining piece of work by one of the Stalin era's most lastingly popular children's writers. *Timur* was set at the time of a war whose precise location and nature was unspecified (but the tale's first readers would certainly have been tempted to identify it with the Finno-Soviet conflict of the previous winter). It showed a group of children settled in a *dacha* area near Moscow turning themselves into a sort of juvenile militia responsible for keeping guard over the homes of officers serving at the front. The leader of the militia was the eponymous hero, Timur. After a series of stand-offs with a gang of child hoodlums led by one Misha Kvakov (whose surname sounds just as ridiculous in Russian as it does in English), the 'Timurites' succeeded in locking a gang member inside a defunct church, on which they posted a notice, *Inside here are the cowards who are robbing peaceful people's gardens at night*. The story concluded with order restored: 'Timur glanced round his comrades, smiled and said: "Wait . . . Let me see . . . Good! Everyone's at peace. That means that I can be at peace as well."'[2]

The activities of 'Timur and his team' were different in every respect from those of Pavlik Morozov, or even Gaidar's own

Timur and his friends lay their plans. (Illustration from Arkady Gaidar, *Timur and His Team* 1940; new edition of 1949)

Malchish. They were low-level, safe, and their target was juvenile hooliganism, rather than the adult crime or aggression that had caused the tragic death of these figures. And Timur's actions were also approved by the father of the two main female characters, Colonel Aleksandrov of the Red Army. At the end of the novel, when Aleksandrov heard about what had been going on, he warmly congratulated the boy hero: 'Their father stood up and, without pausing an instant for reflection, squeezed Timur's hand'.[3] One of the two Aleksandrov girls, Olga, who fancies herself as a social and political authority, has spent the rest of the novel expressing loud disapproval of Timur, but now she is forced to accept that his activities really have been in the best interests of collective existence. In the crucial scene of reconciliation, the senior male character appears not as 'Colonel Aleksandrov', but as 'their father' – a locution that makes him also the parent of the apparently fatherless Timur, the wise patriarchal guide of youth in general.

Timur, then, was a force for social cohesion, as unlike Pavlik as he was like the hero of a Western scouting novel, or indeed the protagonist of a mainstream adventure story such as Enid Blyton's *Famous Five* sagas.

Like other successful artists who not only survived, but prospered, under the Stalin regime (a feat that was admittedly slightly easier for children's writers than it was for their adult counterparts), Arkady Gaidar was gifted with particularly sensitive political antennae. The very name 'Timur', an unusual one in Russia, was probably intended as a tribute not only to Gaidar's own son, but also to Klimenty Voroshilov, whose adopted son (born Timur Frunze) happened to bear this name.[4] At the time when the book was written, Voroshilov was one of Stalin's closest associates, who had recently been portrayed, in Aleksandr Gerasimov's obsequious icon *Stalin and Voroshilov in the Kremlin*, striding shoulder to shoulder, greatcoat to greatcoat, with the leader, against a panorama of Southern Moscow spied over the Kremlin walls. Voroshilov not only had military connections – he was Commissar of War from 1925, and Commissar of Defence from 1934 to 1940, and was promoted to the newly revived rank of Marshal in 1935 – but was a favourite of the Pioneer press, and the recipient of hundreds of letters from children asking for his autograph, or advice on how to live. On the whole, he irritably refused the former, until provided by his assistants, in 1968, with a stack of ready-signed photographs, but he was verbosely generous with the latter: 'Under Communism everybody, everyone without exception, must and will become industrious, conscious, honest, developed in every respect, and, as it says in the [Party] programme, will successfully combine spiritual riches, moral purity and physical perfection.'[5] Voroshilov's rank was stellar; that of 'Colonel Aleksandrov' humble. Yet the military man who took other people's sons under his wing was a distant *alter ego*, invoking the patronage of the highest-placed military official in the Soviet Union for an alternative kind of child hero, a boy who worked in collaboration with adults, carrying out safe, low-level activism, and who limited his agitational and punitive work to subordinates of his own age.

The appearance of Timur marked a blatant, and very obvious, shift in the aims of the Pioneer movement. During the 1920s and 1930s, Pioneer activists had been concerned lest the movement veer too far in the direction of 'scouting' – shorthand for a politically conservative, patriotically oriented children's movement that placed a much greater emphasis on leisure and bourgeois philanthropy than on social activism. The appearance of Timur as an ideal Pioneer hero indicated that the authorities were happy to see 'scouting', in Sovietized form, become the official direction of the Pioneer movement.

The support of the Pioneer authorities for this change in orientation was underlined by the fact that Gaidar's book was promoted far more assiduously than the canonical biographies of Pavlik. This is clear above all by the size of the print-runs – which, in the centrally planned Soviet system, reflected officials' views of how important a book *ought* to be, as well as its actual popularity. Total editions of the canonical biographies of Pavlik Morozov during the 1930s were – considering the fame of the character – surprisingly modest. Solomein's life disappeared after its original run of 10,000 copies. Aleksandr Yakovlev's life was issued only three times, once in 1936, and twice in 1938; the combined print-runs of all three editions totalled 105,000 copies. Smirnov's *Pavlik Morozov* came out only once, in 1938 (the edition reached 50,000 copies); and Valya Borovin's narrative poem, *Morozov Pavel*, was issued once in 1936 with a run of 10,000 copies.[6] These figures, giving a total of 175,000 copies, compared very favourably with those for poets addressing an 'elite' adult audience such as Pasternak (whose books were set at 5,000 copies or so). But they were also significantly smaller than those for Gaidar's *Military Secret* at the period (eight editions running to a total of 555,600 copies between 1935 and 1939).[7] And *Timur and His Team* far outstripped the 1930s lives of Pavlik, and the postwar editions of Gubarev's life (90,000 copies in total from two editions in 1947 and 1948). During the years of the Second World War alone, *Timur* came out in four editions, running to a total of 200,000 copies; thereafter, the number of copies printed *per year* was 200,000–300,000.[8]

In a 1947 vignette of classic books published on the front of an official annual bibliography of children's literature, *Timur* shared the limelight with Krylov's fables, Pushkin's *The Captain's Daughter*, Tolstoy's *Childhood*, Jules Verne, Mayakovsky's children's poems, a volume of Russian folk tales and Kononov's *Tales of Lenin*, as well as a selection of recent works, mostly on wartime themes, by the premier children's writers of the day: Marshak, Abramov, Lev Kassil, Sergei Mikhalkov, Veniamin Kaverin and Valentin Kataev. None of the lives of Pavlik Morozov was featured anywhere, even in the background.[9] The promotion of the two heroes in Warsaw Pact countries was also markedly different: *Timur* was published seven times in East Germany and Rumania in the 1940s, but no book about Pavlik Morozov ever made its way into these important 'Soviet colonies'.[10]

Circulation of the written text was not the only way in which Timur was disseminated to the juvenile public. In 1940, the novel was turned into a blockbuster children's film, directed by Alexander Razumnyi, which was so successful that Gaidar immediately began work on a sequel, *Timur's Oath*, released in 1942, a year after Timur's creator had died on the battlefields of the Second World War. The cinema was immensely popular with Soviet children who had access to a screen – so much so that generations of pedagogical commentators expressed anxiety about its possible corrupting influence. The solution increasingly adopted, from the mid-1930s, was to promote films that could be seen as ideal entertainment for the entire family. Plainly, a film about Pavlik Morozov was never going to be in this category: on the other hand, a movie about a socially conscious, but obedient and charming, small boy had every chance of being well received.

At the same time, it is interesting to note that, when Gaidar's novel first came out, not all the comment on it was blandly commendatory. In 1941, for instance, *Pioneer* magazine published some letters from children complaining that Timur was a bit 'soft' and should have given his antagonists a thumping.[11] The tolerance of even good-humoured criticism of an official novel was quite exceptional, and an indication of just how confident the authorities were that Gaidar's book was genuinely popular with children. Oral history wholly confirms this impression: even adults cynical about every other aspect of Soviet existence usually maintain a sentimental spot for this hero. A man born in Northern Russia in 1935, for example, who spent much of the 1970s and early 1980s as an active dissident, favourably contrasted Timur with Pavlik Morozov: 'At least Timur was trying to help people.'[12] He also remembered having enjoyed the film. Female interviewees of the same generation often go weak at the knees when the boy is mentioned: 'We were adolescents by then [when the film came out] . . . And we were just in love with him,' one woman born in 1931 remembered. 'He was like a lamp in the dark,' another recalled.[13]

A further indication of Timur's genuine popularity was the regular appearance of exhortatory allusions to him in children's journalism, on the lines of 'Timur would never do anything like that' (or 'would always do the other'). For instance, in 1944, a critical article appeared in *Pioneer Pravda* under the title, 'Timur Never Needed a Nanny', criticizing children whose idleness made them resort to deceitful stratagems, such as telling their mother they were too busy with homework to help around the house, and at the same time telling their teacher that housework left them no time for study.[14]

A more active method of encouraging children's desire to imitate their hero was through the foundation of groups of 'Timurites', who collected waste material and scrap metal, delivered post, raised money for fighter planes, helped with child-care, and participated in inspecting black-out provision and other air-raid warden activities.[15] The formation of a self-directed children's secret society like Timur's would have attracted the opprobrium of any Soviet officials to whose attention it had come (and indeed, associations of this kind were rigorously pursued throughout the 1930s).[16] In the 1940s, attitudes to such societies were slightly less repressive, but they were still very much at the borderlines of tolerance. Lev Kassil's *Dear Boys* (1944) was an officially published adventure story centring on a group of schoolboys in a Soviet Russian small town who formed a group called the 'Blue Mountaineers', and later played an active role in anti-Fascist resistance. A critical point in the book was a confrontation between the boys and the woman supervisor of the local Pioneer centre, who was inclined to see their activities as illegitimate; as in *Timur*, this fussy female surveillance had to be corrected by the secretary of the town's Communist Party Committee, who gave the boys a thorough grilling about what they had been up to, but decided that their activities were harmless, and gave them the paternalist seal of approval.[17]

It was not considered appropriate, then, for children simply to organize and run their own societies: such societies had to be approved after the fact, or preferably (in real life, as opposed to fiction), set up with adult encouragement to begin with. However, well-regulated child activism on 'secret society' lines *within* the Pioneer movement, under the strict supervision of adults, was another matter. Accordingly, the Timur movement was not wound down after 1945 (despite another muting of child activism in general at that point), but continued to be encouraged to the end of the Stalin era, as indeed it was for another four and a half decades.[18]

THE LAW OF SILENCE

The publicity given to the Timur movement between 1941 and 1945 throws an interesting sidelight also on Soviet expectations about children's participation in the war effort. In the summer of 1941, not long after the German invasion of the Soviet Union, Arkady Gaidar wrote an impassioned article urging children and young people to learn to shoot and to do their best to defend the motherland directly. 'Take Your Weapons, Komsomol Tribe!', and 'Children and the War', published in late 1941, emphasized that young people's efforts were vital to the war effort. 'Komsomol members, schoolchildren, Pioneers, young patriots, the struggle has only just started: be aware that you will be needed in the fight.'[19] Many teenagers did in fact end up in partisan detachments and in the underground resistance, the most famous cases in point being Zoya Kosmodemyanskaya, hanged by the Nazis in 1942, and the group of Ukrainian teenagers made famous by Aleksandr Fadeyev in his myth-making novel *The Young Guard* (1945).[20] But propaganda directed at children in the Pioneer age range during the war concentrated less on these cases of all-out heroism than on lower-level kinds of contribution to victory, and especially the role of children in keeping a vigilant eye on likely spying activity by foreign infiltrators, and reporting this, as well as any enemy troop movements in the locality, to responsible, patriotic adults. The cliché war story, as published in magazines and newspapers such as *Pioneer* and *Pioneer Pravda*, had a child spotting some suspicious stranger and reporting the sighting to the local Partisan division, or else establishing that the stranger was in fact a member of the Soviet forces in disguise, and passing on vital military information, to receive warm congratulation in return. In Aleksandr Kremensky's 'Night Thunder', published in *Pioneer* magazine in 1942, for instance, boys were rewarded by a local Partisan with sugar cubes and hints about fishing bait in return for information about German troop formations next to their village. In Vadim Kozhevnikov's 'The Correspondence of Warrior Sinukov', a boy guided Partisans safely to the far side of an area patrolled by the Fascists.[21] Factual reports tended to concentrate on children entertaining troops in hospital or collecting scrap, medicinal herbs or some other useful item.[22]

In the years following the war, the same conventions of representation were obtained. In the schoolroom, children were made familiar above all with the activities of valorous adults, such as the crack pilot in Boris Polevoi's novel *A Story about a Real Man* (1947), who taught himself to fly again after losing both legs; or Aleksandr Matrosov, the tough lad from an orphanage who turned into a war hero, blocking the barrel of a machine-gun with his own body in order to save his comrades from slaughter. But they were also acquainted with the heroic achievements of individuals much nearer their own age, and in particular with the life histories of Zoya Kosmodemyanskaya and Volodya Dubinin.

The different paths to martyrdom of these two, as described in the official lives (doubt exists about the extent to which these reflect reality),[23] brought out the continuing importance of age thresholds. Volodya Dubinin, a boy Pioneer, had not fought at the Front or borne arms, though he had taken part in reconnaissance missions organized by the Partisan detachment operating in the vicinity of his native town, Kerch, on the Black Sea. His death was the result of the explosion of a mine when he was on his way to try to help sappers clear the entryways into a local quarry. Zoya, under her *nom de guerre* 'Partisan Tanya', actually saw active service, and was horribly tortured by her captors – enduring beatings, knife-cuts, the excision of a breast – before being led through the snow and hung before a press-ganged audience. Common to both stories, though, was the emphasis on staunch endurance, and the subordination of young enthusiasts to their older comrades.

Increasingly, coverage of child heroes saw them as the product of appropriate socialization, of years and decades of work by dedicated, right-thinking parents. The lives of such heroes turned into a sub-branch of advice literature on family life, stressing the virtues of an all-Soviet upbringing. Lev Kassil and Max Polyanovsky's official biography of Volodya Dubinin, *The Street of the Younger Son*, was interleaved with photographs showing a childhood that was *normalnyi* in one sense of the word – civilized and admirable, to be aspired to – rather than *normalnyi* in the sense of typical. Dubinin, in Kassil and Polyanovsky's portrayal, was a cheerful, lively little boy who had got into all sorts of scrapes, but he also came from a 'good home', with a loving mother, and a sailor father of whom he was deeply proud. And from early days, Volodya had given promise of the heroism to come – as when he defended a younger boy against bullying in the playground.[24]

A similar 'model childhood' was presented with more sententious force in an official life of Zoya Kosmodemyanskaya, and her brother Shura, written by the children's mother.[25] Also credited on the title-page – and to all intents and purposes the ghost-writer for the book – was the teacher and pedagogue Frida Vigdorova, who in the 1960s became famous for her support to Joseph Brodsky during his trial for 'parasitism', but who in the late Stalin era was best known for a diary about her life teaching in a Soviet school. The book set out a template for a successful Stalinist family life. The Kosmodemyanskaya children came from an ideal social background, one where separation from 'backward' peasant roots had been achieved before they were born: their parents were assiduous self-educators from the village who had trained as teachers and moved to the city before the children entered the world. Zoya and Shura had had a perfect upbringing, inculcated with the values of hard work and social commitment by both parents, but with their father as overall mentor and guide. As Kosmodemyanskaya (ventriloquized by Vigdorova) put it: 'Anatoly Petrovich taught me to understand that the force of moral education lay in every small detail, in every tiny action, glance and word'.[26] Each day was calmly ordered, and observed an ideal balance between work and leisure: after supper, the children would read and do their homework while their parents got on with teaching preparation, or with work for the courses they were doing to 'improve their qualifications' (that is, to earn an in-service diploma in teaching methodology). These taxing, but invigorating, duties once completed, the family would settle down to a round of some tranquil but mentally challenging game, for instance dominos, or 'Up and Down', a Soviet version of 'Snakes and Ladders' where ascents were made along the skybound bodies of airliners towards futurist domes floating somewhere in the upper atmosphere.

Naturally, the children had many interests outside the family, all of a politically correct kind. The high points of their early lives were associated with the Pioneer movement: acceptance into the Pioneers; trips to Pioneer camps; playing games taken from *Pioneer Pravda*. As ideal Pioneers, they showed a much more sophisticated range of virtues than Pavlik Morozov, even in the later versions of his legend, including not just commitment to the cause, but a sense of the movement's heroic heritage, and of the decorum best becoming its members. The pair read assiduously about famous Pioneers: favourite books included *Timur and His Team*, and preferred role models the Civil War heroine Tanya Solomakh (from whom Zoya in due course took her *nom de guerre*), and Pavel Korchagin, hero of Nikolai Ostrovsky's 1933 novel *How the Steel Was Tempered*. Shura and Zoya involved themselves in campaigns against cruelty to animals – as promoted by the Pioneer movement throughout the 1930s – and maintained a proper distance from the opposite sex.

Above all, Zoya and Shura were skilled in the kind of emotional management expected of proper denizens of late Stalinist society.

> Both Zoya and Shura revealed their feelings with great reserve, even caution. As they grew up, this trait of character became more and more sharply defined. They feared high-flown language like the plague. They were tight-lipped about expressing love, tenderness, excitement, anger and dislike. I was able to deduce that they had such feelings and inward experiences only from the look in their eyes, their silence, and the way that Zoya would stride across the room when she was distressed or excited.[27]

The central virtue manifested by the two Kosmodemyanskys was less bravery in a flamboyant sense, then, than *not giving anything away*, a virtue that had shaped 'Tanya's' ability to resist her Nazi torturers when she responded to an insistent question about Stalin's location with the bald statement, 'Comrade Stalin is at his post.'

Zoya and Shura Kosmodemyansky were integrated still further into the patriarchy than Timur. By now, parents (provided they had the right ideas) had become the primary instruments of social authority. Lives of model young people were supposed to emphasize 'Communist morality', obedience to adults in private, and in society at large. In 1943 came the imposition of a nationwide set of school rules underlining that deference and subordination to teachers and to other adults were essential. The background to this was the social upheaval brought by the war itself, which had not only orphaned millions of children, but had separated millions of others from their families, and transformed still others into 'latchkey children', left to themselves while their fathers were at the front and their mothers at the munitions factories. Both during the last years of the war, and after it finished, the question of how to impose control on Soviet youth became crucial. But every detail of the Kosmodemyanskys' life history – not just the obvious contrast between their submission and his rebellion – was at variance with the pattern set in legends about Pavlik. The supreme virtue had now become not denunciation, but silence, even at the cost of death. In the circumstances, the virtues of a hero whose most famous action was *telling* all became obscured.

SLIDING INTO HISTORY

During the years of the Second World War, Pavlik was indeed knocked from his recently ascended pedestal as the number one child hero. Coverage of him practically disappeared, and, significantly, when it did surface, was almost always of an oblique variety. In February 1945, for example, *Pioneer Pravda* carried a story about a schoolfriend of Pavlik Morozov – but this time not because of the friendship, but because the friend had himself achieved glory as a war hero.[28] The Second World War also stalled the erection of Pavlik's planned monument in Sverdlovsk, and saw his Gerasimovka monument and museum fall into a parlous condition. 'The house where Pavlik Morozov was born and grew up [. . .] is being pulled down and used for firewood, the window-frames are missing, and the monuments where Pavlik Morozov was killed and at his grave are in urgent need of repairs,' the Sverdlovsk Regional Committee of the Komsomol stated in September 1945.[29]

Once the war was over, however, the late 1940s and early 1950s witnessed a revival of the Pavlik cult, though not to the

Maquette for the monument by Izaak Rabinovich to Pavlik Morozov, 1938. The statue stood in the Pavlik Morozov Children's Park of Culture and Rest from 1948 until 1991. (SCRSS, London)

stellar level that it had enjoyed before 1940. A monument to the boy was finally constructed in Moscow during 1948, to mark what would have been Pavlik's thirtieth birthday, as well as the thirtieth birthday of the Komsomol. However, the project was on nothing like the scale of that first mooted in 1935–6. The statue – still to Rabinovich's by now rather shop-soiled design from the previous decade – did not go up in the revolutionary pantheon of Red Square, or indeed any other area in the symbolic heart of Moscow. Instead, it was placed in the 'Pavlik Morozov Park of Culture and Rest' in the inner-city suburb of Presnya, site of some of the capital's major factories, including the massive cloth mill, the Trekhgornaya manufaktura.

This siting was not a complete snub to Pavlik's memory. Presnya had a significant resonance of its own in Soviet myth, as the site of revolutionary struggle both in 1905, and in October–November 1917.[30] Since the Revolution it had been honorifically known, in commemoration, as 'Red Presnya'. It was also by tradition the place where the very first Pioneer troop had been founded in May 1922.[31] In the 1930s, the Krasnaya Presnya District Committee was considered 'the most prestigious in Moscow'.[32] The Trekhgorka itself – a monstrous hulk of dark red brick down by the Moscow River – was one of the premier enterprises in the Soviet capital, alongside the Moscow car works, or the Hammer and Sickle metal factory. It was the site, for instance, of a flagship day-care centre for children publicized in laudatory brochures showing beaming tots posed on verandas under banners thanking Stalin for a happy childhood. And in 1930, a book of interviews with women workers there had been published which represented the factory as a key place for the sort of self-transformation manifested in Pavlik Morozov's official lives.[33] There was also an established link with the Morozov cult: it was Trekhgorka which had played host to Pavlik's mother, Tatiana, with a delegation of Gerasimovka Pioneers, in 1937 when they visited Moscow.[34]

At the same time, there is no doubt that the new location of Pavlik's monument constituted a demotion vis-à-vis Red Square. It placed him down in the second or third tier of revolutionary martyrs, and – because the park he was in was a *children's* park – emphasized the 'juvenile' nature of his myth. Equally significant, in terms of his rebranding as a purely Pioneer hero, was the list of public figures who attended when the monument was unveiled on 19 December 1948: the secretary of the Moscow Branch of the Komsomol and of the Moscow City Committee of the Komsomol. No senior representative of the Party even at city level appeared in the delegation.[35]

Nevertheless, while 'demoted' in national terms, Pavlik still remained an important figure in his particular niche, that of the Pioneer hero. The fifteenth anniversary of his death in 1947 – coinciding with the twenty-fifth anniversary of the founding of the Pioneers – was given substantial coverage in *Pioneer Pravda*, in the shape of an entire page of commemorative items. The denunciation was mentioned, though in rather coy style –

Pavlik had 'fearlessly told about his father's preparation of forged identity papers' (the revival of the original description of Trofim's crime was no doubt because this particular misdemeanour had more resonance than grain-hoarding to a generation with no first-hand memories of collectivization. 'Forged identity papers' immediately suggested 'spying' and 'treason'). Children were reminded of Pavlik's universal virtues, and especially his kindness to others (helping them with homework, for instance: this motif was relevant to a campaign propagandizing selfless friendship, rather than 'small-minded getting cronies out of fixes', that had been launched in 1947).[36] And they were also reminded of how many famous people had admired the boy.[37]

The year 1947 also saw the publication of a new Morozov biography, this time by Vitaly Gubarev, which was the shortest and simplest, but also the longest lived, official life. The book represented a further blanding-down of the two core motifs, the denunciation and the murder. In the killing scene, Pavlik and Fyodor, two perfect innocents, trustingly attempted to overcome their own feelings of unease when their grandfather and Danila appeared, only to fall victims (by implication – the killing took place 'off-stage') to the enmity of their blood relations:

> 'Got plenty of berries, boys?' Grandpa's voice is hoarse but caressing.
>
> 'Yup.'
>
> 'Show us, then . . . Don't look so sulky with your grandpa.'
>
> Pavel smiled joyfully and took the sack off his back.
>
> 'I'm not sulking, gramps. Have a look at these cranberries. What a size, eh?'
>
> He opened the sack, raised his eyes to his grandfather's face, and stepped back: the old man's face was twisted with hatred.
>
> 'Grandpa, let go my arm, eh? That hurts!'
>
> And at that moment the boy saw a knife in his grandfather's other hand, tore himself free, and yelled, 'Fedya, boy, run! Run, boy!'
>
> But Danila had caught up with Fedya in three giant leaps . . . (p. 64)

The theme of victimization also appeared in the denunciation scene. Pavlik, transmuted to a masculine version of the quivering Natasha from *Fear*, did not even appear before the court. Instead, he confessed his father's misdemeanours to a paternal representative of OGPU in private:

> And Pavel collapses on the broad chest of this man whom he hardly knows, but who is as near and dear to him as family, and trembles from the sobs that have at last overtaken him.
>
> 'Uncle Dymov . . . Uncle Dymov . . .' he whispers, fighting for breath. 'My father is a traitor . . .'
>
> Dymov hurriedly strokes his head and his damp back and says dully: 'Don't, Pasha . . . don't, little boy . . .' and feels a warm tear rolling down his own cheek. 'Don't, Pasha! You're . . . you're a real Pioneer!' (p. 39)

As well as watering down Pavlik's heroics, Gubarev made other changes. For example, he inserted new characters, in particular Pavlik's girl cousin 'Motya' – a tribute, once more, to the theme of appropriate friendship being cultivated in the Pioneer press at the time. The name 'Motya Potupchik' was borne by a real individual, who had been mentioned as a friend of Pavlik's in local Sverdlovsk stories about Gerasimovka published in the mid-1930s. But Gubarev's Motya was a pure invention in terms of her personality, and a decidedly stereotypical one. Fiercely and sentimentally loyal to Pavlik, she was at the same time not his equal in terms of political commitment and resolution, having to be jollied up by him when she was distressed by playground taunts about their attachment ('bridegroom and bride!').

Gubarev's text was in time to win a place as the canonical biography of Pavlik (and was also adapted by its author for the Soviet stage in 1952).[38] But his work did not represent the last word said on the boy in the late Stalin era. In 1950 an entire epic poem by the efficient, if untalented, Stepan Shchipachov (1898–1980) appeared. Shchipachov was another mythographer who had lived through a tough childhood: his autobiographical poem 'The Way' shows him running barefoot through the snow as a small boy, and working as a herdsman from his early years.[39] He also came from Perm province on the western side of the Urals, and so was a countryman, in a distant sense, of Pavlik's. But identification remained at an implicit level: *Pavlik Morozov* (awarded a Stalin prize, second class, in 1951) was not a close study of the actual Gerasimovka events, but a grandiose evocation of a Stalinist historical destiny in the broad sense:

Forests and forests – from the Urals
To the greying tundra, the seas.
The village is lost in forests,
In the skies swirl blizzards and stars.

Try even in thought to encompass
Those distances, those snows,
Where the blizzard stirs and writhes
Like a bear in its winter sleep,
Where the blizzard leaves clawed footsteps
As from house to house it goes.

[. . .] For thousands of kilometres
The snows smoke over the earth.

And in them – above the cities,
Above Oryol, and above Kungur,
Where the path winds through the gashes,
Where blond villagers rack their brains:

Still, next to the village soviets,
The windows flash their glass
Like a bandit's bullet through darkness,
But there is one just cause on earth.

The days, and the weeks, they vanish,
And following on the track
Of thousands of ills, the snowstorms
Press at the kulaks' back.

And in this snowy weather,
Raised up on victory's wings,
Socialism has entered the country:
There is no changing things.[40]

Shchipachov's poem followed the now customary track of generalized mythologization of Pavlik's homeland, and of his family situation. The devoted, if uneducated mother, struggling out in all weathers to take Pavlik food that she had thoughtfully wrapped in a tablecloth (an unknown item in the real Gerasimovka) was set against the severe, anti-Communist father, conflict with whom caused Pavlik distress, rather than exultation. And the epic ended with the patriarchy safely restored, as Pavlik's successor, a boy from a later generation, the Pioneer nominated to take the 'red harvest' to Tavda, shared the cab of a lorry with his father, the adult 'taking the helm' both practically and symbolically.

The twentieth anniversary of Pavlik's death in 1952, which was of course also the thirtieth anniversary of the founding of the Pioneers, saw a further crop of honorific texts. *Pioneer Pravda* ran a still more fulsome set of tributes than five years earlier, with the writer Valentin Kataev turning Pavlik into a fully fledged Stalinist hero. Pavlik, Kataev reminded his young readers, 'gave his life for the interests of his motherland'. His denunciation of his father was passed over with euphemistic embarrassment – the boy had 'even been prepared to stand up against his own father', and a great deal more emphasis was laid on Pavlik as a model in another sense: 'We should be faithful Stalinists, and boundlessly love our great, beloved Comrade Stalin, our father, friend, and teacher, as Pavlik did.'[41] At the stage when Pavlik died, the Stalin cult was in its infancy, and it is questionable whether even a politically active boy would have heard of the Soviet leader, let alone been particularly devoted to him. But with the flowering of the Stalin cult, this too, along with Pioneer ties, electricity and clean white tablecloths, was catapulted backwards into the Soviet past.

Equally wide recognition was achieved by another artefact of the time: Nikita Chebakov's painting of Pavlik confronting his father and grandfather. In the centre of the canvas is the figure of a blond boy in traditional Russian peasant shirt, trousers and boots (having him barefoot, a more likely state in real Russian villages of the time, would not have done at all). Head raised, chin jutting, back straight, he is defiance personified. To the left-hand side of the canvas as one faces it – but ranged so that Pavlik is to *their* left, a symbolically important effect – two men, both bearded, sit at a table under the icon corner, facing their accuser. The younger of the two men, evidently Pavlik's father, has a soft,

Nikita Chebakov, *Pavlik Morozov* (1952). (*Sovetskoe iskusstvo* 1953)

irresolute face, and quails under Pavlik's gaze. Pavlik's grandfather, on the other hand, matches him stare for stare. The picture's meaning is transparent: age and youth are locked in battle, and the former stands for backwardness, darkness and superstition, the latter for progress and light.

The obviousness of the message is matched by the painting's striking lack of sophistication in terms of composition and handling of paint (a feature of most narrative works made under the codes of Socialist Realism, when accessibility to unseasoned viewers of art was a primary virtue). But Chebakov's image was perhaps less straightforward than it seemed, not being devoid, for instance, of visual allusion. For a British viewer, it is tempting to see the piece as a riposte to William Frederick Yeames's *When Did You Last See Your Father?* (1878) – the famous Victorian image of children who put duty to their royal parent above all things, and refuse to denounce him to his Puritan enemies.[42] However, this temptation should probably be resisted: it seems unlikely that Chebakov would have been aware of Yearnes's existence. But there does seem to be a striking parallel, or rather anti-parallel, with one of the most famous *fin-de-siècle* images of

Russian juvenile saintliness, Mikhail Nesterov's painting *The Child Varfolomei's Vision* (1890). In Nesterov's painting, a slim, angular blond boy reverentially looks up to the cowled and bearded saint standing beside him. In Chebakov's painting, Pavel, equally slim and angular, but with his hair bristling rather than flat over his head, defiantly levels his gaze at the bearded elder.

For Chebakov's contemporaries, however, what was important was not his work's location in art history, but its location in ideology. *Pavlik Morozov* received a rave review in *Soviet Art*'s survey of the All-Soviet Exhibition in 1952. 'This painting is unarguably a real achievement on the artist's part and one of the most stirring canvases on show,' the anonymous writer gushed, praising both the handling of the 'warriors for socialism in the person of the young hero', and also of the 'bestial enemies of the working people', his kulak antagonists. Chebakov's painting was given the unusual honour of full-colour reproduction in the magazine.[43] Yet at the same time, the review also brought out a factor that was to become increasingly problematic in terms of the Morozov myth's real impact – its association with a past that was becoming more distant. The canvas, it continued, 'takes us from the contemporary world into the recent past, that is, into the domain of the historical genre'.[44]

From a martyr whose death represented, in extreme form, virtues still relevant to the present day, Pavlik was now declining into a figure from history – and from more distant history than war heroes such as Zoya Kosmodemyanskaya and Volodya Dubinin. What was more, such war heroes fitted better into the 'law of silence' that governed children's own peer-groups than did the legend of the boy who betrayed his father to adult authority.

In the 1930s, children had been worried that they might not have the mettle to do as Pavlik had done; now, models of bravery had altered. Experimenting to see whether one was brave enough to survive torture was a standard feature of the wartime childhood, as in the case of a girl who used, aged ten, to hold her hand to the scalding coils of the heater in the family's apartment until long after keeping it there had become painful.[45] And at least some of the generation who had come to consciousness during the war had little use for Pavlik. In the words of an interviewee born in the mid-1930s, 'I don't remember hearing anything much about Pavlik at school, but we all knew he was a squealer, and I'm grateful to the Soviet school system for teaching me that squealing was something you should never do.'[46] Another man of the same age stated that he was reluctant to believe Druzhnikov's revisionist account of Pavlik's murder, not out of Soviet piety, but because the canonical version at least expressed a kind of poetic justice: 'a dog should die a dog's death'.[47] Attitudes of this kind reflected traditional playground and street values, but were undoubtedly sharpened by Second World War propaganda, which presented treachery as the worst possible crime. How could a boy who voluntarily told all he knew enjoy respect in a culture where the ultimate heroes were those who died without breathing a word?

Timur, on the other hand, was attractive even to those for whom the Pioneer movement smacked of school and compulsion. Where Pavlik Morozov was a 'squealer', Timur 'at least tried to do good and be kind to people'. Children themselves wanted to join 'Timur' bands, but 'Pavlik and the kulaks' games never became popular in school playgrounds. Part of the reason behind this was the fact that Timur was also a hero of the cinema – as in the case of an adult hero extremely popular with children, Vasily Chapaev, who was much better known from the film version made by the so-called 'Brothers Vasiliev' than from the novel by Dmitry Furmanov on which the film was based.[48] For the average child, familiarity with Pavlik's biography did not go beyond rote-learning for Pioneer work, a fact that surely impeded identification with his actions. And by now, war heroes such as Zoya Kosmodemyanskaya and Volodya Dubinin had become more attractive as role models anyway.

In the postwar years, Pavlik never again regained the ascendancy that he had up to 1940. And the revival that was attempted during the post-Stalin era was to prove equally futile, as we shall see.

CHAPTER 7

Pavlik after Stalin

On 5 March 1953, the 'genius of all nations', 'generalissimo' and 'coryphaeus of knowledge', Joseph Stalin, was finally overtaken by an event that no cult document had ever referred to: he died. The leader's demise inspired private glee among some, but public devastation on a massive scale. However, by 1954, some signs of what psychoanalysts term 'reverse transference' were in the air, at least among the Party leadership. Then, in 1956, at a closed session of the Twentieth Congress of the Soviet Communist Party, Nikita Khrushchev launched his all-out attack on the so-called 'cult of personality', the celebration of Stalin's political might and unique human qualities, and a painful reassessment of Stalin's memory and significance began. While this reassessment was slowed down after Khrushchev's fall from power in 1964, Stalin never regained his former position, and was the subject of embarrassment, rather than of celebration.

Children had been a key audience for the Stalin cult itself; inevitably, therefore, the purging of Stalin quotations and laudatory references to Stalin, as well as of 'distortions of history' reflecting the leader's personal obsessions, from school textbooks and other teaching materials, was considered a major priority.[1] Portraits of the leader were removed from schools and from other public places visited by children: in early 1963, the annual financial accounts of the House of Children's Books in Leningrad recorded that over 300 roubles, the equivalent of about £4,500 in today's money, had been expended during 1962 on 'the liquidation' of Stalin images.[2]

But while children certainly experienced the results of such policies directly, everything was done in order to downplay the immense changes in symbolism that had taken place. Children's magazines did nothing to blacken Stalin's name, or even to initiate discussion of the historical significance of his leadership. Some teachers in the post-1956 decades did discuss the Stalin regime with their pupils, but this was a matter of personal initiative, not a stipulation in the school programme, and carried an element of risk for the teachers involved.[3] The dethroning of this particular hero, and of this cult, was not supposed to be interpreted by the Soviet juvenile public as subversive of heroism or cults in a broader sense. Rather, political administrators and educationalists strove for as much continuity with the representational traditions of the past as possible, with pictures of Lenin replacing the icons of Stalin that had formerly ornamented kindergartens, primary schools and Pioneer camps.

Yet, though ruler icons had a high degree of stability, views of children themselves did undergo some change. The preferred child in the Stalin icon had been docile, passively adoring and usually female. The post-Stalin era, by contrast, witnessed a partial rehabilitation of the ideal of the self-assertive child (usually male) that had predominated in the 1920s. The young Partisan heroes who were promoted during the early 1960s were often shown as having taken a more active role than the couriers and monitors of enemy activity who were celebrated in the post-war years: they included, for instance, Lyonya Golikov, who had seen active service with the Partisans, aged only thirteen, and who had been posthumously named Hero of the Soviet Union.[4] A preferred genre in children's fiction was by then the adventure story, usually with a bold boy hero. A popular film of the day, Elem Klimov's *Welcome! And Keep Out* (1964), satirically represented a Pioneer camp as a ludicrously frightful centre of regimentation and prohibition. The hero of the film, who quickly fell foul of authority, and was expelled from the camp (but was concealed there by the other children), was a blond, rebellious small boy. Its anti-hero was a female sneak, the daughter of a major Party official, who spent her time spying on the other children and reporting their misdeeds to the authorities. The high point of the film was a parade honouring 'the Queen of the Maize', in which the tale-telling daughter was supposed to emerge, at the climax, from a large papier-mâché effigy of a corn on the cob, Khrushchev's favourite crop. Parents and children were in fact treated to the spectacle of the tousled blond boy miscreant bursting out of his latest hiding-place, and turning the bogus carnival into a real one. But like Timur, the offender against petty-minded propriety was quickly welcomed back into the patriarchy: the major Party official took a 'boys will be boys' attitude. As it turned out, he disliked sneaking just as much as anyone else.

It is possible that the new fashion for 1920s-style assertiveness partly derived from the personal tastes of the political elite. Khrushchev was on record even in 1936 as saying he had a particular soft spot for rebellious, lively small boys.[5] He, and most of the other Party leaders of the time, had been first exposed to political activity during the years when the feisty child activist was a model. (Khrushchev's party career began in Moscow in 1931.) But it would be a mistake to attribute too much to personal biography. Political expediency underlay the changes as well.

To begin with, the whole of the Soviet representational world (the visual arts, literature, political propaganda) witnessed a move back, in the late 1950s and early 1960s, to the imagery of the 1920s. This was seen as the reassertion of a pure, fundamentalist 'Soviet' culture, from an era before Stalin's rule had led to corruption and decadence. And the need to fill the didactic vacuum left by the dethroning of Stalin himself as the ideal father of the nation's children led to the invention of a new image of Lenin as an amiable and approachable figure, 'grandpa Lenin', often shown bending affectionately towards his audience with an encouraging wave.[6] In 1970, the photo-coverage in *Ogonyok* included an allegedly genuine snapshot of Lenin walking in the park at Gorki and holding hands with his small nephew, Viktor.[7]

The changes were not, though, unidirectional. Discipline remained an essential Soviet value in the post-Stalin era as well. In the words of a 1967 manual for parents,

> Life sternly demands from everyone that he act not with caprice, but in a manner that takes into account the conditions pertaining in, and interests expressed by, the collective and

> society at large. [. . .] The whole structure of family life should teach the child the value of order, of carrying out certain explicit duties, of observing a correct regime, of submitting his own desires to the needs and desires of others.[8]

Role models of submission to the collective, duty and commitment, such as Pavlik Morozov, therefore remained of central importance.

TEENAGE REBEL

For these reasons, the Morozov cult survived not only Stalin's death, but also Khrushchev's denunciation of Stalin's crimes, among which he included not only the organization of the Great Purges, but also forced collectivization. The first year of the so-called 'thaw', 1954, already saw something of a revival of the cult. The memorial to the Morozov boys in Gerasimovka – planned, but never constructed, in the pre-war years – was now finally put up.[9] Pavlik and his brother Fyodor's remains were removed from the graveyard at Gerasimovka to a new site in the middle of the settlement, next to the village soviet and the school, where they were cemented into the pedestal of a heroic statue. This relocation has been interpreted as a further attempt to conceal the OGPU's responsibility for Pavlik's death.[10] However, moves of this kind, resembling the 'translation' of a saint's remains customary in Orthodox practice, were routine in Soviet Communist commemoration of the honoured dead; one might compare the removal of the poet Aleksandr Blok and his wife Lyubov, née Mendeleeva, from the private resting places where they had originally been laid to the Leningrad writers' pantheon, the so-called 'Literary Bridges'. That said, official coverage in the press did not give attention to the 'translation' of Pavlik's remains. It emphasized instead the construction of the monument itself as a feat of wonder, and the monument's role as a focus for Pioneer ceremonies.[11]

The unveiling of the monument was something of a local event, with Komsomol and Party representation only up to provincial level. But another development to honour the cult – the composition of a symphonic poem by Yury Balashkin – had wider resonance.[12] In the following year, 1955, came the promotion of Pavlik to 'Pioneer Number 001' in the roll of honour instituted in the Moscow House of Pioneers by decree of the Twelfth Congress of the Komsomol.[13] An article on children's heroes published in *Pioneer Leader* during 1956 followed suit by giving Pavlik pride of place; it also signalled the rebirth of an early-1930s style Pavlik, who 'did not hesitate' when betraying his father.[14] Several more important publications followed during 1961 and 1962, in the run-up to the fortieth anniversary of the Pioneer movement, falling in May of the latter year. They included a song by Pyotr Gradov and Leonid Bokalov;[15] a three-act opera by Mikhail Krasev, published by 'Soviet Music' publishing house; a new edition of Gubarev's book (which was issued twice, with print-runs of 150,000 copies each time); and an anthology under the title *Pavlik Morozov* (15,000 copies), which came out in the boy's home capital of Sverdlovsk.

Also at this period, Stepan Shchipachov rewrote his narrative poem *Pavlik Morozov* in order to trim it of references to Stalin, and to make the representation of Pavlik less monumental and more immediate. In a combination of both manoeuvres, Shchipachov pruned the courtroom scene at which Pavlik denounced his father, giving the conflict between the two a more intimate, abstract resonance. A passage about filial relationships that had originally figured in the courtroom scene was abridged and relocated in what was now the second section of the poem, 'Mother and Father'.

> The word Father –
> is such a dear one,
> there is tenderness, sternness, there.

In 1950, Shchipachov had continued, 'With this word [i.e. the word 'father']/Transforming its entire life/The people expresses its love/To Stalin.' Now, however, no wider context of patriarchal relations was supplied. Pavlik's dissatisfaction with his father had become an abstract inter-generational split of the sort that was widely represented in official Soviet literature and journalism of the day.[16]

This is not to say that Pavlik was now uniformly a hero of adolescent affront, expressing disappointment that parents were not keeping up with the (in this case political) times. Shchipachov's poem still ended with the scene in which a Pavlik double and his father rode together into the bright future, an ideal of generational co-operation rather than conflict. But in other versions of the legend, especially those from the provinces, the denunciation theme came through more strongly than in many Stalinist renderings of the tale. *Pavlik Morozov*, an anthology of texts published in the capital of his homeland, Sverdlovsk, in 1962, concentrated on scenes showing father and son at loggerheads, including relevant extracts from Yakovlev, Solomein and Gubarev, as well as Sergei Mikhalkov's poem about the young hero 'unmasking' his father.

A similar picture was painted in a new work, E. Khorinskaya's doggerel epic *The Young Drummer Boy* (1958), also published in Sverdlovsk. Here Pavlik recounts his own denunciation to an audience of admiring Pioneers:

> He made fake papers for kulaks . . .
> But why remember the bad!
> I told the judge what he was up to,
> Though inside it made me feel sad.[17]

Although texts published at the centre during the early 1960s tended to place less emphasis on the denunciation than the provincial ones, they sometimes brought out the boy's capacity for self-assertion in another way, emphasizing his role as a freedom fighter. In most ways, Gradov and Bokalov's 'Song about Pavlik Morozov' was heavily dependent on Alymov and Aleksandrov's 'Song about a Pioneer Hero'. It too began with an improbable aerial panorama of the Urals:

> That is not the birds singing, the wind stirring
> Above the mountains, the taiga,
> It is the fame of the young hero ringing
> Above his native Urals.

However, it played on a new element absent from Alymov's original: Pavlik had died not only 'for the happiness of other people', but also 'for this free region' (i.e., the Urals).

The Khrushchev era also saw a proliferation of monuments

to Pavlik Morozov, and of commemorative museums. The Gerasimovka monument was only the first in a clutch of such statues all over the Urals: the Sverdlovsk version, in the university park (previously renamed 'Pavlik Morozov park') was unveiled in 1961, and the Pervouralsk monument in 1962.[18] Pavlik Morozov statues mushroomed in other regions as well, and by the early 1960s large numbers of school playgrounds, even in places remote from Gerasimovka, had their ungainly example, most likely fashioned in bulk, using concrete poured into a mould.[19] If the school did not have a statue, it might well have a camp named after the boy, or a 'Pavlik Morozov' corner; failing that, it was certain to have an 'honorary chronicle of Pioneer history' in which Pavlik's name was listed at Number One.[20]

FROZEN IN BRONZE

Commemorative momentum did not let up with the fall from power of Khrushchev. Solomein's biography was reissued in a slightly reworked version in 1966 (some years after the writer's own death), and was reprinted several times during the late 1960s and 1970s, peaking with an edition of 200,000 copies in 1979. Gubarev's biography remained in print (in editions of up to 200,000) throughout the 1960s and 1970s.[21] New works also appeared: for example, a play by Vladimir Balashov, *The Rowan-Tree Bonfire*, in 1969, and a narrative poem by Mikhail Doroshin, *Pavlik Morozov*, in 1973. Dozens of 'Pavlik Morozov' streets appeared: towns great and small, from Alder to Yakutsk, commemorated the boy.[22] Statues and museums were also created apace. According to the recollection of a woman who worked in the Sverdlovsk Museum of the History of the Revolution during the early 1980s, at this period there were more than 100 museums all over the Soviet Union.[23] Among them, the Gerasimovka museum of course continued to have pride of place, acting as the destination for buses carrying Pioneers from all over the Soviet Union. Many of the delegations brought presents to the museum, sometimes chosen to reflect both the folk traditions of the place that they came from and the character of the hero himself. Typical of these was a wooden painted box carrying incised and hand-coloured portraits of Pavlik and scenes from his life, presented by the Pioneers of Kursk. Other items included a

Assorted gifts from Pioneers to the Pavlik Morozov Museum. (Pavlik Morozov Museum, Gerasimovka)

crystal-mounted clock, various pieces of ceremonial porcelain and a large collection of marching banners.

One could indeed say that Pavlik Morozov was propagandized *more* assiduously during the 1960s and 1970s than in the 1930s, which might be attributed to a kind of compensation mechanism. High Stalinism employed political terror, while affecting not to. Stalin's successors dispensed with such terror on a mass scale, but remained convinced that authoritarian, centralized rule was essential in order to maintain the party's hold on Soviet society. They therefore not only continued to allow a great deal of leeway to the activities of the secret police, but also created new types of social institution meant to encourage surveillance within the community on a voluntary, but formalized, basis. Particularly important was the 'people's militia', a group of vigilantes attached to a workplace or educational institution, operating under the oversight of the Komsomol to maintain public order and prevent its disruption, or 'hooliganism' (the Russian word is used more widely than its English counterpart). The post-Stalin era also saw the ascendancy of the so-called 'comradely court', a type of show trial within the workplace, at which personal misdemeanours such as adultery were as likely to figure as industrial or professional malpractices.[24] Given this background, it is clear why a hero characterized by an unbending determination to impose the right way of thinking upon others should have fitted in.

At the same time, many representations of Pavlik still emphasized his hesitancy about turning his father in. *The Rowan-Tree Bonfire* had him muttering to himself, in bad blank verse, 'No matter what you say, he's still my dad,' and giving his evidence tormentedly at the trial.[25] This laid bare another facet of post-Stalinist culture: the authorities were as worried about disorder and self-assertion among young people as they were concerned to emphasize civic virtue; deeply anxious about what was seen as the desertion of Soviet values in favour of what the cliché of

Mock-up of the classroom where Pavlik was educated. The building in which the museum is now located did not in fact start to be used as a school until 1934. (Pavlik Morozov Museum, Gerasimovka)

the day termed 'corrupt Western influences'. The fact that Pavlik's act of civic virtue was also an act of youth rebellion made it problematic now, just as it had been in the late 1930s and in the 1940s.

This may explain the strange gaps in the publicity given to Pavlik in the post-Stalin era. On the one hand, *Ogonyok*, the most important Soviet weekly news magazine, whose house style lay somewhere between *Picture Post* and *Time*, gave space to Pavlik in its coverage of the various anniversaries of the founding of the Pioneer organization. In 1962, a pull-out centrefold reproduced Chebakov's portrait of Pavlik confronting his father and grandfather.[26] In 1972, a new portrait of Pavlik, his brow wrinkled in fierce concentration, appeared, once again on one of the central pages and in full colour. Even here, though, Pavlik had to take his place alongside other heroes – in 1972, ones from a variety of Soviet 'brother nations', such as Azerbaijan. Certainly, his place

Artist's impression of Pavlik Morozov, published in the spread to mark the fiftieth anniversary of the founding of the Pioneer movement, *Ogonyok*, May 1972.

was underscored as primary: Grisha Akopov, in fact killed two years earlier than Pavlik, was said to have 'repeated' his glorious deed. But there was a sense, as at earlier jubilees, that the past was slipping away: as the jubilee coverage for 1972 all too accurately put it, 'he has been frozen in bronze, this reconnaissance boy of the future'.[27]

Other journals were strangely reticent about the Morozov myth. For instance, when *The Teachers' Newspaper* put out a spread to mark the fiftieth anniversary of the Pioneers, Pavlik did not appear in it.[28] So far as *Soviet Pedagogy* was concerned, he appeared only in the 1972 anniversary publications, not the 1962 ones.[29] Still more surprisingly, there were no special Pavlik materials published during September 1962 or September 1972 in *Pioneer* magazine, or indeed in *Pioneer Leader.*

To be sure, Pavlik continued to be a fixture at discussions round the bonfire and in the school syllabus. From the late 1950s, Gubarev's life was set as extra-curricular reading for class V (twelve-year-olds), and discussions of his life and of the lives of notable Pioneers were recommended as part of the political information sessions held by the 'class supervisor'. (These sessions consisted of a pep talk on a political subject by the 'class supervisor', or of a discussion in seminar format, where pupils reported on items that they had read – books, brochures, newspapers – after an introductory preamble by the supervisor.)[30] Up to the early 1950s, by contrast, the boy had appeared in presentation anthologies, but not in school textbooks, such as *Native Tongue* (*Rodnaya rech'*), which were dominated by material about Lenin and Stalin, and about major adult political events, such as the Revolution, the Civil War and the Second World War. By the early 1960s, knowledge about Pavlik's life was an essential requirement for admission to the Pioneer movement.

FALLING STAR

However, more and more publicity was also given to other heroes, such as war heroes, during this period. The already famous Volodya Dubinin and Zoya Kosmodemyanskaya were joined by a pleiad of other figures, including Valya Kotik, Lyonya Golikov, Adik Neverko (who fought with the Partisans in Minsk province and received the 'For Valour' medal), Trofim Prushinsky (who was bayoneted by the Germans for leading them astray during a search for the Soviet side), Lida Matveeva (who signalled to Soviet tanks in Rostov to warn them of a German ambush, and was hanged by the Germans) and many others.[31] *Sputnik*, a pull-out supplement to the magazine *Pioneer Leader*, published a series of model biographies of such heroes during 1961 which were meant to be collected and stored for instructive reading in the 'Pioneer room' of Soviet schools. Statues were also erected to commemorate them, notably of Lyonya Golikov and Valya Kotik, at the All-Soviet Exhibition of Economic Achievements in Moscow (the monuments were unveiled on 1 June 1960).[32] Stories about revolutionary and Civil War heroes also proliferated: for instance, the fortieth anniversary of the Bolshevik Revolution in 1957 saw *Pioneer* publish a whole article about these in its November issue.[33] One's school might well have a Pavlik Morozov shrine; but it was equally likely to have a corner dedicated to Lyonya Golikov, Volodya Dubinin, Zoya Kosmodemyanskaya, or indeed some adult hero.[34] In anthologies and lists published for the Pioneer jubilees in 1962 and 1972, Pavlik appeared as just one of many different Pioneer heroes, part of a glorious tradition stretching back to the Revolution and on to the present.[35] Pavlik was not even always 'Pioneer 001' where such lists were concerned. In *Soviet Pedagogy*'s spread for the fiftieth anniversary of the Pioneer organization, he did come first in a list of collectivization heroes ('Pavlik Morozov, Kolya Myagotin, Grisha Akopyan [=Akopov], and Kychan Dzhakupov'), but without any details being given; by contrast, Gaidar's Timur got a whole paragraph to himself.[36] And the 1962 jubilee of *Pioneer Leader* contained, not a story about Pavlik, but one dedicated to him: about a boy who exposed the grain-concealing activities of kulaks in his home village.[37]

The 1962 All-Soviet Rally of the Pioneer organization at Artek was similarly eclectic. 'Hero Remembrance Day' included a roll-call of the honourable fallen, beginning with Pavlik Morozov, but including quite a number of lesser-known heroes whose main function was to emphasize the 'friendship of peoples' – many of them came from minor Soviet nationalities. They included Kychan Dzhakybov (a hero of collectivization in Kyrgyzstan), and also Grisha Akopov (now given back his original Armenian surname, Akopyan, as a sign of changing attitudes to the non-Russian population). Pavlik was no longer the representative of 'Russian as preferred Soviet nationality', but a representative of 'Russian as one possible aspect of Soviet nationality'. And the heroes were honoured together in a generalizing ode:

> We honour you, valorous ones,
> You, fearless ones,
> Who gave your life for freedom
> And for the fatherland.[38]

This proliferation of other possible role models was likely to blur the impact of Pavlik for child readers, particularly now that collectivization had faded into the past. Even an official citation for Pavlik in the Book of Honour spoke of his deeds with suspicious vagueness:

> This Pioneer was killed by the kulaks because he fearlessly unmasked their efforts to subvert the organization of a collective farm. When Pavlik found out that his father was at one with the kulaks, the brave, honest boy unhesitatingly spoke out against his father as well. The public interest stood higher for Pavlik than his own private interests.[39]

For those who had little idea what a kulak was, the motivation behind Pavlik's defiance of his father was likely to remain opaque, as indeed was the nature of this defiance. He was just one of a number of different boys who had done something or other admirable back in the early 1930s, when something or other was happening out in the countryside. The significance of revolutionary heroes, or more particularly of Second World War heroes, was a good deal easier to grasp.

The sense that the significance of Pavlik's life was diminishing was deepened by the fact that the 1960s, in particular, was an era characterized by an explicitly modernizing, anti-historical drive. Accordingly, there were various rather comical attempts to update Pavlik's significance, to make him seem more relevant. For example, in late August 1962 (close to the time of Pavlik's thirtieth anniversary), *Pioneer Pravda* printed a story about a boy who could be seen as a contemporary version of

Pavlik Morozov – a Belorussian Pioneer who had allegedly been murdered for his efforts in denouncing the activities of religious 'sectarians' (which is to say, members of a Baptist church).[40] The story illustrated how yet another stigmatized social group had become the obvious suspects when a case of child murder came to light.

Reinterpreting Pavlik as the scourge of 'religious superstition' did not strike at the fundaments of the original myth. It is from some points of view quite surprising that iconoclasm and Bible-bashing did not figure in early versions of the legend, since these were such typical traits of the juvenile activist stereotype of the day. (The only Pavlik interpretation into which they *were* integrated was Eisenstein's *Bezhin Meadow*). However, if the anti-Baptist 'son of Pavlik' was quite in the spirit of the archetype, another modernizing item published a few days later for Pavlik's actual anniversary went close to undermining its rationale once and for all. What, the author wondered, might Pavlik have been doing, had he still been alive in 1962? Might he have been a record-breaking steelworker, perhaps, or a kolkhoz worker, or indeed a teacher?[41] Such counter-factual speculation came from a different world from that inhabited by the original legend, where Pavlik's death was a tragic inevitability. Now, it was seen as a tragic *waste* – not the same thing at all.

In the 1930s, Pavlik Morozov's standing had risen from one among many Pioneer heroes in the struggle against collectivization to the supreme Pioneer hero. Sidelined during the war, he had undergone a renaissance in the early 1950s. While publications continued in the 1960s and 1970s, and Pavlik Morozov remained famous, he had gone back to his original status of one among many Pioneer heroes. A song of the 1970s, 'Hallo, Morozov', gave the game away. Set to the brisk marching rhythm of drums, with French horns standing in as bugles, it declared that Pavlik's deed would live for ever: 'We know, we believe, that you are with us now.'[42] The main association with this kind of formulation, for the post-Stalinist younger generation, was a tribute to a long-dead leader who had gone out of the world when far from 'young' – 'Lenin is always with us.' The effect was to reinforce the feeling that Pavlik was on the shelf.

PAVLIK AND THE NEW GENERATION

In the 1930s and 1940s, whatever children thought of Pavlik, they certainly had a clear idea of who he was and what he had done. By the post-Stalin era, though, despite the efforts of their teachers, many children knew him as a name only. A woman who worked at the Sverdlovsk local history museum in the post-Stalin era remembered receiving sackfuls of letters from schoolchildren that began with the sentence, 'I want to be like Pavlik Morozov.' The next sentence usually read, 'So how can I find out what he actually did?'[43] Sometimes teachers themselves got the facts wrong, or perhaps muddied the water in the attempt to make Pavlik seem more attractive to their audience: one woman born at the end of the 1970s remembers being told at her nursery school that Pavlik had denounced his father because the latter was collaborating with the Nazis during the Second World War.[44]

Evidence collected since the collapse of Communism bears out the picture of confusion about Pavlik's role and significance. A poll of 500 Muscovites aged eighteen or over conducted for the seventieth anniversary of Pavlik's death in 2002 indicated that more than 50 per cent of the sample group either could not remember what Pavlik had done, or identified him incorrectly (as 'a Pioneer hero of the Second World War' or 'a Pioneer hero of the Civil War').[45] In-depth interviewing with informants born since 1945 also indicates a fairly high degree of vagueness about at least the details of the story. For instance, one well-educated and politically aware Leningrader born in 1967, when asked in the summer of 2003 what he had heard about Pavlik as a child, could recall nothing before reading Yury Druzhnikov's book about the boy in 1991, though he was sure he must have been taught something long before that, at school or in the Pioneers.[46]

What is more, the emotions evoked by the name 'Pavlik Morozov' were – in the post-Stalinist generations – generally anything but positive. In the words of one working-class Leningrader who didn't know much about Pavlik but knew what he didn't like about him, 'Pavlik Morozov! Classic stuff! The real Soviet mentality! They rammed that into our heads all right!'[47] Equally, of the 500 respondents in the 2003 survey, only

0.9 per cent agreed that they would be capable of acting like him; 62.6 per cent insisted that they would not, under any circumstances, while over 36 per cent either did not know or answered, 'It depends.'[48]

Once again, such indifference or cynicism towards a Soviet hero should not necessarily be interpreted as a purely post-Soviet circumstance. Already in the late Soviet era, there were signs of a good deal of distaste directed at the phenomenon of the eager juvenile denouncer. Just as in earlier generations, the rules governing children's relations with each other in courtyards and school playgrounds stigmatized the practice of denunciation as disgraceful rather than admirable. Hence, Pavlik could be seen as a hero only in an artificial sense. And, just as in the 1930s or 1940s, the fact of his murder was often seen as disturbing, inspiring a shudder rather than a desire to emulate him.[49]

By contrast, Gaidar's Timur remained hugely popular with the post-Stalin generations. It is impossible to imagine that Pavlik Morozov could successfully have been used as a kind of master of ceremonies and postal confidant, as Timur was in issues of *Pioneer Pravda* published in 1962.[50] 'Timur groups' remained widespread in the Pioneer movement too, encouraged by a growing emphasis on the need to encourage self-reliance and organizational skills in children and Pioneers.[51] Most people who went through the Pioneers in the late 1950s and 1960s, particularly, recall that Timurite activities to do with collecting scrap and helping veterans were a standard part of Pioneer work.[52]

But the currency of Timur went well beyond these semi-official contexts. For instance, children playing improvised games in the courtyards of Russian cities would often spontaneously name themselves 'Timur gangs'. As the Russian psychologist Maria Osorina has pointed out, Gaidar's book cleverly built on the 'secret society' games that Russian children – like their contemporaries in other countries – loved to play; accordingly, the characters and plot formulae from the book easily got imported back into children's day-to-day life.[53] By contrast, Pavlik does not seem to have been the subject of games in this era, any more than he had been earlier, though he had a facetious after-life in blackly humorous ditties transmitted by word of mouth:

Daddy's lying in the street,
Soaked with blood from head to feet.
His little son – oh what a shame! –
Was playing a Pavlik Morozov game.[54]

This piece is interesting for several reasons. It exaggerates the degree of Pavlik's culpability against his father (denunciation has turned into vicious murder), illustrating how what had originally been portrayed as an act of civic commitment was now perceived as an act of violence within the family. It also replaces the annihilation of the son by the annihilation of the father, and points to a widespread phenomenon in the post-Stalin era: the use of humour to defuse horror. The 1960s to the 1980s were the heyday of 'sadistic verses', a genre that starkly represented horrible acts, often by small children, who, innocently happening upon some strange ticking object in the backyard, succeeded in blowing an apartment block sky-high, or who (less innocently) amused themselves by practising Gestapo tortures on the local caretaker.[55] Where all death was seen as absurd, heroic death could only seem even more absurd – those who died in this way had simply not had the intelligence to realize the futility of their own actions.

The tendency to cynicism was reinforced once the postwar generations, who themselves regarded Pavlik without reverence, began bringing up their own children. In the words of a woman born in 1975:

> My father [born in 1950] is a person with a great sense of humour, and so what he said about [Pavlik Morozov] was this: 'Please: they may tell you at school that Pavlik Morozov really is a hero, but don't kid yourself! A person can't be a hero if he betrays his parents. That's really not normal!'[56]

Pavlik did not have the sort of textual after-life that was represented by, say, Agniya Barto's poem 'Uncle Timur' (1958), in which an elderly man who spends his time campaigning for children's playgrounds earns this honorific title from grateful small people.[57] It is notable that when Genrikh Sapgir, who spent reluctant decades publishing as a children's writer because his works for adults would not have got through the censorship, wished to achieve a shock effect by dethroning a child hero, he chose Timur rather than Pavlik. His story 'Timur and Her Team' portrays a warped, spiteful invalid child, confined to a wheelchair, who manipulates her hangers-on to evil effects. The impact of the text – the tasteless portrait of a 'cripple' aside – depends entirely on the sentimental expectations raised by the name 'Timur'. It is difficult to imagine that a story under the title 'Pavla and Her Father' could really have generated more hostility among post-Stalinist intelligentsia readers than, say, Gubarev's original life of Pavlik.

Part of this was to do with a widespread reaction against civic informing more broadly. In 1962, a guest at the dacha owned by Kornei Chukovsky, the famous literary critic, children's writer and journalist, left in the visitors' book a piece called 'The Vigilant Infant', a savagely funny parody of a classic Stalinist genre, the story about a child co-operating with border-guards. Eighteen-month-old Vasyutka, clearly an infant prodigy, rushes one and a half kilometres to the local border-post in order to denounce a strange bearded man he has seen eating bread, gloating, 'Now that mister will get his bottom smacked like he deserves.' The story ends in blissful apotheosis: 'The infant did not hear the approaching thunder of horse-hooves; he was sleeping the sleep of a person who has done all that the duty of a citizen requires.'[58]

Negative reactions to Pavlik were also – particularly among people actually schooled in the post-Stalinist era – part of a much wider disillusionment with school indoctrination and with the ideals put forward in this. Privately, most pupils of the 1960s and 1970s, and a fair number of teachers, were politically apathetic, if not actually cynical, and this mood occasionally came out in public – as, for example, in the following reminiscence about a history lesson:

> A friend of mine got up and said: 'You know how during the Great Patriotic War [the Second World War] soldiers would go into battle, and they'd be shouting, "For the motherland, for Stalin!"? Well, can you imagine if a war started now, do you think people would really go into battle shouting, "For the motherland, for Brezhnev"?' And of course the class cracked up laughing.[59]

To be sure, the war, and war heroes, remained inviolate for many. Zoya Kosmodemyanskaya was still able to inspire, Lev Kassil's *Street of the Younger Son* continued to be read with interest, and war heroes generally were seen by many children with awe.[60] But some children, if the comments they made later are to be believed, now reacted badly even to these. Asked whether he remembered anything about Pioneer heroes, a Leningrad man born in 1960 said in disgust, 'Like filth,' before dredging up two of the Partisan types, Valya Kotik and Lyonya Golikov, from his memory. Asked whether he remembered what they had done, he sighed heavily and continued, 'They blew themselves up, didn't they? [. . .] And they, what do you call it, fought against fascism, the bloody fools!'[61]

Attitudes like this should not be seen simply as post-Soviet wisdom after the event. As early as 1961, the provincial town of Tambov was witness to a scandal over impromptu outdoor performances by a local poet who had chosen a statue as the vantage point for his readings. As the Komsomol administrators anxiously explained, they were objecting not because they were against poetry as such, but because they could not tolerate 'the nasty gobs of spit and cigarette ends that have been rained down on the monument to Hero of the Soviet Union, our former neighbour Zoya Kosmodemyanskaya, a monument to which every spring young and old, the inhabitants of our town, bring the first living flowers'.[62] But there were, evidently, some in Tambov in whom the monument inspired no such reverence, and for whom it had become no more than the eye-catching marker of somewhere to hold public meetings. Where even Kosmodemyanskaya was not sacrosanct, Pavlik, who had always inspired mixed emotions, could hardly survive.

Increasingly, then, material about Pioneer heroes had become the stuff of homework reading and nothing more. In the words of a Leningrad woman born in 1969: 'We had to read about [Pioneer heroes]. If you were going to join the Pioneers, you had to know all about the organization.'[63] Or, as a man nearly a decade older more pithily put it: 'You wrote about it. You ground through it.'[64] This went with a general 'de-heroicization' of child and youth culture. The postbag of the Leningrad section of 'Children's Literature' publishing house was, by the early 1960s, indicating a greater popularity for adventure stories and science fiction than for didactic lives of 'Iron Felix' Dzerzhinsky, the founder of the Soviet secret police, or Sergei Kirov, Leningrad Party leader in the early 1930s. Letters about how inspiring the lives of such long-dead Communists were tended to come from

The monument in Gerasimovka carrying Gorky's command, 'The memory of him must not be allowed to vanish' (the inscription is now almost invisible), September 2003. (Catriona Kelly)

the distant provinces.[65] Rather than to 'heroes', children and young people were now increasingly drawn towards 'idols' – pop stars, including Western ones such as the Beatles, or sporting champions. Younger children felt for the heroes of cartoon films, an immensely popular genre on television, or for the protagonists of traditional folk-tales, princes and princesses. Or they might find their admiration inspired by someone within the family – a mother, for example, heroically combining a full-time job with family duties, and yet always apparently able to shower affection on her offspring.[66]

HIS NAME WILL NO LONGER BE REMEMBERED

Not surprisingly, given this accumulation of cynicism, when the Soviet system did collapse in 1991, the statue of Pavlik Morozov in Moscow, along with the monument to Felix Dzerzhinsky, was one of the first monuments to fall victim to iconoclasts. Since then, Morozov monuments have disappeared in other places, including the boy's home capital of Sverdlovsk. The monuments at Gerasimovka, while still in place, soon fell into poor repair. The one that had suffered the most when I visited in 2003 was a strapping lump of concrete, bearing some vague resemblance to an anvil, on the fringes of the village towards the woods where Pavlik's body was found. Most of the letters once spelling out a quotation from Maxim Gorky's speech to the Komsomol about the boy – 'The memory of him must not be allowed to vanish' – had dropped off, and Gorky's comment was now illegible for anyone who did not already remember what it said. No coach parties visited the museum any more; it had been closed to casual visitors for several years. The exhibition inside had been dismantled, apart from a reconstruction of the schoolroom on the upper floor where Pavlik once studied. What remained of the contents – presents brought by Pioneer delegations, ceremonial banners, photographs and documents – was collecting dust in a side room. Locally, no one much cared: as the chairman of the local collective farm put it, 'We have enough to do to survive.' And inhabitants of the village now valued Pavlik purely in an instrumental sense: because the boy was famous, conditions were better there than in other, comparable, places. They felt they owed the boy the road, the culture club and the local school.[67]

Already in decline during the late Soviet era, Pavlik's cult seemed, by the early twenty-first century, beyond recall. Some people brought up in the 1930s, and once committed to the Communist cause, were still prepared to defend aspects of the cult, associating it with selflessness and social disinterest. 'It was a positive image for the younger generation, a positive image, people strove to live up to it,' a woman born in Sverdlovsk in 1931 insisted in September 2003.[68] Views of this kind were expressed especially vehemently in the right-wing Russian press, where a version of Pavlik as the fervent Pioneer who had *not* 'denounced' his father, but provided witness testimony when the law required him to do so, became popular, and was supported by reference to material in the secret police file.[69]

For others, Pavlik had acquired a symbolic value of another kind: he was held to represent everything most shocking in the Soviet system's mistreatment of children, its capacity to indoctrinate and manipulate the younger generation.[70] Alternatively – following Yury Druzhnikov, the contents of whose book were now known, at first or second hand, to large numbers of people –

Pavlik might be seen as a victim of Soviet power in a more straightforward sense: because he was murdered by the OGPU.[71] Whichever way, the legendary Pioneer had become a fallen hero: the seventieth anniversary of his death in 2002 attracted little publicity, and most of that concerned the cult's decline. The rag-bag of material relating to the boy posted on the Russian Internet around that time included nothing defending the Soviet attitude to Pavlik as a hero, but a good few texts where Pavlik was invoked ironically, for example a song by the rock group Crematorium in which the boy was described as 'a cretin injured by God' and his mother as the sexual partner of 'a whole herd of bold muzhiks'; and a play by Vladlen Gavrilchik that showed Pavlik, alongside Timur, rescuing Pushkin from his fatal duel.[72] An attempt to rehabilitate Pavlik from the beginning of 2004 included vox pop vignettes indicating that only old people knew who Pavlik Morozov was.[73] At the grassroots level, it would seem, the cult was completely dead.

During my own research for the book, I repeatedly encountered, when Russians who were not professional historians discovered what I was working on, a mixture of amusement and incredulity: people in charge of the photocopiers in libraries amazed that I would spend so many valuable dollars having that trash photocopied, taxi-drivers astonished that you could make good money by doing work like that. History may or may not return as farce; in the popular mind, Pavlik Morozov has passed into the sort of history that seems farcical, as farcical as penny-farthings, bloomers and the crinoline. To be sure, attempts to promote some heroes for children persist: the editor of *Pioneer Pravda* (which is still going, though with a much reduced print-run) told me in February 2004 that they particularly emphasize tales about children who have reported suspicious goings-on near the Russian borders.[74] But by and large, children's culture is of a different kind, centring – as in the West – on sport, teen pop and fashion.[75]

The fall from grace of Pavlik Morozov and other Pioneer heroes has often been seen – by liberal Russian commentators, and by Western ones – as a change for the better, a step towards political and moral maturity.[76] To a large extent, this is fair. Whatever the differences between the various versions of the boy's legend at different stages of Soviet history, taking them at face value always required an acceptance of certain fundamental tenets: that collectivization was a historically correct process, and one that enjoyed the support of all right-thinking Soviet citizens; that the legal process by which Pavlik's murderers were arraigned and tried was democratic and just; that children should be indoctrinated into an unquestioning commitment to the political regime of the country in which they were being brought up. On the contrary, collectivization was – in the long run – an economic and political disaster, as well as a cruel assault on the Russian peasantry; the Soviet legal process depended on routine abuse of suspects' and prisoners' rights; and the only admirable aspect of Soviet indoctrination of children was that it did not succeed in generating the loyalty to the system that political leaders and propagandists anticipated it would – because, in requiring *rational* assent to an *irrational* system of government, it left space (despite itself) for scepticism and critical thought, while at the same time inculcating general human values that were likely to encourage self-distancing from political cant.

But if the dethroning of Pavlik as a hero ought to be welcomed, the oblivion into which his story has fallen has to be seen in a less positive light. Most importantly, a thorough, scrupulous review of the trial dossier is long overdue. Whether those executed for the Morozov boys' murders in 1932 were or were not actually guilty, they most certainly did not receive a fair trial, and the *corpus delicti* upon which the sentence was based was without question seriously flawed. In 2001, following a suit for the rehabilitation of the alleged murderers filed in 1999 by Matryona Shatrakova, the daughter of Arseny Shatrakov, the file was reopened, and investigated by Nikolai Vlasenko, deputy director of the rehabilitations department of the Prosecutor General's Office in Moscow. The application for rehabilitation – unlike the vast majority of the half a million petitions of this kind filed since 1991 – was refused. Speaking to an American journalist in 2002, Vlasenko expressed a firm conviction that the original suspects were in fact guilty: 'It was the most savage and extreme crime possible. To take your own grandchildren and slice them open. That's what we know, and that's all we need to know.' Vlasenko also referred to the fact that the case was extraordinarily well documented, 'There are interrogations, residents, witnesses, participants. Don't drag politics into this. It was a terrorist act.'[77]

Clearly, this decision is not intellectually adequate: the materials in the case may represent a fair spread of genres, but this is true also of various other high-profile cases of 1932–3, for example the 'Finnish General Staff' affair, which consists of many volumes of testimony recorded from peasants in Karelia who were supposed to be part of a 'white Finnish' plot to undermine Soviet rule.[78] The fact that abundant documentation was marshalled against those arrested was of course no indication that they were guilty. It is true that there was more hard evidence against the Morozov defendants than, say, in the 'Deaf and Dumb' case mounted in Leningrad during the Great Purges, which was based on allegations that a 'Gestapo agent' named Albert Blum had presented Hitler postcards to a handicapped tradesman, and that this indicated a massive 'Fascist conspiracy' involving dozens of profoundly deaf individuals across the city.[79] Pavel and Fyodor Morozov were definitely murdered: one may doubt whether Albert Blum and the Hitler postcards ever existed. But the investigative procedures in the Morozov case were flawed, and the testimony extracted unreliable. Whether or not the suspects were in fact guilty, their conviction would not stand up in any properly conducted modern court of appeal, and it is high time for this to be recognized. 'Rehabilitation' (the equivalent of a posthumous pardon) might be a problematic decision, given that at least one of the accused (Danila Morozov) does on balance seem to have been involved in the murder (see Chapter 8), and that pronouncing on the innocence of suspects from evidence that was assembled precisely in order to condemn them is an almost impossible task. But a judgement based on the use of torture, forced confessions and invented evidence has to be recognized as unsafe: if one follows the terminology used in Scottish law, the accused deserve – at worst – a verdict of 'not proven', rather than of 'guilty'.[80]

There are all sorts of other areas, too, where reassessment of the Morozov case is important. As I have pointed out repeatedly, the story raises important issues about civic duty that are valid well beyond the context of the Soviet system. The discrediting of the legend – welcome as that was in its own right – was symptomatic of a withdrawal from civic engagement of any kind that has been widespread among post-Soviet intellectuals, and whose effects have been far from wholly positive. Decency and commitment remain more prevalent in the former Soviet Union than the economic situation might suggest would be likely, but are strongly compartmentalized – loyalty stops with the family, an inner circle of close friends, a firm or other place of work. The result is a culture based on fissured, atomized groups, which have become even less porous to outsiders than they were in the Soviet period (when foreigners and other individuals from *outside* the Soviet system tended to be made welcome precisely because official ideology held them suspect), and where there is no consensus whatever about reasonable behaviour. The idea that one might – in whatever circumstances – report a misdeed by a member of such a closed group to the police or government authorities (whose reputation for probity is non-existent) would strike many people as laughable. Therefore, tax violations starve the country of resources, serious crimes – right up to murder – go undetected and unpunished, and private morality is distinguished by a high degree of naked self-interest. Crucial issues of how to create the basis for social trust, and a set of values that might be recognized community-wide, need to be addressed. The final tragedy of the Pavlik Morozov legend was that, in asserting the value of denunciation in a culture where the victims of denunciation were treated unjustly, it helped to create a culture where all social participation came to be seen as collusion with an unjust regime.

Some, at least, of these issues, as well as the history of how the Pavlik myth was created – the history that has been narrated in this book – will be analysed in the displays set up when the Pavlik Morozov museum in Gerasimovka is reopened. In September 2003, it was announced that the Open Society foundation, sponsored by the American philanthropist George Soros, had given a grant of 7,000 dollars to the Ekaterinburg branch of the Memorial association (the group committed to fostering commemoration of the victims of political terror in Russia) in order to help them re-establish a Pavlik Morozov museum of a radically new kind. Now, Pavlik's story would be seen in the context of forced collectivization, and assessed as part of a wider political background. There were plans to obtain the case file on the murders from the FSB, and to make a collection of oral history from the point of view of the repressed.[81]

The story gave rise to a bubble of controversy, with some

suspecting that the museum would be pushing its own ideological line, a simplistically anti-Soviet, pro-Western one, all with the aid of Western money. The fact that the Soros grant came with a prohibition on using the money for 'political' activities created a degree of puzzlement: how, then, was such a deeply politicized subject to be represented at all?[82] Insider comment suggested that the steering committee for the museum was deeply divided, representing all possible shades of opinion about the Pavlik legend.[83] But this is probably a positive development. A subject that has attracted so many vehement, dogmatic opinions and versions, righteously excluding all other versions of the same material, can only benefit from an approach which allows several different perspectives to exist alongside each other, and recognizes that the story of Pavlik Morozov has, in its time, meant many different things.

CHAPTER 8

The 'Real Life' of Pavlik Morozov?

FICTION IN THE ARCHIVES

To the journalists and Pioneer activists that created Pavlik's legend, the question of what Pavlik was really like was of secondary importance. What inspired them was the desire to create a vivid, plausible Pioneer hero in order to celebrate the tenth anniversary of the founding of the movement. The run-up and aftermath to this occasion (it fell in May 1932, just a few months before Pavlik's murder) had been marked by the publication of numerous articles complaining of the dearth of just such heroes in children's literature, and impressing on writers and journalists the need to seek out and portray them. From the first, then, the accepted ideals of heroism were as important as the facts of Pavlik's biography in shaping the lives. Solomein's life, to be sure, included detail that went beyond stereotype: for instance, it made clear that Pavlik's background was Belorussian. Yet his narrative, too, was in its way thoroughly literary, setting out the motifs of the standard early Soviet 'conversion myth'. And later versions of the story – from Yakovlev's life in 1936 to the plays and stories of the 1970s – were equally conventional: their distinctiveness lay in the evolution of the formulas on which they drew.

As the narratives of writers with explicitly literary ambitions, working for the public domain, even supposedly 'documentary' published texts – the articles in *Pioneer Pravda* and in *Pioneer*, and Solomein's biography – were quite different from the material collected for the investigation. This does not, however, make the latter more reliable. Witness testimony is at times contradictory, at times downright fantastic.[1] The investigators had their own tales to tell, and needed to protect themselves from the wrath of higher authorities, who felt that they, as provincial bumpkins, were dealing with the case slowly and indecisively. In the spirit of Stalinist 'self-criticism', local officials attempted to exculpate their faults by grovelling acknowledgement of these.[2] They also – again in Stalinist style – sought a scapegoat lower down the line. On 1 October 1932, Yakov Titov was castigated at a Party District Committee meeting for failing to offer due protection to 'the late Pioneer Morozov', and not taking action when the latter contacted him to complain that he was being bullied by kulaks. It was decided that Titov should be sacked and his file sent to the organs of justice.[3] But at the same time, the secret police and Party authorities engaged in defensive manoeuvres, trying to demonstrate that they had always been aware of what an important case this was. An article by Pavel Solomein published in the Sverdlovsk Pioneer newspaper *Dawns of the Commune* on 8 October 1932 argued that the Tavda administration had heard about the murder only after some delay because there was no telephone line in Gerasimovka, but once they were aware of it, they had leapt into action. 'Everyone started talking. They discussed the question in the bureau of the district committee. Then meetings were held.'[4] Quite obviously, this item had been written 'to order'.

As a matter of fact, it is not at all clear that the Tavda administrators did at first realize what an explosive case the Morozov murders was. After all, it took nearly two weeks for a 'responsible official' even at the local level, to be involved, and the manner of contacting the regional Komsomol authorities (by sending a press cutting) was indeed decidedly lackadaisical. Therefore, documentation which purports to show enthusiastic involvement with the case dating from early September 1932 must be considered suspect. In particular, local inspector Titov – blamed for 'delays' and 'mismanagement' that were not his fault – seems to have indulged in some wholly understandable retrospective creation of paper trails. File H-7825 contains an undated 'Statement' by Titov declaring he has received a visit from 'citizen Pavel Morozov' to report an attack in connection with a dispute over a piece of horse harness 'at 9 a.m. on 26 August 1932'. The statement is signed 'Moro . . .', but the hand in which the signature is written does not look appreciably different from the – uncharacteristically tidy – hand in which Titov has written the rest of the statement (63). Also on file is a chit, originated on 19 September, stating that 'citizen of Gerasimovka Morozov Pavel' had been given a referral to the first-aid point in Maloe Gorodishche 'to establish the extent of the physical damage that he suffered[;] since the aforesaid has been beaten by a certain citizen, [he] should receive medical attention without delay' (54). The chit was issued by the Gerasimovka village soviet, and on the back of it Titov wrote, 'Morozov Pavel neverwent to get lookedat by the doctor Gerasimovka village bekos of not finding no horses because the horses was inthe fields district inspector 8 district Titov.' This note is also signed 13 September 1932 (64). It is likely that Pavlik never reported the beating to Titov in the first place. But once he began to be established as a thoroughly civic character who was always reporting everything, the attitude emerged that he *must* have reported this incident, placing the onus on the local officials to produce documentation, or be considered to have failed in their duty.

Besides deliberate forgery of documents (other instances of this will be mentioned later), the Pavlik Morozov records have

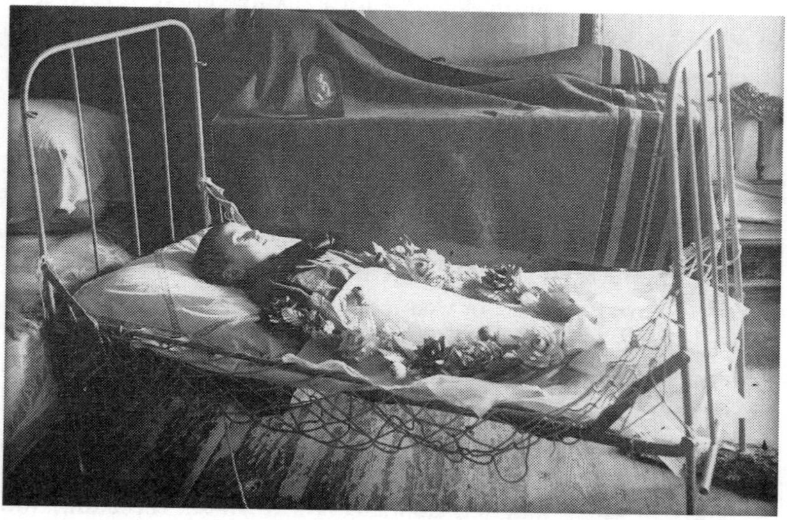

Picture of a child's funeral, early 1930s, erroneously identified as showing Fyodor Morozov. (State Archive of Sverdlovsk Province, Ekaterinburg)

suffered from the tendency of this case to suck everything around into its orbit once it had become famous. The Sverdlovsk regional archive in Ekaterinburg includes an extremely impressive image of the corpse of a child, ceremonially laid out on an iron bedstead, who is identified by the archive's catalogue as 'Fedya Morozov'. Alas, the identification will not hold up. There were few beds in Gerasimovka at the time when the boys were killed, and certainly no factory-made beds of this kind, with immaculate city-produced sheets. One of the main recollections of survivors from the pre-war years is that everything, from soap to clothes to furniture, was home-made.[5] Sergei Morozov had a mattress among his household goods, but definitely not a bed (57 rev.) – Gerasimovka villagers slept above the stove, in the traditional way. Behind the bed that the child is lying on, one can see a framed photograph of a well-fed, well-dressed tot, clearly the younger *alter ego* of the boy on the bed: neither the artefact nor the child's appearance are characteristic of the living conditions of a poor family in a poor village sometime in the mid-1920s. As a record of a child's funeral in the early Soviet era, the photograph is valuable; as an image of 'Fedya Morozov' it unfortunately has no value at all.

Apart from problems with contamination of the documentary records, there are also problems with incompleteness. There was an official procedure for the destruction of protocols, directives and other such documents, presided over by a three-man team consisting of a Party District Committee representative, an OGPU representative and a technician (the person who actually did the work of destruction). What is more, in 1932, the Urals Regional Committee of the CP sent down an order specifically decreeing that all protocols from the previous year should be destroyed.[6] As well as disappearing in this sanctioned manner, material seems simply to have got lost. For example, publicly accessible collections of secret police reports (those held in Party archives) are invariably incomplete, with missing first pages as well as missing issues – a fact that is as likely to have derived from inefficiency as from deliberate efforts to suppress information. Party members who received the reports were barely in a position to cope with the core demands of their job, let alone to worry about recording the details of their day-to-day practices for posterity; meticulous filing of protocols, instructions and the like was hardly a possibility.

Group photograph, Gerasimovka school, 1931: Pavel Morozov, standing in the back row, is marked by the arrow. (Pavlik Morozov Museum, Gerasimovka)

In the circumstances, getting at the most elementary facts about Pavlik becomes difficult. The local museum in Gerasimovka holds what appear to be two basic proofs of existence: a certificate taken from a record in Vladimirovka church, and recording Pavlik's birth on 14 November 1918; and the group photograph taken in Gerasimovka school, in which Pavlik appears in the final row, looking rather timid, lost and unfocused.[7] It seems fairly likely that these two documents are genuine. While the copy of the certificate now available is late (30 November 1965), this does not necessarily undermine its authenticity, but perhaps rather the other way round. The early 1960s were, like the 1920s, a fiercely anti-clerical era, and a faked birth certificate for a revolutionary hero dating from this time would have been unlikely to mention a church as place of registration. Equally, in the second case, the photograph is so distant from official images of Pavlik that, once again, forgery seems unlikely. However, mistaken identity (the wrong child – the wrong class – the wrong school altogether) cannot be ruled out. And the museum certainly holds at least one item that is a clear fake – a portrait of Pavlik with his mother that should be regarded as an artist's impression rather than as a documentary record.

'Pavlik Morozov and his Mother', artist's impression masquerading as a documentary photograph. (Date unknown (?1940); Pavlik Morozov Museum, Gerasimovka)

Oral history – though it turns up useful information about the background to the case – raises just as many problems as the written documentation. The Morozov murders took place so long ago that only a handful of those with direct connections to the boys' family and era are left alive. Of these, the most vehement, Mariya Sakova (sister of Anastasiya) and Dmitry Prokopenko (son of Vasily), gave, in 2003, diametrically opposed accounts of the Morozov family and of Pavlik. Dmitry Prokopenko, who first came to note as an informant about Pavlik's life in the 1960s, and who left an unpublished memoir about him in the Gerasimovka Pavlik Morozov Museum, has a set story which he has repeated many times. He claims that he sat next to Pavlik for four years at the village school, and remembers him as 'a boisterous, active boy' who was the leader in everything, the first Pioneer in the village.[8] Prokopenko is never mentioned as one of Pavlik's schoolfriends in early reporting about Gerasimovka, but this is not necessarily an indication that what he says is inauthentic: those selected as Pavlik's friends in the early 1930s tended to be the children of local Communists or at the very least 'trusties' (such as Karp Yudov and Yakov Galyzov), and Prokopenko, whose family had suffered dekulakization, would not have been considered suitable as a hero's companion even if in reality the two had been best friends.[9] More suspect is the fact that his story is so close, not only in content, but even in style, to official hagiographies of Pavlik (one notes particularly the use of adjectives such as 'active'). When I interviewed him in September 2003, he would not be swayed from the narrow account of his contacts with Pavlik that he has given many times before, though he did produce some new details about more general subjects (the injustices of collectivization; the games the village boys played).[10]

Mariya Sakova's account of Pavlik is much more personal and vivid, yet in a different way 'impure'. She remembers Pavlik as the dirty little boy, covered in lice, that no one wanted to sit next to at school, and the Morozov family as sinister outsiders. Even by the standards of a poor village, 'they lived badly'; Tatiana was a poor housekeeper and Mariya, as a child, was terrified of her – she used to hide under the bed as she went past. But it should be said that Sakova – in an interview that ranged over the conditions of life in Gerasimovka in the old days generally as well as over her memories of Pavlik – took a bleak view of everything mentioned. For instance, she denied that singing and joking ever went on at women's work parties, yet other informants of much the same generation remembered that they definitely did. Equally, Sakova's view of Pavlik was shaped by her conviction that Pavlik, being no hero, must be an anti-hero. This was particularly clear in her description of the removal of his body to a new resting place in 1954. As she remembered, people in the fields stopped working as the bodies were moved: 'Such a stink rose up! Everyone said, "That's them digging up Pavlik."'[11] The recollection is so shocking and vivid that it might seem authentic on those grounds alone. But it is also stereotypical. In Orthodox tradition, an important criterion in the judgement of whether a dead person might be a saint or not was whether his body was incorruptible. In *The Brothers Karamazov*, the rotting of Elder Zosima's body precipitates a bitter crisis of faith in Alesha, who – unlike Dostoevsky – is inclined to take this tradition literally. Sakova's memory of how Pavlik's corpse stank – more than twenty years after it was buried! – may be accurate (this was boggy terrain, after all), but just as likely was prompted by a desire to emphasize how far the boy was from being a saint.

THE DRUZHNIKOV VERSION

We can safely assume that Pavlik really did exist (rumours to the contrary have circulated since the collapse of the Soviet Union, but a properly researched proof of his non-existence has never been set out). It also seems highly probable that he and Fyodor were in fact murdered. They were not, after all, the first children to be the victims of an alleged attack by kulaks, so we are not dealing with the invention of a new tradition; and on the other hand, their murders did not happen close enough to the first such murder, Grisha Akopyan's, for the story's emergence to be explained by inert imitation of a successful formula. But where does one go beyond there? The pitfalls that lie in wait for anyone trying to get back to the detailed facts from sources that are corrupt, fragmented, and at times deliberately misleading, are formidable indeed.

Getting back to these facts is nevertheless what Yury Druzhnikov attempted in his fascinating book about his search for the real Pavlik, first published in 1988. Among the biographers, Druzhnikov takes Solomein on trust, using his biography, as well as Solomein's rough notes of his research for his book, alongside documents from the criminal investigation that he discovered in an unnamed archive (but at least some of which are to be seen in the Pavlik Morozov Museum), and interviews with members of the Morozov family, their relatives and fellow villagers, as the sources for an alternative life of the individual mythologized as 'Pavlik': not a heroic legend at all, but a dismal history of deprivation and exploitation.

The child who in life was known as 'Pashka' Morozov was, Druzhnikov insists, not at all a model of the Soviet 'cultured person'. He was the neglected child of a mother who was a byword for slovenliness. He was slow at his lessons, spoke a thick Belorussian dialect; the dirtiest child in his class, he attended lessons (if at all) with reeking clothes, since he and his brothers used to urinate over each other when they squabbled. So far from being the leader of a Pioneer troop, Pashka was, Druzhnikov thinks, not a Pioneer at all. There was no Pioneer troop in the village during his lifetime, and indeed the village school, first set up in 1930, led a precarious existence in the first years after its founding, closing down for months when its first teacher left, defeated by the harsh local conditions, to reopen only in 1931. Pashka's denunciation of his father to the authorities was not an act of civic obedience, but was motivated by a family feud. His mother had been abandoned by his father when he was about eight, and Trofim Morozov had then begun a second liaison, with a younger woman from the same village; Pashka (perhaps at his mother's instigation) likely betrayed his father to the authorities as an act of revenge. All in all, for the villagers of Gerasimovka, Pashka was in no respect a local hero: his father had been a well-liked kolkhoz chairman, respected for his astuteness in balking the authorities, but the boy was dregs, 'a shithead' and 'a dirty little beggar'.[12] After the murder, 'Pavlik's' grave, officially a shrine, was regularly desecrated by locals: in the words of his mother, Tatiana Morozova, who gave an interview to Druzhnikov decades after her son's death, 'half the village would go and shit on it'.[13]

Equally grim and pathetic were the circumstances of Pashka's murder (as reconstructed by Druzhnikov from documentation that he recognizes to be patchy and compromised).[14] He agrees with the official account of the murder as to place and circumstances: the killing did indeed occur in the woods near Gerasimovka, on a day when Tatiana was out of the village (she was, according to locals, taking a calf to market). The boys had indeed gone off cranberry-picking. But so far as those responsible are concerned, Druzhnikov radically departs from the 'kulak conspiracy' theory. He pours scorn on the idea that the Morozov boys' relatives were responsible. Why would anyone have left the bodies lying in a place close to the village, where discovery was likely, rather than pushing them into a bog, and why would they not have evaded arrest by escaping into the taiga?[15]

The blatant disposal of the bodies indicates, Druzhnikov

thinks, that someone wanted them to be found. This leads him to hypothesize that the children were killed by *agents provocateurs* from the security services working in the region. The idea was to murder some children – any children who happened to be around – as a reason to set up a show trial of kulaks to discredit them in the public eye. He mentions two suspects in particular. The first is Pashka's cousin Ivan Potupchik, who was, Druzhnikov states, a paid informer of the OGPU, and not just a police aide; and the OGPU operative Spiridon Kartashov. Both, Druzhnikov argues, 'had form', so far as behaviour of this kind was concerned. Potupchik was to receive a conviction for rape of a minor in 1961; Kartashov was a pathological sadist who later boasted to acquaintances that he enjoyed bayoneting children or using his horse to trample them to death.[16]

Druzhnikov's reconstruction of the murder goes like this. The 'perpetrator', a professional killer from the OGPU, stops off in a nearby village on the pretence of conducting an investigation, and collects state-of-play details from his local informers. He hears about the planned berrying trip, and the threats against the Morozov boy from his grandfather, and realizes that this looks like a good victim for a murder that will smear dangerous opponents of collectivization in the villages. The next day he goes to the woods, where he bayonets the children to death, finishing the smaller boy off with the butt of his rifle. On 4 September, he calls his informant to the next village and states that he knows a political murder has taken place. The two put together the document on the removal of the bodies. The killing is kept secret for the meanwhile; by the time the boys have been missed and a search has begun, there have been heavy rains, and the evidence at the murder site has been destroyed.[17]

Druzhnikov backs up his account by reference to five documents in particular.[18] The first two are: (a) the protocol from the meeting of the Poor Peasants' Assembly in Gerasimovka on 12 September, laying out the supposed facts of the murders, and demanding that the perpetrators be executed (58, 59–60); and (b) the witness deposition by Potupchik suggesting that Danila Morozov and Efrem Shatrakov committed the murder (29).[19] The other three are: (c) the overview of the state of the investigation as at 16 September 1932, put out by the Tavda office of the Secret Political Section (SPO) of the OGPU (149–51); (d) the

6 September 'removal of the corpses' report by local policeman Titov (7);[20] and (e) a typewritten 'Order' bearing the names of Kartashov and of 'senior plenipotentiary Kulikov', dated 13 September 1932.[21] This states that 'Pavlik Morozov' had been murdered 'because he had been doing work with the Pioneer group and putting up posters calling single householders into the kolkhoz and sticking them on kulaks' fences'. Document (e) also orders that the file on the Morozov murders should be forwarded to the district centre at Tavda.

SLAUGHTERED BY THE OGPU?

Druzhnikov's account is so compellingly narrated as to be almost persuasive on a first reading. But on scrutiny, numerous objections arise. Written clandestinely in the Brezhnev era, the book retains, in its published form, the lack of precision in citation typical of an era when archives and libraries placed much of their material off-limits to ordinary users, and allowed people to see only such books and documents as were deemed to be 'relevant to the subject in hand'. And 'the subject in hand' had to be something of self-evident probity: 'Tolstoy and the Peasant Question', say, or 'Class Struggle in the Factories of Petrograd, 1905–07'. Anyone researching a politically sensitive topic would be able to see relevant materials only through subterfuge (by naming an innocuous theme, and hoping that something interesting would come up), or when someone bent the rules, which meant that specifying one's source exactly would get friends and helpful contacts into trouble. Hence the use of locutions such as 'a certain archive', and a degree of obfuscation about exactly what information came from where. The book also has a sprinkling of small errors, as is inevitable when checking sources is difficult or impossible.[22]

More significantly, Druzhnikov's book is in signal respects unhistorical in approach. It questions the veracity of official sources – perfectly reasonably – yet regularly refers to them in order to cement an argument. And it fails to locate the story of Pavlik firmly in the context of the time when it happened, as opposed to the time when Druzhnikov's book was written. As a political dissident, Druzhnikov himself had abundant experience of the mechanisms of repression in the post-Stalin era,[23] but the analogies which he drew between the working of state institutions in the post-Stalin era and their functioning in the early Soviet era were not always sustainable. The KGB had a deplorable record of arranging political murders in the 1960s, 1970s and 1980s, but even then, not every murder of political importance was necessarily committed by them. And in the 1920s and 1930s, the Cheka and the OGPU had a much weaker institutional base than their post-Stalinist successor organization. Such political murders or attempted murders as they definitely did have a hand in committing were of high-profile individuals domiciled in major cities or abroad (the most famous examples being the spy Ignaty Reis, murdered on the night of 4–5 September 1937 in Switzerland, having been tracked in the months before his death by Sergei Efron, husband of the poet Marina Tsvetaeva; and Leon Trotsky, Stalin's most hated political enemy). It strains credulity to think of the Tavda OGPU, with an abundance of real and threatening political antagonists, going out of their way to arrange a political murder in order to stoke up further conflict in the region. In any case, on 7 August 1932, a law introducing the death penalty for theft of property from collective farms had been introduced, ushering in a period of mass arrests and summary justice, often on next to no evidence.[24] The authorities already had a formidable weapon against their supposed enemies: why should they need an artificial reason to stoke up repression?

Even if they had needed such a reason, the sort of elaborate scenario that Druzhnikov sketches out seems unlikely. The Tavda official world was short of high-calibre material, and neither Potupchik nor Kartashov show – in the interrogation records – any signs of being such material. Indeed, the Party records reveal rather the opposite – about Kartashov, at least. In February 1933, disciplinary action was taken against him for 'crude political mistakes with regard to terminating political actions against kulaks, and also the case he stirred up with regard to the late citizen VISKUNOV and his sloppy attitude to the tasks assigned him'.[25] Rather than the suitable instrument of action against the class enemy, then, Kartashov was, from the authorities' point of view, a bodger and mischief-maker who was too much in league with kulaks for his own good. What impression one has of Bykov from the files also does not suggest an individual likely to have initiated such an operation: he was competent and literate by comparison with Kartashov and Titov, but that does not mean a great deal.

Perhaps, of course, the authorities higher up the OGPU masterminded the operation; but in that case, it seems strange that they let the Tavda operatives bumble on for more than a month, coming to conclusions that differed from those eventually presented at the show trial. In this light, striking also is the fact that Ivan Potupchik, who appeared at the trial, continued to insinuate that Efrem Shatrakov and Danila Morozov had done the murder, and did his best to exonerate Titov from the charges of having beaten the suspects and of having failed to let Efrem Shatrakov sign a protocol (233). The 'conspiracy' at the local level does not seem to have gone further than trying to get a workmate off the hook.

Crucially, too, document (b), on which much of Druzhnikov's argument about the involvement of Kartashov and Potupchik is based, is misdated in the version that he saw. Kartashov's witness interview with Potupchik, according to the version in H-7825, took place not on 4 September 1932, but on 11 September 1932 (29).[26] This later date is borne out by everything in the full case file: Kartashov was definitely in Gerasimovka on 11 and 12 September, but no documents suggest that he was there at any other time. The hypothesis of collusion over the murder followed by collusion over the protocol will not hold up.

Problematic in various senses too is (e), the 'Order' by Kartashov from 13 September, which does not appear in H-7825. To begin with, the style of the document does not resemble the usual format of 'Orders', which had an addressee, a number and an official header. One might contrast the release order for Efrem Shatrakov issued by Shepelev (countersigned by Voskresensky and Prokhrenko) on 14 November 1932. This is headed 'ORDER OF THE PP [Plenipotentiary Division] OF OGPU, COUNCIL OF PEOPLE'S COMMISSARS, USSR, URALS PROVINCE, ON RELEASE FROM IMPRISONMENT AND THE CURTAILMENT OF JUDICIAL INVESTIGATION IN THE CASE OF E. A. SHATRAKOV' (202). There is also some doubt whether Kartashov was senior enough to issue an 'Order': the lowest-ranking official to issue such a document included in H-7825 was Bykov. What is more, the spelling and general presentation of Druzhnikov's document (e) is a good deal more orderly than in the handwritten documents composed by

Kartashov while working in Gerasimovka. Finally, the suspect list given in the Order is curious. It includes Dmitry, Anton and Efrem Shatrakov, Khima and Arseny Kulukanov, Arseny Silin, Danila, Kseniya and Sergei Morozov, and states that Kartashov had decided that the murderers were Danila, Kseniya and Sergei Morozov. But the case file indicates that Kartashov's work with suspects did not take the form that this Order suggests. He did not interview any of the Shatrakovs, the Kulukanovs or Silin; he spent most of his time collecting witness testimony; and the suspect in whose involvement he took most interest was Vladimir Mezyukhin (who was later released). And there are no official documents of early date in which Pavel Morozov is referred to as 'Pavlik'.

It therefore seems likely that document (e) is a fake. Quite who may have forged it, and why, is another issue – but it was certainly composed in retrospect, and in order to indicate that the authorities had been pursuing a consistent line right from the beginning. It may even date from the early 1960s, the point at which Kartashov resurfaced so far as the official history of the Morozov case was concerned.[27]

There really is nothing in the full case file, then, or in the local archives, to suggest that Kartashov and Potupchik were anything other than small cogs in the OGPU machine who were active at the beginning of the investigation, before more senior officials took over. There is no doubt that the authorities in the Urals at this period did exploit murders for political purposes, including murders that might in other circumstances have been seen as acts of self-interest or *crimes passionels*. For example, in January 1931, a woman in Makushinsky district had her throat cut after a drinking bout. When this messy incident appeared in a secret police report, the following gloss was put on it. The victim was a 'collective farmer and activist', who had been lured by kulaks to attend a party, where they had duly taken their revenge upon her for her activities in denouncing them to the police.[28] Possibly this interpretation had foundation, but, given the implausibility of a scenario where an activist under threat would have agreed to go drinking with the very people who were threatening her, it seems much more likely that a squalid drunken assault prompted by sexual or other personal motives was turned into a political crime because it suited the authorities to see it this way. All the same, the distance from creative misinterpretation of killings to actual orchestration of these is large – maybe even insuperable, psychologically and practically speaking.

The OGPU had in any case no need to arrange a murder that could be exploited to political ends; violence was common enough without their meddling. Statistics from 1926 indicate that, while the murder rates in the Urals were about average, those in Western Siberia – lying immediately to the east of Tavda district – were very high in proportion to the area's population (1,432 murders in an area with a population of just under nine million; by comparison, the far more densely populated Central Black Earth Region, with over nineteen and a half million inhabitants, clocked up just 1,443 murders in the same year).[29] The secret police files for Tavda give no detailed statistical breakdowns, but create the impression that the district was very much part of Siberia, rather than the Urals, as far as the level of violent incidents went.

THE 'CIVIC PIONEER': DOES THE EVIDENCE HOLD UP?

There are problems not simply with the 'conspiracy theory' part of Druzhnikov's narrative, but also with other sections of it. For instance, the question of whether Pavlik Morozov actually was a Pioneer is more problematic than it might at first seem. Pavel would not have needed to belong to an official Pioneer troop in order to have *thought* of himself as a Pioneer in 1932 (and to have been considered one in the village where he lived), even though there was no official troop for him to join. It is a mistake to back-project on to the first decade of the Pioneer organization's existence its profile in the 1940s or even in the mid-1930s – an established monolith with institutional bases in schools, trade union culture clubs and apartment blocks, as well as the 'Pioneer houses' and 'Pioneer palaces' that became the flagships of the movement from 1935, and with a hard-and-fast procedure for enrolment (which, from 1932 onwards, was supposed to be executed exclusively as a ritual within schools). In the late 1920s and early 1930s, the Pioneer organization was still in chaotic shape, beset by problems of 'elemental growth' and equally elemental shrinkage (euphemistically known as 'turnover'). It had to rely on inadequately trained or ideologically questionable personnel (including former scout leaders) to act as Pioneer organizers, and was characterized by all kinds of 'voluntarism' and 'parallelism'.[30] At times, the word 'Pioneers' seems to have been used loosely for members of juvenile 'agitbrigades' set up by schoolteachers or other adults to perform ancillary tasks in political campaigns such as the drive to 'transform daily life' (that is, disseminate the principles of hygiene and rational living) in 1927–8, or the collectivization onslaught of 1931–2. The novelist Mikhail Alekseev remembered an 'agitbrigade' of this kind being organized in his village on the Volga in the autumn of 1931: schoolchildren were delegated to visit the houses of peasants who had not yet signed up to the kolkhoz and exhort them to do this immediately.[31]

With or without an agitbrigade or organization, children at this era had ways of hearing about Pioneers, even if they lived in a village. Pyotr Kruzhin (born in a village in Tver' province, 1921) formally joined the Pioneers in 1929, but remembered being aware of the Pioneer movement (from commercial art such as pictures on tooth-powder boxes) and working as an activist (and helping with icon-burning sessions and so on) long before. Thereafter, 'our Pioneer organization was sometimes active, sometimes dormant' for the next four years. Leaders had wildly different ideas of what to do with the children (one drilled them, one took them hunting for herbs, and one did nothing but tell funny stories), and at times when there was no official leader available, Kruzhin would lead the troop himself and enjoy bossing the adults in the village around.[32]

Evidence from Tavda district sketches a roughly similar picture. This was not a place where tooth-powder boxes, even when empty, were likely to circulate in the countryside, but informal Pioneer activity is recorded. In November 1932, responding to the top-level drive for more central control within the Pioneer organization, the District Committee of the Communist Party called a halt to the previously widespread practice of simply letting the Children's Bureau know the names of Pioneer leaders after the fact. Wrong decisions had been commonly made: many of the leaders were too young, many were too inexperienced and some disliked working with children. The Bureau demanded that it be formally notified before groups were set up, and introduced training courses for Pioneer leaders, and a specific programme of Pioneer activities (including indoctrination about political topics such as 'class war', and the struggle with 'national differences', but also games, songs, drama groups and 'living newspapers').[33] The fact that such measures needed to be set in place points to a good deal of unregulated Pioneer activity in the district generally. It cannot be ruled out that one of the Gerasimovka teachers – for example, Zoya Mironova, recorded as a 'Pioneer leader' in the Party cell details in early 1931[34] – had set up what he or she chose to term a 'Pioneer troop' in an impromptu way.

There is also evidence of informal children's agitbrigades in Tavda district. For instance, *Tavda Worker* reported on 28 April 1932 that one had been set up in no less a place than Gerasimovka school. Testimony in the Morozov murders case file also recalls children fly-posting kulaks' fences with the warning: 'A VICIOUS GRAIN-HOARDER LIVES HERE', though whether such information was genuine is hard to say.[35]

Children could also have learned about the Pioneers through written sources. The 1930 primary school reader *New Path* included various pieces of information about the Pioneers. For instance, a picture in the first-year issue, 'I Saw Lenin on the First of May', included a group of Pioneers; the second-year issue had a little story, 'Help', about the Pioneers coming to help out Fedya's mother with her cow, and printed the rousing rally song, 'The Pioneers' March', alongside the 'Laws of the Pioneers'.[36] And one of the very few newspapers received by the Gerasimovka village soviet in 1933 (no information for other years is available) was *Dawns of the Commune*, the Sverdlovsk Pioneer paper – a publication that was particularly insistent on the importance of Pioneers taking the initiative to press home official policy.[37]

DID PAVLIK DENOUNCE HIS FATHER?

The question of whether Pavlik was a Pioneer should be regarded as 'not proven'. Exactly the same applies to an even more important detail of the case, the question of whether Pashka denounced his father in the first place. The case file contains what purports to be a copy of the boy's denunciation, but like all other material there, this needs to be treated with extreme caution. It reads as follows (I have made an attempt to suggest the original spelling and grammar):

> Morozov's son – aged 12. Morozov Pavel Trofimovich. The latter announces during the interrogation of his mother:
>
> > Uncle, my father were up to blaytunt counter-revolutionary tricks, as a Pioneer Ime obliged to tell you, my father int no defender of the interests of October, hes helping the kulaks to escape in every way he can, backing em to the hilt, and as a Pioneer, not as his son I ask you to bring my father to strict ackount for his actions, for in the future there won't be no excuse for no-one to cover up kulaks, and fly in the face of the party, and in addition Ile tell you that my father has helped himself to kulak property, he took a bed off kulak Arseny Kulukanov and wanted to take a haystack off of him only kulak Kulukanov didnt want to let him and said Ide rather the powers that be had it (113).

The piece appears under the title 'Extract from the evidence given by the Pioneer Morozov Pavel Trofimovich on 26 November 1932' (hastily amended to '1931'), and is certificated as genuine by Iskrin, one of the workers at the Tavda OGPU. No source is given, however (no number for the father's case file, for instance), and the copy is not dated. The other documents on which Iskrin's signature appears date from between 1 and 6 November (153, 154, 176, 178), but the denunciation has been placed by the archivist around mid-October 1932, so it is possible (though to my mind, less likely) that it was originated then (at the point when Bykov was managing the investigation). Whichever way, the case file is not the only place where this text surfaced. It was also cited – as a letter rather than a piece of oral testimony, this time – in a report by a district official of the Party organizational section to his superiors in Sverdlovsk.[38] Once again, no source for the denunciation was given, and the official – who did not come from Pavlik's home district, Tavda, but from the neighbouring district of Lower Tavda – knew so little about the Morozov boys' home turf that he even filed the denunciation under a section headed 'Beloyarka Village Soviet', though anyone with local roots would have known that Gerasimovka was not in that administrative area, but constituted a village soviet of its own.

Pavlik's denunciation – in the general sense – had been mentioned in the testimony of some Gerasimovka informants, notably Tatiana Morozova, and – at late stages of the investigation – by Kseniya and Sergei. But no precise picture of how he had made it had been given. In the case of the Shatrakovs' gun, locals reported that Pavlik had gone to the village soviet, and helped Titov with the house search (35, 36); in the case of Kulukanov's hidden goods, he was supposed to have reported to the village soviet (34). But how he denounced Trofim was unclear. The case file and the Party report provide two alternative suggestions: either Pavlik sent a written denunciation (as in the Party report), or he made a statement during oral cross-questioning of his mother (as in the denunciation recorded in file H-7825).

Pavlik can hardly, of course, have done *both* of these things (certainly not in identical words), which might make one wonder about the authenticity of the text in whatever form. Also striking is the similarity of the phrasing in this supposed denunciation and in the 15 October *Pioneer Pravda* article: 'Uncle judge, I am acting not as a son, but as a Pioneer! And I say: my father is betraying the cause of October.'

Of course, it is possible that the newspaper article was based on the Party report or on the OGPU text, but one cannot rule out that the reverse might be the case. The Party report, like the extract from the denunciation in the OGPU file, is undated (the first sheet is missing from the archive record), but the phrase *za sentyabr*, 'in the course of the month of September', is used in it, suggesting that September was complete when it was written. It was standard practice for reports of this kind to be compiled somewhere around the middle of a given month. It is possible that, having learned about Pavlik's denunciation from the first newspaper reports to mention this (that is, those in *Pioneer Pravda* on 2 and 15 October 1932), the author of the report himself sat down and wrote the denunciation, in an attempt to curry favour with the regional administration by emphasizing that he knew more about what was going on in Upper Tavda district than the officials there themselves did. Perhaps the denunciation then found its way from the Party report into the OGPU case file. Or perhaps it was written to order for the latter, and made its way in time into the report (though this second sequence of events seems less likely, first, given that the Party was kept in touch only with the outlines of the investigation, and second, given that the OGPU copy of the denunciation seems to be later than the report).

The denunciation might seem more trustworthy if there were any evidence beyond the case file that a denunciation took place. In fact, there is not, which seems extremely odd. If a kolkhoz chairman had been denounced by his own son for corruptly issuing false identity papers to kulaks in the late summer or autumn of 1931, widespread publicity – certainly at the local level – would have been likely. Early 1931 saw the collectivization and dekulakization campaigns regain momentum after the lull introduced by Stalin's denunciatory speech, 'Dizzy with Success', on 1 March 1930; any material that discredited kulaks was attractive to newspaper editors. But *Tavda Worker* and its predecessor papers carried no such report about a chairman of Gerasimovka village soviet, despite the fact that the village was constantly in the news because of the eruption of some scandal or other.

True, the paper did, on 3 December 1931, report a major scandal that had recently broken in Gerasimovka. Kulaks had 'woven themselves a sturdy nest' in the village soviet, and were trying to subvert grain collection. The kulaks listed were I. Kutsakov, V. Pulyashko, Ermakov, 'the Kulukanovs', Gudumchnin, the Sokovs [Sakovs], and the Naumovs, all of whom had been hiding grain. This was probably the incident that led to Arseny Kulukanov's exile, which was constantly referred to in the investigation. The scandal also seems to fit the time when – according to H-7825 – Trofim Morozov was under investigation (November 1931), but he is not mentioned in the story, which says cryptically, 'The village soviet and [police aides] look on all this with indulgence and are not taking necessary steps.'[39]

One has to bear in mind that newspapers were reticent about revealing the full details of criminal activities on the part of local officials. Only from secret police reports is it possible to establish that Novopashin, Gerasimovka chairman in the summer of 1931, who was denounced in the press for spending too much time with his wife and of cosying up to kulaks, was in fact guilty (in the authorities' eyes) of the far more serious crime of collusion with two men who had robbed two other locals at gunpoint with a revolver, and who had bribed Novopashin with butter and other foodstuffs for his silence. Novopashin had allegedly provided the men with alibis and with character references, and was undergoing criminal proceedings for his misdemeanours.[40] Perhaps the village soviet chairman who was publicly accused of tolerating grain-hoarding was actually under suspicion of some more serious crime? But even police reports are totally silent about Trofim Morozov. Possibly the case was referred to in a report now lost (as mentioned, the sets available for public consultation are incomplete). Even so, it seems strange that records of what must have been a particularly flamboyant case should be so elusive.

Gerasimovka survivors whom I interviewed in 2003 remembered nothing about Morozov's trial, though it was allegedly held in the village school.[41] This is quite possibly a question of their extreme youth at the time: adult witnesses interviewed by Druzhnikov recalled clearly that the trial had taken place in Gerasimovka, one remembering also that Tatiana Morozova had testified against her husband, and that Pashka had joined in to confirm his story – at which his 'uncle judge' had hushed him with the words, 'you're only little, just sit quietly.'[42] On the other hand, the source of this information was the former village teacher, Zoya Kabina, whose role in the case was rather equivocal – like Denis and Ivan Potupchik (the latter of whom she later married), she was a vehement supporter of 'the measures being taken'.

It is hard to agree with Druzhnikov that Pavlik's denunciation 'must be considered a proven fact'.[43] There is no independent record of Trofim Morozov's trial; even establishing that he was ever chairman of the village soviet is a problem. Although it is sometimes claimed that he held this position as many as three times,[44] he appears in no published or unpublished record as the holder of this job. The only written testimony to his association with it is a letter of petition dated 21 April 1930, and now held in the city archive in Irbit, till 1931 the intermediate administrative centre for the Tavda district, where he requests leave to resign as village soviet chairman on the grounds of his poor literacy, and because he had in any case only agreed to do the job on a temporary basis.[45] If this document can be relied upon,

Trofim definitely was the village soviet chairman, but nothing like it can be found to demonstrate his chairmanship at later eras. In the course of preparing a publication of materials from H-7825, a member of staff at the FSB archive attempted to chase up the file on the Trofim Morozov case in Ekaterinburg. He was told that the file had been destroyed in a fire at some point in the 1950s.[46] So no independent corroboration is available from that angle either. It is not even clear under what article of the Criminal Code Trofim Morozov was charged. References in the case file are to 'ten years' exile' (206), but exile was a measure of punishment more often used for kulaks. A sentence of ten years' imprisonment, on the other hand, was a serious penalty (and 'ten years without right of correspondence' was routinely used as a euphemism for execution). But the article of the Criminal Code dealing with the forging of official documents had a maximum penalty of five years' imprisonment; it was only forging of coins and banknotes that carried a capital sentence.[47] Of course, it is possible that Trofim was tried under one of the subdivisions of Article 58; but the absence of publicity for the trial of a major 'enemy of the people' would be anomalous indeed.

There are, to be sure, numerous references in case file H-7825 to the Trofim Morozov case. But these references start to cluster at fairly late stages of the investigation. And they are not consistent. As late as 13 November, Arseny Silin was to state, 'I had no idea that he [Pavel] had told on his father' (197). In the early interviews, only one witness mentioned the denunciation – Tatiana Morozova herself, as part of her evidence against her husband's family: 'my son pavel aged 13 was a pioneer and he told on his father that he was selling documents and he got my husband put in prison for that and that's why the father and mother of my husband got cross on my son that he told on his father' (1). Later, the main evidence about the denunciation of Trofim – alongside Tatiana's stories – came from self-incriminating testimony by Sergei and Kseniya Morozova.

Tatiana Morozova played a significant role in the calumnification of her husband and his family, quickly establishing herself as a trusted source of information. Pavel Solomein, for example, uncritically passed on her stories about witnessing a beating of Pavlik by Danila, and about her own absence from the village of

3 September, in a story under the title 'How Pavlik Died' published in *Dawns of the Commune* on 27 October.[48] At the trial in December 1932, she had an equally weighty role as a witness for the prosecution in a formal sense. In coverage in the press and in official lives of Pavlik, she appeared as something akin to a village Madonna: photographs usually showed her in a plain white headscarf and with a long-suffering expression on her face.[49] She was also later to become the material beneficiary of her son's fame, fêted at provincial events, and sent on special trips to Moscow and elsewhere to meet delegations of Pioneers. She spent the decades after the war, until her death in 1983, living in the exclusive resort of Alupka, in the Crimea, from where she was a frequent visitor to Artek Pioneer Camp, the most prestigious children's leisure facility in the Soviet Union. Well before this (not long after the murders and the trial) she had moved from Gerasimovka itself to Tavda, where her sons were able to receive a better education, and where – according to locals who spoke to Yury Druzhnikov – she was quartered in a room supplied by the OGPU, and had access to special rations as well.[50]

Of course, Tatiana could hardly have known about this glittering future in advance, unless the investigating authorities – as is not impossible – promised her rewards in return for testifying in ways that suited them. But she would have been aware of the danger that she herself could come under suspicion of the murder, or at least of involvement in it, as her mother-in-law Kseniya had. She accordingly had every reason to co-operate with the prosecution of her husband's family, even if he had not (as local gossip asserted) dumped her and her children and gone off with another woman. The denunciation was first mentioned in the context of a long narrative about how Tatiana 'had no friendship with [Sergei and Kseniya] because I was living married totheir son and then in 1931 I split up with him and then my husband started selling documents to exiles' (1). It cannot be ruled out that this story was simply a piece of spiteful gossip on Tatiana's part, an attempt to get the members of her husband's family into trouble. From the point of view of the case investigators, and the tribunal at the trial, Tatiana's testimony reflected badly on Trofim, and indicated her own acuity of judgement and her moral rectitude. But not everyone has been so positive about

Pavlik's mother. She appears not to have been popular in Gerasimovka village, and made a bad impression on some of those who met her in later years, after she had become famous as a result of her son Pavlik's national reputation.[51]

At the same time, arguments from negative evidence are always problematic. It is possible that Trofim Morozov really did – despite his reluctance to keep on the position in 1930 – act as chairman more than once (no detailed records of who was chairman in the individual village soviets of Tavda district survive for the early 1930s). It is possible that one of these times was in late 1931, at a stage when supplying false papers to the dekulakized and to special settlers was a common type of offence by chairmen of village soviets. It is conceivable that he was caught supplying such papers, tried and sentenced to exile or a spell in prison or a labour camp. All of these happenings are possible, indeed likely, in the general political and cultural climate of the Tavda region at the time. Even if all this is accepted, though, there is no proof that he was necessarily denounced by his son. Secret police reports reveal that the commonest way in which the authorities found out about the provision of false papers was at the *other* end of the process – by picking up gossip in special settlement camps from those who had managed to get hold of such papers. In any case, it was easy for kolkhoz chairmen to make enemies, and denunciations against them were particularly common;[52] they were also first in the line of fire if the pace of collectivization was felt to be too slow. Perhaps Trofim simply received a sentence of exile at the point when Arseny Kulukanov, supposedly his crony, was expelled from the village for five years. At all events, there is no need to assume a denunciation by his son, or to propound a tangled family drama, in order to find a reason why Trofim Morozov ended up in trouble with the authorities. Certainly, father–son denunciations were widely reported in the late 1920s and early 1930s, and there is no reason why a boy from Gerasimovka caught up in dreams of setting the world to rights should not have engineered one. Yet there is still nothing to show that this ever happened – and here one comes back again to the fact that the case, had it occurred, would have been such a dream for Soviet propaganda that the lack of publicity looks very odd.

A DIFFERENT KIND OF CRIME

Druzhnikov's version of Pavlik – presenting the boy as definitely the denouncer of his father, but seeing his denunciation as an act of squalid family strife, rather than of disinterested virtue, and presenting his killing as a bestial crime by *pro*-Soviet murderers – is as much a product of myth-making as the official legends about the boy. It rests on an assumption that the truth behind Soviet legends was not just different from the facts as officially stated (fair enough), but diametrically opposed to these. Pavlik was an excellent pupil: therefore, it stands to reason that Pashka was dirty, disruptive and stupid. Pavlik was full of disinterested civic virtue; therefore, Pashka must have acted out of naked self-interest. Pavlik's murderers were kulaks; Pashka's murderers must have been the opposite – the architects of collectivization. At the same time, the Druzhnikov theory perpetuates the idea of the forces of Soviet government as all-seeing and all-powerful, just as Soviet propaganda itself did.

Most importantly of all, the theory shares Soviet propaganda's obsession with conspiracy theories and interest groups. To be fair, the idea of two murderers roaming round bent on killing *any* children in order to provoke uproar is a touch more plausible than the official notion that Sergei and Danila were somehow able to track them down on their return from a berrying trip without apparently knowing exactly where they had gone. To this day, Russians – adults as well as children – sometimes get irretrievably lost in forested country,[53] and running into a person accidentally on purpose would be a near-impossibility. But even the premeditated murder of just any two children would have presented formidable difficulties. What was required: to hang around waiting in a likely spot till two of them turned up (when it might just as easily be six, or nine, or none)? What guarantee was there that locals would immediately blame the 'right' killers, rather than the authorities themselves? What guarantee was there that the bodies would even be found – unless the perpetrators themselves led others to the spot?

The conclusion has to be that this was an impulsive crime, and not a planned one – which would also explain the lack of any attempt to hide the bodies. In this lawless area, the two boys may have been murdered quite fortuitously, by some bandit, maniac or indeed violent drunk. The day when the murders happened, 3 September, was not a saint's day, a public holiday or a 'free day' (a term that came into use during the early Soviet era, when the official length of the week was stretched to ten days and days off did not necessarily fall on the traditional Saturdays or Sundays). However, the date of the boys' murder did coincide with a Saturday two days after the Church New Year, and less than a week after the Feast of the Dormition – in other words, it fell at what would have been a plum time for drinking bouts. That said, the Morozov boys' killer may not even have been human: it is just possible that they were killed by a wild animal (a bear?, a wolf?, an elk or stag?) they had stumbled upon in the taiga, whose gorings or maulings were interpreted, in the overheated atmosphere generated by the death of two small children, as stab wounds.[54]

What is interesting, though, is that no one in Gerasimovka village raised the possibility that the murder was committed by an animal, or by an outsider. Belorussia lies in the western part of the former Russian Empire, the place where 'ritual murder' accusations against Jews had traditionally been strongest, yet no 'blood libel' hue and cry seems to have been raised – though, as is clear from the anti-Soviet material circulating in Tavda, popular anti-Semitism was as strong here as anywhere. Nor did anybody try to blame a 'special settler' – though an escaping settler, coming on two lone children who might have reported his or her whereabouts, would have been a perfectly reasonable suspect. From the first, local opinion was that someone in the community must be responsible.

This search for 'the enemy within', perhaps unusual for a village community in ordinary circumstances, is partly explained by the atmosphere of mutual mistrust prevailing in the early Soviet era, when anyone could come under suspicion as an 'enemy of the people'. The Stalinist 'divide and rule' policy was having its effect on Gerasimovka. In addition, this section of Tavda district, settled only twenty years earlier by people from a quite different area of the Russian Empire (and not all from the same part of it) was an artificial, manufactured community, without deep traditional ties to provide respite from oppression. Most of all, the villagers blamed other people on the principle of 'the best means of defence is attack'. When one reads through the hundreds of pages of collected testimony, it becomes clear that lying was very widespread. Danila – who everywhere reveals a fantastical, attention-seeking streak – seems a particularly unreliable witness. But Sergei Morozov, who unsolicitedly denounced Danila, Vladimir Mezyukhin, and in due course his own wife (who, he said at the trial, had a pre-1917 conviction for theft (223)), comes across as little better. The veracity of Tatiana Morozova, who never told her story about how Kseniya had referred to the children as 'meat' twice in the same way, seems equally questionable.

The fact was that everyone in the village had something to hide – grain hoards that might be discovered, illegal trade in horses and crops, enmity with neighbours and relations. To protect themselves, they regularly made incriminating claims about others: this was meant to prove their 'sympathy to Soviet power' and to divert the uncomfortable scrutiny of the police on to other people. A case in point was Khima Kulukanova, who not only claimed that Kseniya had told her that Sergei had killed the boys, in company with Danila, but who also dredged up a story about her father's pre-revolutionary convictions for 'hooliganism' (125). This tendency to provide servile statements increased as the investigation wore on, and the suspects and witnesses gradually realized just how seriously the authorities were taking the case.

Nevertheless, some patterns of blame among the villagers themselves gradually started to form. By the time of the trial, majority opinion was that those being accused by the authorities had done it (162 rev.). In the beginning, though – till local opinion had started being influenced by official conviction that 'kulaks' had masterminded the murder – the prevailing view of ordinary villagers, as well as the local policemen, was that Danila Morozov, probably in combination with one or both Shatrakov brothers, had committed the murders. This view had already been expressed by Sergei Morozov, in his first interview with the police on 7 September. Sergei's testimony was circumstantial; Danila had been absent for much of the afternoon, and on 5 September he had told his grandfather the boys had been found in the woods, and reported that there were three wounds on one and two on the other. Sergei also considered that the Shatrakov sons must be involved, because they were angry at Pavel for denouncing a gun that they had hidden (12). Other locals echoed Sergei's drift. The villagers held Pavlik responsible for the confiscation of the Shatrakovs' gun by police in July (12, 13, 14, 26 rev., 27, 36 rev.), and were aware of an altercation that had taken place in the street in late August over a piece of horse harness that Pavlik wanted his grandfather to hand over (25).

The villagers widely believed – or said that they believed – Pavlik had been involved in telling on people in the village, and attributed his killing to this. Of course, such an opinion cannot be relied on, any more than the hunches followed by the investigators can. There is no guarantee that Pavlik and Fyodor were murdered at the time when they are supposed to have been, in or near the place where they were found, or for the reasons supposed. If expressed dislike for the boys – as reported at second hand – is anything to go by, most of the village could have perpetrated the killing, or been involved in it, or sought to cover it up. The only villager who almost certainly could *not* have committed the murder was Arseny Silin, who was missing two fingers from his right hand, lost when he was serving in the First World War – this information is available from his medical record (130).

From the interrogation records, and some survivor testimony, also comes the strong impression of a community where violence was both routine, and regarded with relish. The terms of abuse for Pavlik – 'snot-nosed Pioneer' (101), 'damned Communist' (69), 'filth' (192) – jostle grim jokes about the children's bodies as 'meat' (neither Kseniya nor Tatiana denied that an exchange of some kind along these lines took place, though they disputed the substance), and their live selves as 'calves'. And survivor testimony still captures the mixture of prurience and indifference with which the murders were regarded locally. Mariya Sakova remembered that, when the bodies were brought in, the village children – far from feeling frightened, as middle-class city children were when they even heard about the murder – ran eagerly to inspect them. 'His hand was half cut off,' she gleefully recalled of Pavlik.[55]

THE CASE AGAINST DANILA AND EFREM

In principle, the murder could have been committed by a villager, and perhaps particularly a young one. Research by the German criminologist Dieter Arlet on violent attacks outside the home by adolescents suggests an above average likelihood of knives being used; of a woodland site as the place where the murder is committed; and of motives such as anger with the victim, and fear that a misdeed will be discovered if he or she is not silenced. Arlet's case studies also suggest that it is rare for adolescents to make much effort to hide the bodies of their victims – the most elaborate form of concealment is usually to shove the corpses under scrub, or to cover them with leaves. Not surprisingly, therefore, crimes are usually discovered quite fast – more than half, in Arlet's sample, within three days.[56] Of course, this evidence comes from a different era, and a different country, from the Morozov murders; and without the 'control' of information about general preferences among murders of all kinds, it is impossible to judge how specific these adolescent murderers were in terms of their *modus operandi*. But it is worth pausing to consider the possibility of the Morozov murders as the result of youth conflict. It is not intrinsically impossible. Murders of children by other (older) children were occasionally recorded during the Stalin era. On 26 August 1947, for instance, Vasily Shelkanov, aged twelve, was murdered in the woods near the children's home where he lived by a group of fifteen- and sixteen-year-old boys who had taken umbrage at Shelkanov's activities in denouncing them to the children's home authorities (he was president of the inmate soviet in the home).[57]

How much evidence is there to support the idea that Pavlik was murdered by villagers near his own age? Conflicting as it is, the testimony in the Morozov case file seems to agree about one thing: Pavel either did, or was suspected of, a great deal of denouncing. Most recently, he had come under suspicion of being behind the confiscation from the Shatrakovs of their gun. He had also (it is consistently reported) had a fight with Danila Morozov over the horse harness. An encounter between Danila and one or more of the Shatrakovs, on the one hand, and Pavlik and any of his brothers, on the other, could easily have turned into a scuffle. And from name-calling and feinting blows the transition to a much nastier fight, after someone pulled a knife, would have been possible; from there, an escalation into an impulsive, thoughtless, but also vicious, murder, would have been not only possible but likely.

Of the suspects originally preferred by the villagers, Dmitry

Shatrakov can be more or less ruled out. Not only was he able to produce documentary evidence of the appointment at the military conscription point on 3 September that had kept him occupied between early morning and late afternoon (16, 65), but it also seems improbable that he would have made a song and dance about discovering the bodies on 6 September, had he been involved in committing the murders in the first place. Danila and Efrem, on the other hand, look more likely perpetrators. Both in fact did admit to having participated in the murders, though these admissions are of course suspect because they were probably forced out of them. Efrem was, indeed, later to claim not only that he had been beaten by Titov during interrogation, but also that he had not signed the protocol in which he admitted his guilt (231). The former claim is impossible to investigate at this distance, though perfectly plausible; the latter is demonstrably false, since the protocol in question, from 8 September, does in fact bear his signature in the bottom right-hand corner of the reverse side (24).[58]

Whichever way, Efrem Shatrakov quickly went back to denying his involvement in the murder: this was the case at a face-to-face confrontation with Danila on 9 September (23), and also at later interviews with the police. But this may bespeak less the resolution born of innocence than the effects of external circumstances. Once the district administration of the OGPU had become involved, first through Kartashov on 11 and 12 September, and later through the interrogations carried out by Bykov from 16 September onwards, and the narrative about a 'kulak ring' was starting to be elaborated, the police lost interest in the humdrum story of the Shatrakovs' gun and the murders as an act of revenge for it, so that Efrem Shatrakov was never under pressure again. Instead, having been removed from the investigation on 14 November, he started to be used as a witness, in which capacity he appeared at the November 1932 trial, once again denying his guilt, and presenting himself – for the first time since the investigation started – as a friend of Pavel (231).

For his part, Danila was more consistent in accepting the blame, though he did revert to denying involvement at some points of the investigation, for instance, in the early interviews with Fedchenko (172, 174). However, the testimony that he offered was always contradictory and full of odd, improbable detail. He appears to have been easily influenced by what he thought that his audience wanted him to say, or perhaps by what he was being told to say. The most striking demonstration of this is when he claimed at his trial in November that he 'subscribed to newspapers and books and spent time reading them' during his leisure hours. In remote Gerasimovka, where the only copies of newspapers and books were those in the local reading room, this boast was fantastic, and it can have taken nobody in.

Efrem and Danila's confessions certainly do not prove their guilt, then, but they are not clear demonstrations of their innocence either. Unlike some of the later testimony (for instance, Sergei Morozov's confession to Fedchenko (179)), these statements were made in a language close to that of authentic village discourse. In particular, Efrem's tale of how the murders were done is raw, unembellished, and has a horrific plausibility:

> I state that on 3 September I was harowin our field and when Id finished harowin then I went home it wasn't late the sun was high dunno what time weve got no clock and then when I got back I took the harness off of the horses and then took em to the fields And then I went to the field where Morozov danila was harowin and we two had agreed in the morning when I shatrakov was fetchin in the horses And Morozov danila was going to the fields that 3 September and danila he says to me that today the morozov boys are going to get cranberries off the bog and weell kill em or stab em When I met morozov danila [i.e. later that day] Id brought along a little knife and then we went down the path and we met morozov pavel and Fodor not far away from the field in the woods and I went and stuck my knife into pavel into his belly and danil went running after fyodor and he also stuck his knife in his chest in the woods and pavel got away from me and danila came runing up and we got hold of pavel and stabbed him and then we put a sack on his head so that even if he was alive he'd never find his way back home (24).

Danila gave a not dissimilar account of the murder, while denying his responsibility for the actual killing:

> and shatrakov efem came along and we two wentoff together and we met morozov pavel an fodor and I grabbed pavel by the arm and efem stuk his knife in morozov pavel and then fyodor he went running into the woods But pavel he fell down with his head in thebushes and so we dumped him and ran after morozov Fyodor and I morozov danil grabbed morozov fodor and shatrakov stuck his knife in his belly and when he fell down then shatrakov efem cut him in the throat[59] and we ran to the path and morozov pavel wasn't there and then we went home and shatrakov took his knife off home (23).

The telling details here include the fact that the original meeting was on the path, and that both boys then ran into the wood, which would explain the location of the bodies, and the curious positions in which they were found in the post-mortem. Equally, the knife cut to Pavlik's hand is explicable by a desperate struggle with an adversary in a hand-to-hand fight of the kind depicted here, rather than a confrontation with a resolute and well-prepared murderer. Finally, Efrem was the first suspect to give an explanation of why Pavlik had a sack on his head – a detail reverted to only much later in the testimony, when Sergei Morozov claimed to have put this over his grandson's head.

All in all, the descriptions of the murder given by Danila and Efrem at this point were more plausible and circumstantial than those given in later admissions made by various accused persons in the Morozov case, which were less precise about where exactly the murders took place, and about who did what. In his testimony to Fedchenko on 6 November, for instance, Sergei Morozov said:

> When we reached the wood, we saw that Pavel and Fyodor were coming out of it towards us with full baskets of berries. When Pavel Morozov and I had met, I went up close to him and stabbed him in the chest, Pavel shouted out and at that moment Fyodor ran off, I realized he might tell everyone what had happened and shouted to Danilka, 'Hold him.' Danilka threw himself after Fyodor, caught hold of him and held him fast, I finished with Pavel and went up to Fyodor and struck him several more times with the same knife, Fyodor yelled out when I was doing it. After what had happened Daniil Morozov

> ran out of the woods. I finished off the Morozovs, put Pavel's sack over his head, and then went home (179–179 rev.).

This scenario requires one to believe that Danila would have gone out into the woods to execute a planned murder unarmed, a preposterous idea – and the action is presented in a very foggy and abstract way ('Danila threw himself after Fyodor . . .'). The idea of Sergei's guilt is problematic at a practical level too – both given his advanced age (let us remember that the medical report on the form written up when he was first in prison described him as 'elderly and frail' (136 rev.)) and also given the issue of the clothes in which the murders were committed. Only one set of purportedly bloodstained clothes was found at the Morozov household. Even if one accepts that the garments were actually bloodstained, it seems impossible to believe that they could have been worn by two people, one of whom just happened to get his shirt splashed, and the other, his trousers. In a violent attack such as the one launched at Pavel and Fyodor, when the victims had to be grabbed and held still, blood would have been dispersed much more widely. The only tenable hypothesis is that one person alone was wearing the clothes, which – if the measuring test was right – must have been Danila. In the case of Efrem, no incriminating clothes were found, but he had to explain away a knife with apparent traces of blood on it by saying that it was kept in the barn and used for smoothing down the izba floor (which, one assumes, was coated with a primitive flooring mixture of earth and blood) (91). To judge by this quick-witted explanation, and by his interrogation records generally, Efrem was a cleverer and cooler-headed individual than Danila; he may have had the sense to dispose of incriminating evidence in due time.

Perhaps the most telling hint of Efrem's possible guilt, however, is that, when first arrested, he gave his age as fifteen (24). He repeated this to Bykov on 22 September, where his date of birth was given as 1916 (90). In actual fact, Efrem was nineteen or twenty years old at the time (according to an entry in the local church records transcribed by the authorities on 4 November) (188). Birthdays were not celebrated in the Russian countryside until after the Second World War, and births were not registered until a child was christened, which might be months or years after he or she first entered the world. So confusion was definitely possible. Confronted by Bykov with the possibility that he was wrong about his age, Efrem replied: 'I dunno how old I am but my mother said I'm fifteen, I mean, that's my age' (89). But a discrepancy of this order is unlikely to be explained by a simple misunderstanding. Illiterate peasant mothers might not remember what year their children were born in, but they were likely to recall the order in which they were born – and with eight other brothers and sisters, Efrem and his mother had plenty of orientation points regarding his relative age.

There were good reasons why Efrem should have lied. Under Soviet law between 1919 and 1935, offenders below sixteen years of age had a reduced tariff of penalty for many offences, including murder, and were not supposed to go through the ordinary court system.[60] If testimony from a fellow prisoner is to be believed, the alleged Morozov murderers had even been overheard talking about this point in their cell in the second week of October (114). For whatever reason, anyway, the stage at which Efrem was put under pressure by the investigators about his age coincided with his shift to a position of resolute denial that he had been involved in any way with the Morozov murders. The penalty that he faced was no longer a few years in youth custody, but a capital sentence: perhaps this fact – whether he was guilty or innocent – gave him the stamina to face down his interrogators.

The age issue is perhaps the biggest oblique indication that Efrem had an unquiet conscience. But incidental detail in his testimony, and Danila's, indicates that the execution of the murders would have been a practical possibility. Both the young men were agreed that they had been working in adjoining fields on the day of the murders, 3 September (22, 25, 23). Even at a late stage in the investigation (22 September), Efrem Shatrakov agreed that they had met up at some point during the day (90), though he denied that they had had a conversation. In addition, neither Efrem nor Danila had an alibi for parts of the day: there is especial doubt about their movements in the later part of the afternoon. Two witnesses confirmed that Efrem finally left the fields sometime between six and seven (167, 160). Two others saw him near his field not long before this, when he came out to ask Prokhor Sakov for a cigarette (36, 168).[61] But another person,

Afanast Volkov, a lad aged fifteen who was also working in the fields near Efrem, did not see Efrem in the fields when he headed back home at four, though he had seen him there at nine when he began his own day's work (161). There seems to be a chance, then, that Efrem took a break from working in the fields at some point between, say, 3.30 p.m. and 6 p.m., a period when there are no witness statements to cover his movements.[62] For his part, Danila had fewer people around to observe his comings and goings, but if his grandfather's testimony to Titov on 7 September is to be believed, he left the house after returning home for dinner sometime in the afternoon, and returned only after it got dark – in other words, he could perfectly well have met up with Efrem at around four or five (12).

At different stages of the investigation, both Sergei and Kseniya Morozova suggested their grandson was guilty. Their later testimony was (one may assume) to all intents and purposes dictated to them, but it is interesting that Sergei Morozov raised Danila's name as a possible suspect right away, at his interrogation on 7 September (12). Sergei seems to have shared his famous grandson's reputed penchant for telling tales to the authorities – one might compare his unforced accusation to Titov and Potupchik on 12 September about Mezyukhin and Kulukanov's colt (41). But if he really was involved in the murder of Pavlik and Fyodor himself (even at the level of having suggested the deed), it seems odd that he was so quick to implicate his grandson, and thus implicate himself.

My own hunch, then, would be to go for a third version of the 'real' murder story, one lying somewhere between Druzhnikov's hypothesis and the official version of Pavlik's death, and going like this: Trofim Morozov, desperately overstretched by his work as village soviet chairman, and fearful of possible arrest or reprisals, simply disappears from Gerasimovka. He has in any case been getting on badly with his wife, and his extended family – bitterly divided over 'the measures being taken' – offers him no support. Pavel, his eldest son, is left to head the household as best he can. He and his mother and brothers regularly get insulted and bullied by grandfather Sergei living next door, who sees Trofim's departure as a disgrace to them. Rumour has it that Trofim may have been exiled; certainly, nothing is ever heard from him. Pavel himself is neglected, unhappy, perhaps even mentally unstable. But from 1931, the new world of the village school offers him some respite. In 1932, he begins enthusiastically participating in agit-brigade activities, and starts to realize that denunciation is a good way of getting attention from the authorities. He accordingly begins to tell on anyone in the village that he observes doing something that is against the rules.

In harvest season 1932, things come to a head. First, Pavlik is witnessed helping in a house search for the Shatrakovs' gun (in July), and then, at the end of August, he has a squabble over a piece of horse harness with his cousin. The older lads, smarting with resentment, are looking for an opportunity to teach Pavlik a lesson. Efrem gets hold of a knife from the barn that is used only when the floor is remade – it will not be missed – in case it comes in handy. On 3 September, Efrem and Danila are harrowing in adjoining fields, and take a break, at some point during the afternoon, so they can go into the woods for a smoke. Here they stumble across Pavel and Fyodor, just coming back from their berrying expedition. There is a fight, Efrem pulls the knife, and Pavlik is badly injured while trying to defend himself. Fyodor runs away screaming, and Danila knocks him down with some kind of blunt instrument (possibly even a log). Efrem comes over and stabs him, and then finishes off Pavel.

After the killing, Danila and Efrem, panicked, dump the bodies and run, having made only rudimentary – or no – efforts to hide them. They pull the sack over Pavlik's head, to make sure he cannot get away even if he is alive. But Danila, whether out of bravado or a nagging sense of guilt, drops hints to his grandparents about the murders. When the police come round to enquire, everyone assumes that, being minors, the two lads will get off lightly, and little attempt is made (at any rate by the older men involved) to cover up. But it soon emerges that the authorities are pursuing a quite different line – searching for a kulak conspiracy. At this point, mutual recrimination and self-defensive testimony starts in earnest. Soon, the investigators have so many potential kulak suspects – the Knigas, the Shatrakovs, as well as the Kulukanovs and the Silins – that they can barely cope. So gradually the mess of suspects is cleared away, leaving a central core – a group of relations, marital connections and near neighbours – against the background of whose self-serving, clannish machinations the Pioneer hero's preference of civic duties to family ties appears to particular advantage.

The authorities were trying to create order out of chaos, and they were trying to turn Pavlik into a suitable case for Soviet canonization. Therefore, his conflict with his father had to be of a noble, principled kind, and the latter had to be a worthy adversary. Citing a denunciation by Pavlik of Trofim going back to the late autumn of 1931 had serious disadvantages in terms of plausibility – why had Pavlik's incensed relations taken so long to exact revenge when he violated the basic principles of morality in the peasant family? But it fitted the 'youth rebellion' stereotype. It would not have done, in terms of the legend, for Pavlik's father just to disappear – cravenly desert his post, as the Soviet official description would have been. This would have laid bare the serious gaps in the level of government control out in the provinces. No, Trofim had to have disappeared for a good reason – because he was part of the larger world of corruption, sloth and ignorance against which Pavlik had fought so fiercely.

Further speculation, though, is futile. We come back again to the lack of proper pathology reports; to the gaps, contradictions and patent absurdities in the written evidence; and to the faulty and self-interested memories of the now very few survivors. The Gerasimovka old-timers I talked to in September 2003 were determined that those executed for the Morozov murders must have been the actual perpetrators of the crime. In the words of Mariya Sakova, 'They were slaughtered like sheep: who could have done it, if it wasn't their relations?' Folk memory has long ago turned the Morozovs into village monsters – people whom the children hid from when they came down the street, people who lived worse than anyone in a village where life was bitter and hard.[63] And there is, one senses, a self-protective fear among older villagers that others – members of their own families, perhaps – might start to come under suspicion if the case were opened up again.

All in all, it is fair to say that the Morozov murder case is likely to remain open for ever. The boys' bones are covered in concrete, the traces of the crime effaced by more than seventy Siberian winters. Equally elusive is the question of what the 'real' Pavlik was like in life, except in the most general sense – the son of a single mother from a poor village in a marginal stretch of country, who ended his life dying a violent death. Perhaps he had illusions of being a Pioneer, or at any rate a child activist; perhaps he even denounced people, possibly including his father. But the substance of the boy is long gone, evaporated in fantasy, fiction and deliberate lies – as created by Soviet myth-makers, by provincial journalists, by police investigators and, not least, by his fellow-villagers, all of whom were convinced, like their ideological 'betters', that they knew exactly who had committed the crime, and why.

AFTERWORD

The legend of Pavlik Morozov has something in common with a painted box produced as a gift to the Pavlik Morozov Museum in Gerasimovka by a group of Pioneers from Kursk. On the outside, its function appears easy to explain, and indeed rather crude. Once opened, however, the casket proves to hold nothing at all. The apparent purpose of the artefact vanishes: rather than a container for anything particular, the box is a wholly ritual object, an item that once had significance, but in circumstances that have now vanished and can be reconstructed only through speculation.

Just so, Pavlik's legend has, one could say, no ultimate meaning, so fluid did the story prove over the different decades of Soviet power. Every concrete detail of the boy's supposed existence changed – the colour of his hair, the names of his closest friends, the name of the person to whom he denounced his father, the number of other people he denounced, the character of the murder itself. So, too, did the weight given to different motifs – Pavlik as Pioneer hero, Pavlik as model of civic virtue more broadly and, in particular, of fearless denunciation, Pavlik as martyr, Pavlik as victim of the kulaks. The name 'Pavlik Morozov' became what semioticians term a 'floating signifier', constantly shifting in order to accommodate altering ideas about ideal childhood and the nature of juvenile heroism. A guidebook to Moscow that lambasted Rabinovich's 1948 monument to Pavlik as 'a collection of symbols', rather than a portrait of an actual person, had missed the point: this was exactly what the monument was supposed to be.[1]

Most importantly, the significance of the legend changed over time in terms of its ethical associations. For the generation brought up when Pavlik's story was still new, in the 1930s, the boy's actions in denouncing his father and relations at the cost of his own life represented a high ideal of self-sacrifice – unrealizable by ordinary mortals, probably, but none the less worthy of awe. 'In those days we looked straight ahead,' a woman born in the mid 1930s remembered.[2] But at the same time, 'sneaking' in the ordinary sense continued to be considered a contemptible activity among children, just as it always had. Pavlik might be an admirable figure, but he was not – unlike Gaidar's boy hero Timur – a lovable one. And once the war had provided models of children who died rather than betray secrets, Pavlik moved gradually into the background. He now came to stand for Soviet history, for a past that was often dimly remembered. The commemorative aphorism from *Ogonyok* that I quoted in Chapter 7 – 'he has been frozen in bronze, this reconnaissance boy of the future'[3] – precisely captures the embarrassment of trying to evoke dynamic action by means of static, ritualized forms. And, as intellectual dissatisfaction grew in the post-Stalin era, Pavlik came to stand, among those hostile to the established order, for everything that was bad about Soviet history. Yury Druzhnikov's demythologizing book was by far the most elaborate tribute – though of a reverse kind – to the boy that emerged from these years.

Increasingly, too, the abstract content of the myth – its message about self-sacrifice – was out of step with Soviet social values, as official attitudes became more tolerant of materialism and of private values. A man born in 1939 has described learning about the lives of Pavlik and other Pioneer heroes as though they were the laws of Newtonian physics;[4] now, relativity had started to rule the cultural universe, and learning about gravity (in both senses of the word) no longer helped. The contempt and oblivion of the post-Soviet era – when Pavlik's statues disappeared, his museum in Gerasimovka was closed, and some of the streets named after him were hastily given new titles – represented a difference of degree, not a radical change in values.

For anyone interested in how to disseminate civic values by means of role models, Pavlik's myth represents a cautionary tale. The myth created at the cost of suffering (among those accused of his murder) and loss of integrity (among many of those who created the legend), in the long term did not work. Rather than creating a culture where public denunciation was regarded as virtuous, it helped to stigmatize the reporting of wrongdoing; rather than making self-sacrifice seem romantic, it fostered a growing view that self-sacrifice was no longer relevant.

At the same time, the reconstruction of the Pavlik myth is not meant just as a display of archaeological fragments from the distant past. The myth points not only to the logical errors of the Soviet system, but to the dislocation between public outcries about child killings and the actual state of child welfare at the time when these happen. The death of Pavlik and his brother caused national outrage, but at the same time, a blind eye was turned to many, less ideologically seductive, instances of equally terrible child abuse in Soviet society – among children consigned to institutions, for example. It is all too easy – as Benjamin Britten's opera *Peter Grimes* shows us – for child murders to become the subject of scandals that have less to do with children than they have with adults' fears of, and hatreds for, other adults, and their desire to maintain control over *some part* of their daily existence.[5] Such scandals are not historically inevitable – there were, for example, no uproars at all over child killings by strangers in early nineteenth-century Russia. They appear to be characteristic of times and places where anxiety over historical change gets expressed in the desire to maintain some part of life as sacrosanct – which is less childhood as actually

Painted wooden box, 1970s. (Pavlik Morozov Museum, Gerasimovka)

The site of Fyodor Morozov's murder in the woods at Gerasimovka, overgrown with grass and vegetation, September 2003. The pillars of this grave and Pavlik's were traditionally used by Gerasimovka schoolchildren to hide secret letters to each other, and wishes for good exam results, but now they have nothing inside but dry leaves. (Catriona Kelly)

lived than the prevailing view, among adults, of what childhood (*my* childhood) once was (or ought to have been) like.[6]

By extension, there is an ever-present danger that the preoccupation with child welfare may express the desire to regulate children's lives according to abstract principles, rather than to consider what the actual wishes and demands of children might be. A desire to protect children from harm ought to be compatible with an ability to recognize their right to autonomy[7] – which can, *in extremis*, also mean the right to protest against the behaviour of family members. Yet realizing this ideal synthesis in practice may be difficult. In pitting child against father, in showing the child turning to an oppressive state so that he may be liberated from an oppressive parent, the Pavlik Morozov legend presents an impossible ethical dilemma. What *should* Pavlik, in such a situation, have done? Even those fortunate enough to be spared such choices themselves cannot remain unmoved by the question.

NOTES

Dramatis Personae

1 According to the copy of a christening certificate lodged in the Pavlik Morozov museum, Gerasimovka.

2 Khima Kulukanova is stated by her husband to have been sixty years old in 1932 (138); she confirmed this age herself (92). Her mother, on the other hand, said she was fifty-five (132). The former seems more likely, given Kulukanov's own age, and also the fact that Kseniya Morozova got at least one other age wrong.

3 In *One of Eleven* (*Odin iz odinnadtsati*), which is not in fact held in copyright libraries in Russia, but which, assuming it existed, was evidently a book or brochure about different Pioneer heroes. Gubarev's byline is, however, on one of the first newspaper reports about the Morozov case (*PP*, 15 October 1932).

Preface

1 As a nationalist journalist remembered recently, when his first teacher told him and his classmates the story in the late 1940s, 'tears were running down her cheeks. "Poor little children, they should have lived and lived!"' Yury Makhrin, 'Mal'chik, kotorogo nel'zya kaznit', *Pravda*, 27–28 January 2004.

2 A good sense of the 'before and after' of Sverdlovsk is given by two photographs in Harris 1999: compare fig. 3 (1905 Revolution Square in the late 1920s) and fig. 9 (the same square in the 1950s).

3 Harris 1999: 121. (The figure – which is for the whole Urals province – is cited from RGASPI f. 17 op. 120 d. 52, l.59.)

4 Or – caution is essential with every detail in this story – are said to have been found.

5 For the interest of any fungophiles, this was *mokhovik*, Boletus bovinus.

6 In the archive of Memorial, St Petersburg, I checked materials

relating to two cases from 1932–3: the 1933 case of the so-called 'Finnish General Staff', which involved dozens of arrests around Leningrad of individuals allegedly spying for Finland; and case file No. 211776, 'Lube Samuil Markovich and others' (23 August–9 December 1932). The form of the 'acts of accusation' here, and of the interrogation records, arrest dockets and so on, is similar to that in the Morozov case, though more of the material is on printed pro formas – but that discrepancy is fair enough, given that these investigations were directed out of Soviet Russia's second capital, not in the provincial backwoods.

Introduction: Death in the Taiga

1 *PP*, 15 October 1932, p. 2.

2 *PP*, 3 December 1932, p. 1 (the result), p. 2 (the speech).

3 *BSE* (3rd edn), vol. 16 (1974), headword 'Morozov, Pavel'. Similarly, the official history of the Pioneer movement's early years (*Zori sovetskoi pionerii*, 1972: 262), lists Pavlik's murder as a major event in the dateline given at the end.

4 On the Colombo monument, see http://archive.travel.ru/Sri_Lanka/748_TRAVEL.html (accessed 12 July 2004).

5 The Tavda local paper, *Tavda Worker*, had carried material from 17 September 1932, papers in Sverdlovsk from 23 September, and *Pioneer Pravda* itself had printed a first – much more matter-of-fact – report of the case on 2 October. See further in Chapter 4 of this book.

6 In the second *Pioneer Pravda* report, Pavlik was already described as 'bright-haired': *PP*, 15 October 1932, p. 2. The post-mortem report on him describes his hair as 'reddish-brown' (10).

7 The first edition, published in London, 1988, had the title *The Apotheosis of Pavlik Morozov* (*Voznesenie Pavlika Morozova*).

8 The writer Yury Dombrovsky, who suffered interrogation under the Great Terror, lists the interrogator's essential strategies as forced self-incrimination (with interrogation records rewritten to ensure this even if the subject did not oblige), vague and all-embracing charges such as 'hostility to Soviet power', capricious recording of interrogations, grooming of witnesses to provide damning testimony, falsification of 'face-to-face confrontations', and selection of witnesses so they told the 'right' story (Letter to A. G. Aristov, 1 January 1956; Dombrovsky 2000: 573–6). Irma Kudrova, the author of a book about the final years of Marina Tsvetaeva, writes, based on her own experience of interrogation in the 1950s:

I remembered clearly how different the real dialogues in the investigator's room were from the ones written down on paper; how often the record was drawn up after the 'talk' was over, containing scarcely one-tenth of what was said. Even that was formulated by the investigator [. . .] The record does not reflect the investigator's abusive or mocking tone, his provocative lies, threats, and dirty gossip [. . .] Or the hours and hours when the person interrogated is left 'to think things through properly', while the investigators go to eat, take a cigarette break, or simply busy themselves with other matters. Or, if you're stubborn, being dragged from one official to another (Kudrova 2004: 65).

9 This is no doubt fortuitous, as the only photograph of Pavlik that is generally considered authentic (a group image of the Gerasimovka primary school in *c.* 1931) shows a boy with a much more pointed face and a wary expression (see Chapter 8). Of course, it is also possible that the 'artist's impressions' published in *Pioneer Pravda* and elsewhere were modelled on members of Pavlik's family, and Yulianiya's elder siblings, the children of the deputy chairman of the village soviet, would have been obvious models.

10 CK-Gerasimovka 1.

11 As Hava Volovich, who worked as a cub reporter in the small town of Mena, Ukraine, during the mid-1930s remembered: 'The lies weighed me down. There were lies at every step. I'd be sent to interview some old partisan or model worker on a collective farm. He'd have his say, then I'd have to write something different altogether' (Vilensky 1999: 246). Soviet citizens also regularly remodelled their own biographies to make these ideologically appropriate: see Fitzpatrick 2005 for a general discussion of this. On the rules of Soviet heroism generally, see Clark 1978; Clark 1985.

12 See e.g. Rybnikov, *Derevenskii shkol'nik i ego idealy*; Rybnikov, *Idealy gimnazistok*; Rybnikov 1930.

13 Boym 1994: 91. As a matter of fact, the hagiographies of Pavlik provide both secrets (of a political kind, here: Pavlik's father's wrongdoing) and a philosophical (if not metaphysical) conversation – with the 'man from the district centre', i.e. a secret police official, about whether it can ever be right to denounce your father.

14 For incisive comments on the distortions imposed on children's experience by interpretation in terms of the Oedipus myth as family drama, see Deleuze and Guattari: 1972: Chapter 2.

15 Volkov 1979: 208. Cf. ibid., 193, where Shostakovich comments that he is not unhappy about the destruction of *Bezhin Meadow* 'because I can't understand how you can create a work of art from a boy denouncing his father'. Whatever their authenticity as a reflection of the composer's own views, the comments on Pavlik are an indication of commonly held opinions about the boy, especially in the post-Stalin era. Cf. the remarks about Pavlik Morozov in Vishnevskaya 1984: 34–5: 'Children who can barely walk prattle poems and songs – about whom? Pavlik Morozov. And the kindergarten itself bears his name. The message is: if you are good children and denounce your mummy and daddy, then they'll sing songs about you too.' These generalizing assertions are oddly out of keeping with the overall character of Vishnevskaya's memoir, which is immediate and concrete (cf. her recollections of the Stalin cult on p. 35).

16 A. Avtorkhanov, 'A Brief History of the Komsomol', in Novak-Deker 1959: 23.

17 Druzhnikov 1995: 249.

18 On which see further in Chapter 4.

19 Druzhnikov 1995: 254.

20 There is some doubt whether Plato's own view of Euthyphro was as negative as Socrates' filleting of his argument would suggest: one recent commentator has the author of *Euthyphro* closer to the standard Greek position that 'judgment must be proportioned to the offense and not the man' (Edwards 2000: 213–24 – this quotation p. 222).

21 As a leading Russian classicist has observed, Pavlik would have been a hero in Ancient Rome too (Gasparov 2000: 46).

22 Hattonstone 2000: G2 section: 4–5. Hugh Cunningham's eccentric website dedicated to Pavlik Morozov (the factual material of which is taken entirely, with acknowledgement, from Druzhnikov) sees this link of Pavlik with contemporary Western bourgeois ideals of civic responsibility as another indication of the ethical dubiety of the tale (see http://www.pavlikmorozov.com, accessed October 2002).

23 TsA FSB H-7825 t. 1, l. 304. Cf. 'Nikakoi poshchady klassovomu vragu', *TR*, 29 September 1932, p. 2, and the items in *TR* for 20 September 1932, p. 1; 21 September 1932, p. 1; 24 September 1932, p. 1 (of *Smena*); 27 September 1932, p. 2, etc.

24 Traditionally, Jews were the minority that were held to blame for child murders (Dundes 1991); on more recent hysteria, see Warner 1998. Of course, there can be real-life cases where child murderers work in groups, as appears to have happened with the killings of African-American children in Atlanta in the 1980s (Bambara 2000). But such cases are far less common than the pervasive anxiety about them would suggest.

25 Vallely 2003: 12.

26 Kanarsky 1928: 341–54, 51.

27 Trotsky, 'The Struggle for Cultured Speech' (1923), in Trotsky 1973: 53. Lenin is credited with similar views in the newspaper *Vechernie izvestiya Moskovskogo Soveta*'s record of a speech on Red Square, 1 May 1919: see Lenin 1941–51: vol. 29, p. 303.

28 Perel' and Lyubimova 1932: 15 (murder case), 34 (religious instruction). The comparison is not made directly in this book, which gives the two cases without comment. The perpetrator of the murder later had her sentence increased.

29 Kanarsky 1928: 162. For the penalties, see Article 58.2 (ibid., p. 151). See also Rossi 1987: 494–5.

30 See the helpful analysis in Argenbright 2002: 249–75, esp. 251–2; and also Cassiday 2000.

31 M. Gorky, 'Starukha Izergil'', Gorky 1949–55, vol. 1: 356. CK–ATA–Ekaterinburg, 22 September 2003.

32 The most vivid introduction to the Gulag is still Solzhenitsyn's *The Gulag Archipelago*. Applebaum 2003 is an informative and balanced recent survey.

33 Gromov 1998: 189.

34 On Stalin as munificent and wise, see Brooks 2000. For a recent 'naïve' treatment of Soviet history under Stalin, see Amis 2002.

35 Mikhail Alekseev, brought up in a remote village during the 1930s, later remembered how the leader of his Pioneer agit-brigade, delegated to beard a formidably rude and aggressive social outsider, was punched and knocked out by the man, his uncle: 'What have you dragged this pack of young curs over here for?' In another case, the object of agitation restrained himself from physical assault, but wondered loudly: 'What fool sent you over here? Just run away back home, you snot-noses! You're way out of your depth with this one!' (Alekseev 1988: 187). In the village of Murzino, Leningrad province, during the early 1930s, Pioneer troops had to be accompanied back to the station by the local Komsomol organizer and teachers when giving theatrical performances, since there were fears that

otherwise they might be attacked by 'hooligans' (Tsendrovskaya 1995: 89).

36 All these areas of children's existence are extensively documented in the fascinating collection of memoirs *Children of the Russian Emigration* (Petrusheva 1997), based on essays written by children attending schools across the diaspora in 1924.

1. Pavlik's World

1 There is a huge literature on collectivization, and the short sketch here can deal with the process only superficially. Among general studies, particularly vivid is Conquest 2002. Studies of a more academic kind include Lewin 1968; Davies 1980; Viola 1987; Viola 1996. On the aftermath, see Fitzpatrick 1994. For those who read Russian, there is material of immense interest in the various document collections published from the late 1980s onwards, e.g. Danilov, Manning and Viola 1999– ; and the many memoirs by survivors, e.g. Bel'skaya 1994 (an extract is available in Fitzpatrick and Slezkine 2000).

2 This attitude can be seen in e.g. Kaganovich's diary of his visit to the North Caucasus, in Danilov, Manning and Viola 1999– : vol. 2, 369 ff. Cf. the attempt to stop foreign correspondents reporting on the famine in 1933 and 'cooking up vile stories'. 'This must be stopped, and these gentlemen must be prevented from travelling round the USSR. We have enough spies in the USSR as it is' Danilov, Manning and Viola 1999– : vol. 2, 644–5.

3 Tvardovsky 1988: 12. For an equally harrowing account of a family dekulakized still later, in 1933, see Bel'skaya 1994.

4 Viola 1987: 14.

5 See esp. Lewin 1968: 257.

6 Dal' 1880–82: vol. 2, 215.

7 Lenin, 'Doklad o bor'be s golodom', 4 June 1918, Lenin 1941–51: vol. 27, 469; 'Rech' pered agitatorami, posylaemymi v provintsiyu', *Pravda*, 6 February 1918, Lenin 1941–51: vol. 26, 402. For the similarity of views among populists and socialists before 1917, see e.g. Lenin's assessment that the populists were entirely right about the evils of kulaks and 'parasites' (*miroedy*), but wrong in their diagnosis – this was a problem of the capitalist system: 'Ekonomicheskoe soderzhanie narodnichestva i kritika ego v knige g. Struve' (1895), Lenin 1941–51: vol. 1, 354–5.

8 For example, peasants who let out dachas, accommodation for

holiday visitors from the city, were the subject of mistrust and condemnation. Lovell 2003: 113: 'Some villages had given up agriculture and handicrafts and moved over entirely to the dacha economy; such cases were inevitably treated with severe disapproval, as they were seen as contributing to the moral erosion of the countryside.'

9 See Pallot 1999.

10 Conquest 2002: 44.

11 Synonyms of 'kulak' such as *krepysh* (strong man) and *kremen'* (flint) were routinely used in a positive way – to mean someone tough and good at getting things done – though they also had the negative sense of 'miserly' and 'go-getting' (Dal' 1880–82: vol. 2, 189, 207). In the words of Olga Tian-Shanskaya, who carried out extensive ethnographical research in a village in Central Russia during the 1900s, peasants believed it was 'a sin to pile up money'. However, they admired the industriousness and businesslike ways of merchants, though 'by the same token, peasants do not like merchants, of course' (Tian-Shanskaia [=Shanskaya] 1993: 144, 147).

12 Stoliaroff 1986: 43.

13 On 'working for others', see e.g. Danilin 1931: 25, which also records greater support for co-operation among the poorest.

14 Conquest 2002: 44.

15 Hughes 1996: 73–7. (This fining procedure, known as the 'Urals–Siberian Method', was sanctioned at the top level shortly after it evolved and, on 28 June 1929, a clause was added to Article 61 of the Criminal Code making 'failure to deliver grain' a criminal offence.)

16 In one Siberian village, for example, only twenty-nine kulaks suffered expropriations, as against ninety middling peasants and sixty-six bednyaks (Hughes 1996: 110).

17 Conquest 2002: 97.

18 See Viola 1987; Hughes 1996: 139–40.

19 Hughes 1996: 145–6.

20 For a denunciation of the official type, see the protocol of a village general meeting of 10 May 1931, Novosibirsk district, condemning Yakov Nikolaevich Sizov as a kulak on the grounds of his having used hired labour (Hughes 1996: 256–7). Mariya Bel'skaya's family had, before being dekulakized, one cow, one horse and some fowl (Fitzpatrick and Slezkine 2000: 221). For a sewing machine instance, see CKQ-Ox-03 PF 5 B, p. 5.

21 The 'insulting behaviour' document, from the State Archive of Social and Political Documents, Kurgan province, is cited in Bazarov 1997: vol. 1, 130; on confiscations, see the document from the State Archive of Tyumen province (Bazarov 1997: vol. 1, 131). See also first-hand accounts such as 'Victor M.' from the village of Ik in Kurgan, Siberia, in Litvinenko and Riordan 1998: 29–51.

22 Viola 2000: 34–5, 39 (forty-seven child and 11 adult deaths on 189 echelons sent in February 1930).

23 Viola 2000: 40, 42–3, 46, 51); for the Arkhangelsk witness, see Siegelbaum and Sokolov: 1999: 50.

24 Viola 2000: 53.

25 On such a case in Khibinogorsk, 1932, see Bullard and Bullard 2000: 125. However, by the mid-1930s, the situation seems to have relaxed: Starzhinsky 1991: 56 recalls the crèche as being open to all, and indeed as having unfilled places because of the drop in the birth-rate.

26 In June 1933, the head of the Leningrad Region Bureau of the Komsomol Children's Committee wrote to the Komsomol Central Committee to protest at the practice of excluding such children (unless they had been removed from their parents), pointing out that it was quite unfair to discriminate against the children of parents who had proved their loyalty to the state, and asserting that in any case, the educational work of the Pioneer movement was particularly valuable with children who came from questionable backgrounds of this kind (RGASPI-TsKhDMO f. 1 op. 23 d. 1056, l. 21).

27 For a case of this, see the life history of Anna Dubova in Engel and Posadskaya-Vanderbeck 1998: 46.

28 See e.g. TsDOO SO f. 1201 op. 1 d. 18, l. 27.

29 'Victor M' in Litvinenko and Riordan 1998: 47.

30 Litvinenko and Riordan 1998: 50.

31 On open resistance, see e.g. Fitzpatrick 1994: 65–7; Viola 1996. For the report including material on the attacks in the North Caucasus, see Danilov, Manning and Viola 1999– : vol. 2, 369.

32 On slaughter of stock, see e.g. ibid.

33 Bazarov 1997: vol. 2, 63 (cannibalism), 72 (epidemic).

34 Viola 1987: 42–3 (enrolment), 206 (proportion staying on). Some of the 'twenty-five thousanders' did become disaffected, partly because of practical difficulties (the organization of accommodation and duties was often chaotic, and local officials

as well as local populations were hostile), but also because some of them were disgusted by the abuses that they witnessed during dekulakization. Viola 1987: 76, 137 (local conditions); 109, 118 (disgust over abuses, in the former case, undemocratic behaviour of plenipotentiaries at local meetings; in the latter, abuses during dekulakization, 'this is not collectivization, it is pillage').

35 On traditional justice generally, see Frank 1999: Chapter 8. On the use of *charavari* (shaming rituals) etc. against Stolypin farmers, see Pallot 1999: 166–9.

36 On the strategy, see Figes 1988: 156.

37 Lazar' Kaganovich addressing a reception for the 'twenty-five thousanders' in January 1930, quoted in Viola 1987: 65.

38 'Doshkol'naya rabota 1–i Opytnoi Stantsii Narkomprosa. Rabota po obsledovaniyu navykov i mirovozreniya detei. Belkino 1929 – Dobroe 1929 – Krivskoe 1928', RAO NA f. 1 op. 1 d. 294, ll. 66 (bourgeois), 87 (rich/poor), 91 (kulaks).

39 Baranova 1919: 31–4; cf. 'Kak prazdnovali' 1919: 40–9 and a 'free expression' journal, *Novaya shkola*, put out in Pskov Province in the same year.

40 See 'Perechen' kopii postanovlenii Byuro TsK VLKSM po rabote sredi pionerov i shkol'nikov za 1919–28' (typescript held in the Reading Room of RGASPI-TsKhDMO, Moscow), l. 118.

41 According to a 1933 survey, over 40 per cent of teachers were under twenty-three, and over 20 per cent under nineteen; in some areas, such as the Urals, the figures were still higher (48.6 per cent under twenty-three, and 25.4 per cent under nineteen, with a full 10.3 per cent under seventeen). See *Kadry prosveshcheniya* 1936: 188. On teachers generally, see Ewing 2002.

42 For the figure from the 1939 census of 81.6 per cent of the target age group in primary school, see Dunstan 1997: 10. It would be fair to assume that the proportion of children who attended school at some point during their early lives was somewhat higher, since drop-outs, and possibly also children who were over the official age for primary education (yet still receiving this) would not have been included in the census figures.

43 For example, on 14 March 1930, *Pioneer Pravda* ran a piece by Nadezhda Krupskaya calling for rehabilitation for kulak young, while *LS*, in its 27 March 1930 issue, deplored the fact that in some quarters these children were considered appropriate targets for suppression as well.

44 *PP*, 27 January 1930.

45 'The kulak will exult/if weeds and pests/gobble up the crops,/if there is no corn-cutting,/no sacks for the corn (*PP*, 24 June 1930).

46 *Druzhnye rebyata*, 8 (1931), p. 24.

47 This is how dekulakization took place in a 1930 story from *Pioneer*: a commission arrived to visit Lapin, inventoried his property, and dispatched it with the inventory for safe-keeping. 'At the poor peasants' meeting, a resolution to dekulakize Lapin was passed unanimously and the property was handed over to the kolkhoz [. . .] No one in the village, apart from his old cronies, felt sorry for Lapin' (*Pioner*, 8 (1930), p. 38).

48 Bazarov 1997: vol. 1, 78. Irbit district, centred round the old merchant town of Irbit, fell, like Tavda district, the Morozovs' home patch, into Irbit region, but was over 100 kilometres away.

49 *Pioner*, 19 (1930), p. 1.

50 Quoted in Bazarov 1997: vol. 1, 133).

51 Female informant, b. 1920, Pskov province, recorded August 2004, Karelia. Oxf/Lev V-04 PF4A, p. 22.

2. Local Hero

1 *PP*, 24 July 1931.

2 See e.g. 'Pyatiletka na Urale', *Pioner*, 23 (1929), pp. 16–19; or the 'Urals–Kuznetsk Works' board game, where children were supposed to push counters round the region's premier industrial sites: *Pioner*, 3–4 (1934), pp. 8–9. *Pioneer Pravda* created a scandal on 24 September 1931, when it came to light that a group of children from the Volga had been unable to say what the Ural–Kuzbass project might be.

3 Mitreikin 1932: 7–8.

4 On the struggles of local officials, see Harris 1999: 5; on the prison camp contribution to the workforce, Harris 1999: Chapter 4. For press-ganging of peasants to work in lumber production, see 'Vinovnikov k surovoi otvetstvennosti', *Tavdinskaya lesopilka*, 23 November 1930, p. 4, castigating village soviets for not coming up with the required numbers of participants. Kotkin 1995 is an impressive study of a key project, Magnitogorsk, which gives due weight to the idealism and commitment on the ground as well as to control 'from above'.

5 Alymov and Aleksandrov 1937.

6 Ermolaev 1999: 132–81.

7 Treadgold 1957: 147, 255. On the migration generally, see Treadgold 1957: 147–241; *ES*, vol. 23 (1898), 277–80.

8 Gerasimovka does not appear in a list of Irbit district settlements published in 1908 (*Spisok selenii* 1908), and neither does the town of Tavda, indicating how recent the settlement was. Between 1896 and 1913, the population of Perm' province as a whole grew by 800,000, or well over 30 per cent (*Sanitarnyi obzor* 1896: 1; *Sanitarnyi obzor* 1913: 1).

9 CK-Gerasimovka 1; CK-Gerasimovka 2. On the telephone line, see Pavel Solomein in *VK*, 8 October 1932, p. 2.

10 CK-Gerasimovka 1; CK-Gerasimovka 2.

11 R. Lynch, *The Path of Empire* (London, 1903), pp. 235–6, quoted in Treadgold 1957: 143.

12 See the fascinating 1903 memoir by Petr Lazeev (b. 1886), the adolescent son of a family that moved from Tambov province to Tomsk in the 1890s (RGIA f. 803 op. 16 d. 2370, ll. 106–9). Lazeev's father was a martinet who ground the need for education into his children with a stick.

13 TsDOO SO f. 4 op. 8 d. 54, l. 62.

14 Ibid., l. 77.

15 'Ural'skoe oblastnoe-zemel'noe upravlenie. Informatsionnyi byulleten', no.16 (10.1.1931) (GASO f. P88 op. 1 d. 2983, l. 333 and l. 333 ob).

16 Ibid., no. 24 (20.4.1931) (GASO f. P88 op. 1 d. 2984, l. 170).

17 'Otchet Ob-Irtyshkogo obkoma VKP(b): O sostoyanii kollektivizatsii i polozhenii edinolichnikov po Ob-Irtyshkoi oblasti', in Danilov, Manning and Viola 1999: vol. 4, 232.

18 All the informants I spoke to in Gerasimovka replied that land was the reason their parents and grandparents had moved to the Urals: CK-Gerasimovka 1, CK-Gerasimovka 2.

19 In 1930, only ten out of twenty-nine Tavda officials had more than primary education, and this did not include the chairman of the bureau of the district committee, the secretary of the Komsomol district committee, the procurator, the judge or the district investigator. All but five were under forty, and more than a third aged thirty or under, reflecting the general profile of a region where Party membership was more or less confined to the younger generation: 'Spisok rukovodyashchikh otvetstvennykh rabotnikov po sostoyaniyu na 1 iyunya 1930 goda po Tavdinskomu raionu' (TsDOO SO f. 1201 op. 1 d. 7, ll. 49–51). Literacy was particularly poor out in the countryside: see e.g. a 'List of the personal staff of all Members and

candidets [*sic*] of the All-Russian Communist Party (Bolsheviks), gorodishchenskaya [*sic*] cell', signed V. Ivanov (TsDOO SO f. 1201 op. 1 d. 7, l. 107) (materials from the Maloe Gorodishche cell, to which Gerasimovka residents belonged before the cell there was opened in 1931).

20 Ermolaev 1999: 81–2.

21 In December 1933, for example, *Tavda Worker* reported on a clean-up of the local Party with especial reference to 'wolf in sheep's clothing' Ivan Nikitych Kuznetsov. The man had passed himself off as a shepherd's son, and while he had admitted to serving for a while in Kolchak's forces, he had insisted he had done this under duress, before running off to join the Reds at the earliest possible moment. But it had now emerged that his father had owned an iron foundry, and that Kuznetsov himself had been a perfectly normal White soldier who had simply been captured by the Reds. He was duly excluded from the Party. 'Chistka Tavdinskoi partorganizatsii', *TR*, 4 December 1933, p. 1.

22 In mid-August 1932, the Combined Bureaux of the Tavda District Committee of the Communist Party and the Party Control Committee passed a resolution condemning various 'crude distortions of the Party line', including a draconian policy of levying fines on poor peasants as well as kulaks, and mass confiscations of large farm animals, so that 'poor and middling peasants were deprived of their last cow when small animals could have been taken instead'. There had also been illegal confiscation of property and sale of this and of farm animals for private gain, and 'bare-faced administrative mismanagement' (which is to say, bullying and abuse of those with whom officials came into contact) (TsDOO SO f. 4 op. 8 d. 54, l. 76).

23 TsDOO SO f. 1201 op. 1 d. 24, l. 57.

24 For this type of material, see e.g. an item in *TR*, 29 December 1930, p. 4, reporting that one Fadei [*sic*: the name is properly spelt Faddei] Korsakov of Dedlevka village in Beloyarka village soviet had just been prosecuted under Article 79 of the Criminal Code ('predatory slaughter of stock animals') for slaughtering a pedigree pig and marking out two ewes for the kill. The article supplied the additional information that Korsakov had fought on the White side during the Civil War and had been agitating for the collapse of the kolkhoz.

25 See the report by A. Izrailev, plenipotentiary from the Urals Regional Committee of the Communist Party (inspector of

arable and stock farming), early August 1931 (TsDOO SO f. 4 op. 9 d. 953, l. 162).

26 Ermolaev 1999: 89.

27 CK-Gerasimovka 1; CK-Gerasimovka 2.

28 As in the case of Alex Saranin's family: Saranin 1997: 12. The family holdings at Rudyanka, south of Sverdlovsk, included a dye-works.

29 A word of caution should be uttered here. The inventory of household property was conducted as part of an investigation whose purpose was to demonstrate Sergei Morozov's kulak links, and especially the fact that he had hidden property for Arseny Kulukanov. It therefore concentrates on items useful for that purpose. A cart, piece of horse harness and cartwheels figured constantly in witness testimony, and here they are listed. The inventory may have gaps; and perhaps it was also made up from start to finish. However, as the 'everyday details' were one of the few areas of testimony where information was apparently not subject to arbitrary change, there is a possibility that the inventory was in substance genuine.

30 Linen was still a main crop in the Tavda district as late as 1939. See *BSE* edn 1, vol. 53 (1946), col. 398.

31 Ermolaev 1999: 147.

32 According to Kseniya Morozova (103 rev.), she supposed that the boys might have gone to their *aunt's* in Kulukhovka when they disappeared, another detail suggesting this was Tatiana's home. Druzhnikov 1995: 11 gives her brother's name as Onisim Ostrovsky; either this individual under the wrong name (as Andrei Ostrovsky), or another brother, is recorded in the case file as a witness to the discovery of the bodies (6).

33 The oddest omission from interviewing was probably Zakhar Kulukanov, whom Kseniya Morozova described as a friend of Danila's (92), and who was between Pavlik and him in age. Co-operation between two lads who both had grudges against the civic denouncer might have seemed on the face of it likely, but the interrogators were not interested in considering adolescent social networks, only how boys might have been manipulated by kulaks.

34 Certainly, Kseniya Morozova claimed, in response to an accusation that the murderers had met at Silin's house to work up their plots, to have been visiting her sick daughter on 5 September (219 rev.).

35 Efrem himself listed his siblings as Dmitry (twenty-two),

Natal'ya (twenty), 'and six younger ones in my father's family, 3 brothers, Filipp, Mikhail and Ivan, and three sisters, Matryona, Mariya and Anna' (141). Druzhnikov refers to another brother, 'Efim' Shatrakov, but he is a phantom, brought to life by one of the frequent misspellings of Efrem's name.

36 NKVD orders of 1925 and 1928 introduced restrictions on the sale and ownership of firearms, which were traded on the basis of a chit that the person concerned had hunting rights. See *Byulleten' NKVD,* 12 (1925), 93–6, and ibid., 15 (1928), 279.

37 I.e. a traditional steam-bath, somewhere between a sauna and a Turkish bath in terms of humidity levels. A fair number of houses in the country, even humble ones, had such bath-houses, which were traditionally used every week or couple of weeks. This, though, was the best-case scenario: a survey of 1931 indicated that more than 50 per cent of children in villages never visited the bath-house, and were 'utterly filthy' (see *Byulleten' Narkomzdrava* 1 (1931), 35).

38 Druzhnikov 1995: 10; obviously, this is difficult to prove without access to full secret police records.

39 Khima Kulukanova stated at her interrogation on 16 October (125) that her father (i.e. Sergei Morozov) had been convicted more than once of 'hooliganism' in the years before the Revolution. ('Hooliganism' was applied to a wide range of public-order offences, including breach of the peace, criminal damage, damage to public or state property, etc.).

40 This document is included in H-7825, vol. 2, and is placed before l. 1 (it is itself unnumbered). It comprises an order to archive the Morozov murders case file.

41 See e.g. Smirnov 1961: 66.

42 On the Party cell, see TsDOO SO f. 1201 op. 1 d. 16, l. 37. On 9 March, the local teacher, Zoya Mironova, an active *komsomolka* with a record as a Pioneer leader, applied to join the cell, her application being signed by two existing members of the Party (TsDOO SO f. 1201 op. 1 d. 20, ll. 20–23).

43 See e.g. the list of full and candidate Party members for November 1929 at TsDOO SO f. 1201 op. 1 d. 7, ll. 8–9, l. 13, l. 40 (the names mentioned are Ekim Goluzov, b. 1890, and Yakov Orlov, b. 1900). There is also an application on file from 1928 for Grigory Egorovich Mutsuk (alternatively Matsuk), who had moved to Gerasimovka from Vilna Province via Leningrad in 1919, and who had served as chairman of the village soviet in 1924 (TsDOO SO f. 1201 op. 1 d. 6, l. 129).

He was, however, turned down on the grounds of 'not having much to show on the political activity side and having an interest in individual farming' (ibid., l. 130).

44 The cell was under the care of secretary Kuroplyov (the poor man's name translates as Henspit); it had a small hard core of official members, but (if its own records are to be believed) a much larger satellite group of interested local young people who occasionally attended meetings, sometimes rising to as many as thirty-five (TsDOO SO f. 1245 op. 1 d. 2, l. 108: records for meeting on 19 July 1925, with seventeen lads and eighteen 'lases' [*sic*]. Of course, the cell may well have gone out of existence later on, as the absence of continuous records in fact suggests.

45 TsDOO SO f. 1201 op. 1 d. 25, l. 76, 'Spisok sostava yacheek i nalichie chlenov i kandidatov Tavdinskoi partiinoi organizatsii na 20/XI-33 goda', and TsDOO SO f. 1201 op. 1 d. 25, l. 64, 'Perechen' i sostav yacheek VKP(b) v raione' (undated, position in file suggests early 1933).

46 By comparison, at the same time the residents of Gorodishche village soviet were buying in as many as thirty-four issues of *Tavda Worker*, and the residents of Koshuki village soviet, seventy-four. See the 1933 list of newspaper subscriptions at TsDOO SO f. 1245 op. 1 d. 28, ll. 80–85.

47 Over the period January 1930 to September 1933, they generally ranged from 450–500, peaking at 778 in April 1932; predictably, the bulk of the membership (60–76 per cent) was drawn from workers rather than peasants (who made up a maximum of 35 per cent of members during the same period) (TsDOO SO f. 1201 op. 1 d. 25, l. 64).

48 TsDOO SO f. 1245 op. 1 d. 15, ll. 12–13.

49 See his personal file at TsDOO SO f. 1201 op. 1 d. 14, l. 45.

50 TsDOO SO f. 1209 op. 1 d. 1, l. 9.

51 TsDOO SO f. 4 op. 8 d. 101, l. 211 (undated, date estimated from position in the file).

52 TsDOO SO f. 4 op. 8 d. 169, l. 49.

53 TsDOO SO f. 1201 op. 1 d. 26, l. 59: see also *TR*, 24 December 1932, p. 2.

54 TsDOO SO f. 1201 op. 1 d. 26, l. 48. Varygin's name is given in the file as 'Vorigin'; the spelling here has been harmonized with that in H-7825, vol. 2 (see Chapter 3).

55 TsDOO SO f. 4 op. 9 d. 217, l. 37.

56 TsDOO SO f. 1201 op. 1 d. 18, l. 173.

57 Ibid., ll. 20–21.
58 TsDOO SO f. 4 op. 9 d. 217, l. 193. Cf. TsDOO SO f. 4 op. 8 d. 10, l. 22 (a similar report from March 1930, this time with a six-man gang).
59 TsDOO SO f. 4 op. 9 d. 217, l. 45.
60 Ibid., ll. 135–6.
61 TsDOO SO f. 1201 op. 1 d. 26, l. 29 (this for the first half of December 1932).
62 Ibid., ll. 83–7.
63 Ibid., ll. 13–22; TsDOO SO f. 1201 d. 1 op. 18, ll. 43–8.
64 Rumours of coup: TsDOO SO f. 1201 op. 1 d. 18, l. 75; threats to kill: ibid., l. 76; exulting in deaths of activists, ibid., l. 76; informer names: ibid., l. 72; concealing arms, ibid., l. 28.
65 Ibid., l. 37.
66 TsDOO SO f. 1201 op. 1 d. 18, l. 72. See also f. 1201 op. 1 d. 18, l. 104, on the arrest of Citizen Karandashev (Mr Pencil) at Karatunka jetty, the man being found to have various official stamps, some forged, sewn into his trousers, as well as thirteen blank document forms.
67 TsDOO SO f. 1201 op. 1 d. 18, l. 27.
68 For instance, dekulakization was preceded, in 1931 and 1932, by the dispatch of a pro forma to the local village soviet chairman alerting him to the fact that 'in the near future exile of kulaks is to take place in your area, and therefore you are directed to co-operate in every way with the OGPU workers, and to carry out broad campaigns among the local masses, using the spring sowing as a focus' (TsDOO SO f. 1201 op.1 d. 26, l. 9). The order also directed the chairman of the village soviet to contact the secretary of the local Party cell and inform him of his responsibility to regulate the campaign, and emphasized that the exile of kulaks was to be kept 'totally secret' until it started. The example here is dated 11 May 1932, and carries the handwritten signature of Bykov over the typed signature of his predecessor as district plenipotentiary of OGPU, Ushenin, and also the signature of Demin, the head of the secret section of the District Committee.
69 TsDOO SO f. 1201 op. 1 d. 26, l. 37.
70 See e.g. ibid., ll. 19–20, 23.
71 TsDOO SO f. 4 op. 1 d. 101, l. 57.
72 For disciplinary material on drinking, see e.g. TsDOO SO f. 1209 op. 1 d. 1, l. 18; TsDOO SO f. 1201 op. 1 d. 4, l. 45 (drunken accordion-playing); ibid., l. 30 drunken brick-throwing

(comrade Silanov, Irbitskaya OKK doc. No. 636, 16 October 1928). Another kind of bad behaviour – the seduction or attempted seduction of subordinates (what would now be termed 'sexual harassment') is recorded at ibid., l. 64. Material on corruption includes the following: in January 1933, three members of the Komsomol who worked at an orphanage were found to be filching food tokens and selling these on, while in March 1933 two 'recidivist horse-thieves' (this time under the names Parfyonov and Sazhin rather than the Galiudin Galimadinov who had given the police such trouble two years earlier) were found to have escaped from the town lock-up after having concealed a saw in their cell, probably with the connivance of the policeman exercising guard duty (TsDOO SO 1245 op. 1 d. 14, l. 28; TsDOO SO f. 1209 op. 1 d. 1, l. 65).

3. Investigating the Murder

1 TsDOO SO f. 1201 op. 1 d. 24, l. 79.

2 The current file number is H-7825, vols. 1 and 2. The only sheets I did not see were at vol. 2, folios 119–22; these, I was told, had disappeared before the file reached the Central Archive. The staff archivist who told me this also suggested that it was simply a case of messed-up pagination, but that seems unlikely, given the number of missed pages. Possibly they were removed for use at the time the suspects mounted their appeal, or forwarded for use in one of the later cases spawned by the main trial (see below). The file also had a long list of earlier numbers: no. 41, no. 271, no. 374 (when the investigation was in progess), and no. 21612, no. 10155, no. 50930 (archive numbers).

3 A few petitions about quite different subjects have got into the file, probably because the person dealing with the letters as they arrived at *Pioneer Pravda* had been misled by the word *Protest*. See e.g. TsA FSB H-7825 vol. 1, l. 304.

4 A full list of the file's contents, with transcriptions of several documents, is available on the project website for 'Childhood in Russia 1890–1991: A Social and Cultural History', http://www.ox.ac.uk/russian/childhood/html.

5 Partal ligament: *partavaya svyazka*. What the orderly appears to have in mind is the *ligamentum pylori* (from the Greek *pylorus*, a gate-keeper, hence *partovaya* for *portovaya* in the sense of 'entrance'), or ligament of Helvetius, a muscle band running

along the pyloric antrum, i.e. the 'terminal constricted portion of the stomach' (*Churchill's Medical Dictionary*: 1050).

6 In 1926, the medical procedures that orderlies were allowed to carry out included the following: removal of foreign bodies, stitching wounds, tamponization, blood test, placing glass jars on a patient's chest to 'draw off' catarrh, extraction of teeth, lancing boils, treatment of hernias, catherization (*Byulleten' NKZ*, 1 (1926), 62). Surgery was not included; the orderly working on the Morozov case probably had no idea of how to dissect a corpse. Yury Druzhnikov's informants reported that the orderly was reluctant to pronounce on the cause of death etc., and suspected something sinister in this (Druzhnikov 1995: 22), but it is equally likely that the orderly (rightly) felt he was not qualified to deal with a murder victim.

7 Evgeny Devikov, 'Zhertva, no ne geroi: Kommentarii yurista', in Turuntaev 1990: 244. Devikov's article is generally very informative about the procedural eccentricities of the investigation. The first forensic pathology courses in Leningrad were opened only in October 1926 (*Byulleten' NKZ*, 13–14 (1926), 84–5).

8 According to Solomon 1996: 131, cases of murder were regularly left to the beat police at this era, although the latter had no resources to photograph the bodies and no skills in taking fingerprints etc. Druzhnikov 1995: 22 reports from sources in Gerasimovka that the inspection of the bodies in fact took place considerably later than the dates officially recorded, which is possible; whichever way, the quality of the medical evidence is risible.

9 Clearly, only cross-dressing in the reverse direction would have been possible – clothes made for Sergei, who was a big man, could have been worn by his smaller grandson. This is in any case far more likely in terms of practices in traditional peasant households, where children and adolescents often dressed in cast-offs.

10 Rigor mortis normally lasts anything between twenty-four and seventy-two hours, but rapid cooling can inhibit its onset, though it occurs in the ordinary way once the body temperature rises (*Churchill's Medical Dictionary*: 1654). If the children were killed not long before sunset on 3 September, rigor could conceivably have lasted till early on the morning of 7 September, when the examination took place.

11 The statement is dated 11 September.

12 For the information about his relationship with the police, see TsDOO SO f. 1201 op. 1 d. 26, l. 48.

13 A rare exception is the testimony of Sof'ya Efimova, aged twenty-three, given to Fedchenko on 4 November, which simply states that she was at home all day on 3 September and has nothing to say (166).

14 For instance, three-quarters of the cases prosecuted under a law of 7 August 1932, making theft from collective farms subject to the death penalty, were dealt with in less than three days (Solomon 1996: 120).

15 Ironically, given that five members of the Kniga family were to be involved in violence against Komsomol members and police aides in November 1932: see TsDOO SO f. 1201 op. 1 d. 26, l. 48, and Chapter 2 above.

16 See (181–6), which comprises six official forms about property holdings and income for the three Morozovs, Efrem Shatrakov, Kulukanov and Silin. (The forms carry the stamp of Gerasimovka village soviet for 193_, but the year has not been filled in, nor a day of the month supplied. They must, however, date from after 16 October 1932 (when Khima Kulukanova and Vladimir Mezyukhin were released), and before 14 November 1932 (when Efrem Shatrakov was released). Kulukanov's form describes him as a kulak but his land holdings at 2.8 desyatinas are not much larger than one and a half for several others. However his income is given at 442 roubles p.a. pre-1929, and at arrest at 227 roubles (corrected from 22 roubles); tax 23.50 and 55 before 1929. By contrast Shatrakov's income (181 rev.) is 140/160 roubles income, tax 15.14 and 8 (before 1929); Silin's income is given as 220/317 and 18/15 (184). Both are described as 'middling peasants'.

17 Matsuk had either come forward of his own accord, or been asked to, because he was a Party sympathizer: cf. the membership application on file for him from 1928 (TsDOO SO 1201/1/6, l. 129: it was refused: see Chapter 2 above).

18 One of the neighbours later refused to confirm this story (167), but it made its way into the later lives of Pavlik Morozov.

19 Silin originally said that he sold the cloth to Danila in early August, but changed his story at the interrogators' prompting (99), though Danila had been working on the lumber plantations in the taiga over the summer (84) and doing odd jobs, and could perfectly well have acquired the money some other way.

20 It is possible that an undated face-to-face confrontation, co-ordinated by Suvorov, between Sergei Morozov, who argued that Danila was likely to have committed the murder, and Danila, who protested his innocence, also dates from some point on 7 September (21).

21 The early testimony uniformly prefers the verb *dokazyvat'/dolozhit'* (slang for 'to inform') to the more official *donosit'/donesti* ('to denounce').

22 Druzhnikov 1995: 10 gives his rank as 'deputy district plenipotentiary', but it seems unlikely it was so high: Kartashov was not involved in later stages of the interrogation, unlike Iskrin, who is named as 'deputy district plenipotentiary' in the protocols.

23 An undated face-to-face confrontation organized by Titov between Anna Stepanchenko and Kseniya Morozova (38) may also date from 11 September.

24 This man's name was Pavel Yel'shin. In the minutes of the Poor Peasants' Assembly on 12 September, *TR*, 18 September 1932, p. 1, he is described as a 'member of the print *aktiv*' in Gerasimovka.

25 Ignaty Galyzov (34) and Iosif Prokopovich (36).

26 (58) is a typed version of the minute, (59–60) a handwritten version. The minute was also published in *TR*, 18 September 1932, p. 1.

27 TsDOO SO 1201 op. 1 d. 24, l. 73.

28 Of interest at this stage, too, is the involvement of the local teacher, Zoya Kabina, who sat in an interview with the schoolgirl Anastasiya Sakova on 11 September 1932 (31). She was in due course to act as an 'ideological' witness at the trial, giving details of Pavlik's 'Pioneer' activities (see below).

29 TsDOO SO f. 1201 op. 1 d. 24, l. 123.

30 This round of questioning also appears to have taken place in Tavda, though the order issued on 21 October (146) had stated that the prisoners were to be transferred to custody in Irbit. Certainly, Fedchenko interviewed at least one suspect in Gerasimovka itself (160), which would have been a difficult journey from anywhere else but 'the station', as locals called the town.

31 Not on 26 August, or more than a week before the murder, as Danila had claimed (see above).

32 The gloss was provided by the interrogator.

33 'Sledstvie po delu Morozovykh zatyagivaetsya', *PP*, 15 November 1932, p. 1.

34 Very possibly, Vyshinsky made his intervention by telephone – this was a standard method of communication by top officials – and the *Pioneer Pravda* journalists made up the text of the telegram because having access to this seemed more plausible than did a story about overhearing Vyshinsky make the call.

35 Here and later the prosecution case made reference to sheet numbers in the file ('45, 113', etc.), but these are not the ones currently so numbered.

36 On 'fictional' show trials (which had the character of debates, but were taken in deadly earnest), see Wood 2002.

37 'Edinodushnyi protest', *VK*, 25 November 1932, back page; and illustrations, ibid.

38 'Prigovor', *VK*, 25 November 1932, back page.

39 Argenbright 2002: 253.

40 On the stereotypes of such narratives, see Halttunen 1999.

41 On 'campaign justice', see Solomon 1996: 81. Chapters 3 and 4 of this book provide excellent background information on the legal culture that shaped the Morozov case.

42 Examples of leading questions are recorded in the transcript of a face-to-face confrontation between Danila Morozov and Arseny Kulukanov:

> Is it true that on 3 September, the day the brothers Morozov were murdered, you were visited by citizen Morozov and he told you that it was essential to go and look for the Morozovs or report that they were missing, and did you really give him 30 roubles and promise to give him some gold so that Morozov Daniil should tell no one what you had ordered to do in the case of the murder of the Morozov brothers? (153).

Arseny Kulukanov, who behaved in a particularly hard-headed way at interrogations, replied that Danila was lying from start to finish. But it is clear that this interrogation method was intended to put ideas and words into suspects' heads, to provide them with appropriate narratives that they could articulate later. A telling sign of the effects of this technique is the migration of motifs from interviewee to interviewee over the course of time. For instance, on 16 September, Sergei Morozov told Bykov that his wife and Danila had tried to persuade him to pass off the blood on the trousers found at the Morozovs' as the results of a 'bloody flux' that he had been suffering from (107 rev.). But on 23 September, Prokhor Varygin told Bykov that he had overheard Danila saying to Efrem Shatrakov that they must say nothing to the interrogators, even if beaten, and that the blood should be blamed on his grandfather's case of the bloody flux (71 rev.).

43 Had this been an ordinary murder, the question of premeditation would indeed have been crucial, but it was neither here nor there with Article 58.8. Cf. the record of the interrogation of Yakov Titov on 27 September, when Titov stated that he had told Danila and Efrem that, as they were both under eighteen, their punishment would be reduced if they made a full and frank confession (but that he had never beaten or threatened them).

44 On five occasions when suspects were interviewed, there was more than one OGPU officer present in the room: these were the sessions with Kseniya Morozova on 2 and 5 November (154, 173), where one extra officer was present; the session with Danila Morozov on 6 November, where two extra officers were present (176); the session with Sergei Morozov on 6 November, where two extra officers were present (179); and the face-to-face confrontation between Kseniya Morozova and Danila Morozov, on 5 November, at which one extra officer was present (174). At four of these occasions, full confessions were made: in the words of a 'confession protocol' composed after the 6 November interview with Danila Morozov, this had happened 'after much talk had been expended' (178), though in fact the protocol gave only the bald confession as such.

45 In *Istoricheskii arkhiv,* April 2004, note 3, Denis Shibaev gives a different version: the sentence of execution was enacted on only two of those convicted, Kulukanov and Danila (on 21 March 1933), Sergei and Kseniya Morozova having died on 1 and 31 January 1933 respectively. Quite possibly, the earlier date is correct, and the later one was inserted on the notice of the appeal's failure in order to conceal the fact that the execution had taken place *before* the case went to appeal. Equally, this circumstance would explain why the appeal notice – most unusually for an official document – carries no date.

4. Class Warrior, Boy Martyr

1 'Edinodushnyi protest', *VK* 30 November 1932, back page.

2 Literally, 'who have crossed the boundaries of all restraint', 'gone way over the top'.

3 *Sic* To put it more clearly: 'started waiting for the brothers, who had gone to the woods in the morning, to return from there'.

4 Titov, 'Kulatskaya banda ubila pionera Morozova. Rasstrelyat' raspoyasavshchikhsya kulakov i podkulachnikov', *TR*, 17 September 1932, p. 1 (published in *Smena* section). Though signed 'Titov', the story is unlikely to have been the work of the beat policeman of that name, yet there was no other official so called in the district. Probably it was written on his behalf – perhaps by Spiridon Kartashov, perhaps by Pavel El'shin, the local 'village correspondent'.

5 See e.g. *TR*, 18, 20, 21, 24, 27 September 1932.

6 TsDOO SO f. 61 op. 1 d. 793, l. 176.

7 'Kulaki derevni Gerasimovki ubili pionera-aktivista Morozova i ego brata', *VK*, 23 September 1932, p. 2; 'Iz pisem yunkorov', *Na smenu!*, 24 September 1932, p. 3.

8 The archive of *Pioneer Pravda* is currently stored in a closed repository in north-west Moscow, and it is not clear in any case whether it includes material from the early 1930s.

9 E. Smirnov, 'Pavlik Morozov', in Makhlin and Goncharenko 1961: 66.

10 'Zverskoe ubiistvo dvukh pionerov. Nikakoi poshchady klassovomu vragu', *PP*, 2 October 1932, p. 4. There were in fact never more than eight suspects involved, and these were – by the beginning of October – not the same as those in the list published in *Tavda Worker* two weeks earlier. On 15 October, however, *PP*, reported that the killers were Danila Morozov and Efrem Shatrakov – as in the 23 September *VK* article, and 'Dva pionera pali zhertvoi kulatskoi klassovoi mesti', *Na smenu!*, 28 September 1932, p. 3.

11 'Zverskoe ubiistvo', p. 4.

12 'Kulatskaya rasprava', *PP*, 15 October 1932, p. 2.

13 'Kulatskaya rasprava', p. 2.

14 'Soberem podarki derevenskim pioneram v otvet kulach'yu. Ot nashego spetskorrespondenta', *PP*, 17 October 1932, p. 2.

15 'Soberem podarki', *PP*, 17 October 1932, p. 2 (on the prophet and the unwavering resolve of Gerasimovka pioneers); 'Nash otvet kulakam-ubiitsam', *PP*, 23 October 1932, p. 3 (on the donation of notebooks).

16 On the most famous use of aviation, the Cheluskin case, see Petrone 2000: 46–84.

17 The journalists may well have compared their notes with those made by the court secretary, or perhaps even based their accounts on the secretary's notes in the first place.

18 In *Dawns of the Commune*, Pavlik's grandfather hit him with the

harness and threatened him; in the trial protocol, Pavlik's response to this had been to break the windows (224). This was omitted from the newspaper account.

19 *PP*, 27 November 1932, p. 1. The text was the same as the text in the OGPU files and in the OGPU special report for October 1932: see Chapter 5.

20 The final lines of the song in fact read, 'Our young drummer boy has perished/But the song about him will not die.' See e.g. http://dsa.yaroslavl.ru/pioner/start.htm.

21 'Sud nad ubiitsami Pavlushi Morozova', *PP*, 21 November 1932, p. 1; Pavel Solomein, 'Pis'mo iz Gerasimovki', ibid., p. 1; 'Kulaki na skam'e podsudimykh', *PP*, 27 November 1932, p. 1 (on the interrogation of suspects and the funeral). Additionally, *PP*, 29 November 1932, p. 1, carried more material about the trial.

22 E. Smirnov, 'Nikakoi poshchady klassovomu vragu!', 3 December 1932, p. 2; idem, 'Pavlik Morozov – ocherk', *PP*, 17 December 1932, p. 1.

23 See especially *PP*, 3 December 1932, p. 2.

24 O. Shvarts, 'Pavlik Morozov', *Pioner*, 6 (1933), p. 18.

25 Ibid., p. 19.

26 In the original, the quotation reads, 'Starik Morozov pytaetsya prinyat' na sebya "iisusov vid"': 'Vtoroi i tretii den' sudebnogo protsessa nad ubiitsami pionera Morozova', *TR*, 28 November 1932, p. 2.

27 'Vtoroi i tretii den'', p. 2.

28 Shvarts, 'Pavlik Morozov', p. 19.

29 K. A. Schenzinger, *Der Hitlerjunge Quex: Roman* (Berlin: Zeitgeist, 1932).

30 In the book version, Quex is fifteen years old, and seems young for his age. In the film version, his age was, more plausibly, given as twelve.

31 Of course, the story about Pavlik's denunciation was not made up by the *Pioneer Pravda* journalists from start to finish, if one trusts the dating on Bykov's case assessment on 17 September (149–51), and Tatiana Morozova's statement on 6 September (1). But it was given a new centrality.

32 In similar vein, Lidiya Libedinskaya remembered seeing a lachrymose film about a German boy Communist martyr, *The Worn-Out Shoes*, in the early 1930s (Fitzpatrick and Slezkine 2000: 297). There were also original Fascist heroes, e.g. Herbert Norkus, a fifteen-year-old boy allegedly murdered by the Communists in 1931 (Klönne 1990: 58).

33 On *irodstvo* – literally 'tyranny' but playing on the idea of King Herod as a supremely evil child-murderer – see Lifschutz-Losev 1981: 73. The literature analysing the legend of St Boris and Gleb is enormous. A good introduction in English to its significance and history is Lenhoff 1989.

34 A rare early Soviet treatment of the murder, first published in 1925, alluded only to the execution of the Tsar 'and his family', and quoted an announcement made to a workers' meeting in the City Theatre, Ekaterinburg, on 22 July 1918: 'The execution of Nicholas the Bloody is a reply and a stern warning to the bourgeois monarchist counter-revolution, which is trying to drown the workers' and peasants' revolution in blood' – a phrasing which concealed the fate of the other individuals executed alongside (Bykov 1935: 82).

35 'Smert' Ludovika', in Shkapskaya 1979: 84–5; 'Tsar' i Bog! Prostite malym' in Tsvetaeva 1994: 439. Tsvetaeva's poem (published only after her death) pleads for mercy to be granted to those who have killed the Tsar but, by comparing these to the cruel peasant rebel Sten'ka Razin, it brands the killing an act of indiscriminate violence, rather than an 'execution' sanctioned by law. In Sokolov's generally sober and judicious *émigré* account of the Romanov murders, neutrality wavers when the ill-treatment of the Tsarevich is recounted; see e.g. Sokolov 1925: 15, describing the confiscation of the boy's toy gun, or the selection of a close-up of his toys as one of two illustrations of the possessions owned by the Tsar's family discovered by White forces in Ekaterinburg when the town was captured from the Bolsheviks (plate 63).

36 For rumours of the possible survival of Aleksei and Anastasia, see Saranin 1997: 54–6. Saranin also states that there was much gossip about discoveries of gemstones by locals working in the area of Ekaterinburg. The material about not understanding the reasons for the execution of the women and children is taken from an informal interview with a man (b. *c.* 1940), 10 September 2003, Ekaterinburg. This informant also remembered that it used to be rumoured that the cap worn by the watchman at the Ilpatievsky house had once belonged to the Tsar, 'and indeed it did have some kind of royal crest on it'.

37 'Skazanie o Borise i Glebe' (Gudzy 1973: 43, 47).

38 One might compare the small editorial change to the legend of Judas: Danila Morozov was paid in thirty pieces of *gold*, not the canonical silver.

39 For a basic outline of the Yushchinsky murder and the Beilis trial, see *Delo Mendelya Beilisa* 1999: 3–23. More nuanced and more effectively contextualised accounts are Samuel 1967; Tager 1933; Brazul'-Brushkovsky 1913; Rogger 1986: 40–55; Löwe 1993: 284–96.

40 See the unofficial trial transcript (no official court record was kept), *Delo Beilisa* 1913. Engelstein 1992: 300–301, 324–7 has useful observations on the reactions to the trial among conservative, anti-Semitic intellectuals, such as Vasily Rozanov, and on the psychological factors behind the belief in ritual murder.

41 Glagolev in *Delo Beilisa* 1913: vol. 1, p. 31.

42 *Delo Mendelya Beilisa* 1999: 6 (no source given).

43 *Delo Beilisa* 1913: vol. 3, p. 5. Cf. the reference by one of the reporting pathologists, Professor Sikorsky, to the '*muchenie* i umershchvlenie zhertvy' (*martyrdom* and torture of the victim) (*Delo Beilisa* 1913: vol. 1, p. 30). (My emphasis.)

44 *Delo Beilisa* 1913: vol. 3, p. 215).

45 Ibid., p. 271.

46 Ibid., p. 292.

47 The issue of possible involvement by the parents is raised in Brazul'-Brushkovsky 1913: 20–25, but then dropped, and Brazul'-Brushkovsky himself later firmly asserts the 'secular martyr' line: Yushchinsky was tortured to death by the Cheberyak gang because they blamed him for their denunciation to the police (pp. 57–61).

48 For an account of these, see Tager 1933: 279–81. It is interesting that the indirect response among Jews to 'blood libel' may have been to emphasize their own superior care for children: Sherman 2003: 95 argues that the repeated motif of Christians sending their children to learn chess from Jews is to be seen as an unconscious inversion of 'the age-old Christian representation of Jews as monsters who "eat" children'.

49 On this element in the Yushchinsky case, see Brazul'-Brushkovsky 1913: 11–12.

50 In Pavlik's case, both these details originally appeared in Titov's 'Protocol on the Removal of the Bodies' (6), and thence found their way in embellished form into the trial proceedings (e.g. 223). Some also appeared in published accounts of the trial. For example, Shvarts's account in *Pioner*, 6 (1933), pp. 19–20 asserts that the murderers (Sergei and Danila Morozov) dragged Fyodor off 'to the left' after the boys had been killed.

51 For the 'glasses' point see Fisher 1977: 189. On 'glass' as a culinary

measurement, see Toomre 1992: 69, 96 (it equated to approximately 200 ml). On cannibalism as an element of ritual murder, see e.g. the popular English ballad 'The Jew's Daughter', in which the eponymous anti-heroine lures Little St Hugh to her house, and having 'stickit him like a swine' then rolls him up in a 'cake o' lead'. (This ballad, given in twenty-two versions by F. J. Child's *The English and Scottish Popular Ballads*, is discussed by Fabre-Vassas 1997: 134–5. For the use of lingonberry and cranberry (*klyukva*) with roast meat, see Toomre 1992: 511.

52 'Podrobnosti ubiistva dvukh pionerok', *Pravda*, 27 November 1934, p. 6; *Pravda*, 13 December 1934, p. 6. In this case, too, the deduction of the local force seems perfectly reasonable: the killing could perfectly well have been the result of an opportunist attack by local villains.

53 See e.g. *PP*, 3 December 1932. Interesting in this context is the fact that 'kulak' could be used as a term of abuse for Jews (Dal' 1880–82: vol. 2, p. 215).

54 See e.g. the instructions to Pioneer leaders about marking the festival in *Vozhatyi,* 15–16 (1932), pp. 46–7, and ibid., 19–20 (1932), pp. 5–11, 29–34. On the other hand, items in the Pioneer press also recorded that in practice celebrations did not necessarily live up to the plans: see e.g. 'Prospali mezhdunarodnyi prazdnik' (They Sleep-Walked Through the International Festival), *Leninskie iskry*, 18 May 1929, p. 3.

55 See e.g. a piece on the Scottsboro affair: *Zor'ka*, 9 (1932), p. 13; or a regular feature on the virtues of learning German, 'Nemetskii ugolok', running in *Zateinik* during 1932; or an 'international quiz', 'Internatsional'naya viktorina', *Zateinik*, 19 (1932), p. 16. For an example of an anti-racist piece, see N. Frenkel', 'Oktyabryata – tovarishchi detyam trudyashchikhsya vsego mira', *Zateinik*, 5 (1932), pp. 32–6.

56 See Chapter 1 above.

57 For example, the 'Auto-Castrators', a small Orthodox sect, came under assault in the late 1920s as economic predators, exploiters and members of a 'web' of conspiracy and deceit (Engelstein 1999: 210–11). The anthropologist Katherine Verdery has argued that this kind of 'incitement to hatred' was typical of Soviet ideology generally, and traces the nationalist upsurge after 1991 to this aspect of Soviet politics (Verdery 1993: 179–203). One could compare the persistence of anti-Semitic fantasies as an identity-defining marker by exclusion in German

Protestant culture after ritual murder trials ceased in the late sixteenth century: see Po-Chia Hora 1988: 155, 226–30.

58 See e.g. Diderikhs 1991: vol. 1, pp. 283–311: particularly p. 307, 'A Jew has never been known to act on his own', and p. 298, branding Yankel' Yurovsky, the orchestrator of the murder, a 'Jewish monster'.

59 See e.g. a virulently anti-Semitic letter sent by 'A Peasant Man' to Lenin on 7 February 1919, raving about the Bolshevik intention to 'sow the yid faith' in Russia, to teach the Talmud in schools (*Pis'ma vo vlast'*, 1998: 60, p. 95); or a letter from a rank-and-file rural member of the Komsomol member to the Komsomol's Central Committee in 1925 with the information that he hated Jews because 'you've only to read the 24 Protocols stolen from the Central Committee of the Jewish Elder-Leaders (i.e. the anti-Semitic forgery *The Protocols of the Elders of Zion*) to find out what their politics are like' (Letter from K. A. Lebedev, 1 December 1924, TsKhDMO f. 1 op. 23 d. 315, l. 122).

60 I was told by a woman who worked in the 1960s at the Sverdlovsk Museum of the Revolution that colleagues of hers had discovered a cache of arms, along with items suggesting these belonged to a monarchist group, when a former mansion in the city was cleared out so that anything of value could be transferred to the museum (CK-MW-Ekaterinburg).

61 Like the 'ritual murder' spin on Pavlik's death, events of this kind seem to have been more popular at the centre than at the periphery. Anti-religious work in Tavda in the late 1920s and early 1930s took thoroughly practical forms: cf. an item on an 'Anti-Christmas Day' held in Tavda in 1930, which essentially consisted of a patriotically extended shift at the factory and the banning of alcohol sales in the town (TsDOO SO f. 1201 op. 1 d. 9, l. 8).

62 Yakovlev 1936: 186.

63 Smirnov 1938: 75. Note the substitution of the genteel 'chest' for the 'stomach' of earlier accounts. A decade later, Vitaly Gubarev's account pretty well suppressed the murder altogether (see Chapter 6).

64 The second half of the 1930s saw a decline in prominence of the Beilis case itself. According to Gromov 1998: 372, in December 1940 Eisenstein was officially denied permission to make a film based on the popular hack playwright Lev Sheinin's play *The Beilis Affair* (*Delo Beilisa*).

65 *Detskoe kommunisticheskoe dvizhenie* 1932: 37.
66 The painting, now lost, is reproduced in Bown 1998: plate 198. A 'Budyonnovka cap', named after Budyonnyi, the commander of the Soviet Red Cavalry, is a gored fabric cap with a turned-up peak.
67 Lyadov 1934: 4.
68 Babina 1929: 7.
69 P. Solomein, 'Pochemu raiorganizatsii pozdno uznali', *VK*, 8 October 1932, p. 2.
70 P. Solomein, 'Kak pogib Pavlik', *VK*, 27 October 1932, p. 2. Another item on 30 October, p. 1 ('Nikakoi poshchady ubiit-sam') recalled local reactions to the murder – how the return of the bodies to the village reading room had provoked a burst of emotion and a flurry of entries to the kolkhoz, not to speak of much flyposting of kulaks by local schoolchildren.
71 See Druzhnikov 1995.
72 Solomein 1933: 7. Once again, this was an exaggeration: the accepted figure is six (see Chapter 2 above).
73 Solomein 1933: 10.
74 Ibid., 12.
75 Ibid., 8, 22.
76 Ibid., 26–7.
77 Ibid., 29.
78 See e.g. *Pravda*, 5 January 1933, p. 6, 'Nad gustoi taigoi'. For the history of 'luminary metaphors', see Halfin 2000: 116–18.
79 'Kulaki ubili pionera Kolyu Myagotina', *PP*, 21 December 1932, p. 1.
80 *LI*, 21 December 1933, p. 1.
81 Besides Kolya Myagotin, these were N. M. Yagotsk, slaughtered in Kolesnikovo in the Urals in October 1932 for 'denouncing grain-hoarding'; Kh. Stepanov, who had died in 'a vengeance killing by the son of an exiled kulak' (Chuvashiya, October 1932); A. Saratov, an Octobrist and 'son of an active Communist' from Gorky region, January 1933; E. Rybin, 'murdered by an officer's wife' in Samarkand, February 1933; 'Pioneer Girl Ryndlya', murdered out of 'class vengeance' in the Donbass, March 1933; 'Pioneer Varkovin' from Chelyabinsk (November 1932); and one Pal'shiev from the Urals (November 1932). 'Svodka politicheskikh ubiistv pionerov' (RGASPI-TsKhDMO f. 1 op. 23 d. 1056, ll. 1–14).
82 Particularly Tatars, Komi, Bashkirs and Mansi, which last belong among a range of nomadic people traditionally known as

'natives'. It is interesting to note that Solomein's life appeared during 1933–4 in two minority languages for circulation among such groups, Tatar and Komi-Permyak (Solomein 1966: 7 – the colonized sold a myth about the colonizers).

83 *Byulleten' press-byuro TASS na dekabr' 1932* (Moscow: TASS, 1932). (Mimeographed typescript. Held in RAO NA f. 6 op. 1 ed. khr. 56.)

85 In the last three months of 1932, *KP* carried only two small items on inside pages. On 23 November 1932, p. 4, it reported that Pavel, a 'social activist' and his nine-year-old brother Fyodor had fallen victim to kulaks who had been sabotaging collectivization and dominating the village. Pavel's father had come under their influence, but Pavel had received no support when he courageously denounced them. Pavel's murderers were his cousin Danila Morozov and Efrem Shatrakov, son of a kulak: 'class hatred ruptures all ties between people, even the ties of family', the report concluded. Six days later, on 29 November 1932, and also on p. 4, the paper carried a one-sentence report: 'After three days of deliberation, the trial of the murderers of Pioneer Pavlik Morozov is concluded; the ringleaders Kulakanov, Sergei Morozov, Kseniya Morozova and Daniil Morozov have been condemned to death.'

5. All-Soviet Hero

1 M. Gorky, letter to Stalin, 12 November 1931, in Gorky, 1998: 284; letter to Stalin, 1 December 1931, ibid., 290; letter to Stalin 2 August 1934, ibid., 297, 298.

2 An example was the 'Snub-Nose Club' of Irkutsk Pioneers, a writers' group founded in the early 1930s. An article of Gorky's in *Pravda*, 'Boys and Girls', written after the group had sent a copy of their book to him, first brought the group to national attention; it later sent representatives to the First Congress of Soviet Writers (*Baza kurnosykh* 1962: 5–6).

3 M. Gorky, letter to P. Solomein, September 1933 (exact date not given) (Gorky 1949–55: vol. 30, pp. 328–9).

4 See 'Privetstvie *Krest'yanskoi gazete*', *Pravda*, 23 November 1933, p. 2.

5 The article was reprinted in Gorky 1949–55: vol. 27, p. 124, without correction. No doubt to draw attention to Gorky's mistake would have been an extremely risky piece of editorial pedantry, not only because, in the Stalinist view, great writers did not make mistakes, but also because 1952, the year when the

volume went to press, happened to be the thirtieth anniversary of Pavlik's murder.

6 M. Gorky, 'Vpered i vyshe, komsomolets!', *Sobranie sochinenii v 30 tomakh*, vol. 27, p. 124.

7 *Pervyi vsesoyuznyi* 1934: 681. Note also the call by the delegation of Pioneers from the Snub-Nose Club for the construction of the memorial, and praising Gorky for his support, p. 38.

8 See M. Gorky, letter to A. S. Shcherbakov, 19 February 1935, *Sobranie sochinenii v 30 tomakh*, vol. 30, p. 383.

9 See *Kopii postanovlenii sekretariata TsK VLKSM po shkol'noi i pionerskoi rabote za 1935–40 gg* (typescript held in the Reading Room of RGASPI-TsKhDMO), l. 6.

10 RGASPI f. 17 op. 3 d. 968, 'Protokol zasedaniya Politbyuro' TsK VKP(b) ot 17 iyulya 1935 goda: Oprosom chlenov Politbyuro ot 13.VII.35', l. 20 (item 95). My thanks to R. W. Davies for drawing my attention to this decision, and to Denis Kozlov for transcribing the minute.

11 See the observations of Smith 2000: 239–40.

12 Smirnov 1938: 78.

13 The archives of the Moscow City Soviet are closed to the public, so it is possible that there is material here. But if Stalin had made the order, something would definitely have been done about the monument – unless he immediately rescinded it.

14 G. F. Aleksandrov, M. R. Galaktionov, V. S. Kruzhkov, M. B. Mitin, V. D. Mochalov, P. N. Pospelov, 'Stalin, Iosif Vissarionovich', *BSE* (1st edn), vol. 52, col. 618.

15 See Sarah Davies, 'Stalin and the Cult', in Apor, Behrends, Jones and Rees 2004.

16 Amis 2002: 193.

17 See the 'Five-Year Plan of Education and Literacy' published in *Pravda*, 31 December 1932, p. 3.

18 See e.g. the portrait and biography of 'Pioneer girl Elistratova' from Moscow School no. 7, Krasnaya Presnya district: 'Rastet novyi chelovek', *PP*, 25 December 1932, p. 1.

19 'O rabote pionerskoi organizatsii', *Partiinoe stroitel'stvo*, 11–12 (1932), pp. 52–3.

20 See especially Petrone 2000.

21 The first use of the slogan that I have come across is in the coverage to mark the tenth anniversary of the founding of *PP* on 24 October 1935. On page 3 of the paper appeared the banner headline, 'Thank You, Comrade Stalin, for a Happy, Joyful Childhood'. The alternative version, 'Thank You, Dear Stalin,

for a Happy/Joyful Childhood', had a more intimate, sentimental ring, and also directly evoked the paternity of the addressee (*rodnoi* signifies ties of blood as well as ties of affection).

22 Entry to the most popular 'circles', such as ballet, was competitive, and children who had no aptitude would be quietly nudged towards some more 'suitable' activity for them – radio-building, knitting, bird-fancying.

23 A wonderful first-hand account of these is Druskin 1984: see esp. 55–6.

24 See *Deti o Staline*, published for the leader's sixtieth birthday in 1939.

25 See e.g. all the children celebrated in the anthology *Deti o Staline* (1939). The most famous example of someone who became prominent through manual work was Mamlakat Nakhangova, from Tadzhikstan, who allegedly made the cotton yield rocket after she persuaded everyone to pick with two hands. In similar vein, Pioneer work was extremely lackadaisical at one of the most prominent 'model' schools in Moscow, School no. 25. See Holmes 1999: 114.

26 RGASPI f. 17 op. 3 d. 979, 'Protokol zasedaniya Politbyuro TsK VKP(b) ot 19 iyulya 1936: Oprosom chlenov politbyuro ot 29.VI.36', l. 8 (item 19). My thanks to R. W. Davies for drawing my attention to this decision, and to Denis Kozlov for transcribing the minute. The site in question is now occupied by an awful equestrian statue of Marshal Zhukov.

27 Cf. the assertion in Smith 2000: 285, that Gorky's death left the critic Dmitry Sviatopolk-Mirsky, already under attack from 1934, 'dreadfully vulnerable', since Gorky had been his 'protector'.

28 *PP*, 14 November 1938.

29 Gromov 1998: 189.

30 Mikhalkov and Sabo (Szábo), 'Pesnya o Pavlike Morozove', 1937.

31 *PP*, 15 October 1932, p. 2.

32 This section of Solomein's biography contains a comical and revealing error – Pavlik is described as demanding that the troop be set up in October *1932* – a month after he was murdered (*V kulatskom gnezde*, p. 9).

33 Druzhnikov 1995: 149.

34 Yakovlev 1936: 121.

35 Borovin 1936: 18.

36 Smirnov 1938: 9.

37 Korzhavin 1992: part 7, 207.

38 Lyadov 1934: 4.
39 Smirnov 1938: 15–16, 47.
40 For the tie, see *PP*, 4 September 1939, p. 4. A photograph of Rabinovich's maquette appeared in *PP*, 14 November 1938, p. 1.
41 On uniforms as prizes, see Alekseev 1988: 217. Recalling her childhood in a working-class area of Leningrad (Krestovsky Island) in the 1920s, S. N. Tsendrovskaya remembered the Pioneer uniform as a dark-blue sateen skirt; boys would have had shorts in the same fabric and a blouson with thin leather belt: a tie is not mentioned (Tsendrovskaya 1995: 89). Cf. a report from the Tomsk Pioneers in summer 1923 that parents had donated linen for 'shirts and shorts' (again, ties are not mentioned): TsKhDMO f. 1 op. 23 d. 168. In the 1920s, ties of the ordinary kind were regarded as bourgeois appurtenances best eschewed by loyal Komsomol members: Evgeny Evtushenko's father was rebuked for wearing one to a meeting as a student (Evtushenko 1998: 59). Similar attitudes may well have obtained at the Pioneer level. Boris Ignatovich's well-known photograph of a 1 May demonstration in Moscow, 1929, shows Pioneers parading with bugles, drums and banners: only one or two are wearing ties. (It is reproduced in e.g. Morozov et al. 1980: 105. In Steinhoff's film of *Hitlerjunge Quex*, a signal difference between the Fascist youths and the Communist ones is that only the former have neat uniforms and ties.
42 Yakovlev 1936: 8–10.
43 Afinogenov 1977: 226–7. The diplomat Reader Bullard (Bullard and Bullard 2000: 105) saw *Fear* in 1932: 'I saw the play from a side gallery with a view of the whole audience. The sight of the ideal Soviet child did not seem to make them happy.' But as he also got the plot wrong, 'She gives him away to the OGPU and that is the end of Papa,' he may have misunderstood the reaction. It is possible that the audience was moved by Natasha's dilemma, rather than horrified by her action.
44 Eisenstein 1936.
45 On the hair dye, see Bergan 1997: 36.
46 There is not much of the film left, but I quote here from Eisenstein's own description of his work-in-progress: Eisenstein 1936: 31. Interestingly, the restoration of *Bezhin Meadow* carried out by Sergei Yutkevich in the 1960s makes Styopok more like Pavlik than he is in Eisenstein's description.
47 Not, though, in e.g. Lyadov 1934: 4.

48 *PP*, 15 October 1932, p. 2.

49 *Pioner*, 6 (1933), pp. 18–19.

50 Yakovlev 1936: 99, 110. Interestingly, Solomein's biography of 1933 occupies a middle ground between these two positions: when Pavel makes his original denunciation to an official in the village soviet, he does this 'anxiously', but at the trial itself he pronounces 'firmly and confidently, like a well-learned lesson' (p. 18).

51 Smirnov 1938: 46–7, 52.

52 Ibid.: 9; cf. p. 39, which refers to 'savage verbal abuse' and fist-waving.

53 See S. Shingarev, 'Chekletovy – pered sudom obshchestvennosti', *Drug detei* 4 (1930), pp. 9–10. Even in such cases of ill-treatment, it should be noted, Soviet propaganda increasingly fought shy of representing full-frontal confrontations between children and parents. On 17 September 1934, an article in *Pravda* ('Pogovorim o detyakh', p. 3), reported that a schoolboy had written to the magazine *Political Section Activist* complaining about the way that his mother had been treating him. She often spoke to him abusively and had even been known to spank him, though his marks at school were quite good. Readers' responses were quoted, many of which criticized the mother's behaviour but also found the son's problematic – 'Who ever heard of a child being as serious as an adult!' A potential impasse was headed off only when the mother herself independently acknowledged she had been mistaken and vowed to change her ways.

54 Dobrenko 2001b hypothesizes along these lines with reference to case studies of the famous multi-handed propaganda celebration of the White Sea Canal forced labour project, *Belomorskii-Bal'tiiskii kanal: Istoriya stroitel'stva* (1932) on the one hand; and of the writings of Aleksandr Makarenko, particularly *Pedagogical Poem*, which refer in very abstract terms to 'discipline', on the other.

55 *Perechen' postanovlenii byuro TsK VLKSM po rabote sredi pionerov i shkol'nikov, 1936–42* (typescript in RGASPI-TsKhDMO Reading Room), l. 54.

56 RGASPI f. 17 op. 3 d. 968, l. 20 (item 95), 'Protokol zasedaniya Politbyuro'.

57 The only case that I know of is the writer Valentin Kataev's piece for the boy's thirtieth jubilee in 1952 (see Chapter 6 below).

58 See Gorky, 'Literatura i kino', 10 April 1935, SS vol. 27, p. 440.

59 See 'Pioner pomog zaderzhat' narushitelya granitsy', *Pravda*, 27 April 1936. A fictional work of the time is Agniya Barto's long poem *At the Border Post* (Barto 1937), where a boy is rewarded for alerting guards to a marauder with the gift of an Alsatian puppy. For a more humdrum case of Pioneer vigilance, see 'Smelye pionery', *Pravda*, 26 September 1936, p. 6, commending Pioneers who had caught some burglars in a factory. A more Pavlikesque type of civic hero was represented by Gena Shchukin, who had denounced his foster-father's participation in a gang of 'sworn enemies of the people, low-down Trotskyite wreckers', only to be murdered for his pains, and who was the subject of a special book in 1938: Smirnov, *Slavnyi pioner*. But the book was never reprinted, and Shchukin did not appear in later lists of role models.

60 See e.g. *PP*, 4 September 1938, p. 3 – Pavlik denounces on and on, undeterred by beatings; Yakovlev 1936: 130, 140.

61 On this point, see e.g. Shimbirev 1940: 76, 21.

62 On the first case, see Efron and Federol'f 1995: 107–11; on the second, Druskin 1984: 53.

63 Yakovlev 1936: 117.

64 Lyadov 1934: 4.

65 *PP*, 4 September 1938, p. 3. My emphasis.

66 Lurie 1990: xiii.

67 CK, interview with a former editor of children's books for Detgiz publishing house, Leningrad, St Petersburg, August 2001.

68 El. Chernitskaya in *Detskii proletkul't* 1920: 3.

69 See Sats 1925 for a collection of such materials.

70 'Otchet o prodelannoi rabote otryada pionerov No. 1 im. tov. Zinov'eva Tavdinskogo raiona Irbitskogo Okruga s 7go po 20e Maya 25 g.' (TsDOO SO f. 1245 op. 1 d. 12, l. 44).

71 See Chapter 4 above.

72 *PP*, 23 October 1932, p. 2.

73 Gaidar 1946: 172.

74 *Zateinik* 6 (1932), p. 39. Among items publicizing the Pioneer anniversary is A. Smirnov, 'Litsom k pionerdvizheniyu', *Drug detei* 6 (1932), pp. 1–4.

75 *Druzhnye rebyata*, 21–2 (1932), pp. 1–2. The issue was typeset, according to its colophon, on 23 October 1932, that is, eight days after the first big story about Pavlik in *PP*.

76 Officially, the primary school programme was attended by children aged eight to twelve. The presence of so-called 'over-agers' (those more than twelve years old) was common, but such 'over-agers' were commonly asked to leave once they had received a couple of years' schooling so as to make room for others. And by age fourteen or fifteen, a boy would have been considered a candidate for adult illiteracy programmes, not school education.

77 For one of the many pieces on 'coevals', see the picture and story on the entry of some to the Komsomol in 1931: *Drug detei* 1 (1931), pp. 29.

78 See Merridale 2000: 119–22.

79 Lyadov 1934: 4, for instance, ends with a sardonic assault on a number of Pioneer heroes of this kind, for example a boy who had become swollen-headed as a result of catching a thief, and decided that he could himself filch apples with impunity. According to Lyadov, all this stood to reason, since the 'egoist hero' had by definition hived himself off from the collective and the 'unwavering careful supervision of the Party and the Komsomol'.

80 Shif 1935: 16.

81 The changing vision of Pavlik Morozov exemplified an increasing tendency, in the second half of the 1930s, to emphasize 'discipline' in the sense of willing subordination to authority, rather than self-transformation, as the objective of education, and to celebrate sacrifice for its own sake as the ultimate token of Soviet heroism (Dobrenko 2001b).

82 *TR*, 24 August 1933 (published on the *Smena* page), p. 1.

83 *TR*, 3 September 1933, p. 1; *TR*, 16 November 1933, p. 2.

84 *TR*, 3 December 1933, p. 2: 'Only 18 roubles has been received by the fund, from workers at the ski factory, none of the other Komsomol groups have given even a single rouble.'

85 Cf. the standard tautology for Lenin, 'the most human of all human beings'.

86 Petr Zykov, 'Imya, kotoroe nel'zya zabyt'', *TR*, 4 September 1934, p. 3. On the representation of the local through the prism of the centre in Soviet culture generally, see Widdis 2003: 45.

87 *TR*, 4 October 1934, p. 3, 'Ravnenie na kolkhoz im. Pavlika Morozova'.

88 *TR*, 21 July 1939, p. 2; 'Reshenie ispolkoma Sverdlovskogo oblsoveta deputatov trudyashchikhsya ob uvekovechenii pamyati pionera-geroya P. Morozova' (TsDOO SO f. 61 op. 2 d.

1379, l. 5, quoted here from Temnikova and Brovtsin 1996: 136).

89 'Spravka ispolkoma Gerasimovskogo sel'soveta o rezul'tatakh osmotra byusta P. Morozova ego odnosel'chanami', 30 December 1940 (TsDOO SO f. 61 op. 2 d. 1379, l. 9, quoted here from Temnikova and Brovtsin 1996: 136–7).

90 See TsA FSB H-7825, vol. 2, l. 242 (a letter from the director of the Provincial Museum of the Revolution, Sverdlovsk, stating that he has been asked to set up the museum and asking for materials from the case file on the Morozov murders).

91 CK-ATA Ekaterinburg, p. 4.

92 'Na rodine Pavlika Morozova', *PP*, 20 September 1936, p. 3. Compare the letter from Gerasimovka Pioneers to Stalin published in *TR*, 24 December 1934: 'You have given us a happy, joyful childhood,' the children exclaimed, and asserted that everything was perfect in Gerasimovka, though they could do with a few more books.

93 *TR*, 20 January 1934, p. 2.

94 *TR*, 16 November 1933, p. 2.

95 Druzhnikov 1995: 224.

96 Ibid.: 198–200.

97 Ilizarova 1994: 90.

98 Druzhnikov 1995: 143.

99 M. Doroshin, 'Pavlik Morozov' *PP*, 29 March 1933, p. 3. The text was reprinted, with an introduction by Margarita Agashina, in Doroshin 1973.

100 On the invitation (reported ten years after the fact), see *PP*, 2 September 1947, p. 3. This report also suggests (not implausibly) that the cult had the personal support of Nadezhda Krupskaya, the patron of the massive cloth mill, the Trekhgornaya manufaktura, or 'Three Hills Manufactury', usually abbreviated to 'Trekhgorka'.

101 CKQ-E-03 PF2A, p. 4. Cf. a 1938 play by the worker writer Loginova, *Regeneration*, which shows a worker father converted by his activist son (Dobrenko 2001a: 249, 293).

102 Novak-Deker 1959: 125.

103 Tvardovsky 1988: 15.

104 New Year trees – forbidden in 1928 – had started to be tolerated again at the beginning of 1936, but people were still uncertain about the legalities of private ones.

105 CKQ-E-03 PF3A, p. 2.

106 'Perepiska N. K. Krupskoi' (RGASPI f. 12 op. 1 d. 751, l. 17).

107 Borovin 1936: 12–13.

108 For the reference to 'getting off the hook', see Borovin 1936: 12. For a discussion of 'prompting' in Soviet classrooms, and its official status, see Kelly 2004.

109 Other direct responses by children include home-made designs for a monument published in *Dawns of the Commune* in 1939 ('Budem takimi, kak Pavlik Morozov', *VK*, 1 September 1939, p. 1); and a poem included in another issue of the same newspaper where an adolescent reader confessed to the manly emotions that had choked him when thinking about Pavlik: 'I stand, hunched up/And a lump of hot tears tightens my throat' (A. Zhukov, 'U pamyatnika Pavlika Morozova', *VK*, 15 September 1939, p. 4).

110 RGAE f. 396 op. 11 d. 26, ll. 176–176 rev. Quoted here from Siegelbaum and Sokolov 1999: 418–19. Cf. Korzhavin 1992: 8, p. 135. In similar vein, a group of schoolchildren wrote to Molotov in 1942 demanding action against their teacher for unfairness: see GARF f. 2306 op. 70 d. 2753, l. 203 (quoted in Dunstan 1997: 168).

111 Petr Kruzhin in Novak-Deker 1959: 191.

112 Personal information (from an acquaintance of the individual concerned), St Petersburg 2000. How many such incidents actually resulted in arrests is debatable. In the case just mentioned, the girl concerned was stopped on her way to the secret police by her mother, but she might in any case have been ignored by the secret police had she ever reached them.

113 See Rozanov 1913: 236. On parents' powers, see 'O pravakh i obyazannostyakh semeinykh', Article 165 in the 1912 Code (*Svod zakonov Rossiiskoi Imperii*, vol. 10, part 1, 14): parents had the right to chastise 'obstreperous and disobedient children' themselves, and if this failed, to apply to the local juridical authorities to have them dealt with. The likely destination for such a 'trouble-maker' was a penal institution, to which parents could also commit children directly: see e.g. the charter of the Smolensk 'colony-refuge for minors' *Ustav Smolenskoi* . . . 1915: 6.

114 As in the case of Anatoly Rybakov, who returned from a Pioneer rally in *c.* 1924 (when he was thirteen) to find his father verbally bullying his mother (a usual event in the family), and ordered him to stop (which was not). See Rybakov 1997: 26.

115 As in Yury Olesha's classic *The Three Fat Men* (1928). One

might compare J. K. Rowling's Harry Potter stories, in which it is Harry's *step-parents* upon whom terrible revenge is enacted.

116 As in most other countries, Russian children read Grimm and Perrault in bowdlerized versions – a child who had read the originals might have been better prepared for the Pavlik Morozov stories.

117 'Grandfather Trofim' [*sic*]. I suspect that the word in the original song was *batyushka*, 'daddy', and that the informant had inserted the word *dedushka* to replace a word that had escaped her memory (*batyushka* is no longer in common use).

118 CK, interview with ATA, Ekaterinburg, 21 September 2003. Cf. the account by a woman also born in 1931, and from an elite Leningrad home (her father was a Red Army commander): 'That he got killed at the end and all that . . . it all made . . . the most indelible impression on me. [. . .] The fact that he denounced his father and so on [. . .] didn't come into my head' (CKQ-Ox-03 PF6B, p. 13).

119 Avidon in Kent 1997: 189.

120 Though this legend no doubt had different effects on different hearers; my father (b. 1929) recalled feeling bewildered contempt (what was the point of being told this?) when he heard it at the Royal High School in Edinburgh during the late 1930s, but my own reaction to a similar stiff upper lip tale (J. W. Ferguson's *The Story of a Red Deer* (1897), in which the animal hero is instructed by an old stag, 'never, never, lie down and squeal', and eventually drowns himself rather than be torn apart by the hounds) was more like Avidon's: this was clearly heroic behaviour, but would *I* ever be capable of such courage?

121 'Non-denunciation' of certain crimes, including 'counter-revolutionary acts', 'banditry', 'mass unrests' and the forgery of bank-notes carried a sentence of up to six months under a law of 6 June 1927. See Rossi 1987: 233.

122 As argued e.g. in Fitzpatrick 1996.

123 See e.g. A. Dudina in Novak-Deker 1959: 288 (on 'Soviet Border Guard' games on a kolkhoz in Kursk province where she was an activist in the late 1930s).

124 For the quote, see Schenzinger 1932: 404. Klotz 1999: 6265/2 lists no fewer than seven editions of the book between 1932 and 1942. Print-runs are not given. For an understandably grudging acknowledgement of *Quex*'s readability and popularity, see Leutheuser 1995: 96–7. For more information on editions of Pavlik Morozov stories, see Chapter 6 below.

125 As in the case of Nina Kosterina, the arrest of whose father during the Purges fundamentally changed her attitude to the system, and who volunteered in 1941 purely in the hope that her action would save his life. See Kosterina 1968: 190.

6. Pavlik Eclipsed

1 *PP*, 5 September 1940, p. 3; and contrast the issues for 2 September 1937, p. 4, 4 September 1938, p. 3, and 4 September 1939, p. 4. In the provinces, on the other hand, the Pavlik cult retained its force: see e.g. 'Pamyati geroya-pionera Pavlika Morozova', *VK*, 23 August 1940, p. 2; 'Pioner Pavlik Morozov', *VK*, 3 September 1940, pp. 4–5.

2 Gaidar 1946: 298.

3 On the family connection, see Vasil'eva 1997: 21; for evidence of Voroshilov's fatherly attitude to the boy, see e.g. his letter to Enukidze of 29 June 1933 (*Sovetskoe rukovodstvo* 1999: 242), asking Enukidze to obtain a bicycle for him on a trip abroad.

4 Voroshilov's private correspondence for the 1930s and his scribbled diaries contain no references to Gaidar (see RGASPI f. 74, op. 1, d. 295, f. 74 op. 1 d. 41), but he was a noted patron to Soviet artists, particularly in the visual arts.

5 K. E. Voroshilov, letter to Pioneer Evgeny Sheptsov, 6 October 1961 (RGASPI f. 74 op. 1 d. 275, l. 8). For hostility about autographs, see his letter to some pupils from a Moldavian boarding school, 29 December 1966: 'sometimes among young men and women, the search for the signatures of famous people becomes an end in itself, and generates unpleasant competition about who comes first in this activity' (RGASPI f. 74 op. 1 d. 276, l. 223). But contrast ibid., l. 291, a letter of 4 January 1968 which accompanied a signed photograph: this then became standard practice (cf. l. 294, l. 305, l. 307). Earlier examples of Voroshilov's correspondence with children, going back to 1925 (though the letters were usually of a less detailed kind) can be found in RGASPI f. 74 op. 1 d. 274.

6 See Startsev 1941: no. 3330; Solomein, nos. 4161, 4163, 4164 (Yakovlev), 3294 (Smirnov), 419 (Borovin).

7 Startsev 1941: nos. 697–701, 717–19.

8 Startsev 1947: nos. 229–32; Startsev 1950: nos. 307–12 (six edns., one of 200,000 copies); Startsev 1954: nos. 307–10 (four edns., three of 100,000 copies); Startsev 1959: nos. 383–7 (five edns., including ones of 400,000 and 100,000); and so on.

9 See the front cover of Startsev 1947.

10 Klotz 1999: no. 1772.
11 *Pioner*, 3 (1941), p. 3.
12 CK, pers. inf., August 2001.
13 CK-ATA Ekaterinburg, 3–4.
14 L. Morgunova, 'Obkhodilsya zhe Timur bez nyan'ki', *PP*, 28 October 1944, p. 3.
15 See for example *Pioner*, 4 (1942), p. 25 (on collecting bottles to make Molotov cocktails), *Pioner*, 10 (1942), pp. 28–33 (on running crèches, air-raid warden activities, growing vegetables, visits to hospitals, etc.). For further details, see also Rybakov 1984: 69–73; Dunstan 1997: 164–5. According to an official history of the Pioneers published to mark the movement's sixtieth anniversary (*Istoriya VLKSM* 1983: 216), there were over two million 'Timurites' based in Soviet schools by 1944.
16 See Rittersporn 2000: 347–67, esp. 351–2, 359–60.
17 Kassil' 1987: 81.
18 See e.g. 'Imeni Gaidara', *Koster*, 11 (1946), p. 9 (on 'mysterious Timurites' from school, no. 347 in Leningrad helping fetch firewood, etc.). Rybakov 1984: 73–4 and *Istoriya VLKSM* 1983: 295–6, 322–3, also discuss the later history.
19 Gaidar 1946: 374.
20 The first edition of the novel was in 1945. After swingeing criticism in the Soviet press on the grounds that the role of the Party was insufficiently highlighted, etc., it was duly revised by Fadeev.
21 A. Kremensky, 'Nochnaya groza', *Pioner*, 1 (1942), pp. 11–16; V. Kozhevnikov, 'Korrespondentsiya boitsa Sinukova', ibid., pp. 18–19.
22 See e.g. Klava Stepanova, 'My – timurovtsy', *Kolkhoznye rebyata*, 7 (1943), p. 28.
23 For instance, it is now thought that 'Partisan Tanya' and Zoya Kosmodem'yanskaya may not have been the same person, though the execution of the former by the Germans is not disputed; and there is uncertainty about whether 'Tanya' actually faced execution with the Roman stoicism that is captured in the official lives (see below).
24 Kassil' and Polyanovsky 1951.
25 Kosmodem'yanskaya and Vigdorova 1951.
26 Ibid.: 48.
27 Ibid.: 113–14.
28 *PP*, 23 February 1945, p. 2.
29 See 'Postanovlenie Sverdlovskogo OK VLKSM o rabote

domika-muzeya P. Morozova' (11 September 1945) (TsDOO SO f. 61 op. 5 d. 393, ll. 94–6).

30 As early as 1919, the square abutting the Presnya district, whose earlier name was Kudrinskaya Ploshchad', had been renamed Ploshchad' Vosstaniya (Uprising Square).

31 See e.g. *PP*, 15 May 1962, p. 2.

32 Rybakov 1997: 40.

33 Chaadaeva 1932. On the nurseries, see Papkovskaya 1948.

34 On the invitation (reported ten years after the fact), see *PP*, 2 September 1947, p. 3.

35 See *Vozhatyi* 2 (1949), inside front cover.

36 See particularly Valentina Oseeva's extremely popular adventure novel *Vasyok Trubachov and His Friends* (1976).

37 G. Krasnoshchekov, 'Pioner-geroi', *PP*, 2 September 1947, p. 3.

38 See the review in 'Pavlik Morozov', *PP*, 5 September 1952, p. 3.

39 Shchipachev 1976: vol. 1, 74.

40 Shchipachev 1950: 12–13.

41 *PP*, 5 September 1952, p. 3.

42 The image, in the Walker Art Gallery, Liverpool, is accessible on www.liverpoolmuseums.org.uk/walker/collections/19c/yeames.asp/

43 'Sovetskoe izobrazitel'noe iskusstvo v 1952 godu', *Sovetskoe iskusstvo*, 1 (1953), pp. 8–9. The painting appears on p. 11 as a plate.

44 Ibid.

45 CK-ATA-Ekaterinburg, 21 September 2003.

46 CK, informal interview, St Petersburg, 2001.

47 Ibid.

48 See e.g. the recollections of Mikhail Kolesnikov (b. 1918) (*Sovetskie pisateli: avtobiografii*: vol. 5, 292); or of Inna Shikhaeva-Gaister in Fitzpatrick and Slezkine 2000: 371. On Chapaev generally, see Stites 1992: 44–6.

7. Pavlik after Stalin

1 See e.g. the editorial 'Preodolet' posledstviya kul'ta lichnosti v pedagogike', *Sovetskaya pedagogika* 9 (1956), 3–18.

2 'LO izdatel'stva "Detskaya literatura". Otchet ob izdatel'skoi i finansovoi deyatel'nosti za 1962' (TsGALI f. 64 op. 1 d. 166, l. 11).

3 CKQ-SPb-03 PF2B, p. 12.

4 For the brief details of his biography, see e.g. Gusev 1961: 110.

5 N. Khrushchev, 'Kak my organizovali Dom pionerov i detskie parki', *Vozhatyi*, 8 (1936), p. 14.

6 Tumarkin 1983: 260–8.

7 *Ogonek* 16 (1970), p. 9. The quality of *Ogonek*'s reproduction is so low as to make judgement difficult, but the difference in resolution between the picture of Lenin and that of Viktor slightly suggests that this is a photomontage.

8 'Distsiplinirovannost'', in Kondakov 1967: 60, 61.

9 'Postanovlenie Sverdlovskogo OK VLKSM o rabote domika-muzeya P. Morozova', 11 September 1945 (TsDOO SO f. 61 op. 5 d. 393, ll. 94–6, quoted here from Temnikova and Brovtsin, 'Novoe o Pavlike Morozove', *Arkhivy Urala* 1 (1996), pp. 138–9; 'Ob otkrytii pamyatnika pioneru-geroyu Pavliku Morozovu', *TR*, 11 July 1954, p. 2; *TR*, 18 July 1954, p. 2; 'Pamyatnik Pavliku Morozovu otkryt', *TR*, 22 July 1954, p. 1.

10 Druzhnikov 1995: 135–6.

11 'Ob otkrytii pamyatnika pioneru-geroyu Pavliku Morozovu', *TR*, 11 July 1954; 'Pamyatnik Pavliku Morozovu otkryt', 22 July 1954.

12 Druzhnikov 1995: 178.

13 'Lushchie iz luchshikh', *Vozhatyi*, 2 (1956), pp. 4–5.

14 'Lushchie iz luchshikh', *Vozhatyi*, 2 (1956), pp. 4–5.

15 P. Gradov and L. Bokalov, 'Pesnya o Pavlike Morozove', *Vozhatyi*, 8 (1961), p. 54.

16 Shchipachev 1965: vol. 1, 280. For the passage in the 1950 version, see Shchipachev 1950: 36. For Shchipachev's own, somewhat misleading, account of the changes, see his 'Slovo o pionerakh-geroyakh', *Koster*, 7 (1961), p. 7: here he claims that he spontaneously decided the boy's relationship with the father needed reworking.

17 Khorinskaya 1958: 15.

18 V. Vladimirov, 'Pavliku Morozovu – ot pionerov Pervoural'ska', in *Pavlik Morozov*, pp. 136–7.

19 See e.g. the reminiscence of an informant (b. 1949), and brought up in a small town in the Moscow region (CKQ-Ox-03 PF8B, p. 14). Finding out about the composition of Pavlik statues is difficult, as orders do not survive, but run-of-the mill monuments were often mass-produced, since this had the advantage of ensuring that the canons of decency and taste were not violated, as well as of keeping costs low.

20 For instance, a school in Ivanovo province named its camp after Pavlik, and invited Tatiana Morozova to attend the

celebration of the thirty-fifth anniversary of the founding of the Pioneers in 1957: see 'Materialy ob opyte raboty pionerskikh organizatsii shkol Ivanovskoi oblasti' (RGASPI-TsKhDMO f. 2 op. 1 d. 8, l. 120, l. 74). On chronicles, see e.g. 'Informatsionnyi byulleten' Orenburgskogo oblastnogo soveta pionerskoi organizatsii o rabote s pionerami i shkol'nikami' (Jan.–Dec. 1962) (RGASPI-TsKhDMO f. 2 op. 1 d. 249, l. 23).

21 See the figures given in Startsev 1966; Startsev 1970; Startsev 1987; Startsev 1988.

22 A list compiled for me by Vitaly Bezrogov in 2004 indicates that over thirty post-Soviet cities and towns have 'Pavlik Morozov' streets: major cities with such streets include Almaty, Groznyi (in Chechnya), Kazan', Nizhny Novgorod, Perm' and Vladimir. Interestingly, given the 'colonial' status of the legend, two places in the Khanty-Mansiisk Autonomous Region have such streets. Obviously, in the Soviet period, the number would have been greater, as street renamings since 1991 have removed mention of the boy in some places (e.g. Yaroslavl', central Moscow).

23 CK-MW Ekaterinburg.

24 On this type of coercive practice, see especially Kharkhordin 1999.

25 Balashov 1969: 9.

26 *Ogonek,* 21 (1962), centrefold.

27 Ts. Makarov, B. Nikolaev, 'Bessmertie yunykh', *Ogonek,* 20 (1972), p. 8. Grisha Akopov in fact appears here with his real Armenian surname, Akopyan, as became the practice from the early 1960s (see below).

28 *Uchitel'skaya gazeta*, 9 May 1972.

29 *Sovetskaya pedagogika*, 5 (1972), p. 9.

30 *Programmy* 1957. For material on classroom discussions, see Boldyrev 1955: 344 (out of class reading); 266, 305 (discussions).

31 See Gusev 1961: 77–118.

32 *Vozhatyi* 5 (1961), p. 8.

33 *Pioner*, 11 (1957), pp. 18–23.

34 For instance, one prestigious Leningrad language-specialized school had a shrine dedicated to Richard Sorge, a German Soviet agent (CKQ-Ox-03 PF13B, p. 13).

35 See e.g. Gusev 1961; Agapova and Shadskaya 1972.

36 *Sovetskaya pedagogika,* 5 (1972), p. 9.

37 Musatov 1962: 48–58.

38 'Plan podgotovki Vsesoyuznogo sleta pionerov' (RGASPI-TsKhDMO f. 2 op. 1 d. 130, l. 114). At this period, too, the

Komsomol organization was actively collecting material about a wide spectrum of Pioneer heroes for the Book of Honour in Moscow. In 1957, for example, information was gathered from the 1930s press about Kolya Myagotin, and research was done on a number of war heroes, for instance Misha Romanov of Stalingrad, who had affected to surrender to the Germans, but in fact bombarded them with grenades as they approached. And contemporary feats of daring were also chronicled, for instance, the efforts of two Pioneers in Brest-Litovsk to aid the noble Soviet border-guards in their fight against deceitful foreigners, or the successful rescue of children from a fire in Gorky (Nizhny-Novgorod). All these brave and vigilant types duly had their names entered in the Book of Honour. 'Materialy o yunykh geroyakh-pionerakh i geroyakh Oktyabrya . . .' (1957), (RGASPI-TsKhDMO f. 2 op. 1 d. 12, ll. 1–10).

39 'Materialy o zanesenii v Knigu Pocheta Vsesoyuznoi Pionerskoi organizatsii im. V. I. Lenina yunykh geroev-pionerov' (1957–60), (RGASPI-TsKhDMO f. 2 op. 1 d. 131, l. 12).

40 The author of the story, ironically enough, was one 'V. Morozov': 'V novoselkakh pogib pioner', *PP*, 29 August 1962.

41 'On smelym serdtsem pioner', *PP*, 4 September 1932, p. 3.

42 N. Plyatskovsky and N. Peskov, 'Zdravstvui, Morozov!', *Pionerskie pesni* 2 (CD: Bomba Music, Moscow, 2002).

43 CK-ISM-Ekaterinburg.

44 Pers. inf.

45 'Pavlik Morozov glazami moskvichei', *Romir: Rossiiskoe obshchestvennoe mnenie i issledovanie rynka*, http://www.romir.ru/socpolit/socio/09_2002/pavlik-morozov (accessed December 2002).

46 CKQ SPb-03 PF 2A, p. 12.

47 Oxf/Lev SPb-03 PF 17A p. 14.

48 'Pavlik Morozov glazami moskvichei', *Romir: Rossiiskoe obshchestvennoe mnenie i issledovanie rynka*, http://www.romir.ru/socpolit/socio/09_2002/pavlik-morozov (accessed December 2002).

49 An informant I spoke to in St Petersburg in September 2002 (informal interview) recalled that, growing up in a small town in the 1960s, she found the Pavlik memorial 'horrific'. The statue was child size, which underlined its status as a fearful warning of what brutish people might do to any child, including oneself.

50 'Chto posovetuesh', Timur?' *PP*, 29 June 1962, p. 1. Several

items of this kind appeared around the time of the Pioneer rally in late June 1962. For later items, see e.g. 'Kakim by ya byl Timurom' *Nedelya* 21 (1973), 19.

51 See e.g. the reference to Timur work in Ivanovo province (1957) in 'Materialy ob opyty raboty pionerskikh organizatsii shkol Ivanovskoi oblasti' (RGASPI-TsKhDMO f. 2 op. 1 d. 8, l. 95). On encouraging organizational skills, see e.g. 'Spravki ob organizatsii vneklassnoi i vneshkol'noi raboty s det'mi' (March–December 1965, ll. 107–10).

52 See e.g. CKQ-PF8B, p. 16.

53 Osorina 1999: 147–50, 155–7.

54 My thanks to Robin Aizlewood for this ditty, circulating in Moscow during the late 1970s.

55 For a selection of such material, see Belousov 1998.

56 CKQ Ox-03 PF 11B, p. 14.

57 Barto 1960.

58 V. Ardov, 'Bditel'nost' mladentsa', in *Chukokalla* 1999: 342.

59 CKQ SPb-03 PF 2A, p. 11. For a broader discussion, see Kelly 2004.

60 On Kassil', see Oxf/Lev SPb-03 PF 27A, p. 35. On Zoya, CKQ PF8B, p. 14. Other war heroes: CKQ SPb-03 PF 2A, p. 12.

61 Oxf/Lev SPb-03 PF 18A p. 46.

62 'Spravki [. . .] o rabote redaktsii komsomol'skikh gazet' (1961), (TsKhDMO f. 1. op. 32 d. 1047, l. 148).

63 Oxf/Lev SPb-03 PF 16A, p. 67.

64 'Raspisano. Raskatano' (Oxf/Lev SPb-03 PF 18A p. 46).

65 In 1951–2, A. S. German's *Tales of Dzerzhinsky* (1950) attracted twenty-six fan letters, and the top book in terms of number of letters, Vitaly Bianki's *The Great Sea Route* (1950), forty-four. In 1965, by contrast, German's book was down to eleven letters, while William Kozlov's *The President of Stone Island* got fifty-four letters, S. Sakharnov's *Ram and Rum* forty-two, and Yu. Tomin's *A Wizard Walked Round Town* thirty-six. The total number of letters sent in 1965 had also nearly doubled – 4,171 as against 2,192. See 'Byulleten' chitatel'skikh otzyvov, pisem i retsenzii, 1951–52' (TsGALI-SPb f. 64 op. 5 d. 5, ll. 4–7); 'Obzory chitatel'skikh pisem za 1965 god' (TsGALI-SPb f. 64 op. 5 d. 151, ll. 2–8).

66 For cartoon and folk-tale heroes, see CKQ-Ox-03 PF10B, p. 7; for the informant's own mother, ibid. PF11B, p. 14.

67 Impressions gathered on a visit to Gerasimovka, 19 September 2003.

68 CK-ATA Ekaterinburg, 21 September 2003.

69 See e.g. Kononenko 2003; Makhrin 2004. This version of Pavlik's life has unpleasant undertones of anti-Semitism: Yury Druzhnikov is always referred to by full name and patronymic, 'Yury Izrailevich Al'perovich-Druzhnikov', in order to indicate that he is not 'Russian' and therefore must have a desire to undermine the Russian nation.

70 See e.g. Evgeny Devikov, 'Zhertva, no ne geroi: Kommentarii yurista', in Turuntaev 1990: 240.

71 For a full range of views, see Irina Snezhinskaya's thoughtful, and deservedly prize-winning, 1999 TV documentary about Pavlik, *Bez geroya* (*A Film without a Hero*).

72 See 'Pesnya gruppy Krematorii "Pavlik Morozov"' http://www/internettrading.ru/wwwboard/messages10/236.hl, and the commentary in Sergei Avdeev, Aleksandr Bratersky, 'Taina zhizni i smert' Pavlika Morozova', *Khronograf*' html://www.izvestia.ru/community/article 23280; Vladlen Gavril'chik, 'Poet i Tsar'', *Mitin zhurnal*, http://www.initin.com/mjll/gavril.shtml/ (all accessed 13 December 2002). An earlier work in a similar vein is Sergei Stratanovsky's 'The blood of frozen berries, Pavlik Morozov' (1975) (Stratanovsky 1993: 66) (my thanks to Emily Lygo for this reference).

73 Makhrin, 'Mal'chik': the small boys interviewed on Pavlik Morozov street in Lobnya, Moscow province, thought Pavlik was a Second World War hero, a famous historian, a general and a 'squealer'.

74 CK-Grekova-Moscow.

75 See the discussion in Zelensky 1999: 138–60.

76 See Yury Druzhnikov's discussion in the afterword to the second edition of his book, Druzhnikov 1995: 259–65.

77 Reynolds 2002: 1.

78 Sections of the case file are held in the archive of Memorial, St Petersburg.

79 Material from the case is held in the archive of Memorial, St Petersburg. As a result, thirty-five people were executed and nineteen given sentences in prison camps. As early as 1939, the authorities recognized that the case had been a grotesque error, returned the surviving prisoners from the camps, and mounted an enquiry, which laid bare wide-scale falsification of the records.

80 Such a decision has a precedent in the process of reviewing cases from the 1930s. Most of the defendants in the so-called

'Deaf and Dumb' case in Leningrad (1937) were fully rehabilitated when the case was reviewed in 1955, but one, Stadnikov, was cleared 'on grounds of non-proof'. (See the materials relating to the case held in the archive of Memorial, St Petersburg.)

81 'Dzhordzh Soros – Pavliku Morozovu', *Izvestiya*, 4 September 2003, p. 1.

82 See e.g. Platonova 2003: 2.

83 Pers. inf., September 2003.

8. The 'Real Life' of Pavlik Morozov?

1 Cases of contradictory testimony include the following: Anastasiya Sakova told Kartashov on 11 September 1932 that she had seen Kseniya with Pavel and Fyodor on 3 September (31); on 11 November, however, she told Fedchenko that she had *not* seen Kseniya with the boys (169). Sakova's change of testimony seriously annoyed the investigators, who wanted evidence of Kseniya's participation in the murder. Fedchenko registered in the protocol that he believed Sakova was being intimidated (169). But it is also possible that her *first* testimony was the result of intimidation. Besides Kartashov, two other adults were present then – Ivan Potupchik and Zoya Kabina, the Gerasimovka schoolteacher – and it would take quite an assertive child to refuse to make a statement when her teacher told her this was needed. Implausible testimony includes Danila's claims that Kulukanov had gold hidden in his house, as well as the detailed depositions of overheard comments by other witnesses (can one really believe in such razor-sharp ears and such a capacity for total recall?).

2 For instance, on 25 September 1932, a meeting of the District Committee of the Komsomol decided to acknowledge the force of the rebuke administered by the Regional Bureau of the Children's Communist Organization and to depute its chairman to communicate this *nostra culpa* further up the line (TsDOO SO f. 1245 op. 1 d. 14, l. 53).

3 TsDOO SO f. 1201 op. 1 d. 24, l. 105a. See Temnikova and Brovtsin 1996: 134–5.

4 Pavel Solomein, 'Pochemu raiorganizatsii pozdno uznali', *VK*, 8 October 1932, p. 2.

5 CK-Gerasimovka 1, CK-Gerasimovka 2, *passim*.

6 On the destruction procedure generally, see TsDOO SO f. 1201 op. 1 d. 18, l. 7; on the destruction of Urals Regional Committee materials, TsDOO SO f. 1201 op. 1 d. 24, l. 101.

7 Pavlik Morozov Museum, Gerasimovka (the certificate is catalogued SM-MPP, v/f 202; the photograph is not catalogued).

8 See D. Prokopenko, 'Vospominaniya', undated memoir, Pavlik Morozov Museum, Gerasimovka (no catalogue number); CK-Gerasimovka 2 (19 September 2003).

9 For a list of Pavlik's 'official' friends see e.g. 'Tovarishchi Pavlika Morozova v Moskve', *TR*, 20 January 1934, p. 2. They included Motya Potupchik, Pasha Voronov, Nadya Ermakova and Misha Selivestrov. Children from the Potupchik, Selivestrov and Ermakov families are mentioned as among the first Pioneers in Gerasimovka: see 'Zhizn' i rabota Gerasimovskogo pionerotryada', *TR*, 3 September 1933, p. 1.

10 CK-Gerasimovka 2 (19 September 2003). For an example of Prokopenko's previous recollections, see the typescript 'Vospominaniya' (undated) in the Pavlik Morozov Museum, Gerasimovka.

11 CK-Gerasimovka 1 (19 September 2003).

12 Druzhnikov 1995: 174.

13 Ibid.: 225.

14 For instance, he emphasizes (quite correctly) that no proper pathological examination was ever carried out, and that the number of wounds inflicted on the boys varies from report to report (Druzhnikov 1995: 20–21).

15 Druzhnikov 1995: 23.

16 Ibid.: 110–37.

17 Ibid.: 125, 127.

18 Druzhnikov states that (a), (b), (c) and (e) came 'from a certain archive' (they are now held in an unnumbered file at the Pavlik Morozov Museum in Gerasimovka); (d) he knew from a typewritten copy in the Museum of the Revolution in Sverdlovsk. Documents (a)–(d) are also included in case file H-7825, though with one or two significant discrepancies of detail that are discussed below.

19 See illustrations (Druzhnikov: 114, 116).

20 Druzhnikov 1995: 21.

21 See illustration, p. 128 of Druzhnikov's book.

22 For instance, Druzhnikov wrongly states that Sergei Mikhalkov was twenty in September 1932 (p. 11); according to Kasack 1992: 773, he was born on 12 March 1913; he fails to give volume, issue, page and sometimes even year numbers for various periodical references; and occasionally lets through minor contradictions when reporting points of detail (e.g., on

p. 102 he alleges that Sergei Morozov began the search for the boys' bodies ('according to people from Gerasimovka, the search began thanks to the grandfather'), while on p. 127 Ivan Potupchik is said to have organized it ('on the 7 September Potupchik, having received his orders to do so, began a noisy search for the children' – and this though the policeman's report on the finding is given on p. 21 as dating from 6 September). It should be emphasized, though, that here and below my differences from Druzhnikov are not intended to undermine the value of his well-written, gripping and at times very moving book, or of the contribution that it made to a mature reassessment of the Soviet past when it was first published in Russia in 1995.

23 See the biography on www.druzhnikov.com/english/biol.html (accessed 10 October 2004).

24 See Solomon 1996: 113–23.

25 TsDOO SO f. 1209 op. 1 d. 1, l. 64.

26 There is another, but more minor, discrepancy between the document on the removal of the corpses that Druzhnikov cites (p. 21) and the document that appears in H-7825 (6). In the latter, *both* bodies are said to be pointing eastwards; in the former, Fyodor's is said to be pointing *westwards*. (The slip may, of course, be Druzhnikov's: he paraphrases the document, rather than quoting it directly.) The effect is to increase the suggestion that the arrangement of the bodies was carefully organized.

27 Druzhnikov 1995: 118: the item was an article in the Irbit newspaper, *Voskhod*, on 3 September 1963.

28 TsDOO SO f. 4 op. 9 d. 954, l. 210.

29 'Prestupnost' SSSR i soyuznykh respublik po gruppam prestuplenii i otdel'nym prestupleniyam v 1926' (*Statisticheskii sbornik* . . .1928: 890–91 (table 38)).

30 On 'elemental growth' see the comments made at a meeting of the *aktiv* (party activists' group) of the Moscow Komsomol held on 8 October 1924, TsAODM f. 634 op. 1 d. 35 l. 69. For the membership numbers (between 1924 and mid-1926, numbers of Pioneers across the Soviet Union rose from 161,000 to over 1.8 million), see *Direktivy i dokumenty* 1959: 13; RGASPI-TsKhDMO f. 1 op. 23 d. 636, l. 42. After 1926, the rate of growth slowed significantly: numbers had risen only to two million in 1928 (*Direktivy i dokumenty* 1959: 36). On 'turnover', see the report to the Central Committee of the Komsomol at

'Perechen' postanovlenii byuro TsK VLKSM o shkol'noi i pionerskoi dvizhenii 1919–28' (typescript held in the reading room of RGASPI-TsKhDMO, Moscow), l. 148, which indicates that 202,267 Pioneers dropped out of the Komsomol over 1925–6. A report from Stalinsk (Novokuznetsk) in 1925, indicating that the town had fourteen Pioneer troops (i.e. at least 150 Pioneers), but only 280 Komsomol members (Bedin, Kushnikova and Togulev 1999: 383), points to a desire at the local level to sign children up as quickly as possible, without thought for the problems of actually running the troops that had been formed.

31 See Alekseev 1988: 186. The brigade is referred to as a simple '*agitbrigada*' on first mention, and then later on the same page as '*pionerskaya*', as though Alekseev himself were uncertain of its status. The fluid references to this brigade contrast with an absolutely concrete account of the role of the Pioneers at the festival celebrating the bringing-in of the first harvest of the then collectivized village, ibid., p. 218: at this, Pioneer uniforms were presented to the children who were deemed to have performed outstandingly well when acting as guards to the village's standing corn.

32 See Pyotr Kruzhin in Novak-Deker 1959: 185–90.

33 'Prilozhenie k protokolu Zasedaniya Byuro Tavdinskogo Raikomiteta VKP (b) No. 78 ot 14/IX/32: O rabote pionerorganizatsii' (TsDOO SO f. 1201 op. 1 d. 24, ll. 164–7).

34 On the Party cell, see TsDOO SO f. 1201 op. 1 d. 16, l. 37; for the Mironova details, TsDOO SO f. 1201 op. 1 d. 20, ll. 20–23.

35 *TR*, 28 April 1932 (on agitbrigade); (230 rev.) on leafleting: local teacher 'Kadina' [*sic*, for 'Kabina'] reports that when children stuck leaflets on fences, the kulaks would take them off.

36 Mel'nikov and Kalashnikov part 1: 135; Mel'nikov and Kalashnikov part 2: 5–6, 105–7.

37 TsDOO SO 1245/1/28, ll. 80–85. For the other papers, see Chapter 2. On 26 January 1930, for example, *VK* ran a story under the title 'We Set Up the "Red Dawn" Collective Farm', in which a group of Pioneers boasted excitedly about how their work with painting slogans and so on had brought the collective farm into being. And on 21 April 1931, juvenile readers were instructed in detail about the new system of taxation in the villages, which they should explain to their parents. They were also urged to have no mercy on kulaks living locally: 'Kulaks must be named so that they don't wriggle out of paying their dues.'

38 TsDOO SO f. 4 op. 10 d. 267, l. 40. For an impressionistic publication of the letter, dated vaguely as 'no earlier than 3 September 1932', and with various unmarked alterations to and omissions from the original text, see Temnikova and Brovtsin 1996: 133–4. My thanks to Leonid Zakharovsky for kindly presenting me with a copy of this item.

39 'Razorit' kulatskoe gnezdo', *TR*, 3 December 1931, p. 3.

40 TsDOO SO f. 1201 op. 1 d. 18, l. 103.

41 See esp. Mariya Sakova in CK-Gerasimovka 1 (19 September 2003). Sakova expressed certainty that the trial had not been conducted in the village.

42 Druzhnikov 1995: 52.

43 Ibid.: 52.

44 See e.g. E. Smirnov, 'Pavlik Morozov' (Makhlin and Goncharenko 1961: 65): 'It was 1931. Trofim Morozov was elected chairman of the village soviet for the third time.'

45 Pers. inf. from a local historian who has worked extensively in the Irbit archives. Elena Glavatskaya and I were unable to check this story, as the reference had been recorded incorrectly (or the cataloguing system has changed), so that the file is now unlocatable.

46 Pers. inf. 12 April 2004.

47 See Kanarsky 1928: 207, 186.

48 P. Solomein, 'Kak pogib Pavlik', *VK*, 27 October 1932, p. 2.

49 See e.g. *PP*, 3 December 1932, p. 2.

50 On the later life of Tatiana Morozova, see Druzhnikov 1995: 225–31.

51 On Tatiana's unpopularity in the village, see Druzhnikov 1995: 226. This was confirmed when I visited in 2003. For the bad impression after she became famous, see CK-ISM-Ekaterinburg. An informant of mine who visited Artek Pioneer Camp on several occasions in the 1950s remembers that the general attitude was, 'Oh God, not another visit by that dreadful old hag Morozova' (*eta uzhasnaya baba Morozova*) (pers. inf., 2003).

52 Fitzpatrick 1994: 350.

53 The accepted survival technique is to take off one's clothes and turn these inside out, which allows the wood demon to lead one to safety. My thanks to Andrei Zhukov for this information.

54 On the prevalence of banditry in Western Siberia during the 1930s as well as the Civil War era, see Starzhinsky 1991: 118–19. (The young Starzhinsky was narrowly missed by a bullet while

in the taiga, and at first assumed it was a hunter firing at an elk: however, later it transpired that a criminal from the locality had made an attempt to kill the boy, fearing he would be recognized.) On the prevalence of bears in the same region during the 1930s, see Starzhinsky 1991: 90 (though here the argument is that they were too shy to constitute a real danger), and also Druzhnikov 1995: 23.

55 CK-Gerasimovka 1.

56 Arlet 1971: table 107 p. 87 (fixed knife used in twenty-one out of eight-four cases, which is by far the largest proportion of any weapon – the next nearest is a club (*Knebel*), used in nine cases); Arlet 1971: table 91 p. 77 (of thirty-eight cases committed outdoors, twenty-four were in the woods); table 108, p. 88 (in 16.3 per cent of cases, the motive for a killing was anger with the victim, and in 6.7 per cent the fear that the victim would betray a crime). For discovery statistics, see Arlet 1971: table 112, p. 135. Twenty-four cases were discovered in less than a day, and thirty-three (out of sixty-four) in under three days. Arlet does not quantify the concealment methods, but the forty-one case narratives given on pp. 91–123 indicate that only one perpetrator made a serious attempt to conceal the body (by throwing it into a river); the rest made no, or only feeble, efforts to do so. On motivation, see also Alder and Polk 2001: table 7.3, p. 124: around a third of adolescent victims of homicide fall into the 'honour contest' or 'conflict resolution' categories.

57 'Dokladnaya zapiska o detskom dome imeni tov. Budennogo Maslyanskogo raiona, Tyumenskoi oblasti' (22 November 1947) (RGASPI f. 17 op. 125 d. 559, ll. 142–3).

58 To be sure, part of the official concluding formula for interrogation records is missing: instead of reading, 'this record has been set down correctly and has been read aloud to me', it reads, 'this record has been set down correctly'. This may be an unconscious recognition on Titov's part that the due procedures had not been carried out; on the other hand, it is equally possible that it was an oversight, or indeed dictated by a frantic attempt to fit the interrogation record on to one sheet of paper (the signatures and closing formula are crammed below the last printed line of the page, almost reaching the bottom margin). Three decades later, Efrem's brother Dmitry was to return to this episode, which he narrated in the different and potentially more accurate form, that Efrem had been forced to sign a protocol that he did not understand admitting that he had 'taken

part' in the murders. (A. Nagibin, 'Segodnya – 32 goda so dnya gibeli pionera-geroya Pavlika MOROZOVA', *Na smenu!*, 3 September 1964, p. 2).

59 The main injuries to Fyodor described here are consistent with those in the post-mortem report (7) – see also above, Chapter 3. The fact that Danila described these more accurately than the injuries to Pavel may bear out Efrem's story that he (Efrem) killed Pavel, and Danila, Fyodor; or it could be that he simply witnessed this killing close up (I suggest the latter version below).

60 Kanarsky 1928: 51. See also my Introduction above.

61 The first witness, Iosif Protopovich, claimed that this had happened at '17.00 hours' (36); the second, Prokhor Sakov, also suggested that it was at five, but simultaneously claimed it was 'just before sunset' (168), which would time the incident to more like 6.30–7 p.m.

62 Efrem's father claimed that the boy had been back to the house and unharnessed the horses and taken them out to the fields, and then returned, before going out to the Prokopenkos' (17), but his mother said merely that he had been in the fields all day and then at the Prokopenkos'. In any case, a return with the horses, followed by unharnessing and a trip to the fields with them, could have been achieved in half an hour, allowing Shatrakov to reach the Prokopenkos' by the time darkness fell (about 7 p.m.), if he left the fields at about 6.30.

63 CK-Gerasimovka 1.

Afterword

1 Kukina and Kozhevnikov 1997: 72. Cf. the observations of Nancy Condee, 'Pavlik Morozov and the State's Prosthetic', unpublished paper, 1996, p. 2: 'Pavlik was an experience, a form of mass consciousness, proffering a childhood in alliance with the state [. . .] Pavlik was a code for social renewal, ethical rededication, regulated rupture under the watchful eye of a larger state power.' This paper also contains a thoughtful psychoanalytical reading of Pavlik as one of a series of 'otherwise powerless beings' transformed by 'the state's self-interested conferral of alien power' (p. 4).

2 Informal interview, St Petersburg, 2004.

3 Ts. Makarov, B. Nikolaev, 'Bessmertie yunykh', *Ogonek*, 20 (1972), p. 8.

4 Oxf/Lev SPb-04 PF 38A, p. 67.

5 As I was finishing this book, the terrorist attack on a school in

Beslan was producing exactly this reaction in some commentators in Russia: for example, on 7 September, at a meeting on Palace Square, St Petersburg, the film director Aleksei German called for the 'execution by shooting' of the surviving terrorists, on the grounds that anyone who defended himself by holding up a child to fend off bullets and then cut the child's throat deserved to die (news report, 'Rossiya' channel, 10 p.m., 7 September 2004). Obviously, a person who treats a child with the cruelty described here deserves severe punishment; but as Mikhail Piotrovsky, the director of the Hermitage, pointed out on the same programme, it is vital to find out exactly what did go on in Beslan before condemning the hostage-takers to execution – and in any case, turning them into martyrs would be a politically disastrous move.

6 For thought-provoking analyses of child murder scandals, see Morrison 1997; Sylvain Desmille and others in *L'Infini* 59 (1997). In both early twentieth-century Russia, and late twentieth-century Western countries, uproar over child murder accompanied much expenditure of energy about the supposed commercialization of childhood. Tolstoy's *Kreutzer Sonata* (1889) offers a pioneering sight, critically presented, of the 'designer baby', the infant that is the product and vehicle of its parents' venality and egotism. On the supposed commercialization of childhood in the late twentieth century in the West, especially through television, see Postman 1985. In Soviet Russia after 1928, on the other hand, strict state regulation of the market curbed fears of commercialism. Here, it was child abandonment that seemed to threaten 'normal' childhood existence. Not for nothing did the early years when the Pavlik Morozov legend circulated coincide with a crackdown on waifdom and child crime, culminating in a 'clean up the streets' act of 7 April 1935 that introduced full adult penalties for certain crimes, and a decree the following month that 'abolished' child homelessness (by decreeing that all homeless children were to be placed in orphanages). The fate of Pavlik Morozov and his brother, slaughtered while wandering on their own, can be seen as an awful warning of the likely fate of unsupervised children generally.

7 As argued by Michael D. A. Freeman in Alston, Parker and Seymour 1992: 52–71, esp. 66–9.

LIST OF SOURCES

UNPUBLISHED SOURCES

Archival sources

Moscow

RAO NA, f. 1.
RGASPI, f. 17, f. 74.
RGASPI-TsKhDMO, f. 1.
TsAODM, f. 634.
TsA FSB, d. H-7825, tt. 1 and 2. For an inventory of this file, and extracts from documents, see www.mod-langs.ox.ac.uk/russian/childhood/pavlikmorozov.htm

St Petersburg

Archive of Memorial, St Petersburg, case files on the 'Finnish General Staff' (Finnskii general'nyi shtab) (1933); No. 21176, 'Lube S.M. and others' (Lube S. M. i drugikh) (1932); 'The Deaf and Dumb Affair' (Delo glukhonemykh), 1937.
RGIA f. 803.
TsGALI-SPb, f. 64.

Ekaterinburg

GASO, f. 88P.
TsDOO SO, f. 4, f. 1201, f. 1209, f. 1245.

Interviews

Interviews with the prefix 'Oxf/Lev' are part of the research funded by the Leverhulme Trust under grant no. F/08736/A. Interviews in St Petersburg (coded 'SPb', followed by a date code, '02', '03', etc.) were conducted by Alexandra Piir according to a 68-point general questionnaire on childhood which included a question on Pioneer heroes. Interviews in Moscow (coded 'M', followed by a date code '03', '04') were carried out by Yuliya Rybina and Ekaterina Shumilova. Interviews in villages in the Karelia area (prefix 'V', followed by the date code '04') were carried out by

Ekaterina Mel'nikova and Oksana Filicheva. The questionnaire was formulated by Catriona Kelly, Al'bert Baiburin and Alexandra Piir. Interviews with the prefix 'CKQ' were carried out by Catriona Kelly using the same questionnaire. The place code 'Ox' refers to interviews with Russians living abroad conducted in the UK (not necessarily in Oxford), the place code 'SPb' to St Petersburg, 'M' to Moscow and 'E' to Ekaterinburg.

'CK-Grekova-Moscow': interview with Olga Grekova, editor of *Pioneer Pravda*, Moscow, 11 February 2004.

The following interview tapes relating specifically to the Pavlik Morozov legend are also cited:

'CK-Gerasimovka 1, CK-Gerasimovka 2': interviews conducted with residents of Gerasimovka now in their seventies and eighties, 19 September 2003 (four informants, about one and a half hours of tape).

'CK-MW-Ekaterinburg', interview with former museum worker, 17 September 2003 (about one and a half hours of tape).

'CK-ATA-Ekaterinburg', interview with woman born 1931, 22 September 2003 (about one hour of tape).

Interviews described as 'informal' were not tape-recorded: notes were taken afterwards. 'Pers. inf.' refers to casual remarks, also recorded in writing rather than on tape.

Other unpublished sources

Condee, Nancy, 'Pavlik Morozov and the State's Prosthetic', unpublished paper, University of Pittsburgh, 1996.

Prokopenko, D., 'Vospominaniya' (memoirs about Pavlik Morozov). Typescript. Gerasimovka, Pavlik Morozov Museum.

'Svidetel'stvo o rozhdenii Gr. Morozov Pavel Trofimovich'. Typewritten copy of the birth certificate of Pavel Morozov, dated 30 November 1965. Gerasimovka. Pavlik Morozov Museum, catalogue CM-MPP v/f 202 (in Cyrillic lettering).

PUBLISHED SOURCES

Publications about Pavlik Morozov

Contemporary reports on the murder (signed articles are also listed under their authors)

TR, 17, 18, 20, 21, 24, 27 September 1932; 26, 27, 28, 29, 30 November 1932.

VK, 23 September 1932; 8, 15, 27, 30 October 1932; 12, 23, 27, 30 November 1932.

Na smenu! 24, 28 September 1932; 24, 27, 29, 30 November 1932.

PP, 2, 15, 17, 23 October 1932; 14, 21, 27, 29 November 1932; 3, 17 December 1932.

Lives, works of art inspired by the hero, etc.

Alymov, Sergei, and Aleksandrov, Aleksandr, 'Pesnya o pionere-geroe', *Vozhatyi*, 11 (1937).

Balashov, Vl., *Koster ryabinovyi: Massovoe deistvo v shesti stsenakh o Pavle Morozove s uchastiem Sinei bluzy i konnitsy* (mimeographed typescript: Otdel rasprostraneniya dramaticheskikh proizvedenii, VUOAP, Moscow, 1969).

'Besstrashnyi pioner Pavlik Morozov', *PP*, 4 September 1938.

'Bol'shevitskie rebyata', *PP*, 26 January 1934.

Borovin, Valya, *Morozov Pavel* (Vologda: Sevgiz, 1936).

'Budem takimi, kak Pavlik Morozov', *VK*, 1 September 1939.

Byulleten' press-byuro TASS na dekabr' 1932 goda (mimeographed typescript news report: TASS: Moscow, 1932).

Devikov, Evgeny, 'Zhertva, no ne geroi', in V. F. Turuntaev (comp.), *Zavtra budet pozdno* (Sverdlovsk: Sredne-ural'skoe knizhnoe izdatel'stvo, 1990).

Doroshin, Mikhail, 'Pavlik Morozov', *PP*, 29 March 1933.

—, *Pavlik Morozov* (Volgograd: Nizhne-Volzhskoe knizhnoe izdatel'stvo, 1973).

Druzhnikov, Yury, *Donoschik 001: Voznesenie Pavlika Morozova* (Moscow: Moskovskii rabochii, 1995). Also available in English as *Denouncer 001* (New Brunswick: Transaction Publishers, 1996).

'Dva pionera pali zhertvoi kulatskoi klassovoi mesti', *Na smenu!*, 28 September 1932.

'Dzhordzh Soros – Pavliku Morozovu', *Izvestiya*, 4 September 2003.

Eisenstein, Sergei, 'Bezhin lug', *Kolkhoznye rebyata*, 4 (1936).

Gasparov, *Zapisi i vypiski*, (Moscow: NLO, 2000).

'Gotov'tes' k 3 sentyabrya – godovshchine smerti Pavlika Morozova', *TR* (*Smena* section) 24 August 1933, p. 1.

Gradov, P., and Bokalov, L., 'Pesnya o Pavlike Morozove', *Vozhatyi*, 8 (1961).

Gubarev, Vitaly, 'Kulatskaya rasprava', *PP*, 15 October 1932.

—, *Pavlik Morozov* (originally published 1947) (Simferopol': Krymizdat, 1949).

'Iz pisem yunkorov', *Na smenu!*, 24 September 1932.
Khorinskaya, E., *Yunyi barabanshchik* (Sverdlovsk: Sverdlovskoe knizhnoe izdatel'stvo, 1958).
'Kogda zhe budet postavlen pamyatnik Pavliku?', *PP*, 4 September 1937.
Kononenko, Veronika, 'A byl li donos?', *Chelovek i zakon*, 1 (1989), 71–98, 123 (http://rusidiot.narod.ru/facts/pm_p1.html, accessed 12 July 2004).
—, 'Ubit, no eshche opasen', *Sovetskaya Rossiya*, 4 October 2003. (http://www.sovoss.ru/2003/111/111_4_1.htm, accessed 12 July 2004).
Krasnev, Mikhail, *Pavlik Morozov: opera v 3 deistviyakh, 7 kartinakh s epilogom* (Moscow: Sovetskii kompozitor, 1961).
Krasnoshchekov, G., 'Pioner-geroi', *PP*, 2 September 1947.
'Kulak Kulukanov – vdokhnovitel' ubiistva', *PP*, 29 November 1932.
'Kulaki derevni Gerasimovki ubili pionera-aktivista Morozova i ego brata', *VK*, 23 September 1932.
'Kulaki na skam'e podsudimykh', *PP*, 27 November 1932.
Makhrin, Yury, 'Mal'chik, kotorogo nel'zya kaznit'', *Pravda*, 27–28 January 2004.
Mikhalkov, Sergei, and Sabo [Szábo], Ferents [Ferencz], 'Pesnya o Pavlike Morozove', *Pionerskii lager': spravochnik dlya vozhatykh i rabotnikov pionerskikh lagerei* (Moscow: Molodaya gvardiya, 1937).
Musatov, A., 'Bol'shaya vesna', *Vozhatyi* (1962), 48–58.
'Na rodine Pavlika Morozova', *PP*, 20 September 1936.
Nagibin, A., 'Segodnya – 32 goda so dnya gibeli pionera-geroya Pavlika MOROZOVA', *Na smenu!*, 3 September 1964.
'Nash otvet kulakam-ubiitsam: 500 bloknotov na rodinu Pavlushi Morozova!', *PP*, 23 October 1932.
'Otvet obraztsovoi shkoly na ubiistvo pionera Pavla Morozova', *TR*, 20 September 1932.
'Pamyati geroya-pionera Pavlika Morozova', *VK*, 23 August 1940.
'Pamyati yunogo geroya: Pavlik Morozov', *PP*, 4 September 1934.
'Pamyatnik pioneru-geroyu', *PP*, 14 November 1938. [Pavlik Morozov], *Druzhnye rebyata*, 21–2 (1932), frontispiece.
'Pavlik Morozov', *PP*, 5 September 1952.
'Pavlik Morozov', *VK*, 5 September 1937.
Pavlik Morozov (Sverdlovsk: Sverdlovskoe knizhnoe izdatel'stvo, 1962).
'Pavlik Morozov – besstrashnyi pioner', *PP*, 4 September 1935.
'Pavlik Morozov glazami moskvichei', *Romir: Rossiiskoe obshchestvennoe mnenie i issledovanie rynka*, http://www.romir.ru/

socpolit/socio/09_2002/pavlik-morozov (accessed December 2002).
'Pavlik Morozov i seichas zhivee vsekh zhivykh', *Memorial*, 11 (August–September 1999).
'Pioner Pavlik Morozov', *VK*, 3 September 1940, pp. 4–5.
'Pis'mo iz Gerasimovki – Na svezhei mogile', *PP*, 27 November 1932.
['Pis'mo pionerov d. Gerasimovki I. V. Stalinu'], *TR*, 24 December 1934.
Platonova, Valentina, 'O muzee, grante i pionere-geroe', *Tavdinskaya pravda*, 18 September 2003, p. 2.
'Postroim pamyatnik PM', *TR*, 12 October 1933.
Reynolds, Maura, 'Legend of Pavlik Morozov Dies Hard', *Moscow Times*, 13 November 2002, p. 1.
'Rodnye i tovarishchi Pavlika Morozova v Moskve', *PP*, 10 January 1934.
Shchipachev, Stepan, *Pavlik Morozov: poema* (Moscow: Sovetskii pisatel', 1950).
—, *Pavlik Morozov*, in his *Izbrannye proizvedeniya v dvukh tomakh*, vol. 1 (Moscow: Khudozhestvennaya literatura, 1965).
Shibaev, D. A. '"Obozhdite, shenyata-kommunisty, popadetes' mne gde-nibud'." Iz sledstvennogo dela po obvineniyu v ubiistve Pavla i Fedora Morozovykh (1932–1999 gg.)' *Istoricheskii arkhiv* 2 (2004).
Shvarts, O., 'Pavlik Morozov', *Pioner*, 6 (1933).
'Sledstvie po delu Morozovykh zatyagivaetsya', *PP*, 15 November 1932.
Smirnov, Elizar, 'Nikakoi poshchady klassovomu vragu!', *PP*, 3 December 1932.
—, 'Vyshe znamya klassovoi bditel'nosti', *PP*, 17 December 1932.
—, 'Ya kak pioner govoryu zdes' . . .', *PP*, 4 September 1935.
—, *Pavlik Morozov* (Moscow and Leningrad: Molodaya gvardiya, 1938).
—, 'Pavlik Morozov', in N. Makhlin and I. Goncharenko (eds.), *Deti-geroi* (Moscow: Molodaya gvardiya, 1961).
Smirnykh, A., 'V gosti k Pavliku', *VK*, 12 September 1939.
'Soberem podarki derevenskim pioneram v otvet kulach'yu. Ot nashego spets. korrespondenta', *PP*, 17 October 1932.
Solomein, P., 'Pochemu raiorganizatsii pozdno uznali', *VK*, 8 October 1932.
—, 'Kak pogib Pavlik', *VK*, 27 October 1932.
—, 'Nikakoi poshchady ubiitsam', *VK*, 30 October 1932.
—, 'Pis'mo iz Gerasimovki', *PP*, 21 November 1932.

—, *V kulatskom gnezde* (Sverdlovsk: Uralkniga, 1933).
—, *Pavka-kommunist* (Sverdlovsk: Sredne-Ural'skoe knizhnoe izdatel'stvo, 1966).
Sonin, Lev, 'Tragediya v ural'skoi derevne', in V. F. Turuntaev (comp.), *Zavtra budet pozdno* (Sverdlovsk: Sredne-ural'skoe knizhnoe izdatel'stvo, 1990).
Stratanovsky, S., *Stikhi* (St Petersburg: Assotsiatsiya 'Novaya literatura', 1993).
'Stroim pamyatnik Pavliku Morozovu', *PP*, 6 February 1934.
'Sud nad ubiitsami Pavlushi Morozova', *PP*, 21 November 1932.
'Taina zhizni i gibeli Pavlika Morozova', *Mozaika*, 11 September 2003 (http://www.iamik.ru/shownews.php?id+10476, accessed 12 July 2004).
Temnikova, I. V., and Brovtsin, A. V., 'Novoe o Pavlike Morozove', *Arkhivy Urala*, 1 (1996), 133–4.
Titov, 'Kulatskaya banda ubila pionera Morozova. Rasstrelyat' raspoyasavshchikhsya kulakov i podkulachnikov', *TR* (*Smena* section), 17 September 1932.
'Tovarishchi Pavlika Morozova v Moskve', *TR*, 20 January 1934.
'Vospominaniya Tat'yany Morozovoi o Pavlike', *TR*, 3 September 1933.
Yakovlev, Aleksandr, *Pioner Pavlik Morozov. Povest'* (Moscow: Detskaya literatura, 1936).
—, *Pioner Pavlik Morozov* (an adaptation of the 1936 book as a drama) (Moscow: Iskusstvo, 1940).
'Yunyi leninets Pavlik Morozov', *PP*, 4 September 1939.
Zhukov, A., 'U pamyatnika Pavlika Morozova', *VK*, 15 September 1939.
'Zverskoe ubiistvo dvukh pionerov. Nikakoi poshchady klassovomu vragu', *PP*, 2 October 1932.
Zykov, Petr, 'Imya, kotoroe nel'zya zabyt'', *TR* (Komsomol'skaya stranitsa' no. 10) 4 September 1934.

Pioneer heroes

Afinogenov, A., *Strakh*, in his *Izbrannoe v dvukh tomakh*, vol. 1 (Moscow: 'Iskusstvo', 1977).
Agapova, M. I., and Shadskaya, K. I., *Pionery-geroi. K 50–letiyu pionerskoi organizatsii im. V. I. Lenina* (Moscow: Tsentral'naya gorodskaya pionerskaya biblioteka im. M. Svetlova, 1972).
Bagritskii, Eduard, 'Smert' Pionerki', *PP*, 23 October 1932, p. 2.
Barto, Agniya, *Na zastave* (Moscow and Leningrad: Detgiz, 1937).
—, 'Dyadya Timur', *Tvoi stikhi* (Moscow: Detskaya literatura, 1960).

Baza kurnosykh (Irkutsk: Irkutskoe knizhnoe izdatel'stvo, 1962).
Deti o Staline (Moscow: Shkol'naya biblioteka, 1939).
Druskin, Lev, *Spasennaya kniga: Vospominaniya leningradskogo poeta* (London: Overseas Publications Interchange, 1984).
Dubyanskaya, Mariya, 'Busya Gol'dshtein', *LI*, 15 December 1935, p. 6.
Gaidar, Arkady, *Sochineniya* (Moscow: Detskaya literatura, 1946).
Gusev, A., *Yunye pionery. Stranitsy iz letopisi pionerskoi organizatsii imeni V. I. Lenina* (Moscow: Molodaya gvardiya, 1948).
—, *God za godom. Iz pionerskoi letopisi* (Moscow: Molodaya gvardiya, 1961).
Kassil', L., and Polyanovsky, M., *Ulitsa mladshego syna* (Moscow and Leningrad: Detskaya literatura, 1951).
Kosmodem'yanskaya, L., and Vigdorova, F., *Povest' o Zoe i Shure* (Leningrad: Leningradskoe gazetno-zhurnal'noe i knizhnoe izdatel'stvo, 1951).
Kozhevnikov, V., 'Korrespondentsiya boitsa Sinukova', *Pioner*, 1 (1942).
Kremensky, A., 'Nochnaya groza', *Pioner*, 1 (1942).
'Kulaki ubili pionera Kolyu Myagotina', *PP*, 21 December 1932, p. 1.
'Lushchie iz luchshikh', *Vozhatyi*, 2 (1956), pp. 4–5.
Lyadov, V., 'O geroyakh v detskoi literature', *Pravda*, 25 February 1934.
Morozov, V., 'V novoselkakh pogib pioner', *PP*, 29 August 1962.
'O rabote pionerskoi organizatsii', *Partiinoe stroitel'stvo*, 11–12 (1932), pp. 52–3.
Oseeva, Valentina, *Vasek Trubachev i ego tovarishchi* (Leningrad: Detskaya literatura, 1976).
'Pamyati Koli Yakovleva', *LI*, 11 December 1935, p. 3.
Shchipachev, S., *Pavlik Morozov: poema* (Moscow: Sovetskii pisatel', 1950).
—, 'Slovo o pionerakh-geroyakh', *Koster* 7 (1961), p. 7.
—, *Sobranie sochinenii v trekh tomakh* (Moscow: Khudozhestvennaya literatura, 1976).
Smirnov, A., 'Litsom k pionerdvizheniyu', *Drug detei*, 6 (1932).
Smirnov, E., *Slavnyi pioner Genya Shchukin* (Moscow: Molodaya gvardiya, 1938).
Smith, G. S., and Mirsky, D. S., *A Russian–English Life* (Oxford: Clarendon Press, 2000).
'Stalin i Galya [*sic*] Markizova', *LI*, 11 February 1936, p. 1.
'Ubit Pioner Ivanov', *LI*, 15 May 1936, p. 3.

General (childhood and child murder; the Soviet legal system; the Pioneers; Soviet children's literature, etc.)

Alder, Christine, and Polk, Ken, *Child Victims of Homicide* (Cambridge: Cambridge University Press, 2001).

Alekseev, Mikhail, *Karyukha. Drachuny* (Moscow: Sovetskii pisatel', 1988).

Alston, Philip, Parker, Stephen, and Seymour, John (eds.), *Children, Rights, and the Law* (Oxford: Clarendon Press, 1992).

Amis, Martin, *Koba the Dread* (London: Granta, 2002).

Apor, Balasz, Behrends, Jan, Jones, Polly, Rees, E. Arfon (eds.), *Leader Cult in Russia and Eastern Europe* (Basingstoke: Palgrave, 2004).

Applebaum, Anne, *Gulag: A History of the Soviet Camps* (London: Allen Lane, 2003).

Argenbright, Robert, 'Marking NEP's Slippery Path: The Krasnoshchekov Show Trial', *Russian Review*, vol. 61, no. 2 (2002).

Ariès, Philippe, *Centuries of Childhood* (London: Weidenfeld and Nicolson, 1962).

Arlet, Dieter, *Kinder töten Kinder: eine kriminologische Untersuchung* (Hamburg: Kriminalistik Verlag, 1971).

Babina, A., *Kak organizovat' dosug detei* (Moscow: Gosizdat, 1929).

Bambara, Toni Cade, *Those Bones Are Not My Child* (London: The Women's Press, 2000).

Baranova, L., 'Kak my provalili kadetskii miting', *Krasnye zori*, 2 (1919), pp. 31–4.

Bazarov, Aleksandr, *Durelom, ili gospoda kolkhozniki* (2 vols.; Kurgan: Izd. Zaural'e, 1997).

Bedin, V., Kushnikova, M., and Togulev, V., *Kemerovo i Stalinsk: panorama provintsial'nogo byta v arkhivnykh khronikakh 1920–30–kh gg.* (Kemerovo: Kuzbassvuizdat, 1999).

Belousov A. F. (ed.), *Russkii shkol'nyi fol'klor: Ot "vyzyvanii" Pikovoi damy do semeinykh rasskazov* (Moscow: Ladomir, 1998).

Bel'skaya, Mariya, 'Deti Ariny', in B. S. Ilizarov (ed.), *Zhenskaya sud'ba v Rossii: Dokumenty i vospominaniya* (Moscow: Rossiya molodaya, 1994).

Bergan, Ronald, *Sergei Eisenstein: A Life in Conflict* (London: Little, Brown, 1997).

Boldyrev, N. I. (ed.), *Klassnyi rukovoditel': posobie dlya klassnykh rukovoditelei srednikh shkol* (2nd edn.; Moscow: Gosudarstvennoe uchebno-pedagogicheskoe izdatel'stvo, 1955).

Bown, Matthew Cullerne, *Socialist Realist Painting* (New Haven: Yale University Press, 1998).

Boym, Svetlana, *Common Places: Mythologies of Everyday Life in Russia* (Cambridge, MA: Harvard University Press, 1994).

Brazul'-Brushkovsky, S. I., *Pravda ob ubiistve Yushchinskogo i dele Beilisa* (St Petersburg: Tipografiya M. A. Bessonova, 1913).

Brooks, Jeffrey, *Thank You, Comrade Stalin! Soviet Public Culture from Revolution to Cold War* (Princeton: Princeton University Press, 2000).

Bullard, J., and Bullard, M. (eds.), *The Diaries of Reader Bullard, 1930–34* (Charlbury, Oxon.: self-published, 2000).

Bykov, P. M., *The Last Days of Tsardom*, trans. A. Rothstein (London: Martin Lawrence, 1935).

Cassiday, Julie, *The Enemy on Trial: Early Soviet Courts on Stage and Screen* (DeKalb: University of Illinois Press, 2000).

Chaadaeva, O. N. (ed.), *Rabotnitsa na sotsial'noi stroike* (Moscow: Partiinoe izdatel'stvo, 1932).

Chukokalla: rukopisnyi al'manakh Korneya Chukovskogo (Moscow: Prem'era, 1999).

Churchill's Medical Dictionary (New York, Edinburgh, London and Melbourne: Churchill Livingstone, 1989).

Clark, Katerina, *The Soviet Novel: History as Ritual* (Chicago: University of Chicago Press, 1985).

—'Little Heroes', in S. Fitzpatrick (ed.), *Cultural Revolution in Russia, 1928–31* (Bloomington: Indiana University Press, 1978).

Coles, Robert, *The Political Life of Children* (Boston: Atlantic Monthly Press, 1986).

Conquest, Robert, *The Harvest of Sorrow: Soviet Collectivisation and the Terror-Famine* (new edn.; London: Pimlico, 2002).

Dal', V., *Tolkovyi slovar' zhivogo velikorusskogo yazyka* (4 vols.; Moscow: Izd. knigoprodavtsa-torgovtsa M. O. Vol'fa, 1880–82).

Danilin, A. G., 'Pervye shagi kolkhozov byvshego Borovicheskogo okruga', in *Trud i byt v kolkhozakh: sbornik pervyi. Iz opyta izucheniya kolkhozov v Leningradskoi oblasti, Belorussii i Ukraine* (Leningrad: Izd. Akademii Nauk SSSR, 1931).

Danilov, V., Manning, R., and Viola, L. (chief eds.), *Tragediya sovetskoi derevni: Kollektivizatsiya i raskulachivanie. Dokumenty v 5 tomakh* (Moscow: Rosspen, 5 vols., 1999– and continuing).

Davies, R. W., *The Socialist Offensive: The Collectivisation of Soviet Agriculture, 1929–30* (London: Macmillan, 1980).

The Deathless Trumpeter and Other Stories About Young Heroes, trans. Walter May (Moscow: Progress, *c.* 1973).

Deleuze, G., and Guattari, F., *L'Anti-Oedipe* (Paris: Les Editions de Minuit, 1972).

Delo Beilisa: Stenograficheskii otchet (3 vols.; Kiev: Pechatnya S. P. Yakovleva, 1913).

Delo Mendelya Beilisa: Materialy Chrezvychainoi sledstvennoi komissii Vremennogo pravitel'stva o sudebnom protsesse 1913 g. po obvineniyu v ritual'nom ubiistve, ed. R. Sh. Ganelin, V. E. Kel'ner, I. V. Lukyanov (St Petersburg: Dmitry Bulanin, 1999).

Detskii proletkul't: Organ Tul'skoi Detskoi Kommunisticheskoi Partii, 4 (1920).

Detskoe kommunisticheskoe dvizhenie, ed. Ya. A. Perel' and A. A. Lyubimova (Moscow and Leningrad: Narkompros, 1932).

Diderikhs, M. K., *Ubiistvo Tsarskoi Sem'i i chlenov Doma Romanovykh* (2 vols.; Moscow: Skify, 1991).

Direktivy i dokumenty po voprosu pionerskogo dvizheniya (Moscow: Izd. Akademii Pedagogicheskikh Nauk RSFSR, 1959).

Dobrenko, Evgeny (ed.), *Sotsrealisticheskii kanon* (St Petersburg: Akademicheskii proekt, 2000).

—, [2001a], *The Making of the State Writer: Social and Aesthetic Origins of Soviet Literary Culture* (Stanford: Stanford University Press, 2001).

—, [2001b], 'Nadzirat' – Nakazyvat' – Nadzirat': Sotsrealizm kak pribavochnyi produkt nasiliya', *Revue des études slaves*, vol. 67, no. 4 (2001).

Druskin, Lev, *Spasennaya kniga: Vospominaniya leningradskogo poeta* (London: Overseas Publications Interchange, 1984).

Dundes, Alan (ed.), *The Blood Libel Legend: A Casebook in Anti-Semitic Folklore* (Madison: University of Wisconsin Press, 1991).

Dunstan, John, *Soviet Schooling in the Second World War* (Basingstoke: Macmillan, 1997).

Edwards, Mark, 'In Defense of Euthyphro', *American Journal of Philology*, vol. 121, no. 2 (Summer 2000).

Efron, Ariadna, and Federol'f, Ada, *Miroedikha; Ryadom s Alei* (Moscow: Vozvrashchenie, 1995).

Engel, Barbara Alpern, and Posadskaya-Vanderbeck, Anastasia (eds.), *A Revolution of Their Own: Voices of Women in Soviet History* (Boulder, CO: Westview Press, 1998).

Engelstein, Laura, *The Keys to Happiness: Sex and the Search for Modernity in Fin de Siècle Russia* (Ithaca: Cornell University Press, 1992).

—, *Castration and the Heavenly Kingdom: A Russian Folktale* (Ithaca: Cornell University Press, 1999).

Ermolaev, Valery, *Tavdinskoe mestopisanie* (Ekaterinburg: Start, 1999).

Evtushenko, Evgeny, *Volchii pasport* (Moscow: Vagrius, 1998).

Ewing, E. Thomas, *The Teachers of Stalinism: Policy, Practice and Power in Soviet Schools of the 1930s* (History of Schools and Schooling, number 18), (New York, 2002).

Fabre-Vassas, C., *The Singular Animal: Jews, Christians, and the Pig*, trans. C. Volk (New York: Columbia University Press, 1997).

Figes, Orlando, *Peasant Russia, Civil War: The Volga Countryside in Revolution, 1917–21* (Oxford: Clarendon Press, 1988).

Firsov, B. M., and Kiseleva, I. G., *Byt velikorusskikh krest'yan-zemlepashtsev: Opisanie materialov etnograficheskogo byuro knyazya V. N. Tenisheva (na primere Vladimirskoi gubernii)* (St Petersburg: Izd. Evropeiskogo doma, 1993).

Fisher, Ralph T., Jr, 'The Beilis Case', in *The Modern Encyclopedia of Russian and Soviet History*, vol. 3 (Gulf Breeze: University of Florida Press, 1977).

Fitzpatrick, Sheila, *Stalin's Peasants: Resistance and Struggle in the Russian Village after Collectivization* (New York: Oxford University Press, 1994).

— 'Discourses of Denunciation', *Journal of Modern History*, vol. 68 no. 4 (1996).

— *Tear Off the Masks!* (Princeton: Princeton University Press, 2005).

Fitzpatrick, S., and Slezkine, Yu., *In the Shadow of Revolution: Life Stories of Russian Women from 1917 to the Second World War* (Princeton: Princeton University Press, 2000).

Frank, Stephen, *Crime, Cultural Conflict, and Justice in Rural Russia, 1856–1914* (Berkeley: University of California Press, 1999).

Franklin, Bob (ed.), *The Rights of Children* (Oxford: Basil Blackwell, 1986).

Gaidar, Arkady, *Sochineniya* (Moscow: Detskaya literatura, 1946).

Gernet, M. I., *Detoubiistvo: Sotsial'noe i sravnitel'no-yuridicheskoe issledovanie* (Moscow: Tip. Imp. Mosk. Universiteta, 1911).

Gorky, Maxim (Privetstvie *Krest'yanskoi gazete*), *Pravda*, 23 November 1933.

—, *Sobranie sochinenii v 30 tomakh* (Moscow: Khudozhestvennaya literatura, 1949–55).

—, *M. Gorky: neizdannaya perepiska* (Moscow: Nasledie, 1998).

Gromov, Evgeny (ed.), *Stalin: vlast' i iskusstvo* (Moscow: Respublika, 1998).

Gudzy, N. K. (ed.), *Khrestomatiya po drevnerusskoi literature* (Moscow: Prosveshchenie, 1973).

Halfin, Igal, *From Darkness to Light: Class, Consciousness and Salvation in Revolutionary Russia* (Pittsburgh: University of Pittsburgh Press, 2000).

Halttunen, Karen, 'Cultural History and the Challenge of Narrativity', in V. E. Bonnell and L. Hunt (eds.), *Beyond the Cultural Turn: New Directions in the Study of Society and Culture* (Berkeley: University of California Press, 1999), pp. 172–6.

Harris, James, *The Great Urals: Regionalism and the Evolution of the Soviet System* (Ithaca: Cornell University Press, 1999).

Hattonstone, Simon, '"I don't think of him as my father any more"', *Guardian*, 27 November 2000, G2 section, pp. 4–5.

Holmes, L. E., *Stalin's School: Moscow's Model School no. 25, 1931–1937* (Pittsburgh: University of Pittsburgh Press, 1999).

Hughes, James, *Stalinism in a Russian Province: Collectivization and Dekulakization in Siberia* (Basingstoke: Macmillan, 1996).

L'Infini, 59 (1997) (a special issue on *la question pédophile*).

Istoriya VLKSM i Vsesoyuznoi Pionerskoi organizatsii imeni Lenina, ed. V. A. Sulemov (Moscow: Prosveshchenie, 1983).

James, Allison, and Prout, Alan (eds.), *Contemporary Issues in the Sociological Study of Childhood* (2nd edn.: London, Falmer Press, 1997).

Kadry prosveshcheniya: Po materialam perepisi rabotnikov prosveshcheniya v 1933 g. Comp. M. T. Gol'tsman, ed. N. N. Efremov (Moscow: Profizdat, 1936).

'Kak prazdnovali deti 1-e maya', *Krasnye zori*, 2 (1919), pp. 40–9.

'Kak v Tomske sumeli izvratit' postanovlenie pravitel'stva 7.iv.1935', *Sovetskaya yustitsiya*, 29 (1935).

Kanarsky, S. (ed.), *Ugolovnyi kodeks sovetskikh respublik* (Khar'kov: Gos. izd. Ukrainy, 1928).

Kasack, W., *Lexicon der russischen Literatur des 20. Jahrhunderts* (Munich: Verlag Otto Sagner, 1992).

Kassil', Lev, *Dorogie moi mal'chishki. Konduit i Shvambraniya* (Moscow: Vysshaya shkola, 1987).

Kelly, Catriona, '"The School Waltz": The Everyday Life of the Post-Stalinist Soviet Classroom', *Forum for Anthropology and Culture*, 1 (2004).

Kent, Leonard J., A Survivor of a Labor Camp Remembers: Expendable Children of Mother Russia (Lewiston, New York: Edwin Mellen Press, 1997).

Kharkhordin, Oleg, *The Collective and the Individual in Soviet Culture: A Study of Practices* (Berkeley: University of California Press, 1999).

Khrushchev, N., 'Kak my organizovali Dom pionerov i detskie parki', *Vozhatyi*, 8 (1936).

Kincaid, James R., *Child-Loving: The Erotic Child and Victorian Culture* (New York and London: Routledge, 1992).

Klönne, Arno, *Jugend im Dritten Reich: Die Hitler-Jugend und ihre Gegner* (Munich: Deutscher Taschenbuch Verlag, 1990).

Klotz, Aiga, *Kinder- und Jugendliteratur in Deutschland 1840–1950: Gesamtverzeichnis der Veröffentlichungen in deutscher Sprache* (6 vols.; Stuttgart: Metzler, 1999).

Kondakov, M. N. (chief ed.), *Semeinoe vospitanie: Slovar' dlya roditelei* (Moscow: Prosveshchenie, 1967).

Korzhavin, Naum, 'V soblaznakh krovavoi epokhi', *Novyi mir*, 7 (1992); 8 (1992).

Kosterina, Nina, *The Diary of Nina Kosterina*, trans. M. Ginsburg (London: Valentine, Mitchell, 1968).

Kotkin, Stephen, *Magnetic Mountain: Stalinism as a Civilization* (Berkeley: University of California Press, 1995).

Kozhevnikov, R. F., *Pamyatniki i monumenty Moskvy* (Moscow: Moskovskii rabochii, 1971).

Kratkaya literaturnaya entsiklopediya (9 vols.; Moscow: Sovetskaya entsiklopediya, 1962–78).

Kudrova, Irma, *The Death of a Poet: The Last Days of Marina Tsvetaeva*, trans. M. A. Szporluk (Woodstock, NY: Overview Press 2004).

Kukina., E. M., and Kozhevnikov, R. F., *Rukotvornaya pamyat' Moskvy* (Moscow: Moskovskii rabochii, 1997).

Lenhoff, Gail, *The Martyred Princes Boris and Gleb: A Socio-Cultural Study* (Columbus, Ohio: Slavica, 1989).

Lenin, V. I., *Sochineniya* (4th edn.; 50 vols., Moscow: Politicheskaya literatura, 1941–51).

Leutheuser, Karsten, *Freie, geführte und verführte Jugend: Politisch motivierte Jugendliteratur in Deutschland 1919–89* (Paderborn: Igel Verlag, 1995).

Lewin, M., *Russian Peasants and Soviet Power: A Study of Collectivization* (London: George Allen and Unwin, 1968).

Lifschutz-Losev, L., 'Children's Literature, Russian', *Modern Encyclopedia of Russian and Soviet Literatures*, vol. 4 (Gulf Breeze, FL.: Academic International Press, 1981).

Litvinenko, Olga, and Riordan, James (eds.), *Memories of the Dispossessed: Descendants of Kulak Families Tell Their Stories* (Nottingham: Bramcote Press, 1998), pp. 29–51.

Lovell, Stephen, *Summerfolk: A History of the Dacha* (Ithaca: Cornell University Press, 2003).

Löwe, H. D., *The Tsars and the Jews: Reform, Reaction, and Anti-Semitism in Imperial Russia, 1772–1917* (Chur: Harwood Academic, 1993).

Lurie, Alison, *Don't Tell the Grownups: Subversive Children's Literature* (London: Bloomsbury, 1990).

Makhlin N., and Goncharenko I. (eds.), *Deti-geroi* (Moscow: Molodaya gvardiya, 1961).

Malnick, Bertha, *Everyday Life in Russia* (London: George G. Harrap, 1938).

Mel'nikov, M., *Novyi put': Pervaya kniga dlya chteniya i raboty v sel'skoi shkole 1 stupeni*, ed. A. Kalashnikov (9th edn.; Moscow and Leningrad: Gosizdat, 1930).

—, *Novyi put': Vtoraya kniga dlya chteniya i raboty v sel'skoi shkole 1 stupeni*, ed. A. Kalashnikov (7th edn.; Moscow and Leningrad: Gosizdat, 1930).

Merridale, Catherine, *Night of Stone: Death and Memory in Russia* (London: Granta, 2000).

Mikhalkov, S., *Izbrannoe* (Moscow: Sovetskii pisatel', 1947).

Mitreikin, Konstantin, *UKK* (Moscow: Zhurnal'no-gazetnoe ob"edinenie, 1932).

Morozov, S., et al. (eds.), *Sowjetische Fotografen 1917–40* (Leipzig: VEB Fotokinoverlag, 1980).

Morrison, Blake, *As If: A Crime, a Trial, a Question of Childhood* (London: Granta, 1997).

Moskva poslevoennaya (Moscow: Gosarkhiv, 2000).

Novak-Deker, N. K. (ed.), *Soviet Youth: Twelve Komsomol Histories* (Munich: Institute for the Study of the USSR, 1959).

Novaya shkola: Uchenicheskii zhurnal shkol II stupeni Ostrova No. 2 i No. 3 (Pskovskaya gub.), 1 (May–June 1919).

Orme, Nicholas, *Medieval Children* (London: Yale University Press, 2002).

Osorina, Mariya, *Sekretnyi mir detei: v prostranstve mira vzroslykh* (St Petersburg: Piter, 1999).

Pallot, Judith, *Land Reform in Russia, 1906–1917: Peasant Responses to Stolypin's Project of Rural Transformation* (Oxford: Clarendon Press, 1999).

Papkovskaya, E. I., *Kniga o malen'kikh trekhgortsakh* (Moscow: Gos. Uch-ped. giz, 1948).

Perel', Ya. A., and Lyubimova, A. A., *Prestupleniya protiv nesover-*

shennoletnikh 'Okhrana detstva: detskoe pravo' series, issue 9 (Moscow and Leningrad: Narkompros/Gos. Uch.-ped. izd., 1932).

Pervyi vsesoyuznyi s"ezd sovetskikh pisatelei: stenograficheskii otchet (Moscow: Sovetskii pisatel', 1934).

Petrone, Karen, *Life Has Become More Joyous, Comrades: Celebrations in the Time of Stalin* (Bloomington: Indiana University Press, 2000).

Petrovskaya, I. F., *V kontse puti* (St Petersburg: no publisher given, 1999).

Petrusheva, L. I., *Deti russkoi emigratsii* (Moscow: Terra, 1997).

Pis'ma vo vlast' 1917–27: zayavleniya, zhaloby, donosy, pis'ma v gosudarstvennye struktury i bol'shevitskim vozhdyam (Moscow: Rosspen, 1998).

Po-Chia Hora, Ronald, *The Myth of Ritual Murder: Jews and Magic in Reformation Germany* (New Haven: Yale University Press, 1988).

'Pogovorim o detyakh', *Pravda*, 17 September 1934.

Postman, Neil, *The Disappearance of Childhood* (London: W. H. Allen, 1985).

'Preodolet' posledstviya kul'ta lichnosti v pedagogike', *Sovetskaya pedagogika*, 9 (1956).

Programmy nachal'noi shkoly (Moscow: Uchpedgiz, 1945).

Programmy nachal'noi shkoly na 1957–1958 god (Moscow: Uchpedgiz, 1957).

Rittersporn, G., 'Formy obshchestvennogo obikhoda molodezhi i ustanovki sovetskogo rezhima v predvoennom desyatiletii', in T. Vikhavainen (ed.), *Normy i tsennosti povsednevnoi zhizni: Stanovlenie sotsialisticheskogo obraza zhizni v Rossii, 1920–1930-e gody* (St Petersburg: Institut Finlyandii v Sankt-Peterburge, 2000).

Rogger, Hans, *Jewish Policies and Right-Wing Politics in Late Imperial Russia* (Berkeley: University of California Press, 1986).

Rossi, Zhak [Jacques Rossi], *Spravochnik po GULagu* (London: Overseas Publications Interchange, 1987).

Rozanov, Vasily, *Opavshie list'ya*, vol. 1 (St Petersburg: no publisher given, 1913).

Rybakov, A., *Roman-vospominanie* (Moscow: Vagrius, 1997).

Rybakov, N. I., *Gaidar v Arzamase* (Moscow: Sovetskaya Rossiya, 1984).

Rybnikov, N. A., *Derevenskii shkol'nik i ego idealy* (Moscow: Zadruga, 1916).

—, *Idealy gimnazistok: Ocherki po psikhologii yunosti* (Moscow: Prakticheskie znaniya, 1916).

—, *Krest'yanskii rebenok* (Moscow: Rabotnik prosveshcheniya, 1930).
Samuel, Maurice, *Blood Accusation: The Strange History of the Beiliss* [sic] *Case* (London: Weidenfeld and Nicolson, 1967).
Sanitarnyi obzor Permskoi gubernii za 1895 god (Perm': Tip. Gubernskoi Zemskoi Upravy, 1896).
Sanitarnyi obzor Permskoi gubernii za 1910 god (Perm': Elektro-Tip. Gubernskogo Zemstva, 1913).
Saranin, Alex, *Child of the Kulaks* (St Lucia: University of Queensland Press, 1997).
Sats, N. (ed.), *Deti o Lenine* (Moscow: Novaya Moskva, 1925).
Shchipachev, S., *Izbrannye proizvedeniya v 2 tomakh* (Moscow: Khudozhestvennaya literatura, 1965).
Shentalinsky, Vitaly, *The KGB's Literary Archive* (London: Harvill, 1995).
Schenzinger, K. A., *Der Hitlerjunge Quex: Roman* (Berlin: Zeitgeist, 1932).
Sherman, Joseph, *The Jewish Pope: Myth, Diaspora, and Yiddish Literature* (Oxford: Legenda, 2003).
Shif, Al., 'O starshem vozraste, druzhbe i sekrete uspekhov odnogo obryada', *Vozhatyi*, 5 (1935).
Shimbirev, P. N., *Pedagogika* (Moscow: Gos. Uch-ped. giz. 1940).
Shingarev, S., 'Chekletovy – pered sudom obshchestvennosti', *Drug detei*, 4 (1930), pp. 9–10.
Shkapskaya, Mariya, *Stikhi* (London: Overseas Publications Interchange, 1979).
Siegelbaum, L, and Sokolov, A., *Stalinism as a Way of Life: A Narrative in Documents* (New Haven: Yale University Press, 1999).
Sokolov, N., *Ubiistvo tsarskoi sem'i* (Berlin: Slovo, 1925).
Solomon, Peter, *Soviet Criminal Justice under Stalin* (Cambridge: Cambridge University Press, 1996).
Sovetskie pisateli: avtobiografii, vol. 5 (Moscow: Sovetskii pisatel', 1988).
Sovetskoe rukovodstvo: perepiska 1928–1941 (Moscow: Rosspen, 1999).
Spisok selenii Permskoi gubernii: Irbitskii uezd (Perm': Izd. Permskogo Gubernskogo Zemstva, 1908).
Startsev, I. I. (ed.), *Detskaya literatura: bibliografiya 1932–9* (Moscow and Leningrad: Detskaya literatura, 1941).
—, *Detskaya literatura za gody Velikoi Otechestvennoi Voiny (1941–1945)* (Moscow and Leningrad: Detskaya literatura, 1947).
—, *Detskaya literatura: bibliografiya 1946–8* (Moscow: Detskaya literatura, 1950).

—, *Detskaya literatura: bibliografiya 1951–2* (Moscow: Detskaya literatura, 1954).

—, *Detskaya literatura: bibliografiya 1955–7* (Moscow: Detskaya literatura, 1959).

—, *Detskaya literatura: bibliografiya 1961–3* (Moscow: Detgiz, 1966).

—, *Detskaya literatura: bibliografiya 1964–6* (Moscow: Detgiz, 1970).

—, *Detskaya literatura: bibliografiya 1976–78* (Moscow: Detgiz, 1987).

—, *Detskaya literatura: bibliografiya 1979–81* (Moscow: Detgiz, 1988).

Starzhinsky, Pavel, *Vzrosloe detstvo: zapiski syna raskulachennogo* (Moscow: Sovremennik, 1991).

Statisticheskii spravochnik SSSR za 1928 god (Moscow: Statisticheskoe izdatel'stvo TSU SSSR, 1929).

Stephens, Sharon (ed.), *Children and the Politics of Culture* (Princeton: Princeton University Press, 1995).

Stites, Richard, *Russian Popular Culture: Entertainment and Society since 1900* (Cambridge: Cambridge University Press, 1992).

Stoliaroff [Stolyarov], Ivan, *Zapiski russkogo krest'yanina/ Récit d'un paysan russe* (Paris: Institut d'Etudes Slaves, 1986).

Svod zakonov Rossiiskoi Imperii, ed. D. Mordukhai-Boltovsky, vol. 10:1 (St Petersburg: Deyatel', 1913).

Tadevosyan, V., 'Ob ugolovnom protsesse po delam nesovershennoletnikh', *Sotsialisticheskaya zakonnost'*, 4 (1939).

Tager, A. S., *Tsarskaya Rossiya i delo Beilisa: k istorii antisemitizma* (Moscow: OGIZ, 1933).

Tian-Shanskaia, Olga, *Village Life in Late Tsarist Russia*, ed. David L. Ransel, trans. David L. Ransel with Michael Levine (Bloomington: Indiana University Press, 1993).

Toomre, Joyce (ed. and trans.), *Classic Russian Cooking: Elena Molokhovets' A Gift to Young Housewives* (Bloomington: Indiana University Press, 1992).

Treadgold, Donald W., *The Great Siberian Migration: Government and Peasant in Resettlement from Emancipation to the First World War* (Princeton: Princeton University Press, 1957).

Trotsky, Leon [Lev], *Problems of Everyday Life*, trans. anon. (New York: Pathfinder, 1973).

Tsendrovskaya, S. N., 'Krestovskii ostrov ot Nepa do snyatiya blokady', *Nevskii arkhiv*, 2 (1995).

Tsvetaeva, Marina, *Sobranie sochinenii v 7 tomakh*, vol. 1 (Moscow: Ellis Lak, 1994).

Turuntaev, V. F. (comp.), *Zavtra budet pozdno* (Sverdlovsk: Sredne-Ural'skoe knizhnoe izdatel'stvo, 1990).

Tvardovsky, Ivan, 'Stranitsy perezhitogo', *Yunost'*, 3 (1988), pp. 11–29.

Ustav Smolenskoi Gubernskoi Zemskoi vospitatel'no-ispravitel'nogo kolonii-priyuta dlya nesovershennoletnikh (Smolensk: no publisher, 1915).

Vallely, Paul, '*Muti*: The Story of Adam', *The Independent on Sunday*, 3 August 2003, p. 12.

Van Bueren, Geraldine (ed.), *International Documents on Children* (The Hague: Kluver Law International, 1998).

Vasil'eva, Larisa, *Deti Kremlya* (Moscow: AST, 1997).

Verdery, Katherine, 'Nationalism and National Sentiment in Post-Soviet Russia', *Slavic Review*, 52: 2 (1993), 179–203.

Vikhavainen, T. (ed.), *Normy i tsennosti povsednevnoi zhizni: Stanovlenie sotsialisticheskogo obraza zhizni v Rossii, 1920–1930-e gody* (St Petersburg: Institut Finlyandii v Sankt-Peterburge, 2000).

Vilensky S. S. (ed.), *Till My Tale is Told* (Bloomington: Indiana University Press, 1999).

Vilensky, S. S., Kokurin, A. I., Atmashkina, G. V., and Novichenko, I. Yu. (eds.), *Deti GULaga 1918–1956* (Moscow: Demokratiya, 2002).

Viola, Lynne, *The Best Sons of the Fatherland: Workers in the Vanguard of Soviet Collectivization* (New York: Oxford University Press, 1987).

—, *Peasant Rebels Under Stalin: Collectivisation and the Culture of Peasant Resistance* (New York: Oxford University Press, 1996).

—, '"Tear the Evil from the Root": The Children of the *Spetspereselentsy* of the North', in N. Baschmakoff and Paul Freyer (eds.), *Modernisation in the Russian Provinces* (*Studia Slavica Finlandensia, XVII*) (Helsinki: Institute for Russian and East European Studies, 2000).

Vishnevskaya, Galina, *Galina: Istoriya zhizni* (Paris: La Presse libre/Kontinent, 1984).

Volkov, S. (comp. and ed.), *Testimony: The Memoirs of Dmitry Shostakovich*, trans. A. W. Bouis (London: Hamish Hamilton, 1979).

Warner, Marina, *No Go the Bogeyman: Scaring, Lulling, and Making Mock* (London: Chatto and Windus, 1998).

Widdis, Emma, *Visions of a New Land: Soviet Film from the Revolution to the Second World War* (New Haven: Yale University Press, 2003).

Wood, Elizabeth, 'The Trial of Lenin: Legitimating the Revolution through Political Theater, 1920–23', *Russian Review*, vol. 61, no. 2 (2002).

Zelensky, E. K., 'Popular Children's Culture in Post-Perestroika Russia: Songs of Innocence and Experience Revisited', in A. Barker (ed.), *Consuming Russia* (Durham, NC: Duke University Press, 1999).

Zhenskaya sud'ba v Rossii, ed. B. S. Ilizarova (Moscow: Rossiya molodaya, 1994).

Zori sovetskoi pionerii: ocherki po istorii pionerskoi organizatsii (1917–1941) (Moscow: Prosveshchenie, 1972).

ACKNOWLEDGEMENTS

Even the Soviet authorities found the subject of Pavlik Morozov disturbing and bordering on the distasteful. In the circumstances, a dedication to any particular person would be inappropriate, but the absence of a name singled out in this way does not imply lack of consideration for the many individuals and institutions that helped me shed light on his myth.

Comrade Pavlik is based on research for 'Childhood in Russia, 1890–1991: A Social and Cultural History', funded by grant no. F/08736/A from the Leverhulme Trust. My many research visits to Russia during 2002, 2003 and 2004 were also supported by the British Academy (a place on the Academic Exchange programme in 2000, Small Personal Grants in 2001 and 2003–4), by the Ilchester Fund of the University of Oxford, by the Modern Languages Faculty, University of Oxford, and by New College, Oxford. I owe my home institution a huge debt for offering me a year's Special Leave in 2003–4, which left me free to work on Pavlik, and on Russian childhood more generally; I am deeply grateful to Philip Bullock, who took over my teaching and college administration while I was away, and to Mary MacRobert, who helped lighten my load of Finals examining.

Thanks to Stephen Lovell, Gerry Smith, Barbara Heldt, Nicholas Stargardt, Ann Livschiz, and to the audience at the Soviet Industrialisation Project Seminar, CREES, University of Birmingham, for their comments on drafts, and to Anthony Bale for sharing insights from his own work on anti-Semitism and legends about ritual murder in medieval England. David Moon, Judy Pallot and Lynne Viola suggested sources for peasant history generally. Birgit Beumers offered advice, practical support and good fellowship in Ekaterinburg and elsewhere. Yury Druzhnikov's book on Pavlik got me interested in the topic to begin with, and he was good enough to answer my emails about the Pavlik story. Nancy Condee provided me with a copy of her unpublished paper about the myth. Wojciech Jajdelski, Mikhail Leonovich Gasparov and Robert Parker made suggestions about parallels to Pavlik in classical Western thought. Evgeny Dobrenko was a fount of knowledge about Pioneer kitsch, and Stalinist cultural politics generally. I had illuminating discussions with Sheila Fitzpatrick and with Orlando Figes about the historical background to the case, and with Mariya Osorina about children's culture generally. My husband, Ian Thompson, probably now knows almost as much about Pavlik as I do, but has been humorously tolerant of my obsession.

This book is based on extensive first-hand research, and I have directly seen about 95 percent of the material cited. However, various people have helped with checking references, or supplying information that I could not reach myself. Timothy Phillips helped locate materials in *Pioneer Pravda*; Denis Kozlov kindly transcribed the protocols of the Politburo meetings at which a monument to Pavlik was discussed; Polly Jones read through *Komsomol Pravda* and supplied materials on Pavlik's monuments from Soviet guidebooks.

Robert Baldock of Yale University Press, which is publishing *Children's World: Growing Up in Russia, 1890–1991* (to be completed, 'if God grants', in 2005) was good enough to agree that the strange story of Pavlik deserved exposure at greater length than it would have in a large-scale history of childhood: my thanks to him as well. George Miller, at Granta, saw the potential in the book and has been, as in the past, an extraordinarily active editor and source of friendly interest throughout. I cannot say how thankful to him I am.

In Russia, I am particularly grateful to Elena Glavatskaya, for help with locating sources in Ekaterinburg, and for accompanying me on a visit to Gerasimovka and Tavda. Other people who gave valuable aid during my trip to the Urals were Nataliya Reshetnikova, of the House of Film in Ekaterinburg, Irina Evdokimova, director of the local museum in Tavda, and Tatyana Kuznetsova, curator of the Pavlik Morozov Museum in Gerasimovka. The project would not have been possible without the help and advice of members of staff at the Russian National Library, St Petersburg; the Russian State Library, Moscow; the Belinsky Library, Ekaterinburg; the Russian Academy of Education: Scholarly Archive, Moscow; the Russian State Archive of Social and Political History, Moscow; the Central Archive of Public Associations of the City of Moscow; the Central Archive of the Federal Security Service, Moscow; the Russian State Historical Archive, St Petersburg; the Central State Archive of Literature and Art, St Petersburg; the State Archive of Sverdlovsk Province, and the Centre of Public Association Documents, Sverdlovsk Province, Ekaterinburg.

Generous hospitality was offered on my different stays by the staff of the Norwegian University Centre, and by Oleg Golynkin and Mariya Alyokshina, in St Petersburg; by Jonathan Aves and Nataliya Pushkareva in Moscow; and by Mikhail and Tamara Glavatsky in Ekaterinburg. Evgeny Golynkin and Anatoly Chernobaev offered vital aid at the final stages of the project; Lorina Repina and her colleagues at the Institute of General History, Moscow, were extremely helpful in smoothing access to archives. I would also like to offer thanks to my interviewers for the Leverhulme-sponsored oral history project, Aleksandra Piir, Ekaterina Melnikova and Oksana Filicheva, in St Petersburg, and Yuliya Rybina and Ekaterina Shumilova, in Moscow; to Vitaly Bezrogov, for help with arranging interviewing, and for bibliographical and other information; to the interviewees themselves, for their time; to the staff of the European University, St Petersburg; and especially, on many counts, to Albert Baiburin.

INDEX

Numbers in *italics* refer to illustrations.

abortion, 148–9
'Adam', murder of, 11
Adlivankin, Samuil, 132
adolescents, violence of, 250–1
Afinogenov, Aleksandr, 155
agitbrigades, 238, 239, 258
Aizlewood, Robin, 311
Akopov, Grisha, 38, 109, 137, 138, 207, 208, 230
Akopyan, Grisha, *see* Akopov, Grisha
Alekseev, Mikhail, 238, 270
Aleksei, Tsarevich, murder of, 124–5
Alymov, Sergei, xvii, 46–7, 151, 152, 202
Anna Karenina (Tolstoy), 23
anti-Semitism, 39, 126, 129–30, 248
Anushenko, Vasily, 77
'Auto-Castrators', 292
Arkhangelsk, 28–9
Arlet, Dieter, 250–1
Avidon, Yakov, 174

Babel, Isaac, 100
Bagritsky, Eduard, 162, 164
Balashkin, Yury, 200
Balashov, Vladimir, 203
Barto, Agniya, 213, 300
Beilis case, 126–31, 293
Beilis, Mendel, 126, 127, 131
Bezhin Meadow (film), 2, 8, 15, 151, *156*, 156–7, 210
Bianki, Vitaly, 162
Black Hundreds, 131, 311
Blok, Aleksandr, 200
'blood libel' legends, 130, 248
Blum, Albert, 220
Blyton, Enid, 178
Bokalov, Leonid, 201, 202
'border guards', cult of, 214
Boris, Saint, 123–4, 125
Boris Godunov, Tsar, 124
Borovin, Valya, 153, 170–1, 180
The Boy from Urzrum, 44
Boym, Svetlana, 7
Britten, Benjamin, 263
Brodsky, Joseph, 185
The Brothers Karamazov (Dostoevsky), 9, 230
'Brothers Vasiliev', 196
Brutus the Elder, 9
Bulger, James, 137
Bullard, Reader, 298
Bykov, xiv, 62, 74, 77, 86–8, 90, 91–2, 108, 234–5, 252, 255, 256

cannibalism, 31, 128–9
The Captain's Daughter (Pushkin), 180
Chapaev, Vasily, 196
Chebakov, Nikita, xvii, 193–5, 206
Cheberyak, Zhenya, 126, 127
Chekletov, Kostya, 157–8
The Child Varfolomei's Vision (Nesterov), 195
Childhood (Tolstoy), 180
children
  agitation for collectivization, 37–40
  care, xxv, 149
  consumer goods for, 149

children – *cont.*
as heroes, 132–3, 150, 162, 198
martyrdom, 162–3, 184
murder of, 11–13, 126–31, 263
political organizations for, 33–5
in post-Stalin era, 198–200
as prodigies, 150
role models for, 7, 184–7
in Soviet society, 147–50
'Sovietization' of, 36–7
stories for, 161–2
'Timurites', 182
and the war effort, 183–4
see also Pioneer movement; scout movement
Children's Communist Organization, 112
Chukovsky, Kornei, 214
Civil War, Russian, 32, 34, 51
collectivization
child victims of, 42
effects of, 31–2
by force, 25–8
human cost of, 19
rationale behind, 18, 19, 20
as recommended to children, 38
see also 'dekulakization'
colonization, Soviet, 309
Communist Party, in Tavda district, 63–4, 68
'Comrade Churygin' (Zamiatin), 19–20
'comradely courts', 204–5
Condee, Nancy, 319
Conquest, Robert, 42
'The Correspondence of Warrior Sinukov' (Kozhevnikov), 184
Crematorium (rock group), 218
Crime and Punishment (Dostoevsky), 9
Criminal Code (1926), 12, 13, 244
'Cultural Revolution', 6, 37
Cunningham, Hugh, 269

Davis, Natalie Zemon, 71
Dawns of the Commune (newspaper), 63, 107, 110, 113, 117, 133, 224, 239, 245
'Deaf and Dumb' case, 220
Dear Boys (Kassil), 182
'Death of a Pioneer Girl' (Bagritsky), 162, 164
Decree on Mother and Child Protection (1936), 149
'dekulakization', 27–8, 30–1, 51, 242
Denouncer No. 001 (Druzhnikov), 4–5
denunciation
civic, 160–1, 171, 174, 214
distaste for, 212
in the family, 8–10, 40–2, 155, 157, 159, 169, 172–3
in Nazi Germany, 121–3
'Der kleine Trompeter' (German communist song), 123
'designer babies', 320
Devikov, Evgeny, 283
'Dizzy with Success' (Stalin), 30, 242
Dmitry, Tsarevich, murder of, 123–4
Doroshin, Mikhail, 168, 203
Dostoevsky, Fyodor, 9, 230
Druskin, Lev, 160–1
Druzhnikov, Yury, 4–5, 8, 9, 167–8, 196, 211, 230–9, 247, 262, 312
Dubinin, Volodya, 184–5, 195, 196, 207, 208
Dzerzhinsky, Felix, 215, 216
Dzhakupov, Kychan, 208
Dzhakybov, Kychan, *see* Dzhakupov, Kychan

Efron, Sergei, 234
Eisenstein, Sergei, 2, 8, 15, 151, 156, 210
Ekaterinburg, *see* Sverdlovsk
Ekk, Nikolai, 133, 162
electrification, 33
Emancipation of the Serfs (1861), 22
Enukidze, Avel, 179
Euthyphro (Plato), 9, 269

'face-to-face confrontations', 105, 267, 286
Fadeyev, Aleksandr, 183
families
conflict within, 40–2
values, 148–9

'Fat Petya and Thin Sima' (Mayakovsky), 132
Fear (play), 155, 191
Fedchenko, xiv, 62, 74, 80, 92, 94, 105, 106, 252
festivals, Soviet, 176
Filippov, 53
'Finnish General Staff' affair, 220, 267
First All-Soviet Pioneer Rally (1929), 142
First Congress of Soviet Workers (1934), 144, 148
First Experimental Station of Narkompros, 32, 36
First Five-Year Plan (1928–32), 6, 21, 51, 147
Fokin, Pavel, 83
The Foundation Pit (Platonov), 42
Friendly Lads (magazine), 37, 39, 163–4
Frunze, Timur, 179
FSB (formerly KGB), xxx, 70, 221
Furmanov, Dmitry, 196

Gaidar, Arkady, xvii, 162–3, 164, 177, 179, 181, 183, 212
Gaidar, Timur, 179
Galyzov, Efim, xvi, 79, 100, 101
Galyzov, Yakov, 229
Gasparov, Mikhail Leonovich, 269
Gavrilchik, Vladlen, 218
Gerasimov, Aleksandr, 179
Gerasimovka
  appearance and character of, xxvi–xxvii, 48–9, 118–19
  commemorations of Pavlik, 166–7, *216*, 217
  date settled, 276
  farms, 50
  and the kulaks, 53–4, 242
  museum, 203–4, *204*, 217, 221
  school photograph, *227*
German, Aleksei, 311, 320
Gleb, Saint, 123–4, 125
Golikov, Lyonya, 198, 207, 208, 215
Gorky, Maxim, xvii, xxv, 14, 16, *141*, *143*
  on children's affairs, 141–2
  as mentor for young writers, 140, 142
  and the Pavlik myth, 139, 140–5, 153, 160, 167, 217
Gradov, Pyotr, 201, 202
grain requisitions, 21, 25–6
Great Soviet Encyclopedia, 145, 146
Great Terror (1937–38), 88, 98, 158, 169
Grimm brothers, 173
Gubarev, Vitaly, xvii–xviii, 180, 190–1, 201, 203, 207

'Hallo, Morozov' (song), 210
Hamlet, 7–8
Harvest of Sorrow (Conquest), 42
Hate (Doroshin), 168
Hitler Boy Quex (Schenzinger), 8–9, 122, 175
'hobby circles', 149–50
hooliganism, 178, 204, 249
'Horst Wessel Lied', 123
House of Children's Books, Leningrad, 197
How the Steel Was Tempered (Ostrovsky), 186
Hughes, James, 25

identity papers, forgery of, 29–30, 190
In the Kulak's Nest (Solomein), 134–6, 142
informers, 159, 214
International Scouting Movement, 34
internationalism, 129–30, 292
Iskrin, Andriyan, xiv, 106, 240
Izvestiya, 63, 138–9

Kabina, Zoya, xvi, 101, 243, 285, 313
Kaganovich, Lazar, 31
'Karabash' (Bianki), 162
Karabchevsky, P., 127
Kartashov, Spiridon, xiv, 83–4, 85, 108, 232, 234, 235–6, 252
Kassil, Lev, 182, 184–5, 214

Kataev, Valentin, 193
Khorinskaya, E., 202
Khrushchev, Nikita, 197, 199
Kiev, 126
Kirov, Sergei, 44, 215
Klimov, Elem, 198
Kniga, Stepanida, 78–9
Kniga family, 64, 78–9
Kolchak, Aleksandr, 277
kolkhozy, 18
Komsomol, 8, 26, 34, 35, 63
  Tavda District Committee, 112–13
Komsomol Pravda (newspaper), 139
Korzhavin, Naum, 154
Korsakov, Fadei, 277
Kosaryov, A. V., 171
Kosmodemyanskaya, Shura, 185–7
Kosmodemyanskaya, Zoya, 183, 184, 185–7, 195, 196, 207, 208, 214, 215, 306
Kotik, Valya, 207, 208, 215
Kotkin, Stephen, 275
Kotlas, 29
Kovalenko, Pelageya, 83
Kovalenko, Yakov, 101
Kozhevnikov, Vadim, 184
Kozlov, William, 311
Krasev, Mikhail, 201
Krasnaya Presnya, *see* Presnya
Kremensky, Aleksandr, 183–4
Kreutzer Sonata (Tolstoy), 320
Krupskaya, Nadezhda, xviii, 148, 170
Kruzhin, Pyotr, 171–2, 238
Krylov, Ivan, 180
kulaks
  discrimination against, xxii–xxiii, 22, 25–6, 38–9
  dislike of, 24–5, *27*, 50–1
  eviction and forced exile of, 19, 27–9
  origins of, 22–4
  see also 'dekulakization'
Kulukanov, Arseny, xvi
  background and character, 56
  charges against, 86
  conviction and sentence, 104, 107
  exile, 242, 246
  house search, 76, 79, 85, 241, 313
  political convictions, 61
  property and wealth, 60, 79
  as suspect in Morozov murder, 81, 87–8, 90, 91, 92, 93, 94, 95, 96–7, 108, 257
  trial of, 102, 103
Kulukanov, Zakhar, xv, 56, 278
Kulukanova, Khima, xvi, 55–6, 87, 105, 108, 249
Kulukanova, Matryona, 56
Kuznetsov, Ivan Nikitych, 277

Lenin, Vladimir Ilyich
  cult of, 199
  on kulaks, 22
Leninist Sparks (newspaper), 38–9, 137
Let the Shift Begin! (newspaper), 113
Libedinskaya, Lidiya, 289
Likhobabin, xiv, 106
'Literary Bridges', 200
Livy, 9
Lurie, Alison, 161
Lynch, Mayor, 9

McKenna, Sorcha and Vincent, 10
McLaverty, Bernard, 158
Magnitogorsk, 44
Markizova, Gelya, *146*
Master and Man (Tolstoy), 23
Matrosov, Aleksandr, 184
Matsuk, Grigory, 80
Matveeva, Lida, 208
Mayakovsky, Vladimir, 132, 180
Mendeleeva, Lyubov, 200
Mezyukhin, Vladimir, xvi, 59, 78, 84, 85, 90, 91, 236, 249, 257
Mikhalkov, Sergei, xviii, 151, 202, 314
The Military Secret (Gaidar), 162–3, 164, 180
Mironova, Zoya, 239
Mirsky, Dmitry S., 297
Mitreikin, Konstantin, 45, 138
Mokrousov, Stepan Iosifovich, 64
Moor, David, 132
Morozov, Aleksei, xv, *3*, 61, 101, 119, 167

Morozov, Danila, xvi
  background, 58
  case against, 252–9
  conviction and sentence, 104, 107
  as suspect in Morozov murder, 59, 74, 76, 77–8, 80–1, 86–7, 88, 90, 92, 93, 94, 95, 96, 105, 131, 134, 235, 244, 249, 313
  trial of, 102, 117, 119, 123
Morozov, Fyodor, xv
  murder of, 73, 81, 125
  murder site of, *264*
  purported photograph of, *225*, 226
Morozov, Ivan, xv, 55, 57–8
Morozov, Pavel ('Pavlik'), xv
  as activist, 85–6
  biographies of, 134–6, 153–5, 180, 190–1, 203, 223
  birth certificate, 227
  character witnesses on, 101
  children's response to, 167–8, 170–1, 173–5
  corpse, 72–3
  cult of, xxiv–xxv, 2–4, 6–7, 8, 14–15, 16, 44, 116, 137–9, 155, 161, 163–4, 165–8, 187–8, 189, 193, 200–7
  cynicism about, 213
  death certificate, *99*
  decline in status of, 176–96, 207–22
  denunciations, 96–7, 114, 119, 121–3, 137, 157, 159–60, 231, 239–46, 259
  Druzhnikov on, 4–5, 8, 9, 167–8, 196, 211, 230–9, 247, 262
  family responsibilities, 60–1
  friends of, 191, 313
  funeral, 117–18, 123
  and Gorky, 139, 140–5, 153, 160, 217
  memories of, 228–30
  modern attitudes to, xxviii–xxix, 211–15, 217–22
  monuments to, *ii*, 2, *3*, 144–5, 150–1, 166, 187, *188*, 188–9, 200, 202–3, *216*, 216–17
  museum, plans for, 221–2
  myth of, xxii–xxv, 7, 261–5
  paintings of, 193–5, *194*, *206*
  photographs of, 114, *115*, 137, *227*, *228*
  as 'Pioneer Number 001', 201
  psychology of, 7–8
  'real life' of, 228–31, 259–60
  Stalin's dislike of, 15, 147
  wounds, 73, 81
Morozov, Roman, xv, 61
Morozov, Sergei, xvi
  background, 54–5
  charges against, 86
  house search, 76
  political convictions, 61
  as suspect in Morozov murder, 59, 75, 78, 80, 81, 86–7, 91, 96, 102, 105, 119, 131, 134, 249, 253, 254–5, 257
  trial of, 93–4, 95, 102, 103–4, 119
Morozov, Trofim, xv
  absence of during murder, 57, 58
  background, 55
  as chairman of village soviet, 243–4, 246, 257
  denunciation of, 159, 231, 259
  document forging, 58, 86, 96, 190
  exile, 93, 96
Morozov family
  ideology, 61–2
  poverty, 54–7, 60, 135
  tree, xi
Morozov murders
  author's version of, 257–60
  date of, 75
  Druzhnikov's version of, 231–7
  evidence on, 5–6, 71–81, *83*, 84–5, *89*
  file on, xxix–xxxii, 69–71, *70*, 224
    incompleteness of, 226
  forgery of documents, 224–5, 236
  hearsay evidence, 77–81, 84–5
  as an impulsive crime, 247–8
  investigation into, 62–3, 71–96, 105, 223–4
    reopening of, 219
    unreliability of, 220

Morozov murders – *cont.*
  as kulak inspired, 84–5, 87, 97, 107–8, 112, 114, 116, 131
  letters about, 10–11
  local opinion on, 249–50
  OGPU, alleged role of, 232–7
  parallels with other murders, 123–31
  prosecution case, 96–7, 104
  reporting of, 1, 69, 95–6, 110–21, 133–6, 138–9
  as a result of youth conflict, 251
  suspects, 59–60, 76–7, 86, 87, 90, *129*, 236
    alibis, 75–6
    alleged beating of, 106, 252
    charges against, 86
    confessions of, 92–5, 103
  trial, 1–2, 15, 97–8, 100–4, 107, 110, 116–17, 243, 245
Morozov Pavel (Borovin), 180
Morozova, Kseniya, xvi
  alleged beating of, 106
  background, 55
  conversation with Tatiana, 78, 101, 249
  conviction and sentence, 104
  and Morozov murder investigation, 75, 78, 80, 81, 85, 90, 92–3, 97, 101, 245, 249, 257
  political convictions, 61
  trial of, 102, 117, 119, 131
Morozova, Tatiana, xv
  absence of during murder, 75, 231
  conversation with Kseniya, 78, 101, 249
  interview, 165–6
  and Morozov murder investigation, 58, 76, 82–3, 84, 90, 103, 241
  motives, 244–6
  and Pavlik's funeral, 118
  at trial, 100, 101, 119, 243
  unpopularity of, 246, 317
  visit to Moscow, 167
Moscow City Soviet, archives of, 296
murder
  of activists, 137
  by adolescents, 250–1
  of children, 11–13, 126–31, 263
  legislation relating to, 12, 13
  political, 234
  rates, 237
  ritual, 126–9, 248
Myagotin, Kolya, 137, 170, 208

Nakhangova, Mamlakat, 297
Native Tongue (school textbook), 207
Nesterov, Mikhail, 195
Neverko, Adik, 207–8
Neverov, Aleksandr, 162
'New Economic Policy' (1921), 21
New Path, 239
New Year trees, 150, 302
Nicholas II, Tsar, murder of, 124, 125
'Night Thunder' (Kremensky), 183–4
NKVD, 160
Norkus, Herbert, 289
Northern Ireland, 158
Novopashin, 53, 242–3
Novosibirsk, 25
Novyi Mir (newspaper), 169

Oedipus Rex, 7–8
Ogonyok (magazine), 199, 206, 262
OGPU
  actions against kulaks, 26
  alleged role in Morozov murders, 232–7
  and the Morozov investigation, xxxi–xxxii, 5
  in Tavda district, 64
'Old Woman Izergil' (Maxim Gorky), 14
Olesha, Yury, 303
One Day in the Life of Ivan Denisovich (Solzhenitsyn), 169
Open Society foundation, 221
orphanages, 41
Osorina, Maria, 212
Ostrovsky, Nikolai, 186
'overagers' in Soviet schools, 301

'paidology', 7
'Partisan Tanya', *see* Kosmodemyanskaya, Zoya
Pasternak, Boris, 180
Pavlik Morozov (anthology), 201, 202
Pavlik Morozov (Chebakov painting), 193–5, *194*, 206
Pavlik Morozov (Doroshin), 203
Pavlik Morozov (Shchipachov), 191–3, 201–2
Pavlik Morozov (Smirnov), 180
Pavlik Morozov (Yakovlev), 154
Pavlik Morozov Park of Culture and Rest, Moscow, 188
The Peasant Gazette, 63, 139, 171
'people's militia', 204
Perrault, Charles, 173
pests, 39
Peter Grimes (Britten), 263
Pioneer (magazine), 35, 37, 38, 40, 119, 121, 129, 183, 208
Pioneer Leader, 164, 201, 207, 208
Pioneer movement, *xxiii*
  camps for, xxii
  establishment of, 34–5
  First All-Soviet Pioneer Rally (1929), 142
  help to children, 149–50
  murder victims, 137
  neckties, 154–5
  organization, 4, 7, 237–9
  and overturning of family hierarchy, 17
  Pavlik's membership of, 231, 237
  'Pioneer March', *35*
  Pioneer palaces, 150
  and school education, 148
  Sverdlovsk, 113
  and 'Timur', 179–80, 212
Pioneer Pravda
  on Akopov case, 38
  on child activists, 148, 209–10, 218
  founding of, 35
  on Morozov murder case, 1–3, 69, 96, 97, 98, 113–14, *115*, 116–19, *120*, 121, 122, 123, 129
  on Myagotin case, 137
  and Pavlik cult, 161, 189–90, 193, 241
  on Pavlik memorial, 151
  on Soviet festivals, 176
  and 'Timur', 177, 182
Piotrovsky, Mikhail, 320
Plato, 9
Platonov, Andrei, 42
Polevoi, Boris, 184
Polyanovsky, Max, 184–5
populism, 271
Potupchik, Denis, xv, 57, 60, 62, 79, 84, 85, 101, 108, 243
Potupchik, Ivan, xiv, 57, 62, 81, 82, 83, 85, 88, 92, 102, 106, 232, 234, 235–6, 243
Potupchik, Motya, 191, 313
Potupchik, Ustinya, xv, 57
Pravda, 63, 132, 138–9, 141, 143, 149, 161
Presnya, Moscow, 188–9
Prokopenko, Dmitry, *xxvi*, 228–9
Prokopenko, Vasily, 82
Prokopovich, Iosif, 78–9, 94–5
Proletkult, 162
'prompting' in Soviet classrooms, 171
propaganda photographs, *24*, *46*
Prosecutor General's Office, Moscow, 219
Prozerova, Klavdiya, xvi, 101
Prushinsky, Trofim, 208
Pulyashkin, Ivan, 82
Pushkin, Alexander, 180

Rabinovich, Isaak, xviii, 151, 154, 261
Razinkina, Nastya, 128
Razumnyi, Alexander, 181
Rechkalov, xiv, 86, 91
Red Dawns (newspaper), 34
Red Kurgan (newspaper), 40–1
Reis, Ignaty, 234
religion, campaign against, 118, 121, 125
rigor mortis, 72, 283
Road into Life (film), 133, 162
Romanov, Prince Mikhail, 124

Romanov family, murder of, 124–5, 136, 290
The Rowan-Tree Bonfire (play), 203, 205
Rozanov, Vasily, 172
Rybakov, Anatoly, 303

saints, cult of, in Russian Orthodoxy, 229–30
Sakhanov, Sergei, 311
Sakov, Prokhor, 256
Sakova, Anastasiya, xvi, 83
Sakova, Mariya, 6, 228, 229, 250, 259
samosud (arbitrary justice), 32
Sapgir, Genrikh, 213–14
Schenzinger, Karl Aloys, 122, 175
school education
  and the cult of Stalin, 198
  'prompting' in classrooms, 171
  Soviet policy, 147–8
  and 'Sovietization', 36–7
  statistics for, in USSR, 274
  'Study Day', 176
Scottsboro affair, 292
scout movement, 34–5, 179
Second Five-Year Plan (1932–7), 147
Semyonovna, Anna, 170
shaming rituals, 32
Shatrakov, Anton, xvii, 59, 82, 251–2
Shatrakov, Arseny, 219
Shatrakov, Dmitry, xvii, 59, 76, 81, 82, 85, 251–2
Shatrakov, Efrem, xvi
  background, 59–60
  case against, 252–9
  as suspect in Morozov murder, 76, 77–8, 80, 81, 82, 87, 88, 91, 92, 95, 134, 235
  at trial, 101–2
Shatrakov family, 278–9
Shatrakova, Matryona, 219
Shatrakova, Olga, xvii, 59, 82
Shcherbakov, A. S., 144
Shchipachov, Stepan, xviii, 191–3, 201–2
Shelkanov, Vasily, 251
Shepelev, xiv, 62, 94, 95
The Shift (newsletter), 110–12
Shkapskaya, Mariya, 124
Shmakov, A. S., 127
Shostakovich, Dmitry, 8, 269
show trials, 2, 13, 97–8, 100, 204–5
Shvarts, Oleg, 119, 121, 157
Silin, Arseny, xvi
  background, 56–7, 60
  denunciation of, 96, 101
  innocence of, 250
  and Morozov murder investigation, 76, 79, 81, 88, 90, 91, 95, 105, 108, 244
  at trial, 103, 104
Silina, Matryona, 56, 59
Skalkina, Olya, 128
Smirnov, Elizar, xviii, 2, 98, 113–14, 118, 121, 145, 153, 157, 180
'Snub-Nose Club', 295
'social prosecutors', 107
Socialist Realism, 141, 175, 194
Solomakh, Tanya, 186
Solomein, Pavel, xviii, 133–6, 140, 142, 153, 168, 180, 203, 223, 224, 230, 244–5, 299
Solzhenitsyn, Alexander, 169
'Song about Pavlik Morozov' (Gradov and Bokalov), 201, 202
The Song of a Pioneer Hero (Alymov), 46–7, 151, 202
Soros, George, 221
Soviet Pedagogy (newspaper), 207, 208
Soviet Union
  festivals, 176–7
  maps of, *xviii*
  promotion in, 43–4
  terror in, 158–9
'Sovietization', 33, 36
'special settlers', 66–7
Sputnik (magazine supplement), 208
spying, 160, 190, 218
Stalin, Joseph, *146*
  on *Bezhin Meadow*, 15, 151
  breadth of interests, 145–6
  and children, 146–7
  on collectivization, 21

cult of, 6, 176, 193, 197
death of, 197
'Dizzy with Success' speech, 30, 242
on the kulaks, 27
on prosperity of Soviet citizens, 149
'The Year of the Great Breakthrough', 26
Stalin and Voroshilov in the Kremlin (Gerasimov), 179
State Prosecution Service, Moscow, xxix, 70
Steinhoff, Hans, 122
Stepanchenko, Anna, xvii, 81
Stolypin reforms (1906), 23–4
A Story about a Real Man (Polevoi), 184
The Street of the Younger Son (Kassil and Polyanovsky), 184–5
Suvorov, xiv, 76, 81, 82–3
Sverdlovsk (now Ekaterinburg), xxv, xxvii
political processions in, *52*
Svetlov, Mikhail, 123
Svyatopolk, 123–4, 125

Tager, A. S., 130
The Tale of Boris and Gleb, 125
Tambov, 215
Tashkent the Abundant (Neverov), 162
TASS, 138
Tatars, 133
Tavda district
appearance of, xxvi–xxvii, xxvii–xxviii
attacks on Party activists, 64–6
character of, 48
farms, 50
maps of, *xxi*
special settlers, 66–7
Tavda Worker (newspaper), 51–3, 63, 69, 112, 114, 116, 121, 165–6, 167, 239
The Teachers' Newspaper, 207
Tian-Shanskaya, Olga, 272
Timoshenko, Fyodor, xvii, 91
'Timur and Her Team' (Sapgir), 214
Timur and His Team (Gaidar), 177–83, 186, 218
Timur's Oath (Gaidar), 181
'Timurites', 182, 196, 212
Titov, Yakov, xiv, 62, 71, 72, 79, 81, 82, 88, 102, 106, 224–5
Tolstoy, Leo, 23, 180, 233, 320
Treivas, Fruma, 168
Trekhgornaya manufaktura ('Trekhgorka'), 188, 189, 302
Trotsky, Leon, 12, 234
Trusov, xiv, 106
The Tsarist Regime and the Beilis Affair (Tager), 130
Tsendrovskaya, S. N., 298
Tsvetaeva, Marina, 124, 234
Tvardovsky, Alexander, 169
Tvardovsky, Ivan, 19
Twentieth Congress of the Soviet Communist Party (1956), 197
'twenty-five thousanders' movement, 26–7, 32, 273–4

'Uncle Timur' (Barto), 213
Uralkniga (Uralbook), 166
Uralmashstroi (Urals Machinery Works), 44
Urals
drug abuse in, xxvii
forced labour in, 45–6
industry in, 44–6
maps of, *xx*
prison camps in, xxvii
The Urals Worker (newspaper), 63
Ushenin, xiv, 62–3

Varygin, Prokhor, xiv–xv, 64, 77, 78, 81, 85–6, 100, 101
Verdery, Katherine, 292
Verne, Jules, 180
Vigdorova, Frida, 185
Vishnevskaya, Galina, 269
A Visit to the Tank Drivers (painting), 132
Vladimir, Prince, 124
Vlasenko, Nikolai, 219

Volkov, Afanast, 257
Volkov, Konstantin, xvii, 100, 101
Volovich, Hava, 268
Voroshilov, Klimenty, 179
Vyshinsky, Andrei, 158

'War Communism' (1918–21), 21
'The Way' (Shchipachov), 191
The Way to the Kolkhoz (newspaper), 63
We (Zamiatin), 19
Welcome! And Keep Out (film), 198–9
When Did You Last See Your Father? (Yeames), 194
Wood demon, 317

Yakovlev, Aleksandr, xviii, 131, 144, 151, 152, 155, 157, 180, 223
Yakovlev, Kolya, 137
Yeames, William Frederick, 194
'The Year of the Great Breakthrough' (Stalin), 26
The Young Drummer Boy (Khorinskaya), 202
Young Guard, 166
The Young Guard (Fadeyev), 183
'Young Talents' contest, 150
Young Worker (newspaper), 25
Yudov, Karp, xv, 64, 79, 229
Yudov, Yakov, 101
Yudova, Stepanida, xvii, 78
Yurovsky, Yankel, 293
Yushchinsky, Andrei, 126, 127, 131
Yutkevich, Sergei, 298

Zamiatin, Evgeny, 19–20
Zhukov, Andrei, 317